The Black Press

1827–1890

The Black Press

1827–1890

The Quest for National Identity

EDITED WITH AN INTRODUCTION

by Martin E. Dann

G. P. Putnam's Sons   New York

*In memory of those who have died in the
struggle for black liberation*

I am deeply grateful to the entire staff of the Schomburg Collection; to Professor Herbert Aptheker, who kindly read the original manuscript; to Professors John Weiss, Philip Foner, Eric Foner, Allan Schaffer, and Otto Lindenmeyer, for their valuable advice; and above all, to Clamma, for everything.

Preface

I HAVE limited the selections contained in this anthology almost exclusively to those black newspapers available on microfilm at the Schomburg Collection of the New York City Public Library. These papers were largely collected and photographed as a project of the Committee on Negro Studies of the American Council of Learned Societies under the direction of Professor Armistead Scott Pride.*

There are, however, additional newspapers scattered throughout the United States and Canada, in libraries, historical collections, and personal archives, which have not been included. No accurate figures on the distribution of these black newspapers have been found. Frederick Douglass, in his autobiography, said that his paper reached 3,000, and T. Thomas Fortune mentioned in his paper that the New York *Freeman* reached 5,000.† Whatever the printing, it is clear that these papers reached far more people. Papers passed from hand to hand or, in the time-worn tradition, were posted in a local pub or other common meeting place. In this way, a single paper may have been (and probably often was) read by a hundred people.

The basic criteria for selection were that the document had to be written by a black man or woman and that they had to be an original contribution to a black newspaper—that is, edited and published by black men. Many valuable articles were not included because the author was white or because the article was from a book or white newspaper. This was done to maintain consistency. Other articles

---

* See Armistead S. Pride, "A Register and History of Negro Newspapers in the United States, 1827–1950" (PhD, Northwestern University, 1950).

† Warren Brown, in his MA thesis "Social Change in the Negro Press, 1860–1880" (New School for Social Research, 1950) says that the *Elevator* (San Francisco) printed 800 copies weekly (according to the issue of May 5, 1865), the *Planet* (Georgetown) printed 280, and the *Missionary Record* printed between 720 and 1,000 (according to *Rowell's Newspaper Directory,* 1873).

which are available in other documentary histories were also omitted.

During the first six decades of its existence, the black press established itself as an indispensable part of the developing black community. Because of the large amount of material available in the years that follow I have chosen to end the anthology with articles up to, but not including, 1890. This decision was dictated solely by the attempt to present as careful and complete a selection of the available material in a single volume.

Despite the tremendous importance of Frederick Douglass throughout this period, his journalistic contributions have not been included in this collection owing solely to the fact that much of his work is now readily available. The reader is referred to Philip S. Foner's comprehensive four-volume study *The Life and Writings of Frederick Douglass* (1950). Significant articles and much important information on black history are also available in Herbert Aptheker's excellent two-volume work *A Documentary History of the Negro People in the United States.*

Most newspapers subscribed to exchanges—that is, a newspaper would subscribe to other papers in return for subscriptions of their paper. Generally, basic news items (especially international news) were taken from large white daily papers and reprinted. There are, therefore, many articles printed in white papers (notably Garrison's *Liberator*) which were obtained originally from black papers. Except for one entry, such material is not included in this collection.

Contents

Introduction

THIS collection of articles has been selected from black newspapers between 1827 and 1890. Their common theme is the black man's quest for a national identity. Because these articles are drawn from the pages of the black press, they demonstrate that the history of black people in this country is *not* merely one of failure and hopelessness. The writings of black journalists reveal a history of struggle and survival in the face of the deliberate attempt by white American society, as a whole, to destroy the integrity, the strength, the culture—in short, the national identity—of black Americans.

White people in this country have usually taken their American nationality for granted, even when they were not born here. In its better moments, America offered full and equal status to all who came to its shores, and asked in return only their loyalty. America was, at least in myth, a "melting pot." Black men and women, however, have been the exception to this pattern. For them, the quest for their place in American society came in the face of one of the most brutal experiences of oppression known to man; the enslavement of millions of people and the continuing, absolute rejection by a country they called home.

The history of black people in America is one of self-determination and self-definition, to be included as "Americans" with full citizenship rights or to be granted the privilege of establishing a separate and independent political entity. And these concepts were more crucial for black people than any other people who lived here because the overwhelming majority of white people attempted to strip them of their language, customs, religion, to destroy their institutions, to prohibit their education—in effect, to refuse to recognize that black people had *any* rights which white people were bound to respect. Such attempts to force black people to sever every tie with their past, to degrade, exploit, and proscribe them, to keep them powerless and dependent, simply underscore the observation that white America had no place for its black citizens. The quest for national identity is a response to this oppression, and it was an expression of the demand for autonomy. It did not mean that black people were trying to imitate white society, but that they were defining their place in American society. It affirms all those qualities which colonialism negates and destroys—the will to create a meaningful life, the ability to resist, the search for self-awareness.

Two currents in black intellectual history evident in the black press converge repeatedly: a response to white racism and an assertion of self-determination. And it is in the concept of black nationality that both reach a watershed. Both were inextricably linked and developed almost simultaneously, and both were directed toward the same goal of freedom, equality, and racial pride that had been denied to black people. In the face of attempts by American society to repress any movement toward black self-determination and to crush any sign of self-defense, two distinct (but interrelated) programs appeared in the early nineteenth century and extend into our own time:

(1) inclusion—the desire to be recognized as citizens, to change the basic nature of this country from racist to egalitarian, the demand for equality—in short, to work through the system;

(2) exclusion—the separationist response to racism, oppression, and terrorism, leading to various forms of resistance, including foreign and domestic colonization—in short, to avoid the system.

The decision to take one path or another depended on the individual's perception of these two alternatives. But it is important to remember that these choices were not mutually exclusive and existed conjointly. The final aim of both was manhood, dignity, and self-respect—the goal with which black nationalism has become synonymous.

The distinction between these two alternatives is not as clear as the above implies. But as poles in a field of action, they prescribe the structure within which we may begin to understand the quest for national identity in terms of a positive response to the recognized corruption, injustice, and racism within the system. It is a mistake to view this experience simply as a reaction to repression. To do so ignores that aspect of the black society and press which fought to assert its independence, to establish an ethnicity, and to retain the inherent qualities of the race. Black demands for reform, the hope that the American system would change if it understood what it was doing to black people were, in a sense, idealistic, but consistent with the assertion of black people that they were both black and American. The struggle for national identity thus challenges the constant attempts of the society to deprive black people of their rights as citizens, to deny black people their humanness, and to degrade their African cultural heritage. As being black came to mean someone alien from the American system, the black press exposed the condition white America demanded for acceptance: to deny one's blackness, to deny one's identity.

For black people, the concept of national identity was not limited to allegiance to American ideals, but was a consciousness of their heritage and worth, an individual response to a unique condition. National identity involved an awareness of a collective responsibility, a resistance to racism, and a commitment to self-definition and self-determination. National identity, often proclaimed as "a nation within a nation," meant the protection of both the individual and the community against a hostile government and people. There were exceptions, but in the main, the contract that bound white citizens to the government never existed for black people. The basic rights of participation in political power, civil rights, a share in the benefits of the system, and the protection of the government were extended to black people only under duress, if at all. Thus, the quest for a national identity takes place against the attempt by a white nation to enslave or destroy, to exploit or exclude a black nation in its midst.

In this context, the black press provided one of the most potent arenas in which the battle for self-definition could be fought and won. By stressing the primacy of racial pride and thus forging ethnic solidarity, the black press became, along with the church, a central institution in the black community. Black editors and their correspondents, as leaders in the community, not only were able to communicate information vital to the community and necessary for its cohesion, but also were often the only educational resources available. Indeed, black papers were usually the only source of information about the repression of the black community since white papers rarely printed such information.

In presenting the material of the black press from 1827 to 1890, an attempt has been made to construct categories intended to illuminate the central themes of the period:

—The role of the black press as seen through the eyes of its editors

—The place of black people in history and the importance of resistance to their liberation movement
—The black man in the political process and the struggle for civil
rights
—The black reaction to colonization, and efforts to establish black
communities in the West
—The struggle of black people in the American labor movement to
gain equality
—The creation of a strong black community, based on independence, self-help, and opposition to racism and oppression.

The black press was the focal point of every controversy and every
concern of black people, representing as it did the strengths and mutual reinforcements which united the black community. These endeavors were a consistent and realistic attempt to put black people in
a position where they could overcome white racism and develop, in
spite of a hostile environment, with an awareness of their capabilities.
It was in this attempt to define the black American's link with his past
and to develop the sense of cohesiveness that we observe the clear
enunciation of racial pride. The demand is not for assimilation, but
for equality; not for imitation of white people, but for the right to live
in freedom. The quest for a national identity meant the recognition of
being part of the larger black community with whom individuals
shared a continuity of experiences, with whom they shared a common
history of oppression—and for whom the promise of self-fulfillment
would be realized.

THE ORIGINS OF THE BLACK PRESS: NEW YORK

Much of this early period of black history has been obscured by
controversies over the nature of government. Black people, however,
were not a neglected subject by any means. "Liberal democrats" and
the conservative majority (led by Martin Van Buren) were united on
at least one issue: Free blacks were *not* to enjoy the same rights as free
white men, and the institution of slavery would be protected. The
ownership of property (rather than existence) was considered the basis
of citizenship, suffrage, and social and political recognition.

By 1821 universal suffrage had been defeated, and the New York
Establishment, the Albany Regency, was even more deeply entrenched. White society and privilege were powerful and well protected. By 1824, however, the Albany Regency was under attack.

Demonstrations were held against the oligarchs with shouts of "Huzza for the people!" The "people's party," which won the election of 1824 with broad popular support, had championed political equality and governmental reform. But the "people" meant "white," and universal male suffrage (established in 1824) did not include black people. Social equality for the white man was the cornerstone of this new politics, as much as political disfranchisement and social ostracism of black people.

Though slavery was officially abolished in 1827 in New York, the state was still a happy hunting ground for kidnappers. The Fugitive Slave Law, enacted in 1793, which sanctioned the kidnapping of runaway slaves anywhere, anytime, without any legal protection for slaves, was the law of the land. Prejudice was rampant in every aspect of political, social, and economic life.

Attempts to write off the free black population became more difficult as they began to demand full citizenship rights. Unable to reconcile the inclusion of black people into the political or social system, white Americans proposed a number of solutions for the "Negro Problem"—solutions which were, in varying degrees and in one form or another, efforts to enslave, segregate, or exclude black people in the United States. One of these solutions, proposed by the American Colonization Society, was the deportation of all free blacks to Africa.

The American Colonization Society, organized in December, 1816, was supported by some abolitionists and most proslavery men. As early as 1788, when the Philadelphia Free African Society opposed the suggestion made by the Negro Union of Newport, Rhode Island, that free blacks remove themselves to Africa, most black people opposed any such colonization schemes. In a letter to Paul Cuffee, an active supporter of colonization, in 1817, James Forten (a wealthy black sailmaker and abolitionist) told of a meeting of 3,000 black people in Philadelphia where a unanimous vote was taken against the American Colonization Society. Despite widespread black opposition, the society was able to gain supporters among "liberal" whites—and was successful in promulgating its programs. It became evident to black leaders that only through their own instruments of communication could they effectively combat the growing support for the Colonization Society. They were, from the outset, opposed by every institution in the white community—the churches, the papers, the politicians, the legal system—and they were hampered by financial strains and divisions within their ranks.

Despite these formidable obstacles, in the late winter of 1827, two black men, one a recent graduate of Bowdoin College and the other a young militant minister, joined forces to publish the first black newspaper in the United States. At its offices at 6 Varick Street (later at 152 Church Street) in New York City, Jamaican-born John Russwurm, the second black man to graduate from a college in America, and the Reverend Samuel Cornish originated what was to become one of the most significant institutions of the black community in this country— the black press. The paper was called *Freedom's Journal,* and, as is true of every birth, it was the expression of a force and energy that could no longer be contained.

It is significant that the paper originated in New York, rather than Boston or Philadelphia, both of which had large black populations. In the latter two cities the white community was more sympathetic to the black man, and Philadelphia in particular boasted one of the strongest white abolitionist groups. In New York, however, several newspapers were vituperous in their attacks on the black community and abolitionists as well. It was largely in response to these challenges and out of the growing black protest movement that the first black abolitionist paper emerged.

The New York black community lived in the area of today's City Hall. Although observers often described its poverty and crime, it also had an African Society of Mutual Relief, a theater, numerous churches, and the African Free School.

Antebellum black papers were not written for the slave population, but for ex-slaves and free black citizens, largely in Northern states, who were becoming upwardly mobile. The concerns of its editors were directed primarily to the conditions at home, to kidnappers in New York, to various methods of self-help and self-improvement, to self-defense, to the colonization controversy rather than to conditions in the South upon which they felt they could have little direct influence.

Freedom's Journal tried to steer a middle course in the constant debates over colonization, but it became increasingly difficult to maintain such a position. It may very well have been the result of tensions raised by the society's activities that prompted Samuel Cornish, the senior editor, to resign only six months after the paper had begun.

With John Russwurm as sole editor, the paper printed articles in favor of the society (usually by whites, notably John H. Kennedy of Philadelphia) and against the society (usually by black men). Cornish became the general agent of the paper; in this capacity he was responsible for promoting it. Over the course of the life of the paper it grew from a circulation in eleven states and twenty-four agents to fourteen states and almost twice as many agents. Though no articles appear with Cornish's name, he did advertise plots of land for sale 70 miles from New York City as the basis for a black agricultural community.

Russwurm continued to publish the paper until March 28, 1829, when it ceased publication. A recent convert to the goals of the American Colonization Society, he soon left for Liberia where he became editor of the *Liberia Herald* and then superintendent of public schools. From 1836 until his death in 1851, he was the governor of the Maryland Colony at Cape Palmas.

Two months later, on May 29, 1829, Samuel Cornish resurrected *Freedom's Journal* under a new name, the *Rights of All*. The paper reflected a new sense of militancy, as shown by Cornish's vibrant attacks on racism and a powerful "Appeal to the Colored Citizens of the World," written by the Boston agent for *Freedom's Journal,* David Walker. One year later the first National Negro Convention was held in Philadelphia.

The black convention movement began in 1830 and lasted until the end of the nineteenth century, but it was most influential during the three decades prior to the Civil War. These conventions were composed of the leading black men of the day, many of whom were connected with black newspapers. This may account for the importance placed on black papers by the conventions and their sponsorship of them. It was at the conventions that the calls for justice and demands for reform were hammered out—and it was in the black press that their resolutions and proceedings were printed. The national conventions were held each year between 1830 and 1835, after which time they were held irregularly, largely because it was believed that they were not as functional as the smaller state conventions. Not only did they seek to present a consensus of the black community, but they were the basis of an organized political response to American racism and were effective in uniting the free black population of the North.

Prior to the Civil War, these conventions were held only in the North, because such gatherings of blacks in the South were prohibited. But with the end of the war, this institution was carried to the South, and during Reconstruction such conventions of black people were common occurrences. The black press was a crucial factor in bringing leaders together and in disseminating information about these meetings.

The inauguration of the *Weekly Advocate* in January, 1837, represented a new stage in the developing national identity within the black community. Its name was changed to the *Colored American* a month later, when Samuel Cornish became its editor. The new name is significant of a controversy, which had been going on within the convention movement, on the proper reference to black people, Negroes, colored Americans, Anglo-Africans, Africans, or Afro-Americans. As an extension of the convention movement, the name "Colored American" probably represents a consensus.

Like its predecessors, the *Colored American* was dedicated to racial pride and unity, now with a greater awareness of and emphasis on political considerations—especially obtaining full civil rights. As was true of many other black papers, the participation of a high proportion of religious leaders gave this paper a particular interest in religious matters and at times a greater emphasis on "morality" than on "political action."

In June, 1839, Cornish resigned, and Charles B. Ray, the former general agent and pastor of the Bethesda Congregational Church, became editor. Philip Bell, the proprietor, continued to work with the paper. Throughout its history, the *Colored American* was supported liberally by Arthur Tappan, a white abolitionist associated with William Lloyd Garrison.

The colonization controversy was now largely settled for the black community (though it remained important for whites), as their interest turned to measures of self-help and Western and Northern migration. Political interests took precedence as the numerous conventions pressed the appeal for an end to slavery and full citizenship rights for black people. Black abolitionists were organizing antislavery societies, increasing numbers of blacks were finding their way to freedom in the North, and through local conventions and aided substantially by the black press, new organizations were emerging, and black people were uniting in common cause against tyranny, exploitation, and oppression.

Relatively little information has been found in this early period of the black press. The most extensive listing of antebellum black newspapers (most of which have not been found) was collected by Martin Robison Delany in his *Condition, Elevation, Emigration and Destiny of the Colored People of the United States,* published in 1852. Delany edited his own paper, the *Mystery* (Pittsburgh), was an assistant editor with Frederick Douglass on the *North Star*, and was a prolific contributor to many other journals throughout his lifetime. The following extract from his pamphlet is contained in a lengthy footnote.

During the last twenty years, there have been, at different periods, published among the colored people of the United States, twenty odd newspapers, some of which were conducted with ability. Among them, the "Colored American [1837–42]," in New York city; Samuel E. Cornish, Philip A. Bell, and Charles B. Ray, at different times, Editors. "The Demosthenian Shield," issued from a Literary Society of young colored men, in the city of Philadelphia. "The Struggler," by Philip A. Bell, New York, out of which the "Colored American" took its origin. The "National Reformer," an able monthly periodical, in pamphlet form, in Philadelphia; William Whipper, Editor. "The Northern Star," a Temperance monthly newspaper, published in Albany, N.Y.; Stephen Myers, Editor, still in existence—changed to —— [possibly *The Elevator*, 1842]. "The Mystery [1843]," of Pittsburgh, Pa.; Martin Robison Delany, Editor—succeeded by a committee of colored gentlemen, as Editors. The "Palladium of Liberty," issued in Columbus, O., by a committee of colored gentlemen; David Jenkins, Editor. "The Disfranchised American," by a committee of colored gentlemen, Cincinnati, O.; A. M. Sumner, Editor—succeeded by the "Colored Citizen"; Rev. Thomas Woodson, and William Henry Yancey, Editors. The "National Watchman [1842]," Troy, N.Y.; William H. Allen and Henry Highland Garnett [Garnet], Editors. Another issued in New York city, the name of which, we cannot now remember; James William Charles Pennington, D.D., and James McCuen [McCune] Smith, M.D., Editors: the issue being alternately at Hartford, the then residence of Dr. Pennington—and New York city, the residence of Dr. Smith. The "Excelsior," an ephemeral issue, which appeared but once, in Detroit, Mich.; William H. Day, Editor.

The "Christian Herald," the organ of the A. M. Episcopal Church, published under the auspices of the General Conference of that body; Augustus Richardson Green, Editor, and General Book Steward. This gentleman has, also, written and published several small volumes of a religious character; a pamphlet on the Episcopacy and Infant Baptism, and the Lives of Reverends Fayette Davis and David Canyou. The "Elevator," of Philadelphia; James McCrummill [McCrummell] Editor. The "Ram's Horn [*ca.* 1846—48]," New York city; Thomas Vanrensallear [Van Rensselaer], Editor. There is now a little paper, the name of which we cannot recollect, issued at Newark, N.J., merely a local paper, very meager in appearance. "The Farmer and Northern Star," in Courtland [Cortland], N.Y., afterwards changed to the "Impartial Citizen [*ca.* 1848]," and published in Boston; Samuel Ringgold Ward, Editor. "The

North Star [1847–50]," published in Rochester, N.Y.; Frederick Douglass, and Martin Robison Delany, Editors—subsequently changed to the "Frederick Douglass' Paper"; Frederick Douglass, Editor.

A number of gentlemen have been authors of narratives, written by themselves, some of which are masterly efforts, manifesting great force of talents. Of such are those by Frederick Douglass, William Wells Brown, and Henry Bibb. . . .

There are, in addition, a number of papers omitted by Delany:

The People's Press, Troy, New York, in 1843, edited by Thomas Hamilton and John Diaz.

The Clarion (which succeeded the *Watchman*), Troy, New York, in 1842, edited by Henry Highland Garnett.

The Elevator, Albany, New York, in 1842, edited by Stephen Myers.

The Genius of Freedom, New York, 1845–47, edited by David Ruggles.

The Mirror of Liberty, New York, 1837–(?), edited by David Ruggles.

The National Reformer, New York, in 1833, edited by William Whipper.

The Colored Man's Journal, New York, New York, 1851–60, edited by Louis H. Putnam.

The Aliened American, Cleveland, Ohio, from 1852 to 1856, edited by William H. Day, Samuel R. Ward, and the Reverend J. W. C. Pennington.

The Christian Recorder (succeeded the *Herald*), Philadelphia, in 1856, edited by Bishop Jabez Campbell (1856–68), Bishop Benjamin F. Turner (1868–84), Reverend Drilee (1884–   ).

Mirror of the Times, San Francisco, in 1855, edited by Mifflin W. Gibbs and J. H. Townsend.

The Pacific Appeal, San Francisco, in 1862, edited by Philip A. Bell.

The Herald of Freedom, Cleveland, Ohio, in 1855, edited by Peter H. Clark.

Following the Civil War, black people began to look with new hope to political institutions for a redress of grievances, for inclusion in the political life of the country, and, perhaps most crucially, for the protection of the federal government. Heartened by modest attempts at political reform (under Radical Reconstruction), the black press

reflected a cautious optimism. As before, its task was not only to vindicate the black community, to prove that black and white could live
and work together, but also to provide the mechanism for self-elevation. Black newspapers printed information on such subjects as farming, business practices, household hints, and meetings of local interest.
At the same time, the editors displayed a growing wariness of the
white community. When the South tried to impose the Black Codes in
1865 as *de facto* reenslavement, the press resisted and argued stren-
uously, but in vain, for its rights as black Americans. For a brief period in the late 1860's and early 1870's it seemed that black people
might be given a chance. But such hopes were crushed when Hayes, in
order to win his election (in 1876) to the Presidency, promised the
white Southern leaders that he would not interfere with their attempts
to suppress the black population. Yet despite a growing mistrust of the
North and the federal government, the black community, led by their
press, remained loyal to the Republican Party, under which they had
achieved "emancipation."

By the later 1870's several forces converged to impose new forms of
servitude. The need for cheap labor on the plantations, on the railroads, and in the mines and the threat of black equality in the society
led to the establishment of two institutions: the convict-lease system
and the sharecropping system. Under the former any black man,
woman, or child arrested for any offense was sent to a prison farm,
where his or her labor was bought by private companies at a few cents
a day to pay the "fines." It is not surprising that when the demand for
labor was high, the number of arrests was correspondingly high.

Under the sharecropping system, a man and his family were to get
a share of the crop in return for advances on food and supplies and
were required to turn over most of what was produced to the landlord.
Since the landlord also kept the books, it was impossible for a share-
cropper to come out ahead; with debt being inherited, the family endured prolonged subjection.

At about the same time, the Ku Klux Klan had begun to be active,
and despite some attempts to legislate against the Klanners under
President Grant, they gained power. Black papers printed the daily instances of brutality and outrage that occurred—often in the face of
their destruction—and called for protection and resistance, without
success.

As the black man's faith in the political system and his loyalty to
the Republican Party was used time and again to deprive him of any

semblance of self-determination and as his rights as a citizen were continually eroded, the black press reflected his efforts toward winning immediate objectives in education, employment, and politics. Though independent political action was proposed by more daring black editors in the 1870's and 1880's, the tendency was successfully resisted, and black people remained (when they could) Republicans. Black editors, who were, almost without exception, Republicans (and who were often supported by the Republican Party), struggled to consolidate gains and power in their party and called on party leaders to renounce their racism and hypocrisy.

When black people began to advance substantially, white people became more hostile and repressive. They instituted a reign of terror, sanctioned by law and custom. Wherever black people were becoming independent and powerful, white people organized to destroy them. Where black people potentially held the political balance of power, white people refused to allow them to register, or vote. With the symbol of the Republican Party as the party of emancipation strongly embedded in their experiences, black people went to the polls only to be refused the ballot and, if they persisted, to be murdered.

Despite these conditions, black newspapers continued to press for an egalitarian system and urged resistance to oppression. By their continued emphasis on various forms of self-help, they were able to sustain in the black community the strength to resist and hope of the future. The editors, who were often self-educated, brought to their community a spirit of racial pride and encouragement that were essential factors in keeping the community together. Their stress on individual achievement and unity among black people, their attack on forms of racism and exploitation thus placed them at the focal point in the social, political, and economic changes that were taking place.

Black papers, by their very nature, reflected a definite sense of immediacy and, at times, a tendency to deal with problems at an *ad hoc* level. Furthermore, the black press was often representative of the portion of the community which was articulate and accumulating property and becoming upwardly mobile. Thus the black press was in a position of trying to hold onto their gains while pushing for change and opposing white racism.

The black press throughout its history brought to its readers an awareness of oppressive conditions, while it emphasized the successes of black men and women. Black newspapers urged their readers to work for their own progress, for recognition in their professions as black men and women, with dignity and self-respect. The accomplishments of black people as doctors or lawyers, teachers or workmen, became a major theme in these papers. In such a way, the press was able to instill a positive sense of the progress and future of black people which was imperative to resisting persistent attempts by white racists to undermine the black community.

The following is a series of brief biographical sketches of prominent black editors:

PHILIP A. BELL edited the *Weekly Advocate* for one month in January, 1837, until Samuel Cornish took over and changed the name of the paper to the *Colored American.* In 1838, Cornish, Charles B. Ray, Philip Bell, and Stephen Glouster (of Philadelphia) became the editors. In 1857 Bell moved to San Francisco, where he edited the *Pacific Appeal.* In 1865 he published the *Elevator* until it was absorbed into *Mirror of the Times.* In 1880, Bell became the doorkeeper of the California Senate. He died in April, 1889, at the age of eighty-two.

WILLIAM CALVIN CHASE was born in Washington, D.C., on February 2, 1854. His father was a blacksmith and prominent in the community. He attended Howard University and subsequently was connected with the Boston *Observer,* the Washington *Plaindealer,* and the *Argus* until he joined William V. Turner on the Washington *Bee.* On December 23, 1882, Chase became the editor of the *Bee.* Later he was appointed recorder of deeds (a patronage position) by Frederick Douglass.

PETER HUMPHRIES CLARK was born in Cincinnati and for more than thirty years was employed there as a teacher and principal of black schools. He worked on Frederick Douglass' paper in Rochester, New York, and later published his own, the *Herald of Freedom,* in 1854.

EDWARD ELDER COOPER was born in the South before he moved to Indianapolis. From 1882 to 1886 he worked for the United States mail service, after which he worked on the Indianapolis *World.* On July 14, 1888, he began the publication of the Indianapolis *Freeman,* the first black illustrated newspaper. In 1893 he began publishing the *Colored American* in Washington, D.C.

SAMUEL E. CORNISH was senior editor of *Freedom's Journal* in 1827. When he left the paper to John Russwurm's control, he became general agent and moved to Bellville, New Jersey. In 1829 he returned briefly to New York to publish *Rights of All,* which did not last long. He was active in the convention movement, as well as a minister of the First Colored Presbyterian Church, which he had organized in 1821. He was editor of the *Colored American* in 1837 and 1838.

JOHN W. CROMWELL was born in Portsmouth, Virginia, on September 5, 1845. He was graduated from Howard University Law School in 1874. On March 16, 1876, he became editor of the *People's Advocate* in Alexandria, Virginia.

CHARLES HOWARD DAY was born in Lorain, Ohio, and was graduated from Oberlin College in 1849. He was a leader of black youth during the 1830's, and for the next three decades he was an active organizer of and participant in the convention movement. Prior to his assuming the editorship of the *Aliened American* in Cleveland, Ohio, in 1853, he published a paper in Detroit, Michigan, called the *Excelsior.* In 1853 he was designated vice-president of the National Negro Convention, which was primarily responsible for the establishment of the *Aliened American.* In 1855 he moved to an all-black settlement at Buxton, Ontario. In 1871 and 1872 Day and Cassius Brown edited the *National Progress* in Harrisburg, Pennsylvania. In 1872 he was appointed clerk in the Pennsylvania State Department.

WILLIAM L. EAGLESON was the editor of the *American Citizen* in Fort Scott, Kansas, in 1878 and co-editor of the *Kansas Herald* in Topeka the following year. In the early 1890's he moved to Langston City, Oklahoma, where he became the editor of the Langston City *Herald.* He was active in the black colonization movement and during the 1890's organized several other projects to establish all-black towns.

TIMOTHY THOMAS FORTUNE was born in Marianna, Florida, on October 3, 1856. In 1869, because of Ku Klux Klan raids, the family moved to Jacksonville, where Thomas learned to set type in the *Daily Union.* He worked in the post office and in 1875 was appointed to a mail route. He resigned this commission after a year and went to Howard University, in Washington, D.C., where he stayed for two years before returning to work on the *Daily Union.* In 1881 he went to New York to work as a typesetter on the *Weekly Witness,* along with William Walter Sampson. In 1879, together with Sampson and George Parker, he took over the *Rumor.*

The following is an account by Fortune of how he started his career in journalism. This was printed in the New York State Commission, National Negro Exposition 1915 (at Richmond, Virginia).

. . . In 1879, when I took hold of *Rumor,* together with George Parker and William Walter Sampson, it was much run down, as Mr. Parker had exhausted his resources, and they had been considerable, in the effort to publish a weekly illustrated newspaper on the order of Harper's Weekly. Mr. Parker was a man of limited education, but possessed the literary and artistic temperament in a very large measure. . . .

I did not care for the name, and other things associated with it, and soon changed the shape from the magazine to the newspaper, and the name from *Rumor* to the New York *Globe.* For some time, Mr. Sampson and I set the type of the *Globe* at night, working on the *Weekly Witness* in the day to be sure of our living expenses and that the paper would come out on time. There was no time to write articles, so I used to set one "out of my head," and dictate one to Mr. Sampson at the same time. We used to work in this way from 7 till 12 o'clock at night. . . .

On November 8, 1884, the *Globe* was discontinued after an internal dispute with the Reverend W. B. Derrick, who had bought out Mr. Parker and become a co-editor; this resulted in the paper being sold at auction. On November 22, 1884, Fortune started a new paper, the *Freeman,* with Jerome B. Peterson. On October 8, 1887, Fortune left the *Freeman,* to take a job at the New York *Sun,* and turned the paper over to Peterson and his elder brother, Emanuel, Jr. A week later the name of the paper was changed to the *Age.* Thomas returned to the paper in 1891, after the death of his brother, and continued to contribute to both the *Age* and the *Sun* until his mental breakdown a few years later. He died in 1928.*

EDWIN F. HORN was born in 1859 in Tennessee. In 1878 he published *Our Age* in Evansville, Indiana. A few years later he moved to

* The most complete account of Fortune's life is a BA thesis by A. Terry Slocum, "Timothy Thomas Fortune, a Negro in American Society" (Princeton University, 1967).

Indianapolis and, along with E. E. Cooper, founded the *Colored World,* which later became the Indianapolis *World.* In 1880 he was an alternate delegate from the First District in Indiana to the Republican National Convention held in Chicago. In 1887 he edited *Justice* in Chattanooga, Tennessee.

HENRY J. LEWIS, probably the first black political cartoonist, was brought up in Pine Bluff, Arkansas. In 1879, when he was twenty-five years old, his sketches appeared in *Harper's Weekly.* He moved to Indianapolis, Indiana, where, beginning in 1889, his cartoons were printed regularly in the Indianapolis *Freeman.*

IRVING GARLAND PENN was born in New Glasgow, Virginia, in 1867. His family soon moved to Lynchburg, Virginia, where he attended school. He left high school but passed a teacher's examination and taught in 1883 and 1884. In 1886 he worked for the Lynchburg *Laborer.* He subsequently worked for the Richmond *Planet,* the Virginia *Lancet,* the Knoxville *Negro World,* and the New York *Age.* In 1891 he published *The Afro-American Press and Its Editors.*

JAMES WILLIAM CHARLES PENNINGTON was born in Maryland, and in 1829 the family moved to Brooklyn. He educated himself and became a minister before moving to Hartford, Connecticut, where he had a congregation, was an active abolitionist, and participant in the convention movement. He then traveled to England and the West Indies and returned to New York, where he became pastor of the Shiloh Presbyterian Colored Church. In 1840 he was elected president of the Connecticut State Temperance and Moral Reform Society. In 1841 he published *A Textbook of the Origins and History of the Colored People* and in 1849 published *The Fugitive Blacksmith.* In 1849 he was a delegate to the Peace Congress at Paris, attended the National Levee at the mansion of the Foreign Secretary of State, de Tocqueville, and was given a Doctor of Divinity degree by the University of Heidelberg. In 1853 he became pastor of the Prince Street Presbyterian Church in New York. In 1859 he became pastor of the Second Colored Presbyterian Church, Newton, Long Island, and correspondent to the *Weekly Anglo-African.*

JEROME B. PETERSON was born in Brooklyn on September 12, 1859. His mother was from South Carolina, and his father was a white minister. During the draft riots of 1863, Peterson's father was almost lynched and escaped with the aid of the crew members of the ship upon which he operated a barbershop. Both the mob and those who saved him were Irish. Afterward he took his family to England, where they stayed for two years, until the war was over.

Peterson attended a black elementary school and later the New York Evening School on West Thirteenth Street in New York City. After graduation he worked at the Freedmen's Bank (185 Beekman Street), a branch of the national bank established to aid newly freed slaves. Peterson rose to the position of clerk before the bank failed in 1877. When this occurred, Samuel Harris, the manager, went into the brokerage and law business and took Peterson with him as his assistant.

In 1887 Peterson became associate editor of the New York *Freeman* and later became co-editor of the paper (now called the *Age*) along with Fortune.

In 1904 he was appointed U.S. consul to Puerto Cabello, Venezuela. He resigned after a year to return to the *Age*. In 1906 he was appointed deputy collector of Internal Revenue and ten years later was appointed stamp deputy at San Juan, Puerto Rico, where he remained until 1919. He was demoted (owing to political changes) to storekeeper gauger, a post which he held until he retired in 1931 at the age of seventy-two.

PINCKNEY BENTON STEWART PINCHBACK was born in 1837 and at the age of eleven entered Gilmore's High School in Cincinnati, where he remained for two years. In 1848 his father, Major William Pinchback, died, and Pinckney took various odd jobs. From 1854 to 1861 he worked on steamboats on the Mississippi and Missouri rivers. He went to New Orleans in May, 1862, and organized an all-black unit, the Corps d'Afrique. He was made captain of the group but resigned his commission a year later because of discrimination. In 1867 he organized the Fourth Ward Republican Club and was sent to the Louisiana Constitutional Convention in 1868. He was elected president pro tempore of the session of 1871 and became the first lieutenant governor when O. J. Dunn, the incumbent, died. He filled the office for only one month. He also took over the office of Governor Henry Clay Warmouth when the latter was debarred on account of impeachment proceedings. Although elected a U.S. Senator by the Louisiana legislature in 1873, he was denied his seat. From 1870 until 1882 he edited the *Weekly Louisianian,* at times turning over the operation to T. DeS. Tucker, Joseph D. Kennedy, and J. M. Vance, Jr. In 1890 he moved to Washington, D.C.

WILLIAM A. PLEDGER was born near Jonesboro, Georgia. In 1869 he worked for the Western and Atlanta Railroad. He taught school for five years in Athens, Georgia, and was appointed to a government position before entering Atlanta University. After graduation he edited the Athens *Blade* (along with W. H. Heard) and was then appointed surveyor of customs at Atlanta. He was removed from office under Cleveland and edited the Atlanta *News* and Atlanta *Defiance* (again with Heard). He was active in the Afro-American Council and Republican politics and in 1890 was appointed inspector of immigration at Savannah. In 1894 he was admitted to practice law. Though he was referred to as "Colonel," there is no indication of military service, and the title may have been honorary.

CHARLES B. RAY became co-editor of the *Colored American* in 1838 after having been a general agent for the paper. He became the senior editor, a position he retained until the paper ceased publication. Ray had been active in the Underground Railroad and was the pastor of the Bethesda Congregational Church in New York City. His daughter, Cordelia Ray, was a corresponding editor to various papers, including the *New Era.*

MAGNUS L. ROBINSON was born in Alexandria, Virginia, on November 21, 1852. He worked there as a baker until 1868, when he entered Howard University Law School. He could not finish, however, because of poor health and taught school while working on various local papers before he and his brother established the *Virginia Post* in 1880 in Harrisonburg. In January, 1888, he, together with Frederick Douglass, Jr., began publishing a Republican paper, the *National Leader,* in Washington, D.C., and was subsequently appointed to minor political offices as a reward for his loyalty to the party. In 1890 he moved the *National Leader* to his home, thereafter calling it *Zion's Leader.*

DAVID RUGGLES published two papers, the *Mirror of Liberty* in 1837 and the *Genius of Freedom,* 1845–47. In addition, he was the secretary of the New York Vigilance Committee and in that capacity rescued many blacks who were kidnapped or threatened—one of these being Frederick Douglass. An advertisement for a grocery store appeared with his name in *Freedom's Journal* in the fall and winter of 1828. In the *Weekly Anglo-African* of 1860, he advertised his services as a hydrotherapist in Northampton, Massachusetts. He apparently moved to California during the Civil War, for in 1865 his name appeared as treasurer for the *Elevator* in San Francisco.

JOHN B. RUSSWURM was born in Port Antonio, Jamaica, in 1799 and was graduated from Bowdoin College in 1826. In 1827 he and Samuel Cornish founded *Freedom's Journal*, which lasted until March, 1829. He soon left for Liberia, where he became superintendent of the public schools and editor of the *Liberian Herald*. From 1836 until his death in 1851 he was governor of the Maryland Colony at Cape Palmas.

JOHN P. SAMPSON, editor of the *Colored Citizen* in Cincinnati during the Civil War, was a public school teacher in New York City.

JOHN SHUFTEN was born in 1840 in Georgia. He was graduated from Howard University, having studied literature and law, as well as medicine, and was admitted to practice before the United States Supreme Court. He edited the *Colored American* in Augusta, Georgia, in 1865 until it was taken over by the *Loyal Georgian*, edited by J. E. Bryant.

H. C. SMITH was born in Clarksburg, West Virginia, on January 28, 1863. He was an accomplished musician and composer before he began publishing the Cleveland *Gazette* in 1883. In return for his active support of Ohio Governor (later Senator) J. Benson Foraker in the state election he was appointed deputy oil inspector.

SAMUEL RINGGOLD WARD was born a slave on a plantation in Maryland. He was a teacher and an agent for the *Colored American* in Newark, Pennsylvania, from 1837 to 1840. He moved to Cortland, New York, where he was the pastor of a Congregational church and where he also edited the *Farmer and Northern Star*. While in New York, he helped organize the Liberal and Free Soil parties in that state. In 1850 he edited the *Impartial Citizen* in Boston, and in 1853 he was a co-editor of the *Aliened American*. Although the chronology is unclear, Ward apparently moved in the early 1850's to Canada, where he lived at the time of his work on the *Aliened American*. Since he had been a conductor on the Underground Railroad in Buffalo and Syracuse in 1851 and 1852, he may have been forced to emigrate because of his activity. He lectured for the Anti-Slavery Society of Canada and traveled to England in 1853. He published his autobiography and shortly thereafter moved to Jamaica, in the West Indies, where he died in about 1865.

The Black Press

1827–1890

The Role
of the Black Press

ALTHOUGH *the black press tended to relate to those forms of racism and oppression of immediate concern to its constituents, rather than to present systematic analyses or reports from Southern plantations, it did provide information on slavery as an institution which had been reprinted from white papers or from already published works. There was no question of its opposition to every form of slavery—the black press attacked it vigorously. Perhaps because it was a well-known subject and because the press saw its primary role as improving conditions in its communities, directly affecting the black people of the North, one finds relatively little about conditions in the South. The black press in the North identified strongly with its enslaved brothers in the South but apparently felt it could be of greater help in unifying the local communities, thereby gaining political strength.*

Efforts were constantly made through the black abolitionists and their conventions to press the government at both state and federal levels to outlaw slavery in the country as a whole. In a very direct way, through the Underground Railroad, black and white abolitionists helped escaped slaves, and vigilance committees composed of blacks were effective in preventing kidnappings and frustrating slave hunters.

The main theme which runs through the entire history of the black press is the need for self-definition, for self-determination and, most important, the need to speak for themselves.

With the following presentation to its readers the first black newspaper, Freedom's Journal, *was born.*

TO OUR PATRONS

In presenting our first number to our Patrons, we feel all the diffidence of persons entering upon a new and untried line of business.

But a moment's reflection upon the noble objects, which we have in view by the publication of this Journal; the expediency of its appearance at this time, when so many schemes are in action concerning our people—encourage us to come boldly before an enlightened publick. For we believe, that a paper devoted to the dissemination of useful knowledge among our brethren, and to their moral and religious improvement, must meet with the cordial approbation of every friend to humanity.

The peculiarities of this Journal, renders it important that we should advertise to the world our motives by which we are actuated, and the objects which we contemplate.

We wish to plead our own cause. Too long have others spoken for us. Too long has the publick been deceived by misrepresentations, in things which concern us dearly, though in the estimation of some mere trifles; for though there are many in society who exercise towards us benevolent feelings; still (with sorrow we confess it) there are others who make it their business to enlarge upon the least trifle, which tends to the discredit of any person of colour; and pronounce anathemas and denounce our whole body for the misconduct of this guilty one. We are aware that there are many instances of vice among us, but we avow that it is because no one has taught its subjects to be virtuous; many instances of poverty, because no sufficient efforts accommodated to minds contracted by slavery, and deprived of early education have been made, to teach them how to husband their hard earnings, and to secure to themselves comfort.

Education being an object of the highest importance to the welfare of society, we shall endeavour to present just and adequate views of it, and to urge upon our brethren the necessity and expediency of training their children, while young, to habits of industry, and thus forming them for becoming useful members of society. It is surely time that we should awake from this lethargy of years, and make a concentrated effort for the education of our youth. We form a spoke in the human wheel, and it is necessary that we should understand our pendence on the different parts, and theirs on us, in order to perform our part with propriety.

Though not desiring of dictating, we shall feel it our incumbent duty to dwell occasionally upon the general principles and rules of economy. The world has grown too enlightened, to estimate any man's character by his personal appearance. Though all men acknowledge the excellency of Franklin's maxims, yet comparatively few practise upon them. We may deplore when it is too late, the neglect of these self-evident truths, but it avails little to mourn. Ours will be the task of admonishing our brethren on these points.

The civil rights of a people being of the greatest value, it shall ever be our duty to vindicate our brethren, when oppressed; and to lay the case before the publick. We shall also urge upon our brethren, (who are qualified by the laws of the different states) the expediency of using their elective franchise; and of making an independent use of the same. We wish them not to become the tools of party.

And as much time is frequently lost, and wrong principles instilled, by the perusal of works of trivial importance, we shall consider it a part of our duty to recommend to our young readers, such authors as will not only enlarge their stock of useful knowledge, but such as will also serve to stimulate them to higher attainments in science.

We trust also, that through the columns of the FREEDOM'S JOURNAL, many practical pieces, having for their bases, the improvement of our brethren, will be presented to them, from the pens of many of our respected friends, who have kindly promised their assistance.

It is our earnest wish to make our Journal a medium of intercourse between our brethren in the different states of this great confederacy: that through its columns an expression of our sentiments, on many interesting subjects which concern us, may be offered to the publick: that plans which apparently are beneficial may be candidly discussed and properly weighed; if worth, receive our cordial approbation; if not, our marked disapprobation.

Useful knowledge of every kind, and everything that relates to Africa, shall find a ready admission into our columns; and as that vast continent becomes daily more known, we trust that many things will come to light, proving that the natives of it are neither so ignorant nor stupid as they have generally been supposed to be.

And while these important subjects shall occupy the columns of the FREEDOM'S JOURNAL, we would not be unmindful of our brethren who are still in the iron fetters of bondage. They are our kindred by all the times of nature; and though but little can be effected by us, still let our sympathies be poured forth, and our prayers in their behalf, ascend to Him who is able to succour them.

From the press and the pulpit we have suffered much by being incorrectly represented. Men whom we equally love and admire have not hesitated to represent us disadvantageously, without becoming personally acquainted with the true state of things, nor discerning between virtue and vice among us. The virtuous part of our people feel themselves sorely aggrieved under the existing state of things—they are not appreciated.

Our vices and our degradation are ever arrayed against us, but our virtues are passed by unnoticed. And what is still more lamentable, our friends, to whom we concede all the principles of humanity and religion, from these very causes seem to have fallen into the current of popular feeling and are imperceptibly floating on the stream—actually living in the practice of prejudice, while they abjure it in theory, and feel it not in their hearts. Is it not very desirable that such should know more of our actual condition; and of our efforts and feelings, that in forming or advocating plans for our amelioration, they may do it more understandingly? In the spirit of candor and humility we intend by a simple representation of facts to lay our case before the public, with a view to arrest the progress of prejudice, and to shield ourselves against the consequent evils. We wish to conciliate all and to irritate none, yet we must be firm and unwavering in our principles, and persevering in our efforts.

If ignorance, poverty and degradation have hitherto been our unhappy lot; has the Eternal decree gone forth, that our race alone are to remain in this state, while knowledge and civilization are shedding their enlivening rays over the rest of the human family? The recent travels of Denham and Clapperton in the interior of Africa, and the interesting narrative which they have published; the establishment of the republic of Hayti after years of sanguinary warfare; its subsequent progress in all the arts of civilization; and the advancement of liberal ideas in South America, where despotism has given place to free governments, and where many of our brethren now fill important civil and military stations, prove the contrary.

The interesting fact that there are FIVE HUNDRED THOUSAND free persons of colour, one half of whom might peruse, and the whole be benefitted by the publication of the Journal; that no publication, as yet, has been devoted exclusively to their improvement—that many selections from approved standard authors, which are within the reach of few, may occasionally be made—and more important still, that this large body of our citizens have no public channel—all serve to prove the real necessity, at present, for the appearance of the FREEDOM'S JOURNAL.

It shall ever be our desire so to conduct the editorial department of our paper as to give offence to none of our patrons; as nothing is farther from us than to make it the advocate of any partial views, either in politics or religion. What few days we can number, have been devoted to the improvement of our brethren; and it is our earnest wish that the remainder may be spent in the same delightful service.

In conclusion, whatever concerns us as a people, will ever find a ready admission into the FREEDOM'S JOURNAL, interwoven with all the principal news of the day.

And while every thing in our power shall be performed to support the character of our Journal, we would respectfully invite our numerous friends to assist by their communications, and our coloured brethren to strengthen our hands by their subscriptions, as our labour is one of common cause, and worthy of their consideration and support. And we most earnestly solicit the latter, that if at any time we should seem to be zealous, or too pointed in the inculcation of any important lesson, they will remember, that they are equally interested in the cause in which we are engaged, and attribute our zeal to the peculiarities of our situation; and our earnest engagedness in their well-being.

Freedom's Journal, New York, March 16, 1827

With the following concluding assessment, Freedom's Journal *ceased publication. Its editor, John Russwurm, soon left for Liberia, where he died in 1851.*

The time having arrived when our connexion with the *Journal* is about to be dissolved, we feel it our duty to offer, for the last time, a few words to the candid consideration of those friends who have been kind enough to patronize our feeble attempt, to dispel the clouds of ignorance and folly which surround us as a community. If we cast our eyes at home, in our own land, or abroad, in foreign lands, we find none so low and degraded—so dead to all the noble feelings which actuate intelligent and immortal beings. In the bosom of the most enlightened government, we are ignorant and degraded; under the most republican government, we are denied all the rights and privileges of citizens, and what is still worse, we see no probability that we as a community will ever make it our earnest endeavor to rise from our ignorance and degradation. The vain and idle things of the moment occupy our minds and woe betide the being who has the temerity to denounce them, and tell us that we should aim at employing our time more profitably. . . .

The principal objects which we have ever had in view, have been the dissemination of useful knowledge; the defence of our community; the necessity and advantages of education; and lately, the expediency of emigration to Liberia. It is admitted that for a community to become eminently virtuous, it is highly essential that there should be a general dissemination of knowledge, and for the attainment of this, the press is a powerful auxiliary in the hands of enlightened and virtuous men. But we are apt when taking a view of the objects which are made subservient to human happiness to forget this, as if society could exist in its present happy state without its aid. We would then inculcate upon our readers the necessity of extending a patronising hand to the support of whatever is calculated to promote their happiness, and to improve their minds. It is admitted, that the standard of education is deplorably low, and that some general movement should be made towards raising it—but what avail all these admissions, without an effort to do something; for it is a fact, that while the rest of the community, are daily making higher attainments in knowledge, we remain almost stationary, with prejudices increasing daily. It is not our province here to enquire why prejudices should be in the pathway of the man of colour, all we know is that they are there, and are ever likely to remain, until the theories of our African Symmes shall take place, and produce a general amalgamation. In many things, it is our duty to experiment until we arrive at the truth; but unless we have reasonable hopes for a favorable issue, they are all useless; hence then, we conclude that all efforts here, to improve the mass of coloured persons must prove abortive; and this conclusion we adopt from the evidence of our own eyes.

In our efforts to improve our condition; we have endeavored to place before our readers every thing which had the least tendency to improve them morally, by portraying virtue in the most alluring colours, and depicting vice and folly unadorned with any of those flimsy veils with which their votaries are ever desirous of arraying them. We have kept nothing back through fear; when time and occasion called for a defence against the attacks of vile men whose aim was principally to hold us up as beings devoid of all principle, we have boldly come forward in defence of our brethren from a principle of duty; when our vices or follies deserved censure, we have not been backward in giving it; discarding all motives of self-interest, relying wholly upon the justness of our remarks and the necessity and sense of duty which prompted us to offer them.

Education being the principal mover to every other improvement, we have laboured constantly to place its advantages in the most striking light by citing the blessings which have flowed from it in other portions of our country, where it is more generally enjoyed and appreciated. We have endeavored by holding up ignorance to view, and the evils which befall society from such a state, to render our readers more sensible than ever of the imperious necessity that more general efforts should be made for the education of our rising youth, for it is upon them only that all our hopes for the future respectability of our people are fixed; they are last stay of the departed glory of Ancient Africa—if we neglect them *now,* we must never expect to see them qualified to act their part in life, any better than we have. . . .

. . . Generally speaking, an editor's office is a thankless one and if so among an enlightened people: what could *we* expect? We are therefore not in the least astonished, that we have been slandered by the villainous—that our name is byword among the more ignorant, for what less could we expect? Prepared, we entered the lists; and unvanquished we retire, with the hope that the talent committed to our care, may yet be exerted under more favorable auspices, and upon minds more likely to appreciate its value.

Freedom's Journal, New York, March 28, 1829

With John Russwurm gone, Samuel Cornish, the former co-editor of Freedom's Journal, *resumed his journalistic activities. As the new editor, he changed the name of the paper and, in the following prospectus, clearly indicates the source of his disagreements with Russwurm.*

TO OUR PATRONS, AND THE PUBLICK GENERALLY

In offering the first number of this paper for your perusal, we deem it necessary to state its object and the manner in which we purpose to conduct it.

Viewing this great Republick as composed of so many different grades and capacities, the Editor considers that there is great room for, and that it is all important that he as well as others, should contribute his mite towards the improvement of all its parts, every constituent must become perfect, as far as human perfectability goes, before the body politic can be made perfect. Under this view of the subject, the Editor feels that he is as much interested in the general improvement of Society, as any other citizen; and hopes through the divine blessing to devote these pages and his other humble abilities successfully, to the general benefits of Society. But as humanity and more especially the principles of the gospel of Jesus Christ, inculcate sympathy and love, to the oppressed and afflicted, this Paper will more especially be devoted to the rights and interests of the coloured population. It will at all times give a correct representation of that people, in opposition to the persecuting, slanderous accounts, too often presented to the publick eye, it will be the constant aim of the Editor, as far as in his power, to remove the many abuses which exist among his brethren, to promote habits of industry and economy, and to inculcate the importance of an improved education. In endeavoring to accomplish these objects, he will elicit the united intelligence of his brethren and the friends of his colour, and act under the influence of that intelligence. Virtuous characters, instances of laudable ambition, attractive science, etc. will constantly be through these columns presented to his readers, with the view of exciting the spirit of emulation, in everything noble, everything virtuous and good.

It may be asked by some, if such are the views of the Editor, why did he withdraw from the editorial responsibilities, which he assumed some time ago? I answer, were it practicable his conduct on that occasion, could be supported by abundant and satisfactory reasons; but it is otherwise. The Editor hopes that neither his friends nor brethren will prejudge the future by the past, but will give this paper a fair trial, and let it stand or fall by its merits.

And as all are interested in the various objects presented in this address, he humbly solicits the patronage of all, and should any circumstance lead to the least impropriety, he hopes his friends will not be backward in suggesting it. And he promises a reform.

A word on another subject and I am done, the sudden change of the late Editor of "The Freedom's Journal" in respect to colonisation, has excited much astonishment, and led to many inquiries; to me the subject is equally strange as to others and I can only dispose of it, by classing it with the other novelties of the day. I conclude by saying my views, and the views of the intelligent of my brethren generally, are the same as ever in respect to colonisation; we believe it may benefit the few that emigrate, and survive, and as a missionary station, we consider it as a grand and glorious establishment, and shall do all in our power to promote its interests, looking toward the glorious period, when civilization and religion shall have spread over the vast and important continent of Africa. But as it respects three millions that are now in the United States, and the eight millions that in twenty or twenty-five years will be in this country, we think it in no wise calculated, to meet their wants or ameliorate their condition.

The Rights of All, New York, May 29, 1829

Junius C. Morel's name occurs frequently among leaders of the early convention movement. Though there is no evidence that he actually published a paper, the following proposal, written by him and John P. Thompson, indicates his attitudes.

THE AMERICAN

We believe that whatever measures are used, or resorted to, having for its objects the removal of our active, free born Colored Population out of these United States, ought, by all true Philanthropists, to be considered and treated as measures taken to perpetuate Slavery, with its baneful effects, in this great Republic.

The primary objects of the *American* shall be, to convey useful and wholesome information to our colored Brethren and at the same time endeavor to stimulate them in the paths of education and virtue. Religion, Morality, and Temperance being the three greatest steps in civilization, shall always find a conspicuous place in our sheets. The Constitution of these States shall be respected by us, whilst we shall unceasingly cry against Slavery in any manner, firmly believing there exists no such term in the Philanthropist's Vocabulary, as Humane Slaveholders. The sheets of the *American* shall never be polluted by advocating such pithy Philanthropy as is set forth by the American Colonization Society and its emissaries. For before God we know of no other home for the native born man of color, than these United States. The true interests of our brethren shall be faithfully watched and zealously advocated. Under such impressions and with these promises, we have deemed it expedient to call our friends and brethren to support us in our undertaking, resting perfectly satisfied that they are sensibly convinced of the utility of establishing such a vehicle in this city. The first number of the *American* will appear as soon as a sufficient number of subscribers are obtained to warrant the publishing.

[Philadelphia, May 30, 1831]

The *Liberator,* Boston, July 2, 1831

Eight years after the Rights of All *ceased, a new paper, the* Weekly Advocate, *was inaugurated, published by Samuel Ennalls and Philip A. Bell. It was soon to have the Reverend Samuel Cornish, the co-founder of the first black newspaper and vigorous opponent of colonization, as its editor.*

The addition of another Paper to the list of those already before the Public, may be, and is probably considered by some persons of common observation and superficial reflection, as unnecessary and uncalled for; but numerous, however, as we freely allow them to be, it is believed by many of our people, that there is still a vacancy to be supplied, a chain to be filled up; and that there is NOW a clear opening for one of a different character, which shall be devoted to the moral improvement and amelioration of our race. After the most mature deliberation we have commenced the noble enterprise. Our paper, though somewhat small in size, will be found valuable in contents. The advantages of the present undertaking are not to be estimated by words, they are incalculable. If the Press, a "FREE PRESS," be a foe to the tyrant—if its blessings be so great and innumerable; the Question naturally presents itself, why do we not have one of our own? We now have a Press and Paper under our own entire control and we call upon our friends, one and all, to come forward and assist us in this work and labour of love, and share in the consequent blessings thereof. Are there not hundreds among you, who will welcome the Advocate as a Friendly Visitor?—Philanthropists! shall we have LIGHT, clear and irresistible Light on all the important topics of the day, or shall we live and expire in the gloom of ignorance, with the lights of science shining around us.

The *Advocate* will be like a chain, binding you together as ONE. Its columns will always be the organ of your wishes and feelings, and the proper medium for laying your claims before the Public. What then, in the name of common sense, is wanted to enable us to GO FOR-

WARD, in the successful prosecution of this new enterprise?—Judging from numbers, we are abundantly able. O how often have we been insulted and degraded, and how frequently do we feel the want of an ADVOCATE among us! Those of us who shall be instrumental in establishing such a paper, will reap a *rich reward in their own bosoms*— not in silver and gold—but in the intelligence and improvement of our race in intellectual knowledge and refinement. And when time has consigned us to our honoured graves, the good we have done will live after us. Future generations will partake largely and freely of the fruits of the tree planted by our bounty, rise up and call us blessed. . . .

. . . We need scarcely say, we are opposed to *Colonization.* It matters not to us what features it may assume whether it present itself in the garb of philanthropy, or assumes the mild and benign countenance of Christianity, or comes with the selfish aspect of Politics; we will believe, assert and maintain (So help us God!) that we are opposed to the exclusive emigration and colonization of the People of Color of these United States. We hold ourselves ready, at all times to combat with opposite views, and defend these our principles to the last! In regard to TEMPERANCE, we go the whole in this good cause. But our motto is *Temperance in all things.* We shall advocate Universal Suffrages and Universal Education, and we shall oppose all Monopolies, which oppress the poor and laboring classes of society. . . .

We need not say that our entire dependence for support is upon the colored portion of this great community, when we tell them that the *ADVOCATE is their paper,* in every sense of the word—that it will advocate their just claims and rights—sustain them in every proper appeal to manly generosity and justice. And as the cause of IMMEDIATE EMANCIPATION is based on incontrovertible right, we shall at all times, take it up with resolution, and defend it with firmness. We trust we possess sufficient moral courage to assert THE TRUTH and maintaining it at all hazards. We shall neither be frightened or coaxed from our duty. The empty threats of the oppressor we despise. We shall, however, always point out that course to the friendless and unprotected, which will bring *happiness* to the mind, and will give such advice as will prove useful to all in the wearisome journey of human life.

The people of color have often said among themselves. We want an Advocate of our own—devoted particularly to our own interests—

conducted by ourselves, devoted to our moral, mental and political improvement, containing the news of the day, and a variety of scientific and literary matter; and ONE in which we can make known our various and respective occupations in life, through the medium of advertising. To such we say. Look here! Today you have spread before your eyes the desideratum you have so long, and ardently prayed for. Here is your ADVOCATE and FRIEND. . . .

The Weekly Advocate, New York, January 7, 1837

At the height of the convention movement, the newly formed Weekly Advocate *reaffirmed the need for an independent spokesman for the black community.*

. . . Those who have seen the *Advocate,* have expressed their sincere desire that it should become general among us. And who can assign a reason why it should not? Heads of families! do you not want such an *Advocate* and *Friend,* to cheer your leisure hours; and impart useful and moral instruction to all the members of your family; and as a body, how often have you been insulted and degraded, and your dearest rights trampled under foot; even your own private habitations have been invaded, and the unsuspecting young man or woman to whom LIBERTY was sweet; has been KIDNAPPED and carried far away from the light of home! Truly, "No man seemeth to care for our souls." Where is *that paper* you can emphatically call *your own?* We give you the *Advocate,* for a little more than the expense of its weekly delivery at your doors. Let us then have your united support, accompanied with your prayers for our prosperity, and we shall by so doing accomplish two great and important objects. 1. Insure our own personal happiness and strengthen the foundation of future knowledge. 2. Refute the slanders of our enemies who tell us "No such paper is wanted; nor will it ever be supported by the coloured population." A grosser libel was never perpetrated on our people.

The Weekly Advocate, New York, January 14, 1837

The Weekly Advocate *was changed as an indication of the emphasis on their demand for full citizenship rights to the* Colored American, *and was directed toward the unification of the various black communities.*

PROPOSALS AND PLAN OF A NEWSPAPER
FOR THE PEOPLE OF COLOR.

"THE COLORED AMERICAN"
Rev. Samuel E. Cornish, Editor

ONE DOLLAR & FIFTY CENTS per annum
always payable IN ADVANCE

This paper is designed to be the organ of Colored Americans—to be looked on as their own, and devoted to their interests—through which they can make known their views to the public—can communicate with each other and their friends, and their friends with them; and to maintain their well-known sentiments on the subjects of Abolition and Colonization, viz.—emancipation without expatriation—the extirpation of prejudice—the enactment of equal laws, and a full and free investiture of their rights as men and citizens.

It is well known that our paper, being thinly scattered over the country, in small communities, remote from, and unknown to each other, without any means of cultivating acquaintance, and interchanging views and feelings one with the other—has operated to their disadvantage, and retarded improvement. The publication of *"The Colored American,"* therefore, will open a channel of communication for the interchange of thought, and through which light and knowledge may flow to instruct, enliven and fertilize all.

But further, to promote the welfare of our brethren and friends, and to secure for the paper their general and united support, *"The Colored American"* is established on the following basis, viz.—That when the monies received from Subscribers shall be sufficient to cover actual expenditures the surplus to go (through the hands of a Board of Supervision) for the general good of the colored people—to sustain agents and lecturers for the improvement of the free, and to free the enslaved.

It may be shown, that in this way, if every colored person who is able, *will take the paper and promptly pay the price,* a large sum of money may be collected and expended to bless and benefit our brethren;—enough to support all the lecturers and agents who are now so much needed, to visit, to lecture and to instruct them. To prove this, look at the fact—that there are in the city of New York about 16,000 *free* people of color; in the State, 44,000; 22,000 in New England; 18,000 in New Jersey; 38,000 in Pennsylvania; and in a word, nearly 200,000 in the rest of the States. Now it is plain that if *every one that can do it* (and what industrious man or woman is there that cannot?) were to pay the small sum constituting the price, viz. *a dollar and a half,* the whole together would amount to a large sum, enough to defray all expenses, and leave a handsome balance with which to promote the holy cause of abolition. Let *all,* then, come up to the support of the paper as *one man.*

"United we stand, divided we fall."

P. A. BELL, Proprietor
SAMUEL E. CORNISH, Editor

The editor, aware of the diversity of opinion in reference to the title of this "Paper," thinks it not amiss here to state some reasons for selecting this name, as more appropriate than any other. Many would gladly rob us of the endeared name, *"Americans,"* a distinction more emphatically belonging to us, than five-sixths of this nation, and one that we will never yield. In complexion, in blood and in nativity, we are decidedly more exclusively "American" than our white brethren; hence the propriety of the name of our paper, *Colored American,* and of identifying the name with all our institutions, in spite of our enemies, who would rob us of our nationality and reproach us as exoticks.

But why colored? some have said; why draw this cord of cast? Because the peculiarity of our circumstances require special instrumentalities and action. We have in view, objects peculiar to ourselves, and in contradistinction from the mass. How then, shall we be known and our interests presented in community, but by some distinct, specific name—and what appellation is so inoffensive, so acceptable as COLORED PEOPLE—COLORED AMERICANS.

We are written about, preached to, and prayed for, as *Negroes, Africans,* and *blacks,* all of which have been stereotyped, as names of reproach, and on that account, if no other, are unacceptable.

Let us and our friends unite, in baptizing the term "Colored Americans" and henceforth let us be written of, preached of, and prayed for as such. It is the true term, and one which is above reproach.

Why we should have a paper.

1. Because the colored people of these United States have to contend with all the multiplied ills of slavery, more cruel in its practice and unlimited in its duration than was ever before upon any people; and we are proscribed and pressed down by prejudice more wicked and fatal than even slavery itself. These evils not only pervade the length and breadth of the land, but they have their strong hold in the Church of Jesus Christ, where they abide and act themselves out, contrary to all its holy precepts. Colored men must do something, must make some effort to drive these "abominations of desolation" from the church and the world; they must establish and maintain the Press, and through it, speak out in *thunder tones,* until the nation repent and render to every man that which is just and equal—and until the church possess herself of the mind which was in Jesus Christ, and cease to oppress her poor brother, because God hath dyed him a darker hue.

2. Because our afflicted population in the free states, are scattered in handfulls over nearly 5000 towns, and can only be reached by the Press—a public journal must therefore be sent down at least weekly, to rouse them up. To call all their energies into action—and where they have been down-trodden, paralyzed and worn out to create new energies for them, that such dry bones may live.

Such an organ can be furnished at little cost, so as to come within the reach of every man, and carry to him lessons of instruction on religion and morals, lessons on industry and economy—until our entire people are of one heart and of one mind, in all the means of their salvation, both temporal and spiritual.

3. Because without such an organ, we never can enlist the sympathy of the nation in our behalf, and in behalf of the slave; and until this is done, we shall have accomplished nothing, nor shall we have proved ourselves worthy to be free men and to have our grievances redressed. Because the wise and good awake and consecrate themselves to our cause, we ourselves must have proclaimed our oppression and wrongs from the HOUSE-TOP. When did Greece and Poland win the sympathy of the world; after they had published their wrongs, asserted their rights and sued for freedom at the hands of their oppressors. Then, and only then, were they worthy to be freemen, nor should *we* expect the *boon,* until we feel its importance and pray for its possession. With us this is to be a great moral struggle and let us brethren be united in our efforts.

4. Because no class of men, however pious and benevolent can take our place in the great work of redeeming our character and removing our disabilities. They may identify themselves with us, and enter into our sympathies. Still it is ours to will and do—both of which we trust are about to be done, and in the doing of which, this journal *as an appropriate engine,* may exert a powerful agency. We propose to make it a journal of facts and instruction. It will go out freighted with information for all—it will tell tales of woe, both in the church and out of the church; such as are calculated to make the heart to bleed and the ear to burn. It will bring to light many hidden things, which must be revealed and repented of, or this nation must perish.

The Colored American, New York, March 4, 1837

The editor of the Champion of Equal Rights, *John G. Stewart, had published a paper in Albany, New York, during 1831 and 1832, entitled the* African Sentinel and Journal of Liberty. *No copy of either paper has been found, but these documents represent an indication of his interests and activities.*

PROPOSALS

For publishing in the city of New York, a Weekly Paper, to be entitled THE CHAMPION OF EQUAL RIGHTS by *John G. Stewart*

THE proposed publication will be devoted to the interest and advancement of the People of Color in the United States, and conducted upon the principle of "Justice to all men." The subscriber is fully aware that to elevate the condition of the man of color in this country must be by the infusion of a spirit of political and commercial enterprise, and to that end this paper shall studiously aim. In brief, this publication shall be every colored man's newspaper, though it shall not be void of interest to men of all colors. We will at all times endeavor to disabuse the public mind in relation to the character and conduct of the colored people generally in the city of New York and other places, where, through the hostility of the pro-slavery press, the motive of the colored man is impugned, and his too often unimpeachable moral character aspersed with impunity.

This paper will contain, independent of a general summary of the news of the day and other interesting miscellaneous matter, a con-

densed portion weekly of the history of the colored race from the earliest ages. It will also contain Biography and Sketches of character of
those Africans, and People of Color, who have distinguished themselves in ancient and modern times; but more particularly those of our
own country. We would here take the occasion to state for the information of the public that this paper, with the exception of the speci-
men number, will not be issued from the press until one thousand
good subscribers are obtained to warrant its publication. However, we
are confidently assured that that number can be obtained immediately
in the city of New York alone, and we feel assured that half that number may be obtained among our friends in Albany and its vicinity. It
is believed that this paper will effect for the colored man in a political,
literary and commercial point of view what the *Colored American* is
calculated to effect in a moral and religious view. This paper will
therefore not come in collision with any similar print; but pursue "the
even tenor of its way" uninfluenced by sectarian or party views. With
these brief views we submit our prospectus to an enlightened public.

We cannot conclude, however, without respectfully requesting our
friends and the friends of the colored man generally throughout the
country to exert themselves a little to obtain subscribers for our paper,
and send their names to the subscriber in New York, free of post-
age. . . .

The Colored American, New York, November 10, 1838

*The dilemma of having to choose between the lesser of two objection-
able candidates in an election brought Reverend Cornish and his succes-
sors into conflict.*

. . . But says Bro. Cornish (in effect) you are bound to vote for the
best of two men, though both may be bad, to prevent the greater evil;
and he might strengthen his argument by saying, the good order of society requires it, for if you do not vote for the lesser, other men will
vote for the greater and elect him. Be it so then. We have no right
whatever to involve ourselves in the greater guilt by sustaining the
greater sin. But if you vote for neither, you disfranchise yourself,
which you have no right to do. Granted that we have no right to disfranchise ourselves when we can vote and not involve us in guilt—
when we cannot without sustaining moral evil as in slaveholding, we

are bound to disfranchise ourselves. If other men will do wrong the guilt be on their heads.

Finally, so long as abolitionists disregard this rule in voting and vote for party without regard to their abolition principles, so long will they be guilty, and so long shall we have slavery in some of its forms amongst us. We may create an universal conscience upon the moral bearings of slavery; but until that conscience directs our votes in strict accordance with out principles, we shall have slavery nevertheless.

This is our political abolition, and only a long absence from home has prevented us from making an exposition of our creed before.

The Colored American, New York, November 9, 1839

The Aliened American *grew out of the Ohio Conventions of Colored Citizens, which met periodically to discuss the oppressive conditions of their people and to formulate alternatives. From 1849 to 1852 the conventions appointed committees to establish a newspaper, based on the popular joint-stock principle, but no one was willing to assume the task. At last, Charles Howard Day, Samuel Ringgold Ward, and J. W. C. Pennington agreed to accept the position.*

. . . There are, in all the United States, but two newspapers conducted by Colored Americans, and those in New York State, while west of New York State, reside the majority of the Colored Americans of the Free States. This portion of our fellow citizens, deprived, for consecutive years, by what is miscalled Law, of almost every right dear to freemen, and because thus deprived, made helpless, comparatively—this class of native-born citizens, thus treated worse than foreigners—have had no mouthpiece to speak for them. This paper speaks for them, first through its name—*Aliened American.* Born under the United States' Constitution, and entitled by it, to all the rights and immunities of other citizens, the State and National Governments have not only disfranchised, they have ostracized—have made them aliens—through their Law, their Public Opinion and their Community Regulations.—Our color has been, generally, a mark of degradation, no matter how learned, how eloquent, or how well-disposed we have been. In the honorable instances of communities and individuals where color has *not* been regarded a crime, it has often been owing to our becoming better known.

What we propose to do by this paper is to make our way where our personal presence would be excluded, and by appealing to the judgment of men, to induce them to act towards us as they would desire us to act, were our conditions reversed. This paper, therefore, will endeavor to represent Colored Americans by insisting that Manhood is not justly measured by the color of the hair, the shape of the nose, or the hue of the skin.

Another object of this Periodical, is to aid the *educational* development of Colored Americans; to assist in the enforcing of an appreciation of the benefit of *trades* [industrial education] and to aim at our Social Elevation. We have a work to accomplish, which, however Law may facilitate, it can never, itself, wholly finish. "Self effort" nerving our hearts, we can remove every just ground for reproach, and faster than ever before, *live down* the already shallow excuses for our oppression.

But we speak not for ourselves alone. We speak for Humanity. If Humanity be a unit, wherever it is cloven down, whenever the rights common to human beings are infringed, there do we sympathize; and reserving to ourselves the decision as to the *how* and the *when,* we shall do our part to relieve that Humanity. Our humble advocacy rests not upon the accident of color. We claim for all and especially for all Americans, equal justice before American Law; and are willing to stand or fall by its just application, under the Constitution of our common country.

The Aliened American, while it will give prominence to Literature, Science, and Arts, will be a faithful transcript of the News of the week. Its Foreign and Home Correspondence, (for which ample arrangements have been made,) will weekly bring us in connection with all parts of the World.

In the Foreign Department we have secured the valuable services of Dr. S. C. Murray, formerly of New Bedford, Mass., but now of Canada West, who intends to remain in the Old Country for two years. One other gentleman, whose name we are not permitted to give, is expecting to sail for Europe, shortly, and will be a regular contributor to our columns.

In the Home Department, we are able to announce as Corresponding Editors, Samuel R. Ward, Esq., of Toronto, Canada West; and Rev. J. W. C. Pennington, D.D. of New York City.

Among our regular contributors we are permitted to name Rev. Amos G. Beman of New Haven, Conn., Dr. Martin R. Delany, of

Pittsburgh, Pa., and a host of good and true men from among us, in all departments of life; and others, from our white friends, whom we need not now mention.

Considering the amount of reading matter in our columns and the price $1.50 per year, we furnish the cheapest paper now published among us. While we heartily desire to see every one of our papers sustained, we look especially to our Western friends, for a support worthy of their numbers.

Finally, in nailing our colors to the mast, in the name of the Aliened American, we have accepted an office from which, for two years past, we have turned away, hoping and laboring for some other person to assume the responsibility. We are not here of our own seeking. The voice of twenty-five thousand oppressed ones has called us forth, to these duties; and being thus called, we claim an indulgence and forbearance, such as brothers alone can give. With the continued, constant, substantial support of our friends, we can still face the enemy, and our heart never fail.

The Aliened American, Cleveland, April 9, 1853

The author of the following "Salutation," Samuel R. Ward, corresponding editor of the Aliened American, *was a recent emigrant to Canada.*

I came to Canada to enjoy greater liberty, than the Black Man ever had, or ever will have, in my native country, but I came, also, to enjoy, in the bosom of my family, an exemption from the toils to which the best 13 years of my life had been devoted, and to which the living of my dependent family had been sacrificed. Neither to travel and lecture, nor to edit a paper, in whole or in part, was my determination. I commenced lecturing, however, just 48 hours from my arrival hither, and I have been at it ever since. And I am requested to edit one paper, to act as corresponding editor of another, and, I am regular contributor to a third. So the determinations of my manhood, in these matters, have proven little more stable than the soap bubbles, and cobhouses of my boyhood. To the charge of fickleness to which this statement may subject me, I reply, simply, that one of my earliest and firmest determinations, one yet unshaken by years of poverty, and progressing premature old age, was *to serve my own people, to the extent of my very limited ability,—whensoever, howsoever, and wheresoever, I might have opportunity.* Therefore, though I have not a penny to invest in newspapers, while poverty and bankruptcy forbid my devoting other hours to this service than those I can spare from the toil needed to support and educate my large family, I am as ready now, as I was fourteen years ago, when a young man, to do, cheerfully, what in me lies, in the promotion of our sacred cause. Hence, my acceptance of the humble post, to which the fondness of my friend W. H. Day, Esq. assigns me, as one of his corresponding editors of this Journal.

I feel less responsibility in the matter, because of the well-known efficiency of Mr. Day, on whose ship, I simply engage for a voyage, as second mate, and because, to keep up my nautical (if not *naughty*) figure, the pious and learned Rev. Dr. Pennington, is the first mate of our gallant vessel. The former gentleman I have known from *his* boyhood, and the latter has known me from *mine.*—From both, I have always received the kindest, warmest friendship and I take great pleasure in saying, with all the inferiority I feel, in comparison with those gentlemen, I am proud of the distinction of being, in so intimate a sense, a fellow-laborer with them—a subaltern to them.

Before saying more, I beg leave to intimate, that though a resident of another country, from choice, and ardently attached to the Institutions and Government of my adopted country, I shall not in this Paper, say aught savoring of discourtesy towards my American Brother, as such, nor shall I suffer myself to give a British coloring to any of the subjects I shall herein discuss. In the maintenance of this resolution, I shall be guided no more by my sense of propriety, than by the fact that I am editing a British newspaper, in which I have ample scope for saying all the British things I desire to give publicity to.

The Black People of Ohio, in particular, and of the Great West in general are the most progressive of our people, in the United States. Neither in America or in Europe is there to be found an example of a people who are a very small minority in a State, robbed of so many civil and political rights, and liable to so many outrages, who have made so much progress as these people have during the past quarter of a century. The pauper classes of Europe, find all manner of civil equality and general encouragement. They may rise to any distinction, or enjoy any honors or emoluments after which they may lust. That they should make progress in a country that fosters and shelters and encourages them; that they should vigorously and successfully labor to enrich, adorn, defend, and build up a country thus endeared to them, is not for a moment to be wondered at. Nor is it so great an achievement on their part after all. They find a country ample for their residence, a soil rich in exhaustless resources; and *liberties already fought for and won* by others, ready to their hand, and for their enjoyment. But the Black Man escaping from the savages of Slavedom, finds here discouragement, disfranchisement, prejudice, Negrohate, in every nook and corner of every locality, and almost in every individual wearing a sort of whitish skin. In spite of all this, the noble Blacks of the West, are progressing, I repeat, as rapidly as any class of poor people, however free in the land. If greater riches are to be found among our people, in the Eastern and the Southern States, they have been a longer period acquiring their wealth, and it is much less equally distributed.

The learning, talent, energy, and enterprise of the Western Blacks, I think, place them on a par with those of any other portion of the Union. And it is less flattering than historical, to add, that no portion of Disfranchised Americans have shown themselves more keenly alive to their needs and wrongs, nor more ready to put forth efforts for their redress and supply. This is new to nobody. The question now mooted and to be settled, is, how long shall this important, increasing, progressive, class of American-born citizens be trodden under foot? Or, is it possible to excite in our Anglo-Saxon Spoilers, so much of a sense of justice, as shall wipe out our wrongs? Shall the great fundamental principles of this Republic, ever be practically applied alike to whites and to blacks? Shall the Religion of the country, ever show itself to be that "wisdom which descendeth from above" and which is "without partiality"? To propose, to meet, to discuss, and in some sort, to settle this question, this paper is started. With such objects before it, what black man, what friend of the outraged Negro race, will hesitate to accord to it its needed share of support?

I hope that all who read this Journal, and who reflect upon the objects to which it is devoted, will see, that the questions we discuss, involve the Honor of the country as much as the prospects of the Blacks. For if Republican Institutions are to be despised, if Profession and Principle are to be, in America, two *distinct,* not only, but *antagonistic* entities; if hypocrisy is always to be written in legible characters, upon the figurehead of American Democracy; if complete, unchecked, eternal supremacy, is to be given to the Despotism now controlling this question, then, *not* upon the Blacks, will descend the indignant scorn of an on-looking world; the well-earned infamy of a practical affiliation with Alexanders, Napoleons, Metternichs, and Haynaus, of the Old World, will not settle like clouds of blackness upon *the oppressed,* but upon the oppressors shall this deep and dreadful disgrace descend, by the award of universal verdict. And when the God of the Poor and Needy shall arise to overwhelm this people, by the inflicting of long deferred but too well deserved judgments, at the hands of the *spoiler* and not the *spoiled,* will an account for all this iniquity be required.

The Aliened American, Cleveland, April 9, 1853

On the eve of the Civil War the new sense of urgency was reflected in this paper, edited by Thomas Hamilton. A literary magazine with the same name was also published by Hamilton.

OUR PAPER

In issuing *The Weekly Anglo-African,* we hope to supply a demand too long felt in this community. We need a Press—a press of our own. We need to know something else of ourselves through the press than the every-day statements made up to suit the feelings of the base or the interests of our opponents. We need something more than the general news or the mere gossip of the hour, such as is usually presented to us through the press, in general. Our *cause* (for in this country we have a cause) demands our own advocacy.

The powerful and influential journals around us certainly have but little especial interest in, nor can they present our case as it should be presented—surely, as we can present it ourselves. The English, the Germans, the Irish, the Welch, the French, and others, in this country, though by virtue of position, receive far more at the hands of the community and the press than we do, or as yet can hope to; and yet each of these find it necessary to have an especial *organ* of their own, through which to direct the minds, efforts, and actions of their class. And we too need a good journal in this vicinity, through which to utter our own thoughts and disseminate all those great truths that underlie the immutable principles of RIGHT and JUSTICE, from our own stand-point. We are aware that there is a difficulty in forcing home upon our people a conviction of this truth. Nevertheless, if there be any one thing that should fasten itself in the minds and hearts of our people, it is the indisputable necessity of *sustaining* and *reading* a good journal directed especially to their true interests. Such is to be THE WEEKLY ANGLO-AFRICAN; and as an earnest of our pledge, let us be a little more specific of our aim.

First, We shall through its columns strive to set forth our cause in a true and clear light, by a thorough and impartial review of our condition, past and present. As a people, we have been too long groping in the mists of an uncertainty, that brought us upon quicksand and stones of stumbling; and when the mists and vapors cleared away, we have found ourselves but shipwrecked mariners, incapable even of taking heart again for tomorrow. We shall therefore by the light of the past and the *actual* of the *present,* endeavor to point the right path for our people, both free and enslaved throughout the land.

Secondly, We shall direct the attention of the masses to industry, to perseverance, to economy, to self-reliance, to the obtainment of substantial footing in the land of our birth.

Thirdly, We shall direct attention to the cause of education among us—that is, that kind of education really essential to our present condition and future development—discouraging wholly that kind of ephemeral nonsense too often mistaken by many of us for education, but which blasts the hopes and prospects of too many of our youth.

Fourthly, We shall continually call attention to the subjects of *agriculture* and mechanics, and other elevating employments, urging our young men to be content with a frieze coat and check shirt, and a half a loaf, in the pursuit of these, rather than with lace jackets, tinselled hats and well-fed persons, to be satisfied in the occupancy of menial and unelevating and undeveloping employment.

Fifthly, We shall endeavor by a continuous correspondence from nearly every city and town in the country, to connect and keep astir our whole people, thus bringing them together weekly, to compare notes and learn of each other's prosperity.

Sixthly, We shall give, from time to time, a brief account of the resources, employments, and thrift of our people about the country, and also short biographical sketches of note-worthy colored men.

Seventhly, Of all that transpires in our common country or throughout the world that will have any bearing upon our cause, we shall take a view so broad and so comprehensive that none will fail to see either the danger or the advantage and be thus enabled to act accordingly.

Eighthly, We shall, with all our heart and strength, oppose error and wrong, and strive to promote justice and virtue, wherever we find them.

Thus shall we hope to present a paper that will meet the wants and have the cordial and united support of a generous public.

The Weekly Anglo-African, New York, July 23, 1859

Black settlers in Canada formed small but highly important colonies, mainly in southern Ontario. They published a number of newspapers, perhaps the best known of which by the Shadd family. The prospectus for the paper appeared as follows. The paper was published in several cities in Ontario during the 1850's. Osborn Perry Anderson, printer's devil to the publisher, Israel Shadd, was the only Canadian black at the Harpers Ferry raid in 1859.

THE PROVINCIAL FREEMAN
AND
SEMI-MONTHLY ADVERTISER
Is published by I. D. Shadd & Co.
Chatham, C.W.

The "Provincial Freeman" will be devoted to Anti-Slavery, Emigration, Temperance, and General Literature. It will open its columns to the views of men of different political opinions, reserving the right, as an independent journal, of full expression on all questions of projects affecting the people in a political way:

Not committed to the views of any religious sect exclusively, it will carefully observe the rights of every sect at the same time that a reservation shall be made in favor of an existing difference of opinion as to the views or actions of the sects respectively.

As an advertising medium, as a vehicle of information on Agriculture, and as an enemy to vice in any and every conceivable form, and a promoter of good morals, it shall be made worthy of the patronage of the public.

The Weekly Anglo-African, New York, November 5, 1859

The New Orleans Tribune *was one of the earliest black newspapers in the South and was printed three times a week, in French and English. The paper was an official organ of the Republican Party.*

OUR PLATFORM

. . . For colored soldiers who partake of the perils of our armies on the battlefields, we want equal treatment with the white soldiers. We claim for them fair chance for promotion, fair board of examination, and admission of colored officers to all positions and ranks, according to their merit and valor.

For colored laborers who want entire freedom and self-disposal of themselves, we want that they be as free as white men in contracting for their labor, going from place to place and enjoying the earnings of their toils.

For colored ministers, we claim the same respect that is accorded to white clergymen. . . .

For colored children, we want that they shall be received in the common school. . . .

For the colored woman, we claim the same regard as for the white one. . . .

For the colored men generally, we claim the right of suffrage, and thereby the right of self-taxation and self-government. . . .

The Tribune, New Orleans, March 5, 1865

The Black Republican, *edited by Dr. S. W. Rogers, was an organ of the Republican Party in the final days of the Civil War and during Reconstruction.*

EDITOR'S ADDRESS

Today, from the delta of the Mississippi, from the city of New Orleans, we offer to the consideration and acceptance of the American people, a newspaper conducted by American colored men.

The Black Republican Newspaper Association by which our paper is issued, is composed, with few exceptions, of American colored men, most of whom were bondmen. The editor of the *Black Republican,* now a freeman, was born, and has lived most of his life, a slave.

Agreeably to the terms of the prospectus printed in another column, the object of the *Black Republican* is the elevation and advancement of the people of color, and the establishment of liberty and justice for all men.

We think that *Black Republican* is a proper name for the newspaper organ of American colored men.

We mean to maintain our race—not deny it. The name of our paper asserts at once our race and our principles.

White men may be monarchists, aristocrats or oligarchs, but American colored men should be nothing but Republicans. In the prevalence of Republican ideas and the establishment of Republican institutions, are the hope and the safety of our people.

As we have fought for these ideas on the field, and have suffered for them through revolution, so shall we proclaim and defend them on the forum and through the press in the face of all foes whatever. Admitting the fact of complexion, we still ask nothing on that account, and shall yield nothing. As men, we require whatever belongs to man. By the help of God our paper will be an instrument, however humble, to unite our people, to bind them to the great Government that gave us freedom, to restore the National power, and establish it upon the rock of freedom and justice, and to strengthen the hands and gladden the spirit of our beloved chief magistrate, Abraham Lincoln, in whose heart is the cause of the poor. We shall give our cordial support to the men and the measures that looked to the restoration and enlargement of free Louisiana, upon the grounds of liberty and equality.

We shall seek to obtain our rights; not by overleaping them in pride or anger, but by such patient and steady steps as may best secure them.

Without further promises or declarations we present the *Black Republican* to the people.

The Black Republican, New Orleans, April 15, 1865

The Weekly Defiance, *edited by C. H. Brown, was taken over on February 24, 1883, by the Reverend W. H. Heard and W. A. Pledger. It indicated a renewed determination in the Southern black community to receive its rights.*

. . . The *Defiance* made its first appearance on the 13th of August, 1881, since that time it has never ceased nor hesitated to speak for the rights and privileges of our people. The *Defiance* has always been found denouncing the many outrageous wrongs that are daily perpetrated on our race. There is not a society in this city that but should feel themselves interested in this enterprise; for it has done much for the success and elevation of them all. Remember, citizens, that Atlanta is the capital city of Georgia and the colored citizens pay over $3,000 taxes on real estate, which is more than any other county in the state can say. So there is no excuse for not sustaining this paper. . . .

The Weekly Defiance, Atlanta, October 24, 1882

The Weekly Pelican *was edited by John L. Minor and was staunchly Republican in editorial policy.*

. . . Not since the dark days of Reconstruction has the Republican party in Louisiana been so sadly in want as in the present time, of a firm, staunch, and unswerving advocate of these eternal principles of equal rights and equal justice to all men—principles hallowed by the blood of many; and, perhaps, there never were presented as now, such signs of good omen for the starting and continuance of an able wide-awake Republican newspaper. . . . *The Pelican* will advocate protection to American industries, thereby benefitting the wage-worker, upon whom rests the stability of our government; the improvement of all waterways of sufficient importance to require government aid; the education of the people under the aid and fostering care of the National Government; the building of railroads and the enactment of judicious laws in their behalf; the passage of laws beneficient to the working man and the capital of the country; and last but not least, free speech, a fair ballot, and an honest count. . . .

The Weekly Pelican, New Orleans, December 4, 1886

At a time when women were fighting for their rights in American society, some black women were recognized as important and equal members of the black press. The following is only a partial list of these women.

WOMEN AS JOURNALISTS

Portraits and Sketches of a few of the Women Journalists of the Race.

The Negro woman's history is marvelously strange and pathetic. Unlike that of other races, her mental, moral, and physical status has not found a place in the archives of public libraries. From the womb of the future must come that poet or author to glorify her womanhood by idealizing the various phases of her character, by digging from the past examples of faithfulness and sympathy, endurance and self-sacrifice and displaying the achievements which were brightened by friction. Born and bred under both the hindrance of slavery and the limitations of her sex, the mothers of the race have kept pace with the fathers. They stand at the head of the cultured, educated families whose daughters clasp arms with the sons. The educated Negro woman occupies vantage found over the Caucasian woman of America, in that the former has had to contest with her brother every inch of the ground for recognition, the Negro man, having had his sister by his side on plantations and in rice swamps, keeps her there, now that he moves in other spheres. As she wins laurels he accords her the royal crown. This is especially true in journalism. Doors are opened before we knock, and as well equipped young women emerged from the class-room the brotherhood of the race, men whose energies have been repressed and distorted by the interposition of circumstances, give them opportunities to prove themselves; and right well are they doing this by voice and pen. On matters pertaining to women and the race, there is no better author among our female writers than

Mrs. N. F. Mossell
Her style is clear, compact and convincing. Seven years teaching in Camden, N.J. and Philadelphia, her present home, and the solid reading matter, viz: The Bible, "Paradise Lost," The Atlantic Monthly and The Public Ledger, which was her daily food while under her father's roof, gave her a deep insight into a human nature, and the clear mode of expression which makes her articles so valuable to the press. Her career as a writer began many years ago, when Bishop Tanner—then editor of The Christian Recorder—was attracted by an essay on "In-

fluence" which he requested for publication. Short stories followed, and from then to the present, she has been engaged constantly on race journals. "The Woman's Department" of the New York Freeman was edited by her with much tact and The Philadelphia Echo is always more readable when containing something from her pen. For three years she has been employed on the Philadelphia Times, The Independent, and Philadelphia Press Republican, following the particular lines of race literature and the "Woman's Question." Mrs. Mossell's experience in journalism is that editors are among the most patient of men, that the rejection of an article by no means proves that it is a failure, that sex is no bar to any line of literary work, that by speaking for themselves women can give the truth about themselves and thereby inspire the confidence of the people. Besides newspaper work her home life is a busy one, assisting her husband, a prominent physician of Philadelphia, whose own literary life has been an incentive to her. Spare moments are given to the completion of a book, on a race question, which will soon be launched on the current thought and society.

Mrs. Lucretia Newman Coleman
is a writer of rare ability. Discriminating and scholarly, she possesses to a high degree the poetic temperament and has acquired great facility in verse. Her last poem, "Lucille of Montana," ran through several numbers of the magazine Our Women and Children, and is full of ardor, eloquence and noble thought. Mrs. Coleman has contributed special scientific articles to the A. M. E. [African, Methodist Episcopal] Review and other journals, which were rich in minute comparisons, philosophic terms and scientific principles. She is a writer more for scholars than for the people. A novel entitled "Poor Ben," which is the epitome of the life of a prominent A. M. E. Bishop, is pronounced an excellent production. Mrs. Coleman is an accomplished woman and well prepared for a literary life. She was born in Dresden, Ontario, went with her missionary father to the West Indies where he labored a number of years, thence to Cincinnati, O., where he was pastor of a church, and after his death she went with her mother to Appleton, Wisconsin, to take advantage of the educational facilities. After graduating from the scientific course of Lawrence University she devoted her time to literary pursuits, and now ranks with the most painstaking writers.

Miss Ida B. Wells (Iola)

has been called the "Princess of the Press," and she has well earned the title. No writer, the male fraternity not excepted, has been more extensively quoted; none have struck harder blows at the wrongs and weakness of the race. T. T. Fortune (probably the "Prince" of the Negro press) wrote after meeting her at the Democratic Conference at Indianapolis: "She has become famous as one of the few of our women who handle a goose-quill with diamond point as easily as any man in the newspaper work. If Iola was a man, she would be a humming independent in politics. She has plenty of nerve and is as sharp as a steel trap."

Miss Wells' readers are equally divided between the sexes. She reaches the men by dealing with the political aspect of the race question, and the women, she meets around the fireside. She is an inspiration to the young writers and her success has lent an impetus to their ambition. When the National Press Convention, of which she was Assistant Secretary, met in Louisville, she read a splendidly written paper on "Women in Journalism or How I Would Edit." By the way, it is her ambition to edit a paper. She believes that there is no agency so potent as the press in reaching and elevating a people. Her contributions are distributed among the leading race journals. She made her debut with the Living Way, Memphis, Tenn., and has since written for the New York Age, Detroit Plaindealer, Indianapolis World, Gate City Press, Mo. Little Rock Sun, American Baptist, Ky. Memphis Watchman, Chattanooga Justice, Christian Index, and Fisk University Herald, Tenn., Our Women and Children Magazine, Ky., and the Memphis papers, weeklies and dailies. Miss Wells has attained much success as teacher in the public schools of the last named place.

Mrs. W. E. Mathews (Victoria Earle)

Ten years ago "Victoria Earle" began taking advantage of opportunities offered for acting as "sub" for reporters employed by many of the great dailies. She has reported for the New York Times, Herald, Mail and Express, Sunday Mercury, The Earth, The Photographic World, and is now New York correspondent to the National Leader, D.C., The Detroit Plaindealer, and the Southern Christian Recorder. Under various nom de plume she has written for the Boston Advocate, Washington Bee, Richmond Planet, Catholic Tribune, Cleveland Gazette, New York Age, New York Globe, and the New York Enterprise, besides editing three special departments. Reportorial work is her forte, yet her success in story writing has been great. She contributes to the story department of Waverly Magazine, The New York Weekly and Family Story Paper. "Victoria Earle" has written much; her dialect tid-bits for the Associated Press are much in demand. She has ready several stories which will appear in one volume, and is also preparing a series of historical text books which will aim to develop a race pride in our youth. She is member of the Women's National Press Association and no writer of the race is kept busier.

Miss Mary V. Cook (Grace Ermine)

Whatever honors have come to Miss Cook are the results of persevering industry. She has edited the Woman's Department of the American Baptist, Ky. and the Educational Department of Our Women and Children in such a manner as to attract much attention to them. Her writings are lucid and logical and of such a character as will stand the test of time. Aside from journalistic work her life is a busy one. She has appeared on the platform of several national gatherings and her papers for research, elegance of diction, and sound reasoning were superior. She holds the professorship of Latin in the State University, her Alma Mater, yet however great her mental ability, it is overmatched by her character. Her life is the crystalization of womanly qualities. She moves her associates by a mighty power of sympathy which permeated her writings. She is a good newsgatherer and is much quoted, is a native of Bowling Green, Ky., where her mother, a generous hearted woman who sympathizes with her aspirations, still lives. Miss Cook is interested in all questions which affect the race.

Lillial Akbeeta Kewus (Bert Islew)

Those who know much about the newspapers of the race, know something of Bert Islew's Budget of Gossip in the spicy "They say Column" of The Boston Advocate. Bright, witty, sparkling, one would not think Bert Islew's career antedated only three years and that she was barely twenty when she caught the public ear. The early atmosphere she breathed may have developed a public spiritedness. Was born in the home of Hon. Lewis Hayden,* that good man whose

* Lewis Hayden was born a slave in 1816 but escaped to Canada in 1844 and then moved to Detroit, where he lived for two years, establishing a church and school for

name is closely associated with the Crispus Attuck monument. When but thirteen years old and in the graduating class of the Bowdin Grammar school she entered a prize essay contest and carried off the third prize, although the other contestants were older High School pupils and graduates. This fired her ambition, and soon after graduation she wrote a novel entitled "Idalene Van Therese," which, for lack of means, is unpublished. Then came her successful career with The [People's] Advocate. In addition to her newspaper work, she has for several years been the private stenographer and secretary to the widely known Max Eliot, of the Boston Herald. This position calls for proficiency, and Bert Islew's record for taking down copy verbatim is among the highest in New England. Then, too, her position in the Herald office calls for special articles and reportorial work, which she does creditably. She is recognized in all circles for her ability, and works side by side with editors and reporters without an iota of distinction being made.

Mrs. Amelia F. Johnson

In the mild countenance of Mrs. Amelia Johnson can be read the love and tenderness for children which was demonstrated last year by the publication of the Ivy, an eight-page journal devoted especially to the interests of our youth. It was a good paper filled with original stories and poems and information concerning the doings of the race. Mrs. Johnson is keen, imaginative, and critical, story writing is her forte. It is a part of her nature to weave her thoughts into pleasing imagery. Even when a child she would follow the scratches on her desk with a pencil and tell wonderful stories of them to her seatmate. She has written many of them at different times and is now engaged in writing a story book to be used in Sunday-school libraries. Many short stories from her pen find snug resting places in corners of weeklies. There is a vein of wit and humor in her sayings—a pith and transparency which makes her articles extremely readable. Of all the writers before the public, none of them possess in a higher degree the elements of a skillful critic. She has contributed to the Baptist Messen-

---

blacks. He moved to Boston, where he became a militant abolitionist and conductor on the Underground Railroad. He was Grand Master of the Prince Hall Masonic Lodge. During the Civil War he recruited black soldiers and throughout his life fought for women's rights and temperance and against discrimination. He died on April 7, 1889, in Boston.

ger, Md., The American Baptist, Ky., and Our Women and Children Magazine. Mrs. Johnson was educated in Canada—taking a thorough French course—and has taught both French and English branches in Baltimore, her present home.

Miss Mary E. Britton (Meb)

To the ready pen of Miss Mary E. Britton (Meb) is due many of the reformatory measures which have given the race equal facilities on railroads in Kentucky. The energy and resolute vim of her character is traced in her writings, especially when advocating woman's suffrage and the same moral standard for both sexes. She has studied language from the standard English and American authors and her diction is remarkably chaste. Miss Britton was editor of the "Women's Column" of the Lexington Herald, contributes special articles to the Courant—the Kentucky educational journal—the Cleveland Gazette, the American Catholic Tribune, the Indianapolis World and Our Women and Children Magazine. Her own ambition to excel prompts her to inspire others and nearly all her articles have this savor and was exhibited in those written for The Ivy, the children's paper. The local papers of Lexington, Ky., her home, and the Cincinnati Commercial have published and commented on her articles.

Miss Ione E. Wood

There is a dash of freshness, a breezyness in Miss Wood's writings, a clear, decided ring which will yet be heard in louder tones. She has pronounced views on total abstinence and is an enthusiastic member of the Woman's National Suffrage Association. She contributed several stories to The Ivy and now edits the Temperance Department of Our Women and Children magazine. Miss Wood will make a clever reporter. She is now tutor in Greek in the Kentucky State University.

Miss Kate D. Chapman

sends from her faraway Dakota home spritely poems and other contributions to racial journals. She is only eighteen, but the public is becoming familiar with her bright thoughts and unique expressions. She has read much and will write much. Her contributions have appeared principally in The Christian Recorder and Our Women and Children. Her ambition was stirred when but five years old by receiving a book as reward for committing a poem. She will devote her talent to juvenile literature.

Occasional Contributors—Among those who do special work and contribute valuable articles to weeklies and monthlies are Mesdames Francis E. W. Harper and L. F. Grimke [Angelina], Philadelphia. Cora C. Calhoun, former editor of the Woman's Department in the Chattanooga Justice; Olive B. Clanton, New Orleans; Lavinia E. Sneed, Ky.; Josephine Turpin Washington, Selma; Misses Georgia M. DeBaptiste, Ill.; Julia K. Mason, D.C.; Alice Henderson, Ark., and Meta Pelham, one of the essentials on the Plaindealer staff.

Editors—The Western Herald was edited by Mrs. Amos Johnson, Keokuk, Ia.; The Lancet, by Miss Carrie Bragg, Petersburg, Va.; The Musical Messenger by Miss Amelia L. Tighlman, Montgomery, Ala.; The St. Matthew's Lyceum, by Mrs. M. E. Lambert, Detroit, Mich.; The Ivy, by Mrs. A. E. Johnson, Baltimore, Md.; and Miss A. E. McEwen is Assistant Editor of the Herald, Montgomery, Ala.

This article includes only a few of our writers. When we remember the very difficult circumstances of the past, the trials and discomforts of the present, we are indeed cheered with the prospects. In the busy hum of life it is difficult to make one's way to the front, and this is true of all races, hence, we are not at all discouraged since our sisters have had such ready access to the great journals of the land. When the edge of prejudice shall have become rusted and worn out, the Negro woman shall be heard most potently in the realm of thought, till then shall we strive.

LUCY WILMOT SMITH
In the Journalist.

The Freeman, Indianapolis, February 23, 1889

THE BLACK SAMSON ASLEEP

There is a poor blind Samson in the land   And shake the pillars of the common weal,
Shorn if his strength and bound in bars of steel   Till the great temple of our liberties
Who may in some grim revel raise his hand   A shapeless mass of wreck and ruin lies.

The Freeman, Indianapolis, October 5, 1889

The Black View
of American History

ALTHOUGH *most white historians until recently have largely ignored the significance of black people in American history, black editors throughout the nineteenth century were writing of the contributions black people made to the making of this country. Often it was in the form of countering the racist myths that found ready acceptance in white America.*

In response to the dual roots of American society, colonial exploitation and institutional racism, the black press found in black history the affirmation of its strengths and the roots of its struggle for liberation and nationalism. Black people saw, in the history of resistance to oppression, the confirmation of their manhood and dignity. Though militant calls for resistance appear predominantly in the Northern and Western press, there were numerous instances when the Southern press provided the means for black organizing. Whenever there was the threat or occurrence of a black uprising, the press was the first to be destroyed. Despite the obvious dangers, black editors continued to assert their demands and urged their readers to stand for their rights.

The slave revolts in Haiti (1791) were still fresh in the minds of all when this article was written. It is an example of the persistent attack against the internal slave trade, which many white abolitionists neglected in favor of attacking the foreign slave trade.

From a correspondent at Newbern, N.C. of the date of Sept. 10, 1828, we learn that a few days ago a vessel was launched from a public wharf in that place with a cargo of Slaves, bound for Elizabeth City, N.C. or Norfolk, Va., thence to be re-shipped for New Orleans. To hear the screams and moans of them and of their bereaved parents left far behind was enough to pierce the hardest head.

It was but yesterday that another vessel, loaded with these unfortunate and miserable beings (the Cain of these slave holding states) departed from our wharf for the places above mentioned. The scene was really distressing. It is not our desire to harrow up the feelings of our readers by frequent allusion to these scenes but we consider it our imperious duty to place all such open violations of the laws of God and nature before them.

It is high time that the citizens of the Union should arise as one man and put an end to a traffic which all civilized nations are at present endeavoring to abolish: we do not mean the foreign slave trade alone; we refer to our and their internal slave trade. In our humble opinion, the thousands which are annually appropriated for the suppression of the foreign slave trade, is to be considered but a secondary object, while our domestic slave trade is suffered to be carried on from one State to another. We may declaim as much as we please upon the horrors of the foreign slave trade, but we would ask, are the horrors of the internal slave trade less—are the relations of life less endearing in this country than in Africa—are the Wood folks of the South less cruel than the slavers on the coast? Surely not—surely the natural heart of man is the same wherever he has the power to domineer over his fellow man, to bind him hand and foot, and sell him like beasts of burden and when he pleases, to destroy him.

It is our earnest wish that the subject of domestic slavery may continually be placed before the public, and though the subject is a hackneyed one, its intrinsic merits are such, that it can never lose its importance in the estimation of the man of true feeling. To the patriot it is one of peculiar interest, as being incorporated with the welfare of the Southern part of the Union, for unless efforts are made to stay its evils, the day will come when all we have read of Spartacus and his servile band—of the horrors of the revolutionary scenes of St. Domingo will be reacted before our eyes.

Freedom's Journal, New York, October 17, 1828

References to black men of the past as sources for cultural pride were common in the papers and central to their message.

Before our people can occupy the position which the law of God, and the genius of the age bespeak for them, there are many things to be done, many purposes to be sought out, and accomplished. Should they commence the work industriously and skillfully, the promise of God, the leadings of His providence, and the signs of the times assure success. They have all the natural requisites to make them, in science and renown, what ancient Egypt once was.

The pinnacle of earthly glory, with all its shining attractions is before them. What Cyprian, Augustine, Origen, Tertullian, and others in the Church were, colored men may be again. What Hannibal of old was, in honor and military prowess, some of our sons may be, and as Hanno and Terence, excelled in the literary annals of the world, so may we, at least in our posterity. Take courage then brethren. The God of benevolence, the bountiful benefactor of all mankind has given to us, as much physical strength and intellectual power as to any other men.

The first thing to be done by our people in the elevation of their moral and civil condition is, to change long standing habits and throw off useless practices.

The effects of slavery may be seen in the useless, vulgar, and sinful habits and practices, into which many of us have fallen.

They must be broken off. Our population should be equal to any other, in refinements. The elements are within themselves. They possess all the natural properties for cultivated refinement, and taste that the French nation possess, with more stability of character.

We should cultivate honesty, punctuality, propriety of conduct, and modesty and dignity of deportment. These should characterize our intercourse with all men.

The second thing is, untiring habits of industry, the dint of perseverance. In this matter we have been much gainsayed. Our detractors have often unjustly accused us of imbecility and idleness. The facts are, motives have been withheld from us. We have had to labour against fearful and paralizing odds. But thanks to Providence, the tables are turning. Life, liberty and the pursuit of happiness are being conceded to all men.

Our colored population should not be *least nor last* in their efforts, but like the oppressed Jews in Europe, be prodigies of unceasing effort and of undying enterprize.

The third thing is, rigidness of economy.

We intend no disparagement to colored men when we say in this matter, we have been greatly deficient, and are deeply criminal. Fine dress and luxurious living seem to have been the summit of our ambition.

We should spend little upon our outward-man, nothing for superfluities; but husband EVERY DOLLAR for the purpose of elevating our character, and improving our condition.

The fourth thing is cultivation of our intellect. Herein is our great deficiency. O! *Spirit of slavery, unholy prejudice against color, what hast thou done!* Thou hast entered the colored man's intellectual world, and despoiled its inhabitants of the image of God. The repair of the ruins, brethren is our citadel of strength. . . .

Every opportunity should be improved—every means brought into requisition. The Sabbath and the week day school should be taxed, and the mid-night lamp made to contribute its portion. Public Libraries, Lectures and Debating Classes should be established. . . .

We mean by intellectual cultivation, the accumulation of knowledge, extensive and solid. Such as will qualify us for all the situations and occupations of freemen. . . .

The Colored American, New York, May 6, 1837

Stephen Myers, editor of the Northern Star and Freeman's Advocate *and prominent black abolitionist, directed his temperance paper to the self-elevation of the black community.*

. . . The first effort, then, which humanity dictates, is an endeavor to induce government to exert every means in its power for the purpose of putting a stop to the cruel separation of families, by selling off at intervals the husband from his wife, and the children from their parents—if this is not done, and it is asking little of the philanthropy of the age, revolution will but the sooner break out— When the slaves are least prepared for freedom, and the horrors of war will then, too late for remedy sound its terrific blast far and wide. The first efforts of revolution may perhaps be put down, but a successful one will follow. . . .

The Northern Star and Freeman's Advocate,
Albany, N.Y., March 17, 1842

The systematic destruction and denial by whites of the role black people played in history as soldiers was the result of their fear of uprisings. Black journals were thus one of the few sources of information available on this subject.

. . . The [Crimean] war in Europe which has just halted in its strife has not been too without its lessons. . . . That thus in the service of their masters, they, the subjects, might learn the lesson by which to insure their own complete redemption from every fetter that now binds them by the mere will of these tyrannical masters, that the subjects shall learn to be the master—the master of himself, the peer of any man—this is his lesson, and as he is pursuing his task, he is gradually gaining confidence in his own strength and prowess. . . . We have been slow to believe in our own prowess. . . . All claims to courage and coolness under circumstances of difficulty, or danger having been denied the black man, we ourselves have taken it for granted that we have none. . . . In the French Army, two classes of soldiers have attracted much attention; one only however on this side of the water, viz.: the Zouave. The other, the Turcos, who are genuine blacks from Africa, besides being the most soldierly looking men in Europe today, for fierce force and daring have no superior in the world, or out of it. . . . Let prowess no longer be denied the black man; rather let it from this day forth be remembered that loyalty and courage are among the component parts of his nature and that the one under a just sense of right and the other under circumstances of danger, can and will be manifested whenever and wherever occasion demands. This is our lesson.

We wonder whether the wild Africans now being imported on our Southern border are of materials such as could, in a certain event, be manufactured into a regiment of Turcos.

The Weekly Anglo-African, New York, July 30, 1859

There were some who counseled restraint and relieving pressures on the government to abolish slavery in all its forms. But this meant ignoring laws which, in effect, denied the black man's claim to manhood.

. . . Cease agitation? Yes, when you repeal the Fugitive Slave Law, reverse the Dred Scott decision, and give us the right of citizenship in the free States, abolish slavery in the District of Columbia, break up the internal slave trade between the slave states, and guarantee unto us the privileges which the Federal Constitution guarantees to all men. Then, and not until then, may you expect us to be silent. . . . When the people of our common country shall be willing to accord to us the political rights which are enjoyed by other natives of the soil, we shall then be prepared to cease warring against the government and rebuking the church of its hypocrisy. But just so long as the enemies of the colored men's rights is to be found skulking behind the pillars of the church, and seeking security in the strong arm of the law, we can never remain silent. . . .

The Weekly Anglo-African, New York, August 20, 1859

The place of the American black man in the history of his country was an important ingredient in the development of a national identity. The development of such a "black history" represents a critical step in this process.

. . . The *negro* was the *primum mobile* of the Florida war which cost us forty millions of dollars. Sambo ran off from his Georgia master and sought liberty among the Everglades and protection among the savages, which he could not enjoy in the place of his birth. The United States Government, which has long been the servile tool of the negro-drivers at the instance of the latter, declared war against the Seminoles, with a view of getting back the runaways and breaking up their haunts.

A *negro* was at the bottom of the Mexican war. The South, seeing that the free states of the Union were likely to outnumber the slave states, because the territorial possessions were chiefly north of the Missouri line, resolved to procure territory out of which they could make slave states, so as to keep up the balance of power in the Senate of the United States. The Government therefore declared war on a feigned issue with the Republic of Mexico, and at a cost of 150 millions of money procured California and Mexico. It was then that the tide of the affairs of slaveholders turned. For the first time, though not the last, they missed a figure in their calculations, and California and New Mexico are both devoted to freedom. . . .

It is the inevitable *negro* that has blown out and chilled the furnaces of Pennsylvania and stopped the rolling mills, and spread desolation among her iron interests. We have coal, iron ore, and limestone in such inexhaustible abundance that we could supply the iron wants of half the world; but we have no adequate tariff to protect those interests from foreign competition. The North . . . cheerfully pay 30% more for Southern sugar than they need pay for the West Indian article, merely to fill the pockets of a few hundred sugar manufacturers in Louisiana. But when we ask in return that the iron interests in the North shall receive protection, why, that is a horse of another color.

In the halls of Congress, the *negro,* his servitude and his freedom are the staple of three-fourths of the speeches delivered. The *negro* builds up and plucks down—makes and unmakes—political men at will. It was the *negro* who occasioned the attempted massacre of Sumner upon the floor of the Senate chamber, and then occasioned the premature deaths of Brooks and Butler, the guilty principal and accessory to the assault. The *negro* sentenced to political death and damnation most of those public men who broke down the Missouri restriction and passed the Kansas-Nebraska Bill, and he has just begun to wreak his vengeance on Senator Douglas, the leader of the gang.

Does the American wish to relax his features, stiffen in the pursuit of business by an hour of hearty and recreating laughter, he goes to see Sanford and Christie's opera troupe where Sambo convulses his audience with *negro* wit. Does he wish to regale himself by hearing the tones of exquisite music, he listens to the far-famed *negro* melodies, which strange to say, constitute the only American music we have. . . . It is not the climate of the South, so much as the *negro* that gives the Southerner his affable manners, his softness of voice, and his eloquence.

What name has attracted more attention in courts, legislatures, governors' messages and on the stump, than that of Dred Scott, the *negro* of Missouri? What personage has become so world-wide and renowned in literature as "Uncle Tom"? . . . All over America, all over

Europe, and in far off Asia, the *negro's* lament is heard in the plaintive language of Uncle Tom. . . .

The Weekly Anglo-African, New York, September 17, 1859

John Brown's raid on Harpers Ferry in 1859 stirred a revolutionary consciousness among black men and women and encouraged them in their struggle against slavery and oppression.

In all ages and in every department of effort for the true advancement of mankind have been found men in advance of the masses. These are the outposts—they stand in the foreground of their times; many of them are in so far in advance that they may be regarded as living and acting in the future. Misunderstood, hated, denounced, traduced, and often deprived of life, though invariably in the right, they find few bold enough to espouse their cause and fewer still willing to become co-laborers with them. It was so in the days of Christ; and it was so before; and it has been so ever since. Coming up to their standpoint long after these men had passed out of sight and it is still receiving their doctrines, and acting up to their teachings that society does them justice.

Such is the position of John Brown, and the other captured survivors of the twenty-two, and "they were right" will yet be the verdict of coming history.

John Brown is one of the age, and a man of the American continent. He is far in advance of thus much of the country in which he has lived, and being full of well-spent years and of brighter hopes today than ever of the ultimate success of the great work of liberation of the bondmen—the highest aim of his life—he is now ready, if need be, to be offered up. Talk as we will—call him fanatic, madman, traitor, our word for it—Brown could not help it. It was his mission. He was impelled by an unseen hand—a hand notwithstanding, points the destinies of nations. . . .

The Weekly Anglo-African, New York, November 5, 1859

Brown had hoped his actions would spark widespread revolts among the slaves. As an event, free blacks saw its prophetic impact, and indeed, it

helped shift the struggle against slavery from nonviolent abolitionism to militant resistance.

Passions often blind men to such an extent that they not infrequently fail to attend to their real interest; often to the neglect of an examination even into the cause of the hindrances that lie in their way. This is true as often of communities as of individuals, and the South in this respect have made a gross mistake.

Let us instance at this time but two points. First: that within the last quarter of a century a change has been coming over the Northern mind in relation to the subject of slavery, and of this change the South has persistently refused to make herself acquainted. She has persistently refused to study, read, or even look into what is termed Abolition publications and Abolition journals. She has persistently shut out all true knowledge and all proper light on the subject, and is today almost utterly ignorant of both the nature and extent of this great change—of the great advance made in the North on the subject of man's rights. Her servile press and paid menials among us here in the North for the sake of their tenure of office, have not been true to the South in that matter. So far from stating the real facts as they have transpired, and keeping the South posted, they have deceived her by continually stultifying the truth and when the Harper's Ferry affair occurred, it was like a shock of thunder. The South was not prepared for such a result, nor has she even yet opened her eyes to the depth or extent of sympathy felt in the North for the poor oppressed bondmen in their midst, notwithstanding the hard endeavors of the political and otherwise interested journals to gloss it over.

These journals may talk as they will, laws for the punishment of offenders and those who dare to meddle with the peculiar institution may be summarily executed, severe codes for the government of the poor slave may be enforced, demagogues may plot and politicians may plan, notwithstanding all the feeling that justifies American slavery is daily growing less and less, and rests today on an incalculably feebler foundation than ever before.

But to our second point: The Abolitionism of the North, so far from making war on, or being inimical to the institution of slavery, has been for the last twenty years its great safety valve; the escape pipe through which the dangerous element incident to slavery found vent. Prior to the existence of Abolitionism, outbreaks and fearful mutterings and threatenings among slaves were frequent and to the holders alarming. We can all trace back to the Nat Turners and the Denmark Veazies* and others. The slave then had no hope of deliverance except by his own right-arm however feeble. He saw no farther, and believing that it was appointed to man but once to die, felt willing to do so or gain his liberty. But when Wm. Lloyd Garrison and his co-adjutors enunciated the doctrines of abolitionism and non-resistance, the slave received a new and far different lesson. He was taught to hope for deliverance—to feel that he was not forsaken nor forgotten—that someday, however distant, he would be enabled to lay aside his chains and be acknowledged a man. With these hopes the fierceness of his passions subsided, he agreed to submit to his hard task, and thenceforth up till recently but little comparative discontent has been manifested, and yet the South, to this important fact has also been blind. Let them henceforth read Abolition journals and Abolition literature—let her read our paper, if she wishes to study and know the signs, and interpret the meaning thereof, as they appear in the moral horizon of the North, be wise.

The Weekly Anglo-African, New York, November 5, 1859

One of the most militant of black abolitionist papers, the Weekly Anglo-African, *consistently emphasized the necessity of resistance to oppression. Its title reflects the growing sense of identity as both African and American.*

. . . Our Anglo-African blood, at any rate, will not permit us to cease hostilities at that point. We must insist on going farther on, no more patching up of wrongs, no more compromises with wrong-doing. We must continue united, and never cease wrestling with the giant evil of Slavery till we have rid the land of it—till the bondman shall stand free and disenthralled—a man. We must insist upon all this, before we shall be willing to ensure that peace and tranquility now so earnestly sued for. . . .

The Weekly Anglo-African, New York, November 12, 1859

---

* Denmark Vesey led an uprising of slaves in 1822; Nat Turner led an uprising of slaves in 1831.

Stirred by John Brown's raid, the black community rallied to his defense. Throughout the black community special prayer meetings were dedicated to Brown.

Here in the North we spend annually thousands of dollars in catching and punishing thieves and robbers, preventing theft and robbery. But John Brown and his few surviving followers, on the other hand, are to forfeit their lives for simply endeavoring to obtain and restore stolen chattels to their proper owners—to restore the slave to himself.

What right has Virginia to protect theft and punish with death him who, from honest conviction, attempts to do just what every law of right, humanity, and true religion prompted him to do? What is to be done with every other species of interest? But it may be claimed that the law stands in the way of all such attempts. What right has Virginia to legalize theft in the bodies and souls of men? It was a mercy to the property holders that the stolen goods—the chattels—did not tumble out of the state through the breach made by Brown; and as one step makes way for another, it may occur to the chattels someday to make a breach for itself. With an eye to this possiblity and the future, John Browns who may take into their heads to again break into the State of Presidents, or some other of her sister States, it is now proposed that the whole South wheel out of the Union, and build a strong barrier against future inroads and set up for itself. Out of what materials this barrier is to be rendered does not appear.

Whatever may have been the mistakes of the South on the subject of slavery, and the sentiments of the North upon it, we scarcely think it will be guilty and blind enough to add the fatal error of disunion to the already fearful list, or accept from their Northern toadies advice leading to that end.

For a State like Virginia, whose partition gives way at the slightest touch of the arm of an aged man, whose inhabitants become frantic before the face of twenty-two men, whose military find it impossible to collect their scattered senses sufficiently to make even a semblance of resistance, whose authorities lose all dignity, and the sleep of whose inhabitants has been murdered—to talk of wheeling out of the Union, is one of the thinnest and meanest scarecrows ever set up before the eyes of sensible men.

The Weekly Anglo-African, New York, November 19, 1859

Encouraged by the actions of John Brown at Harpers Ferry, black editors became even more insistent on direct confrontation to end slavery.

THE IRREPRESSIBLE CONFLICT

No matter what way we turn our eyes, we find an irrepressible conflict going on, and one which has been going on since the foundation of the government. It is everywhere rife in the land and to evil doers is fearful. In church and in state, in the moral circle, in the social circle, there it is, ceaseless and irrepressible, and will so continue till the last vestige of human oppression is extinct, or society itself in the land is destroyed. This conflict is between right and wrong—between human bondage and human oppression on the one hand, and human freedom and equality on the other—between the robber of rights and the robbed.

If society places itself clearly on the side of wrong, it will, in this conflict in the end destroy itself; if on the side of right, then human bondage and oppression must come to naught in the land, and that right speedily. Men's feelings, religion, education, and interests are all deeply enlisted on the one side or the other of this subject, and it is impossible now to retire from the great conflict. The conflict is onward and irrepressible. It is vain to deny it. For our part we have no fears for the ultimate result. As much as we love country, government, law and order—yea, even life itself—we love liberty, right, equity, and justice more. In the former we have nothing so dear to us but we are willing to give up—yea, even sacrifice—for the full securement of the latter. For these we would contend, if need be, unto death. . . . There has been and ever will be, a conflict. It was manifested—openly and loudly manifested—at the adoption of the Constitution, and so also during the Revolution, and subsequently down to the Missouri Compromise, and then with a violence not even yet forgotten. . . . and so down to the stirring hours of Brooks and Sumner, and of Douglas and Nebraska, and to the rubbing out of the Missouri Compromise by the latter day traitors; to Cuba and Mexico, to the revival of the African slave-trade, and to the advance of Abolitionism in the North, and the spread of free and liberal sentiments generally. Thus may we learn something of the irrepressible conflict going on in the country, from the commencement down; and yet, in all this, we have presented its political aspect only.

The same conflict, irrepressible and onward, is and ever has been between the master and the slave, and the church and the slave—between sordid interest and enlightened conscience—between a low, servile press and an enlightened community. Repress this conflict? Conquer it? What arm is sufficiently powerful—what force, either in the press, or in the government, or in the combination of demagogues is equal to the task. All these may patch up, plaster over, smooth down, hem in, and cover up or smother out to the utmost; but they cannot check an atom of the conflict. Like a terrible volcano, it will break out with tenfold violence and tenfold fearfulness. . . .

The Weekly Anglo-African, New York, December 3, 1859

John Brown, the subject of this intimate description, was mourned deeply by the entire black community as a brother. But they also understood that it was not Brown alone who frightened the whites.

. . . A plain old man, who sat but yesterday in that chair at our fireside—a real homebody, yet somehow a homeless wanderer—speaking of them in bonds "as bound with them," narrating his duty to "do unto others as he would that they should do unto him," a gleam in his cold blue eye as he spoke of slaveholders, a bowie-knife in either bootleg, a volcanic repeater doubled up in his side pocket, quietly asking if we would be "willing to sleep under a tent" with him; we miss him a week or two, and he has "settled the case" for Kansas. He comes our way again, sits in the same quiet chair, himself more restless than before, his smooth-shaven face covered with a long beard, his iron-grey hair bristling up, and just possibly a wilder gleam in his cold, glittering eye. . . .

. . . John Brown did not frighten *all* Virginia; there are in that State some half million of slaves and we have no reports that they were terrified. The probabilities are that they felt and yet feel a glow of John Brown's spirit flashing through their dark bosoms; and it was to crush that spirit, and prevent the chance of a rescue from the slaves themselves, which caused Gov. Wise to call out his imposing military display. . . .

. . . Virginia would never have trembled at seventeen, nor seventeen hundred white men in arms, had they been all John Browns; it was the five black men armed to the teeth, and the hundred thousand black men in their midst armed with a quarrel just, who caused the Virginians to tremble and shudder.

Mr. Beecher* must have read the papers, must have read that there were twenty-two invaders, seventeen white and five black. Why does he omit all mention of the latter? Were they not men? Did not a few of them hold sixty whites imprisoned in an out-building incapable of defense? Was not one slain at the door of the engine building? Were not two others found defending that building to the last, with John Brown and his sons?

How does the record stand? The sixteen white men who crossed the bridge at Harper's Ferry with their brave commander, had three alternatives all of which happened to them, defeat, death, escape—and of the sixteen at least four escaped. The five black men who followed John Brown like the heroes of the German myth, knew that for them there was no re-crossing of the dark river, they went forth to their death with a faith as pure and a heroism as exalted as any of their companions; but one of them has escaped—those who did not fall in the fight, did on the day we now commemorate, stand up in their hard won shackles and receive the heroic greetings of their heroic leader as he went forth to his death, leaving but one traitor behind him, and he a white man. . . .

. . . John Brown has struck his blow against the living iniquity of our land. Whether that blow will be as deep and lasting, as it has been sudden and powerful, time alone can tell. . . .

The Weekly Anglo-African, New York, December 10, 1859

Memorial meetings were held throughout black communities in the North to commemorate John Brown's martyrdom. At one of these, held in Shiloh Church, New York City, its pastor, the Reverend Henry Highland Garnet, delivered this sermon. Garnet was born in 1815 and was a leading black abolitionist in New York City. At the end of the Civil War he moved to Washington, D.C., where he was pastor of the Fifteenth Street Presbyterian Church. In 1881 he was appointed minister to Liberia. He died there on February 13, 1882.

* The Reverend Henry Ward Beecher was a white minister who spoke against John Brown's raid.

The day has come in which the nation is about to suffer a great crime to be perpetrated against the cause of liberty. Today John Brown is to offer up his life a sacrifice for the sake of justice and equal human rights. Henceforth the Second day of December will be called "Martyr's Day." I am not a man of blood. I hold human life to be sacred, and would spare even a man stealer if he stood not in the bondman's path to freedom. Often have I indulged the hope of seeing slavery abolished without the shedding of blood; but that hope is clouded. . . . The withered hand of an old man whose hairs are white with the frosts of nearly seventy winters has given the death blow to American slavery. . . . Hero, martyr, farewell!

The Weekly Anglo-African, New York, December 10, 1859

Thomas Hamilton, the editor of the Weekly Anglo-African, *used the occasion of John Brown's trial and execution to remind his readers of another famous event in the history of liberation struggles, the Nat Turner insurrection.*

There are two reasons why we present our readers with the "Confessions of Nat Turner." First, to place upon record this most remarkable episode in the history of human slavery, which proves to the philosophic observer that in the midst of this most perfectly contrived and apparently secure system of slavery, humanity will out, and engender from its bosom, forces that will contend against oppression, however unsuccessfully; and secondly, that the two methods of Nat Turner and of John Brown may be compared. The one is the mode in which the slave seeks freedom for his fellow, and the other mode in which the white man seeks to set the slave free. There are many points of similarity between these two men: they were both idealists; both governed by their views of the teachings of the Bible; both had harbored for years the purpose to which they gave up their lives; both felt themselves swayed as by some divine, or at least, spiritual impulse; the one seeking in the air, the earth, and the heavens for signs which came at last; and the other, obeying impulses which he believes to have been fore-ordained from the eternal past; both cool, calm, and heroic in prison and in the prospect of inevitable death; both confess with child-like frankness and simplicity the object they had in view—the pure and simple emancipation of their fellow men, both win from the judges who sentenced them, expressions of deep sympathy—and here the parallel ceases. Nat Turner's terrible logic could only see the enfranchisement of one race, compassed by the extirpation of the other; and he followed his glory syllogism with rude exactitude. John Brown, believing that the freedom of the enthralled could only be effected by placing them on an equality with the enslavers, and unable in the very effort at emancipation to tyrannize himself, is moved with compassion for tyrants, as well as slaves, and seeks to extirpate this formidable cancer, without spilling one drop of christian blood.

These two narratives present a fearful choice to the slaveholders, nay, to this great nation—which of the two modes of emancipation shall take place? The method of Nat Turner, or the method of John Brown?

Emancipation must take place, and soon. There can be no long delay in the choice of methods. If John Brown's be not soon adopted by the free North, then Nat Turner's will be by the enslaved South.

Had the order of events been reversed—had Nat Turner been in John Brown's place at the head of these twenty-one men, governed by his inexorable logic and cool daring, the soil of Virginia and Maryland and the far South would by this time be drenched in the blood and the wild and sanguinary course of these men, no earthly power could stay.

The course which the South is now frantically pursuing will engender in its bosom and nurse into maturity a hundred Nat Turners, whom Virginia is infinitely less able to resist in 1860, than she was in 1831.

So, people of the South, people of the North! Men and brethren, choose ye which method of emancipation you prefer—Nat Turner's, or John Brown's?

The Weekly Anglo-African, New York, December 31, 1859

In reply to the New York Herald, *which criticized the manner and means of black resistance, the editor, Thomas Hamilton, defended the right of insurrection, and self-defense.*

If there be any two things beyond all others that men should value and preserve, they are life and liberty; and if there be a question as to which shall be sacrificed, we unhesitatingly say life, and the civilized world echoes back the answer, life—sacrifice life and let liberty live. Without liberty, of what value to the possessor is life?

The Anglo-African insurrections that have occurred in this country within the last two hundred years . . . are but the uprisings of a people keenly sensible of their oppression, and willing to sacrifice life in their endeavor to throw it off and substitute liberty therefor. . . .

. . . oppressed men resolving to liberate themselves make use, and are justified in that use, of the best means in their power to that end.

. . . Precisely so the slave has no arms, no implements of warfare of any kind. He is a slave—a perpetual slave—and yet having resolved to be free wisely makes use of the best means in his power to that end. He resorts, and justifiably resorts, therefore, to the tinder-box, the match, and the torch. These are the only weapons of warfare left him. He has no choice, no election, and therefore is not to be blamed. Give him something better, something more in keeping with the science of war, and the art of using it, and he will not be backward in accepting even such terms. But until this is done he cannot afford to attend to niceties of scientific warfare. The contest is too unequal, and the stake too heavy. Oppression, with all its accursed concomitants, is on the one side, and liberty and manhood, with all their joys and glories, on the other.

We wonder what white men would do under the same circumstances; and yet we are among those who think that one set of men who have chained and hoppled another, and debauched their women, and stole their children, are rather bad judges of what niceties their victims should use in their endeavors to release themselves from such a hellish thraldom. . . .

. . . Truth prompts us to say that some of the most remarkable instances of kindness and generosity to be found on the pages of history are recorded of these deeply injured and long outraged men towards many of the whites during these outbreaks, and no amount of historical perversion and newspaper lying can make out to the contrary. The fact is, what is so laboriously put forth by the satanic press to show the brutality of the blacks in these instances of uprising, are but the full settlements with the white fiends who had treated these poor unfortunates throughout their whole former life with the most shocking cruelties and horrid brutalities, which were not forgotten on these days of reckoning. . . .

The Weekly Anglo-African, New York, January 21, 1860

The constant insecurity of black people who managed to escape to the North was increased by laws and a legal system aiding slaveholders.

It is a curious fact not generally known, that New Jersey has a Fugitive Slave Law of her own, enacted in 1793 and re-enacted with modifications in 1836, and 1846. The slaveholder, or his agent can apply to a Common Pleas judge and the arrest will be made by the sheriff and the question of property decided by three judges. The law is in accordance with the interpretation of the Federal Constitution which makes the restoration of fugitive slaves the duty of the State. New Jersey has also a law authorizing a slaveholder to take his slaves through the State, and make a temporary residence with them.

The Weekly Anglo-African, New York, February 18, 1860

At the close of the Civil War, many legal restrictions were placed on Southern black people by whites who feared a wave of revenge if the slaves rebelled.

. . . The black code of Louisiana is as bloody and barbarous as the laws against witchcraft, as foolish and unjust as that obsolete divorce law, and as far behind the spirit of the times as either of them. It has been practically repealed by the authority of public sentiment ever since the occupation of Louisiana by the national forces. . . .

The Tribune, New Orleans, July 21, 1864

In answer to those white Southerners who looked back to "the Union as it was," the emancipated black man posited a future of liberty.

. . . Still there was a black spot on the National escutcheon, which, fostering and gangrening, kept pace with the growth of the country. Six hundred thousand slaves in 1790 had increased in 1860 to four millions. A peculiar institution had fastened itself and though opposed to every political principle upon which the Federal System was founded, it defied every effort of the people either to modify, or abolish it. Entrenched behind the Constitution, its upholders and apologists badly held the reins of government; and allying themselves with the party of Progress, adopting the principle to rule, or rain, [reign] they determined to destroy the Union, or destroy themselves. Profiting by the election of a minority candidate to the Presidency, they rushed the slaveholding states into a revolution, inaugurated civil war, embarked in an attempt to subvert the Union, initiated a reign of terror throughout the South and brought about the present condition of things. . . .

It was quite natural for all the people who were attached to the Union and who were not interested in the ownership of slaves to see in the early stages of the rebellion the speedy destruction of the entire system. Its utter incompatibility with free government was made manifest by the war; and though ministering perhaps to the physical growth and prosperity of the Free States, it was opposed to every correct principle of social and political relations, and only served to retard the slave states in their development and progress. Such was the rapid rise of these opinions that they soon spread over the entire country. Even under what is called the "War Power" of the Executive, those opposed to the institution soon found in the Constitution itself, the means for its destruction; and a timid President, waiting servilely attendant upon public opinion instead of bravely leading it, after many haltings and delays, at last launched his Proclamation of Emancipation, and virtually, by this diliatory step, with which a Jackson would have begun the war, ended it. For, ever since then, the fate of the rebellion, so far as the contest at arms was concerned, has been doubly and trebly assured. Two hundred thousand black soldiers are now in the National armies. No longer under the stars and stripes is the expression of an opinion hostile to slavery punished by hanging, tar, and feathers, rolling in bales, social tabooing, or the trial and imprisonment prescribed by Louisiana statutes. We are fortunately free now, even while still under all the restraints of martial law, to proclaim slavery both a curse and a sin, even from the housetops.

If then it be asked, restore us to "the Union as it was," the manifest reply is that it is impossible; for how could such a Union be brought about. Could you say to the 200,000 black soldiers, good, gentle, quiet, patient, docile creatures, do for the sake of the Union of white men, return to your owners and be again slaves! Submit to be again property! Give them your labor for their husks! Cower down into slaves, and sacrifice yourselves for the benefit of an Oligarchy such as the world has never before seen or felt! We think even a slaveholder would hesitate in making such a preposterous request; and that even he, with all his foolish notion of the "divine institution" and of the inferiority and stupidity of the colored man would know the certain answer he would receive. . . . They must have free speech, free schools, free press, free religion, free government, free individual development; for each of these is as indispensable to their existence as free air. . . .

The Tribune, New Orleans, September 20, 1864

At the close of the war, with Southern society at the point of collapse and marauding gangs roaming town and country, terrorizing the black population, the Army was the only source of protection. Although not particularly militant, the Tribune *was led to advocate measures of self-defense.*

The Freedmen's Aid Association will meet this evening, and will have under consideration several important propositions. Up to this time the interests of freedmen or more generally of the colored people have been very imperfectly protected. Efforts have been made by the competent authorities; but however sincere these efforts were, they have not been adequate to the urgency and the difficulties of the situation. All over the state, the Freedmen are threatened in their lives, robbed of their liberties and deprived of the fruits of their toils and labor.

. . . In many parts of the State, a system of terror has been inaugurated, to keep down the Freedmen; several have already been murdered and many more will be if we do not resist. The right of self-defense is a sacred right. We read in the American Constitution that it is an immunity of its citizens of the Republic that they can bear arms. Assassins are not brave; and a few cases of self-defense followed by the punishment of the would-be murderers, would be sufficient to plunge into a solitary terror the slavocrats of the parishes. These people must be taught to respect the lives of their fellow citizens.

But, to avert the recurrence of murder and ambush it would probably be sufficient to send a few companies of colored troops into the worst parishes. The presence of our armed brethren, wearing the United States uniform, would do a great deal toward bringing the slaveholders to their senses. The black regiments carry with them the vivid and forcible image of the revolution, i.e. of the elevation of the downtrodden race to the level of citizens. . . .

The Tribune, New Orleans, July 18, 1865

Black editors warned of reactionary forces in the South who sought to reestablish quasi-slavery through the Black Codes.

The rampant spirit of rebellion is not dead; it still burns with all its hellish fires and is only awaiting the propitious hour to begin anew its treason against the Government, which from all evidences before us, we can readily see is now rapidly hatching.

Every action of the conquered, but not subdued reconstructed States plainly shows that although reconstructed, they are not repentant, nor is it likely they ever will be, until all the present generations of traitors and their issue are either extirpated or exterminated. . . .

The Elevator, San Francisco, October 13, 1865

The threat of slave revolts did not end with the Civil War, but became even more real among Southern whites who were no longer able to marshal all the forces of repression.

Constant fears are expressed by former slave masters of an insurrection among the freedmen. They are extremely anxious about the holidays, and want the military sent to every part of the state to overawe the anticipated insurrections. Poor fellows! They have fanned a flame which they now fear is to consume them. . . . Acts of injustice like the holding of our fellowmen in slavery, very naturally suggests to guilty parties fear of retaliation. . . . Nothing short of a deliberate attempt to re-enslave them can ever create an insurrection and as any such attempt would be treason, the freedmen would still be found loyal to their government.

The Leader, Charleston, December 24, 1865

Justifications for equality were directed not simply to the prejudices of white readers, but also to reinforce a positive black self-image, black pride, and black identity.

. . . if character is the standard of manhood, we cannot see any just reason for withholding the titles of manhood on account of his physical nature. It is not because a person is six feet high that he is a 'man,' nor because he has a big brow and thick straight hair, but because he has the *moral* qualifications of a man. Why then exclude a person from this position because he has a *black face?* If he displays the moral character of a man with a *white face,* who, in the judgment of his fellows, is deserving of the title, 'man' in its fullest sense, common sense and justice demand that he receive the same honorable distinction. . . . It is quite customary to hear the remarks that 'the negro is fit for nothing,' that 'he cannot be taught anything,' and that 'he cannot advance in the scale of humanity.' If this is really so, how very foolish for men to sit down in legislative halls and make laws to prevent him from learning anything, and advancing in the human scale, when these men, in their own minds, are convinced that he *cannot* do what they are determined he shall not get a chance to do. . . .

The Colored American, Augusta, Georgia, December 30, 1865

Apprehensions of reactionary tendencies in the South were not unwarranted, as indicated by the following incident. Such occurrences became more common as they went unpunished.

We are informed that a most fiendish outrage was committed near Hamburg, S.C., one night last week by five *white* men, disguised with masks. They went to the house of Chandler Garrot, a colored man, and each violated the person of his wife, a colored woman. They then went to the shop of Wesley Brooks, a poor colored man, and robbed him of $60, nearly all the money he possessed.

Comment upon the conduct of these men is unnecessary. Why do not our city dailies mention some of the outrages committed daily and nightly by white men against the freedmen? If a freedman commits an offense against a *white* man, it is immediately heralded, but when the freedmen suffer, the world seldom hears of it. . . .

The Loyal Georgian, Augusta, January 27, 1866

Black papers were quick to remind the whites that without the help of black soldiers, the Union Army would have lost.

. . . We are no lovers of hero worship, neither do we believe in defying anything human; but we *do* believe that those men who went into the field to put down treason and rebellion have earned at least the poor compensation of their country's gratitude. To say that the colored troops did not do much towards subjugating the rebels, is to say what they, the rebels themselves do not believe. It is even probable that the war would have been yet on the government's hands had it not been for our black soldiers. . . .

The Colored Tennessean, Nashville, March 24, 1866

The following is one of a series of articles entitled "The Negro and American Literature" by George Rice.

. . . The foreigner brings to this country the legends, traditions, and customs of his fatherland; and generations must intervene before his ideas lose their national cast, and he becomes Americanized. With the negro, it is different. His traditions and legends have yet to be woven. New creations peculiar to the race have yet to be made from constant association with American ideas and customs. He approaches the nearer to the true national type than the races we received from foreign immigration, since they bring with them and maintain to a greater or less extent, the customs of their respective countries.

The negro is as much an American as he is a negro. He has his own marked traits of character; but surely, his ideas, manners and customs are American, in the full sense of the word, as much as those of his white contemporaries.

The American Government based one of its proudest pillars of strength upon the negro's broad shoulders, thus unwittingly making him an important and necessary part in the foundation of the national structure. His life was thrown as the last measure of salvation, into the breach of the nation's disasters; his labor was necessary for the nation's development; and the election of a colored Senator [Blanche K. Bruce] proves that his mind is necessary to make the nation's laws. We have yet to see him—and this will come as naturally as all the rest —take the part that waits for him in the great field of American literature.

The New Era, Washington, D.C., March 3, 1870

In the rewriting of black history it was important to show that black people earned whatever rights were granted to them. The author of the second letter is Lewis Douglass, the eldest son of Frederick and corresponding editor of the New Era.

If a colored child is maltreated, its parents or guardians have the right, in every State of this Union at present, of at least *seeking* a remedy in the courts. But if the mind of the child is poisoned with the knowledge of being proscribed . . . there is no redress. When we ask for redress, we are told that the progress already attained is so wonderful and unexpected that we ought to be content with what we have, or at least be cautious how we endanger the future by asking too much. . . . We have gained nothing that we have not earned. Military necessity was the parent of our freedom, and anti-slavery philanthropy was simply a name in which the deed was christened. . . .

The New Era, Washington, D.C., March 24, 1870

. . . At this juncture, the black man is allowed to fight, simply because it was absolutely necessary; the Union armies were being defeated on every battle-field, the "flower of the Northern youth" were not coming up to die for the freedom of the black man as rapidly as the safety of the nation demanded, hence the sable soldiers took places in the decimated armies of the Union, and their pay was to be that of which they had been robbed, viz. their freedom. . . .

We hold that the right of the black man to freedom always existed, and that the United States, in depriving him of the exercise of that right, committed a gross outrage upon him, the full measure of which can never be determined, so monstrous has been its evil effects; and that allowing him, after much importuning on his part, to take up arms and assist in preserving the union of States, does not place him under deeper obligations to the people of the North than they are under to him. . . .

The New Era, Washington, D.C., April 7, 1870

The Supplementary Civil Rights Bill was an attempt to provide enforcement procedures for the vaguely worded Fourteenth Amendment by prohibiting segregation in public transportation, accommodations, and schools. Although it became law in 1875, it was declared unconstitutional in 1883. (The name of the paper was changed on September 8, 1870, from the New Era *to the* New National Era.)

The legislation necessary to complete the work of doing justice to erase what has been, by brutal outrage, compelled to contribute to the wealth of this great nation, will have been accomplished upon the passage of the Supplementary Civil Rights Bill. There can be no peace in the nation while the law acknowledges favored classes or fails to afford protection to all of whatever race, color, or previous condition. Senator Sumner's Bill is in the interest of peace. Its aim is to give equality of rights with other citizens to the 600,000 colored voters of this nation and those whom they represent.

The oppressors of the black race in this country, in order to make that oppression lasting, rebelled and attempted to destroy the nation whose tendencies seemed toward liberty and justice. The war of that rebellion was marked on the part of the rebels with a cruelty and horror that would have well accorded with the warfare of the most barbarous people on earth. . . . The steadfast loyalty of the black man to the Union, his devotion to her soldiers and trustworthiness as guide, or scout for our army, his noble bravery and daring as one of the nation's armed defenders brought upon him all that the cowardly hate of the Southern chivalry could invent in the way of torture and murder. For the aiders and abettors of the Ku Klux, the murderers of Union men, women, and children, is proposed a general amnesty; a proposition which meets with great favor by Senators from the Southern States. For the loyal and outraged black man is asked manhood rights; the same protection and regard for his rights, privileges, and comforts as is accorded to those who have left nothing undone tending to the destruction of the government and the strengthening of tyranny. . . . The Supplementary Civil Rights Bill is of far more real value to the good name of the nation, than is the amnesty proposition. The one is to place the nation firmly upon the foundation principles upon the Declaration of Independence, and gives to all races and colors, regardless of previous condition of servitude, the power to vindicate their rights by law. The second, without the enactment of the first into law, exalts rebels, assassins, and demons above the loyal black men and women of the South. The climax of injustice and outrage upon the colored people of this country, will have been sapped, when the Congress of the nation, failing to secure all rights for all, gives amnesty to those who clutched the nation by the throat and bringing to their assistance all the instrumentalities of their barbarous and brutal natures, only failed to destroy her because of the timely aid of the strong arm of her black soldiers.

The New National Era, Washington, D.C., January 18, 1872

D. Augustus Straker is probably the author of the following letter (signed only with the initials D. A. S.). He was a professor of common law at Allen University, in South Carolina, and later moved to Detroit, where he was a prominent lawyer and judge. He published The New South Investigated *(Detroit, 1888) and was a frequent contributor to the* New National Era.

Whenever a great moral work is to be done history furnishes us with the evidence that a great man has been raised up to accomplish it. More than a score of years ago the West Indian Islands were degraded by the barbarous and inhuman institution of slavery. . . .

Samuel Jackson Prescod, a negro, fought the cause of his race manfully, by day and by night, disregarding offices, scorning to be ap-
peased . . . until the Negro in the West Indies should be freed in word
and deed. . . . Prescod died but a few months ago, Assistant Judge of
the Court of Appeals, the peer of his associates and respected, nay es-
teemed, by all men.

Just so in this country, if not so now it will be so in a very short
time. Today is of great import to the negro in the history of the American States. His inalienable rights are denied him. . . . Give us our
rights for right sake, and not because of any special advantage which
may derive by association.

The New National Era, Washington, D.C., January 18, 1872

*The author of the following article was Mrs. Faith Lichen, a corre-
spondent of the* Era.

Reader, were you ever a colored boy? Have you ever gone to school
with your heart thumping tramp, tramp the boys are marching and
been obliged to walk around a crowd of white boys because they
chose to put themselves right in your path and had it leap into your
throat by a "cuff the nigger"—yelled into your ears and after doing all
that one pair of fists could do against half-a-dozen other pairs, were
you unmercifully beaten (two or three policemen passing meanwhile)?
. . . Have you ever studied Smith's Geography with a carefully cut
card held over that very worst type of the Negro presented in painful
contrast to the most perfect of the Caucasian on the opposite page?
Have the words "superior to all others," referring to the latter, ever
stuck in your throat while pride made you "go down," while some
other boy no more ambitious but less sensitive "went up"?

Have you ever tasted the sweet revenge of sticking pins into the
eyes of that soul driver in the picture of a cotton field at the head of
the lesson on Georgia? No! Then you don't know what a jolly experience belongs to nine-tenths of the free born colored men in this land
of liberty; then you can't see the necessity for all this commotion
among them about the Supplement to the Civil Rights Bill. You who
do not know what it is to have been kicked in byways, hooted on
highways, dragged off railways, driven to the decks of steamboats,
hurled from the communion table in your Father's House, to your

agony and humiliation, your wretchedness and despair, you cursed
God and—lived.

The New National Era, Washington, D.C., January 25, 1872

The author of the following letter was J. P. Sampson, editor of the Colored Citizen, *published in Cincinnati, "in the interest of colored soldiers
assisted by government and sanitary missions." It was, apparently, a joint
stock company, which published weekly during the Civil War. The editor
noted that the printing was done by white men because no black men were
available.*

. . . There is a degree of cringing servility eminently patronizing in
every effort we make to gratify an insane prejudice of caste, by giving
assurance that we do not want equal rights in social matters, making
an issue outside of the subject of a right regulated by statute law. I
would give no indemnity; I have no apology to offer for any relation
growing out of a right so justly ours. Must one class of American citizens governed by consent be deprived of public comfort incorporated
under our laws in order to foster the prejudices of another class, and
to prevent them from being brought together in a social way—a matter wholly impossible except by the intelligent consent of the parties?
Should this right, by some affinity result in friendship and social relation with any white fellow citizen, I would demand equal rights and
respect in that relation as in any other. I would demand it by every
sentiment of honor. The man or woman, white or colored, who would
demand less is void of proper self-respect. . . . Sooner or later we
must have no separate legislation to suit the proscriptions which society makes; all are known as Americans and in its title as citizens of a
common country we demand a common law for suffrage, education
. . . I would not demand it as a reward for valor on the battlefield,
but in the name of home by nativity, none will be known to the law by
peculiar habits of race. . . .

The New National Era, Washington, D.C., January 25, 1872

*The debilitating nature of Southern society is described in the following
letters. The first is by Sarah Thompson, from Memphis, Tennessee. The*

second is by A. W. Shadd, a graduate of Howard University Law School and brother of J. D. Shadd, speaker of the House of the Mississippi legislature in 1871. Their father, I. D. Shadd, an early abolitionist and active participant in the convention movement, moved to Canada prior to the Civil War and settled near Chatham, Ontario, where he edited the Provincial Freeman.

. . . Last winter on coming from Cincinnati to this city, myself and four small children . . . we were not allowed to enter the ladies sitting room in Louisville, Ky. Therefore, to keep ourselves warm, we were obliged to walk to and fro in front of the depot in the sleet and while my dear children were suffering and crying from the severity of the cold. In faltering accents, one of them inquired of me "Why is this, ma? What have we done? Why can't we go in there and get warm just like the others?" . . . We had committed no offense. Our only crime was being American negroes.

The New National Era, Washington, D.C., February 15, 1872

. . . The Southern gentleman rents the land to his former slave at about the whole value of the land each year, and thus practically sells his land each year, recovering it at the end. This high-toned gentleman, this soul of honor, does more—he "furnishes" the people on his plantation, buys provisions, and sells to the poor colored man at an advance of 50 to 100%, agreeing to wait for his pay until the crop is picked out and ready for market. A little judicious exaggeration of the account usually attends these operations, and at the end of the year, the colored man frequently finds that he has nothing due him for his year's labor. . . .

The New National Era, Washington, D.C., October 3, 1872

This was written by J. Sella Martin, the founder of the New Era *and pastor of the Fifteenth Street Colored Presbyterian Church in Washington, D.C.*

Good riddance to the Negro! For 250 years he has been a thorn in the flesh. The 15th Amendment has extracted him. . . . Let the blood of Crispus Attucks* cry no more from the ground, as the consecrating libation of our revolution, against the nation which held his descendants in slavery. Thou old saint, hero and martyr of Harpers Ferry, let thy soul betake itself to rest! We have followed thy marching on to the end of battle, and to the day of victory!

. . . We are poor and contentment in our poverty means the neutralization of our ballot. Bound by poverty to the soil of the monopolists with the fetters of capital, independence in feeling when circumstances arise becomes impossible. We must be owners of the soil; and we need to acquire those habits of economy which will make the nation see our deserts in granting land, and keep us under an ever-present sense of the need to hold it when we get it. Rooted and grounded in the soil, we will be steadied by considerations of our responsibilities; and many of the old traces of oppression will fall from us while truthfulness, honesty, sobriety and industry will take their places . . .

The New National Era, Washington, D.C., February 10, 1870

Richard T. Greener, the author of the following letter, was a correspondent of the Era *and later one of its co-editors. He was the first Negro to graduate from Harvard (1870) and was a professor at the University of South Carolina during Reconstruction and dean of the Law School at Howard University (1879–82). He was later appointed U.S. consul at Bombay (1898) and Vladivostok. A staunch advocate of migration to Western lands, he was instrumental in organizational work enabling many to leave the South.*

. . . It is scarcely necessary to revert to the struggle which, starting with the foundation of the government, has embodied for the contest for our rights the symbol for liberty and equality. It has been said that our history in this country has been its romance; but it might have been as truly said, I imagine, that it has also been its tragedy. The slave ship, the slave hut and pen, the overseer's whip and the burning tears of separated husband and wife, and the equally cruel caste and proscription which has hounded the negro when free from the cradle to the grave have mingled in far unequalled proportions the romantic with the tragic. They will live in the history of the country, not to be cherished with vindictive feelings by us, but to be read as warnings against injustice, to be cited as sad examples of that perversion which

* The first man, a black, to die in the Boston Massacre in 1770.

noble principles may undergo, when the children drift from the teachings of the fathers, when expediency and wrong are substituted for right. . . .

The New Era, Washington, D.C., May 5, 1870

❃

Black settlements on the frontier of Kansas grew quickly during the last years of Reconstruction. Their papers reflect the growing sentiment of active self-defense—the only practical response to Southern repression.

The way the devils of the South are treating the colored people is an outrage to even the half-civilized people of that portion of our Union. If our advice could be heeded by our people in the region spoken of above [Nashville] we would say to them leave, but never move until every plantation owned by the devils who take so much pleasure in warning them to get out are laid in a bed of ashes.

For colored men to expect protection from the government is mere nonsense while Hayes is President, and for them to look for protection from the rebel State governments is foolishness; and for them to attempt to protect themselves by openly resisting or fighting is out of the question. Hence, the only feasible plan is for each man to provide himself with a box of matches and a quart of coal oil, and at night quietly and carefully steal out of their cabins, and while the brutes are sleeping with their families around them dreaming of the terror they have scattered among the colored people, just economically scatter their oil upon the most inflammable parts of barns or houses and then make the best use possible of the matches, and then lite out for dear life. Just let this plan be tried in a dozen localities and we feel sure that a very sudden stop will be put to all this Southern deviltry.

Now we expect the Northern press will go into spasms when they read this advice, but we expect it will be taken in more than one place nevertheless. For 200 years we were driven like brutes by these wretches of the South and we can no longer bear up under their treatment. Hence, we recommend *coal oil* and *matches* as the only certain cure.

The Colored Citizen, Fort Scott, Kansas, November 9, 1878

❃

Black communities supported their own militias for self-defense. After the withdrawal of federal troops from the South in 1877, white officials began to disband black militias.

ATTENTION

Many of the prominent colored citizens of this city [Topeka, Kansas] having signified their desire to organize and maintain a militia company we have determined to go ahead and perfect such an organization, and we invite all colored men who favor such a step to call at the Colored Citizen printing office and leave their names and when a sufficient number have done so we will call a meeting and consummate the organization.

W. L. EAGLESON

The Colored Citizen, Topeka, Kansas, November 9, 1877

As conditions worsened in the South, and the great "Exodus" of freedmen began from the South to Kansas in 1879, the outspoken editor of this Kansas paper urged his readers to follow the example set by John Brown.

WANTED, A FEW BLACK JOHN BROWN'S

Brutal murders and barbarous outrages, in the South are still continued. Almost every day a fresh outrage perpetrated by the demons of some one of the same Southern States, is reported. Such a thing, as a black man finding any security for his life provided he dares assert his manhood, in that devil-ridden country, is out of the question. . . . There is no such thing as justice, none in all the South, that is, where there is a black man interested; if one works for a white man he is systematically swindled out of his wages, and if he protests, his life is taken from him, as ruthlessly, as if he were a brute. If he goes into the courts he finds, Judges lawyers, and juries all against him, and if he attempts to stand up like a man and demand a trial, that's fair and impartial, he is given quickly to understand that, in that country, that old demon Judge Taney's decision is in full force, that a "black man has no rights that a white man is bound to respect." . . . The fact is, the ex-rebels of the South never mean to permit the colored people to act in anything independent of their dictation, and it will yet be found out, that the loyal people of the North, who fought the late war to a successful termination, will have to say in language too thunder like to be misunderstood, that they did not spend *billions of money, and shed rivers of blood for naught.* The war is not yet over, and if the American people imagine that the black people of this country will always submit patiently, and we came near saying, foolishly to the inhuman treatment that they have had to endure since the day they were first stolen from their native land and landed upon the shores of this cruel country, they will, the first thing they know, wake up and realize a state of affairs too horrible to contemplate. The South today is nursing a wind, that before they know it will turn upon them as the most terrific whirlwind that has ever been known in the history of the world. They will yet learn that "whatsoever a man soweth, that shall he also reap." The civilized world, has long since given the Black American credit, for being the most docile, patient, and forebearing human, upon the Globe, but his long association with his white brethren, is beginning to tell upon him, and he is fast coming to think and feel that he has suffered enough, and that it is about time that something of immunity from further persecution ought to be accorded him, and naturally enough he is looking to the people who broke his chains, and loosed his shackles, to see to it, that he is made secure in his person and property, and so soon as it gets through his brain, that he is always to suffer and never be protected by the strong arm of the Government, he has always revered and for which he has always been ready to shed his blood, from the day that Crispus Attucks, fell in defense of the flag of his country down to the butchery at Fort Pillow,* and even on down to the successful termination of the late war for the Union; and that courts of justice are mere traps that serve to, induce him to bring in his cause to the end, that he may be more easily and systematically murdered, he will then at last get the right conception of his duty, before his eyes, namely to bring about such a conflict, as will *wake this whole country up,* from one end to the other. All that is needed is a few Black John Brown's . . .

The Colored Citizen, Fort Scott, Kansas, January 4, 1879

---

* On April 12, 1864, the fort was captured by the Confederate Army, and after surrendering, nearly half of its black and white defenders were massacred.

Various forms of institutionalized racism were established, but none so cruel as the convict-lease system. Black men, women, and children were arrested on any charge, convicted, and sentenced to labor farms, where their work was bought by companies seeking cheap labor. When these private concerns needed more labor, there were more arrests. The great industries of the South were thus built upon a new form of slavery.

. . . the convict slaves are leased out to men who entirely control them, who have to pay but 6¢ per day for their hire, and only $200 if one escapes. A white man with money can bribe his way out, but there is no chance for the poor unfortunate colored people. . . . If the colored man breaks a contract, he is sentenced to 12 months on the chain gang. . . . We hope that so long as these outrages continue, the colored people will continue to leave the South until those in power will see the error of their ways and repent in sackcloth and ashes and accord equal justice to all.

The Kansas Herald, Topeka, February 13, 1880

T. Thomas Fortune, the editor of the Globe, *was a rare journalistic crusader, counseling militant resistance to oppression and also providing a serious center for political organizing, which culminated in the creation of a protective organization, the Afro-American League.*

. . . When murder, usurpation, intimidation, and systematic wrong are practiced in open violation of law; when the Negro who steals from society what society steals from him under the specious cover of invidious law is hung upon the nearest oak tree, and the white villain who shoots a Negro without provocation is not so much as arrested— when society tolerates such an abnormal state of things, what will the harvest be?

The question of the illegal suppression of a tremendous voting population is not a race question; it is a national question, defined minutely in the federal constitution. . . . A people invite destruction or violent contention by permitting fundamental laws to be abused, by permitting common rights to be usurped by an arrogant and violent class. The people of the United States will find all too soon that they are playing on top of a volcano which is liable to erupt at any moment. . . .

The Globe, New York, January 13, 1883

In the North, exploitation of black people was of a different nature.

. . . The Civil Rights bill* was proposed to break down the prejudices of the whites, not the prejudices of the blacks. . . . White men stand ready at all times to make money out of colored people honestly when they are compelled to, dishonestly as often as they possibly can. And when the black man prefers to do his own work, or refuses to be robbed, the cry is raised that "The negroes are drawing the color line." Let them draw it! Let them be as mean and cunning as white men. The survival of the fittest is what Darwin considers the best proof of the capacity of a race, and if we are to survive in this country, we must draw the line on the arrogant white man just as he draws it on us. He used it to make money during the slave regime; he has used us to make money and power for him since the war—he is never satisfied unless he is using us. The *Globe* means war to the knife on the white man's greed, selfishness, and subterfuge, and the only way to be successful in this warfare is to use the very same weapons that the white man uses. . . .

The Globe, New York, May 5, 1883

The following article originally appeared in the New York Globe *and is a response to the growing apprehensions by whites of more militant and successful efforts by black organizations to develop unity and racial pride around issues of self-determination, national identity, and political equality.*

What we want in religion is absolute equality of worship and when we can't get it in the white churches, we organized churches of our own; hence the AME [African Methodist Episcopal] church. . . . We want absolute equality in the public schools—mixed scholars and mixed teachers—and if we can't have it, we want colored schools

---

* In 1883 the Supreme Court outlawed the Civil Rights Acts of 1875, which sought to provide some protection for black citizens against segregation. By 1900 most Southern states had legalized separation of the races.

taught by colored teachers. We want absolute impartiality in newspaper treatment, to publishing and editing newspapers for ourselves—hence *The Globe* and *The Recorder,* and other papers, published to proclaim the wrongs and demand redress for the people. . . . Show us one black president of a white college in this broad land; show us one black professor in any white college in this country; show us one black preacher with a white flock; show us one black editor running a white newspaper. On the other hand, we have white presidents of black colleges from Maine to California, and from the Pacific to the swamps of Alabama, and white professors in black colleges by the hundreds; we have an army of white ministers who grow fat by feeding black souls, and we have a newspaper, or so reported, to be run by white men, or by their cash. Who has drawn this line? Certainly we have not. Then if we did not draw it, should we not make those who did draw it respect and observe the conditions implied in the erection of the barrier? Obviously. We believe in doing unto others as they do unto us. If a man slap us on the right cheek, would we turn to him the left one? Not much. If a man steal our cloak would we give him also our coat? Not if there was a policeman near at hand. If a man ruthlessly shove us out of his house, would we extend to him an invitation to dine and lodge in our house? Not much. Idealism is good, but practical "hard pan" is not to be ignored.

The Gazette, Cleveland, August 25, 1883

T. Thomas Fortune, editor of the New York Globe, *was acutely sensitive to the mechanism of exploitation that worked against the poor of all races. Though not sanguine about the solution of racial problems, he urged a unity among all workingmen on the basis of common resistance to their oppression.*

. . . There are men in this country who own more than the aggregate wealth of all the small farmers of the South—the five and ten acre farmers. But how did they get it? Honestly, dollar by dollar, cent upon cent? Not at all! They got it by robbery and perjury and forgery. No man can in his lifetime honestly amass $2,000,000, or $50,000,000. And yet we have men whose wealth rivals the thievings of princes with millions of subjects obedient to their behests.

The blacks of the South are not the only poor of that section. The mass of the blacks are poor and so are the mass of the whites. The few rich men live upon the labor of the poor and keep them poorer. There is no sentimentality about this relation of the wealthy and the poor, but there is much error. . . .

The blacks of Georgia are poor and there are few exceptions to the rule; the whites of Georgia are poor, but there are exceptions to the rule—that is the only difference. It is the same in New York as in Georgia. One-fourth of the population of the whole country depends upon the labor of the day for food and clothing and shelter. We are in our "minority" as yet. Then why should it be expected of us that we should own magnificent stretches of land, imposing buildings and conduct lucrative business. If we had robbed the editor of the Atlanta *Constitution* of his labor for 200 years, as he has robbed us of ours, we would not expect him to own the whole country 20 years after we had been made to restore to him his freedom.

But it is useless to expect fair play from that quarter. It is almost futile to expect a white man to do justice by a colored man at any time. To rob him of his freedom and his labor has been the pastime of these men ever since they forced him to come among them.

Three-fourths of the entire population of Georgia labor to enrich the remaining one-fourth; yet this little fraction says it owns and manages all the wealth and business and bears all the burdens of taxation of the majority. . . . The three-fourths who labor and the one-fourth who appropriate that labor will come to an understanding some day. Let the white men of the South force the question. Let the black man and the poor white man meet that issue as it should be met.

The Globe, New York, October 13, 1883

When the Civil Rights Bill was declared unconstitutional, black men and women voiced their opposition and demonstrated. Then, as now, the problem was one not of law and order, but of justice.

There appears to be some serious trouble over the Civil Rights decision. Five hundred colored men are reported to have been under arms at Austin on the 29th. and the Governor was appealed to to furnish militia to protect the public peace. The protection was furnished, of course, though colored men have appealed in vain for protection from mobs and assassins. No blood is reported to have been spilt. The restlessness of the colored people of the South should be a warning to the people of the country that injustice, and lawlessness, and mobocracy on the part of the whites are becoming more and more intolerable to the colored people. When the uprising comes, no one stops to inquire the cause—every effort is made to suppress it. The only way to cure the restlessness of colored men is to deal justly by them. No half way ground will avail. We have been wronged, and unless they are healed, the country will be disturbed by our restlessness for the next century. We desire peace and order and fraternity, but how talk of these when wrong and outrage walk abroad in the noonday and assassination and intimidation lurk in the shadows of night. Men may cry Peace! Peace! But there is and can be no peace unaccompanied by honest and impartial justice.

The Globe, New York, November 3, 1883

T. Thomas Fortune's call for militant resistance to oppression shares the same insight developed by Frantz Fanon (in his Wretched of the Earth) *that ". . . the 'thing' which has been colonised becomes man during the same process by which it frees itself."*

. . . There is but one way to put a period to the force and violence of a Bourbon [Southern Democrat]—use more force and violence than he uses. As he believes in brute force, he respects it, even when it is used by those he hates and stabs in the dark. . . . Let the colored man stand his ground. There is far more honor in dying like a free man than living like a slave. . . .

The Globe, New York, November 10, 1883

Emigration was a form of protest, but to the editor of the People's Advocate, *if one couldn't, or didn't want to, leave the South, he could fight.*

. . . Emigration is a mild and peaceable solution of the vexed question; while the reasons for it are being promulgated, the colored people are being robbed, cheated, insulted, bulldozed and murdered. . . .

We can afford this no longer. We performed the labor at the South and we should demand respect and consideration. We feed the indolent pride-blown autocrat and deserve their gratitude. We have increased the cotton crops steadily, until the yield has reached prodigious figures, and we deserve commendation. But what do we get? The blood of our fathers is the price we receive for our labor. Profane thresholds we receive for our fidelity and forbearance. Night is made hideous with the yells of denunciations and anathemas directed against us, wild, racking in blood; mad rapine and organized bands of relentless murderers, track us to our homes, our churches, our places of business and our public meetings, and there is no retreat, no succor, no commiseration for us. We submit to this or take the only alternative—defend ourselves with our manhood, our valor, and if need be with our blood. We are shot down like dogs, let us shoot back. We are cheated out of our earnings, let us demand remuneration, and apply the torch when the demand is not acceded to, and the means of removing the subject of the contention. We can no longer afford to lie supinely upon our backs to be treaded upon by ruthless robbers.

If our homes are invaded, let the shotgun protect them (the sentiment of the North seems powerless in that direction); if our rights are denied, let a navy-six [revolver] be their arbiter; if our property is destroyed, let the torch be applied until devastation, destruction, blood, tears, and misery and starvation serve to teach the whites that justice must be done. . . . When this is done we will at least have earned the title of *men* and will receive the sympathy, if not the support, of our white friends.

The People's Advocate, Washington, D.C., November 24, 1883

Incidents such as the following were used by Fortune to emphasize the importance of self-defense as a right of free men.

. . . At Yazoo City, Mississippi, last week, a white merchant and a colored butcher had an altercation. The white merchant acting upon the natural cowardice of his race in such matters, declined to settle the dispute in an honorable hand-to-hand fight, but posted off after his friends. The colored butcher did the same. When the white man returned with his friends the colored man and his friends, without standing to be shot proceeded to stand and shoot. As a consequence, "three of the best citizens of the place were killed outright," and others were wounded. And the whole gang of them, on murder bent, should have been killed outright. When a man takes violence as his weapon he should die by violence. "An eye for an eye, a tooth for a tooth," the accepted law of retaliation.

But the matter did not rest here. The citizens "rose up as a man," took the law in hand, and lynched the colored men, who had been lodged in jail. The colored men fought the mob to the bloody end, and died like heroes. And so brave men always die.

Two hundred white men flooded Yazoo City to defy the law and to avenge men who had invited the death they deserved. In a warfare of this nature, where brute force and cruelty are the only rules observed, let both sides carry to its logical result the cowardice of the fight. Let the torch vindicate the outrages of the mob and the shotgun. . . .

The Supreme Court of the United States, a beggarly apology for wisdom and fairness, declares that such lawlessness and murder are without the jurisdiction of the National Government; that if the State affords the victim no protection he need not look to the National Government. Then, where shall he look, pray? To the mercy of the mob, the humanity of the murderer? No; let him use the same weapons that other oppressed people use—let him use the dagger, the torch and the shotgun. There is no other appeal; no other argument will avail. The State denies protection; the National Government declares it has no jurisdiction. Then shall black men, free and independent, made in the image of their Maker, stand up as cowards to be shot by ruffians made of the same clay, with no more rights, human or Divine? Perish the thought! A race of cowards would thus sink their manhood, but free men never!

The Globe, New York, January 5, 1884

Little more than a century after the American Revolutionary War, black editors, like Fortune, appealed to the same ideal as did the Founding Fathers.

. . . Papers all over the South proclaim, in justification of murder and mob villainy that the black man must be kept down, and he must not be permitted to enjoy the privileges and immunities guaranteed by the Constitution of the Union, that there must be one law for the white man and another for the black. The fountains of justice are made inaccessible to the black man; judges and juries no longer throw around him the presumption that he is innocent until proven guilty; mobs sit in judgment and pass sentence from which there is no appeal; the community, speaking through the newspapers, the echoes of the people, justify crime and incite to lawlessness—anarchy walks abroad, and the man who can shoot straightest or use the dagger most unerringly is the dispenser of human life. We appeal from the *arbiter dictum* of irresponsible cutthroats and murderous editors to the forum of American reason; we appeal to the innate justice of the law of the land; we appeal to the manhood and the courage of the black men of the South. It is bad enough to be denied equal political rights, but to be murdered by mobs—denied the protection of life and limb and property—the thing is not to be endured without protest, and if violence must be met with violence, let it be met.

The Globe, New York, January 12, 1884

The hypocrisy and corruption of the judicial system generally, and in the South particularly, reflected the depth of racism at the highest level. A proposal by whites to establish segregated juries was met by renewed demands by blacks for justice and equality.

To be tried by a jury of one's peers is the legitimate right of every citizen of our government, a right which finds sanction in the fundamental principles of our organic law. But too often the judgment of American courts, unlike that of any other country is even yet in this boasted land of pure Christianity construed to suit the views and caprices of a perverted public sentiment. . . . Packed juries can never subserve the demands of the law, for when a white jury is chosen solely to the exclusion of a single colored person to try white persons for offenses against colored men, there is strong evidence of injustice and when an entire colored jury has been impaneled to try colored men at times, it offers a precedent that is at once dangerous and subversive of the designs of a jury sworn to duty. But what is the design in selecting a jury composed chiefly of colored men to try colored culprits? What does it mean? It proposes interposition between white and black in the exercise of rightful authority for the former against the latter. It means to establish an unwarranted practice in order to justify a precedent in choosing a white jury to try, what sentiment may deem to be exceptional cases, in which are involved the liberty and happiness of some despot lord. . . . When the precedent is once established and the purpose is accomplished, then argument becomes needless, for it can be claimed that colored men presided over cases concerning one of their own and should not now complain where white men are required to do the same. . . .

The Gazette, Cleveland, February 23, 1884

As reports of mob attacks against the black communities of Danville and Copiah, Virginia, were revealed, the black press urged self-defense as the only realistic alternative.

. . . For conscientious political opinions, righteously declared or understood, men and their wives and children have been shot, hanged, or otherwise murdered. Appeal after appeal have been made to high heaven for a cessation of such wrongs without effect. Our government seems powerless to check this onward march of terror and to avoid and defend the shedding of innocent blood, there is need of reformation, and if in the near future the movement is not initiated we are loath to longer see our people thus made a target for the chivalrous and hot blooded southerners, who in many instances are so brave that they go by night to the homes of their victims and there display their valor? Our appeals for years having been unanswered, the only thing left us is to take the law in our own hands and thereby thoroughly establish our liberty and independence. During the war we were called and gladly did we respond, and taking up arms went to the front, and right manfully did we battle for the dissolution of that accursed system of slavery. That our work was effective thousands of maimed and generally used up rebels, "because of negro bullets," speak too loudly to be denied. The southerner knows full well the power of thorough negro organization and proper discipline, and since during all these years the government has failed to protect its people from all these terrible outrages of which Danville and Copiah are only typical illustrations of their cussedness. The only thing left us is to ask the northern whites to remain neutral, and if every dark-hued man in this country will respond voluntarily to our notion of righting this matter there will be no need of the passage of the Ex-Governor's resolutions. We will try to establish ourselves by force and might (as persuasion has failed) in the territory which we believe God in his dispensation of places and things intended for the colored men—we mean the south. If the colored men of the south and of the north unite, and as heretofore suggested, the whites of the north remain quiet, we will either put a stop to this hellish affair or die in the attempt. Time for decisive action is ripe. We have suffered too much and too long in silence. The mode suggested seems the only alternative left us or we must continue to die like curs in a pen. Therefore, if our much oppressed people will only organize, and unless the whites of the north interfere, we feel competent that we can teach the bourbons of the south a lesson that they will not forget soon as they seem to have forgotten the late war, which was fully five years too short to exterminate entirely the accursed rebels of our country and murderers of innocent people. It must ultimately come to this. We find no rest at our firesides, nor at our labors. Why then longer stand and be slaughtered like beasts of prey? We ask only for an equal showing. Arm us equivalently and then we will meet shot gun to shot gun, rifle to rifle, pistol to pistol, cannon to cannon, man to man, on an equal plain. After such an event this trouble will be settled. We therefore would suggest that the colored people throughout the Union at once organize. Especially in the south would we have the leading spirits take hold of this matter and effect organizations that will do them credit. We of the north will not be found wanting. We are men and freemen clothed with the rights of other beings and by God endowed with the power to think and act. Let us not then longer submit to be like sheep, driven at will, but when struck, strike back and with interest. We love our country, its constitutions and its laws, but we love our lives and liberty better, and like other nationalities we must protect and defend the things that so vitally concern us. If the constitution, laws and powers that be are inadequate to defend us, then we who are so greatly concerned must form laws for our own protection. If this course is adopted it will save the government the useless expenditure of thousands, yes, millions of dollars for annual investigations, which only tend to solidify the north against the south, but does nothing toward protecting the colored man in his enjoyment of life, liberty, and happiness. Sound the tocsin along the line that we may all prepare for self-defense. *"Sic Semper Tyrannis."*

The State Journal, Harrisburg, Pennsylvania, March 1, 1884

"Revisionism" in historical writing was common among black editors who constantly sought to dispel the myths of American democracy and justice, while exposing racism. The theme of self-preservation in the face of such conditions was an important link between protest movements and those of self-help.

. . . The colored people of this country came here not of their own accord; they were kidnapped from their land by pirates who were protected by the laws of nations which professed to love God and revere justice. . . . Abraham Lincoln was never an abolitionist in the broad sense of the term; he was a colonizationist. Expatriation was the panacea which he deemed would settle the slave question. He became the father of abolition because the exigencies of the war left him no alternative . . . It is not necessary in this address to recapitulate the incidents of Reconstruction history which naturally led up to the finality of 1876. It is sufficient to know that anarchy prevailed in every Southern state; that a black man's life was not worth the having; that armed bodies of men openly defied the Constitution of the U.S. and nullified each and every one of its guarantees of citizenship to the colored man. With the absolute control of the Federal Government, the Republican Party permitted armed insurrection to prevail from 1868 to 1876, and during that period thousands of black men—loyal to the government and loyal to the party—were shot down like sheep. . . . This temporizing policy permitted terrorism to run rampant; permitted the rule of the majority to be overturned; permitted the black man to be slaughtered and despoiled of all his rights. . . . Black men of the U.S., rely upon yourselves in the future; place no more confidence in demagogues, white or black; seek out the men among you of true intelligence, honesty and courage and stand by them. . . . Self-preservation is the first law of nature and the black man in official position is more likely to stand up for his own and your rights than a white man who owes his elevation to your votes. . . . You have your own future in your hands. . . .

The Freeman, New York, December 6, 1884

The right of self-defense was a constant theme in the black press and became especially important as the federal government, under a policy of benign neglect, allowed the Southern states to engage in the repression of black citizens.

. . . Colored men of the South, turn on the light! The columns of the *Freeman* are open to you for a clear, forcible, manly ventilation of all your grievances and there is not a cutthroat within range of Mason and Dixon's lines who can gag us or compel us to suppress the facts of the brutality and cowardice which every day disgrace Southern civilization, and we ram this defiant statement into the wide mouth of the mayor of Salisbury [N.C.], and honestly wish that it could choke him. Let the colored men of the South protest against the rule of the mob and the degradation of the machinery of the law. Let them protest! It is a reproach and an insult to our manhood that we allow ourselves to be shot, outraged and lynched without one word of protest, or the uplifting of a finger in self-defense. Stand up for your rights, and if they be denied you by the courts of law, defend yourselves with the same arguments used to outrage you. What is fair for the one is fair for the other, and if the white scamps lynch and shoot you, you have a right to do the same. . . .

The Freeman, New York, July 18, 1885

In a period often characterized as a nadir in black history, the black press provided a striking contrast in its militancy and its efforts toward unifying the black community.

Mississippi white men have managed in times past to make for themselves a reputation for cold blooded murderous villainy only surpassed in cruelty and recklessness by that of the white men of South Carolina. It is not any more a question of politics, it is simply a question of reckless villainy, defiance of established law, and the infamous acquiescence or connivance of the State and local authorities. When the constituted authorities of a State, or county, or municipality wink at murder, it is high time to question the power or the disposition of the State to give to its citizens that Republican form of government guaranteed to them by the Federal Constitution, and in the absence of such Republican form of government, to proceed to arm themselves for self-protection. . . .

What are the unprotected colored citizens of Mississippi to do? Arm themselves to the teeth, organize into secret bodies, and measure out to lawless white men the same measure they receive. There is nothing else left to do. They have no protection in the Federal Courts; they are denied justice in the State Courts; they are murdered in the very temple of justice by outlaws who are shielded in their villainy by state and county authorities. There is nothing left for them to do but protect themselves. Let them do this.

The Freeman, New York, March 27, 1886

One of the most important functions of the black press was to provide its readers with information about lynchings and other forms of oppression (subjects usually ignored by white papers) and to encourage resistance.

The lynching of five colored men at Yorkville, S.C. . . . by armed men is but another heinous crime which, from time to time, have been practiced upon the Negro. Even the judge on the bench, in instructing the Grand Jury, said that "It was [the lynching] one of those things which the law could not reach, and therefore it would be useless for them to lose their time in attempting to ferret out the perpetrators." Well, if the law can't reach the rascals, if justice can't overtake the ruthless slayers of black men and women, the only recourse the colored man has is to protect himself and to remember the old law, "an eye for an eye, and a tooth for a tooth."

The Weekly Pelican, New Orleans, April 9, 1887

The black press often printed incidents of outrage against the black community.

In St. Bernard's Parish, La., May 4, a plantation overseer by the name of Green, known to be a Louisiana desperado who has figured in two or three killing scrapes, had a quarrel with Robert Smith, a colored laborer, and threatened his life with a knife in his hand, advancing on Smith, who picked up a stick laying near by and stood Green off. Green became enraged and armed himself, and at night, accompanied by two other white companions, went to Smith's cabin and broke open the door. Smith knew Green's voice and suspected his mission and as the door fell in he opened fire on the first man who appeared and Green received the contents of Smith's revolver, and was mortally wounded from which he died. The other two white men returned the fire and ran, slightly wounding Smith. Smith was arrested next morning. At noon a lynching party composed of white men went to the jail and demanded the keys which were surrendered to them without trouble. They took Smith out and hung him to a tree in broad daylight without being masked. Smith is the seventh colored man mobbed in the South last week as follows: Kentucky mobs one and shoots one, Georgia one, Louisiana one, Mississippi one and Virginia one. There are from six to eight colored men or women murdered by white men in the Southern States weekly. There seems to be no other redress for us but to organize into protective unions in defense of our parents, wives and children, whose lives are in jeopardy every day at the hands of these Southern white desperadoes. The white press doesn't publish half the crimes committed upon colored people by their white brothers. I premise they are ashamed to put them on record.

The Freeman, New York, May 15, 1886

Instances of resistance were often not as obvious as open confrontation, especially in confinement of the convict labor camps.

Nashville, Tenn. A diabolical attempt to murder the keeper and guards of the County Farm was discovered Sunday. The County convicts are leased to the proprietor of the farm and four of them conspired to murder him and the guards and thus effect their escape. Arsenic was smuggled into the prison at the farm as cigarettes, and placed in the drinking water. Ten men including the proprietor and four guards were prostrated, but so far none of the cases have resulted fatally, although several victims are in a precarious condition. One of the conspirators has made a full confession.

The Western Cyclone, Nicodemus, Kansas, April 21, 1887

A recurrent expression throughout black history is the appeal by the black man to the federal government for intervention on his behalf.

There have been colored men that would die rather than take the treatment inflicted upon them and the only chance to get rid of them was to overpower them by bands of KKK by the hundreds or place them in prison and a mob of people make an arrangement with the proper officers and drive the unprotected man from his cell and take his life. How long will the government of the State and the United States suffer such wrongs to go unnoticed? The constitution of the United States provides for the protection of the citizens of the United States and still my people have suffered more from the heel of oppression from the taskmaster in that way since 1861 than they have in the hundred years before. We are law-abiding people and have suffered more than any nation and have not yet resorted to violence. . . . A government that will not protect its people is not worthy to be called a government.

The Benevolent Banner, Topeka, Kansas, July 23, 1887

A proposal by the editor of the National Leader, *Frederick Douglass, Jr., to build a statue to John Brown met with opposition from T. T. Fortune, editor of the* Age.

. . . There is another, a forerunner of John Brown, if you please, who stands in more need of our copper pennies to be melted down into a monument to perpetuate his memory than John Brown. We refer of course to Nat Turner, who was executed at Jerusalem, Southampton County, Virginia, for inciting and leading his fellow slaves to insurrection long before John Brown invaded Kansas and planned his unfortunate raid on Harper's Ferry.

Nat Turner was a black hero. He preferred death to slavery. He ought to have a monument. White men care nothing for his memory. We should cherish it. . . .

The Age, New York, January 12, 1889

The editor of the New York Age draws the color line over our proposition to erect a monument to the memory of the life and the character of John Brown and suggests that Nat Turner stands more in need of one. We have no fault to find with his suggestion; but when he slurringly remarks "that whenever colored men move that somebody's memory be perpetuated, that somebody's memory is always a white man," he helps to sustain the charge made against us by the white men of the South, "that it is the colored people who draw the color line." We have always been of the opinion that the character and good acts of a man were worthy of emulation and perpetuation, and not his color. . . .

Nat Turner has been dead many years, and the editor of *The Age* has never found time to suggest a monument for him until now, and he only suggests it now in opposition to one being erected in honor of John Brown, because he was so fortunate or unfortunate as to be born white. Prejudice among the white people of this country is dying out, but the editor of *The Age* would encourage it among the blacks. . . .

The National Leader, Washington, D.C., January 19, 1889

. . . 'That Nat Turner has been dead many years' is almost equally true of John Brown. John Brown lost his life in urging and leading an insurrection of slaves. Nat Turner at an earlier date did the same. The conduct of the one was no more heroic than the other. The whites have embalmed the memory of John Brown in marble and vellum and Fred Douglass Jr. now wants colored people to embalm it in brass; while the memory of the black hero is preserved neither in marble, vellum, nor brass.

What we protest against is Negro worship of white men and the memory of white men, to the utter exclusion of colored men equally patriotic and self-sacrificing. It is the absence of race pride and race unity which makes white men despise black men all the world over. . . .

We yield to no one in admiration of the character and sacrifices of John Brown. The character and sacrifices of Nat Turner are dearer to us because he was of us, and exhibited in the most abject condition the heroism and race devotion which has illustrated in all times the sort of men who are worthy to be free.

The Age, New York, January 26, 1889

William Calvin Chase, editor of the Washington Bee, *gave the following speech before the National Colored Press Convention on March 6, 1889.*

. . . For upwards of two hundred years the colored people have been made the objects of the most bitter hatred and tyranny. No task was too laborious, no tendency was too humiliating for the slave. A life of unequalled toil lay before him, a past black with the shameless atrocities of a hard and wicked master. Everything essential to the make-up of a proper manhood or womanhood was denied the slave, and the influence which conspire to destroy individuality were fostered by the whites, then beset with their awful consequences among them. Whether the last traces of African individuality was destroyed in the vortex of conspiring tendencies it is difficult to say. Surely when the Negro emerged from slavery he brought but little sin in common save the stripes of brutality together with ignorance and poverty. Such a condition was the logical consequence of slavery—a life of intense misery and deprivation; a standing monument to the cupidity and tyrannical spirit of past times. Today we are in a condition to appreciate the forces which have operated against the liberty and equality of our people. By the few lessons we have learned while in the enjoyment of a new estate, we can form some conception of the possibilities which lie before us and the only means by which they may be realized.

We occupy a peculiar place in the busy American body politic. We are included in the basis of representation; we are taxed and made to conform to all the rules and regulations governing society, but we have no real representative force and practically nothing to say with regard to taxation. Our votes are not counted and our lives and property are subject to the fiendish caprice of lawlessness and crime. The prejudice which operate against us are fed by a vicious sentiment which favors non-interference with State sovereignty even when the assertion of such presumed sovereignty overrides the power and authority of the Federal government—a sentiment which permits State authority to interfere in Federal as well as in State elections. . . .

Our condition demands not so much a leader as it does a more widespread manifestation of moral heroism and physical courage. It demands that a manly defense be made against the encroachments of unauthorized power, greed and vice. It demands that when our homes are invaded the shot gun shall be the direct resort in their protection; when our rights are invaded the navy-six shall play an important part in their arbitrament as it does in their denial; that when our property is destroyed that the torch of retaliation shall be lighted and applied until devastation, destruction, blood, tears, misery and starvation shall teach our white oppressors that the colored man whose Heaven-erected face the smiles of love adorn can and will fight and die as well as submit and suffer and is being taught to assert his rights by the dreadful instruments of revenge. Our condition suggests the further adherence to the republican party as a lever toward our elevation. . . .

The Bee, Washington, D.C., March 9, 1889

. . . The Negro has meekly asked that his rightful privileges be respected, that he be secure from injury as to person, or property in the exercise of his prerogatives; he asks that the law shall be obeyed. There will come a time when he will cease to bend the knee in supplication. He will lose faith in the effectiveness of persuasion and amicable methods. He will demand his own. If the government is so hedged in by States rights agreements that she cannot protect him, the courageous blood of L'Ouverture,* of Attucks, and of Turner, though cooled by years of oppression will surge anew in his veins, and the Negro may take the law into his own hands. A revolution would ensue beside which the popular disturbances of history would pale into insignificance . . .

The Freeman, Indianapolis, March 2, 1889

* Toussaint L'Ouverture, a leader of Haitians in their struggle against European colonialism during the last decade of the eighteenth century.

ETHIOPIA TO UNCLE SAM

ETHIOPIA—See how my people are murdered, maltreated, and outraged in the South, and you, with a great army and navy, are taking no measures to prevent it. Will the day of retribution never come?

UNCLE SAM—The administration is engaged just now in rewarding the faithful (appointing them to fat offices). When this is over we shall look into your case.

The Freeman, Indianapolis, September 21, 1889

The Black Man
and Politics

From the very beginning, black people saw politics as the mechanism by which they might achieve equality. No other subject raised such controversies among the black editors. In the period prior to the Civil War black editors split sharply: Some emphasized the more general "moral reform" of society, while others spoke of the necessity for political action. It was in the conventions of black men during this formative period that efforts toward political organization were developed. The black press, which was often the voice of these conventions, clearly reflects the political concerns of the black community.

Following the Civil War, the black vote became crucial in elections. Recognizing this, the Southern white governments effectively disfranchised the black voter. The black press resisted such efforts and generally displayed a fundamental loyalty to the Republican Party.

The heritage of the black political experience as reflected in the press may be seen as a dichotomy between the failure of the political institutions to include black people and the struggle of black people to develop indigenous leadership. The role of the black press in this dialectical process may be viewed in terms of its attempt to reconcile a desire to work with the existing system and the fact of their real exclusion. Black Americans were thus confronted with a caste system which they sought to change and an unresponsive political system from which they were alienated. The need to create institutions which would protect them and which would provide them with the rights of citizens was constantly being undermined by the very real experience of being used by the system. The black press in the nineteenth century sought to counter this condition by reinforcing the fact that black Americans were entitled to the same rights as anyone else. Although basically moderate in its political stance, the black press did lay the foundations for an ethnic political grouping which would work toward some form of integration.

The elections in New York, as in many other "free" states, barred most free blacks from voting by qualification tests, intimidation, etc. But Cornish here spoke to the reluctance of those who did not exercise their privilege.

The period of our State Election is at the door—Our views of that subject are the same as they have been for years. We have always said, that every coloured man who possesses the right, with becoming modesty, should approach the polls and there judiciously throw his weight into the political scale; and I cannot but deeply censure that part of our coloured population who are blessed with the various necessary comforts of life, and yet have not secured to themselves this privilege. We have but few coloured voters, yet we have more than 1000 individuals in this city who could with ease, secure to themselves that privilege—and were they in this particular to act as men and republicans, they would soon find themselves more respected.

True it is, the convention who altered the constitution of this State, acted in my opinion, very wrong and illegally in requiring of the coloured man, qualifications which were not required of the white.

It is plain that a State has the right of appointing the qualifications of its voters, and it is equally plain, that it has no legal right to require of A. a six feet stature and not to require of B. the same requisite, and if this proscription had been contested by the coloured people, before the Supreme Court, it must of necessity have been removed. Yet, as it was no doubt considered by the honorable Convention, as a matter of expediency, rather than one of law and justice, and as the coloured population at that time, had been rendered politically insane, by some designing political demagogues among the whites, it was more judicious to submit to the injustice, and secure to themselves the easy requisition.

The coloured population of most of the other free States, do not labour under the same disadvantages with us of New York, in this particular.

Our advice to them is participate in your rights as citizens, but *be temporate, be prudent, be modest.* Set an example for the whites, who are already, too many of them, politically half crazy.

The Rights of All, New York, October 16, 1829

The primary goal of the Weekly Advocate *was to establish the place of black people as an equal part of the American fabric.*

FREE MAN OF COLOUR

What an empty name! what a mockery! Free man, indeed! when so unrighteously deprived of every civil and political privilege. Free indeed! when almost every honorable incentive to the pursuit of happiness, so largely and so freely held out to his fairer brother, is withheld from him. A freeman! when prejudice binds the most galling chains around him, drives him from every mechanical employment, and situations of trust, or emolument; frowns him from the door of our institutions of learning; forbids him to enter every public place of amusement, and follows him, wherever he goes, pointing at him the finger of scorn and contempt. Is this to be a freeman? Is this to be a participant of the freedom of a country boasting to be the freest under the canopy of Heaven? What a sad perversion of the term freeman! No man of colour, be his talents, be his respectability, be his wealth what they may, enjoys in any sense, the rights of a freeman. That liberty, and those privileges which of right and according to the principles of our CONSTITUTION, ought to be his, he enjoys not. Persecuted, and degraded, he wanders along through this land of *universal liberty and equality,* a desolated being. His, no station of honor, power, or fame! Too often the virtuous and intelligent man of colour, must drag out an ignoble life, the victim of poverty, and sorrow. Then unwept for—but by a few of his persecuted race drops into the grave.

How long shall this cloud of unholy oppression darken his way? How long shall the sons of persecution brook the insults of a natural brother? How long shall true American citizens be deprived of their legitimate privileges and freedom, be to them, but the "baseless fabric of a vision." If forever, then roll back ye dark ages of ignorance, for "Ignorance then would be but bliss." We trust, however, that the day is not far distant when oppression and prejudice will cease their unhallowed war, against the innocent and unoffending, and that every man of colour will not only nominally, but in reality, enjoy all the blessings and privileges of freemen, native AMERICAN FREEMEN.

The Weekly Advocate, New York, January 14, 1837

The following editorial was written in response to a statement by President Martin Van Buren, who in his inaugural address opposed any attempt to abolish slavery.

So then it has come to this! The President of the United States, clothed in the constitutional power of his high office, in the contest now waging between Liberty and Slavery, plants *himself* in the breach, to conciliate the conscience-stricken contemners of our country's honor and the rights of man. . . . By this act, he has secured the trumpeting of America's shame to the ends of the earth. Does he vainly think he can stay the progress of public sentiment, or abate the force of truth? He is a foolish man if he thinks so! No! long before he descends from his high elevation, the growlings and mutterings of public opinion now heard in the distance from Europe, from the West Indies—from the East, the North, and West, will become too deep and powerful for resistance—and he will be obliged to obey it, or be driven from his position, as obnoxious men are sometimes driven from the public age. . . .

The Colored American, New York, March 11, 1837

The political balancing act prior to the Civil War was primarily over the question of admission of states to the Union as "free" or "slave."

For the last four or five years, certain classes of our northern citizens have been more than ordinarily interested in our GLORIOUS UNION! They have resisted the compunctions of conscience, the warning voice of Abolitionists, and the mandates of God, by crying out "the Union, the Union is in danger!"

A Union with a vengeance to it!! What is the Union worth if it must be maintained at the expense of the liberty of the north? A northern citizen cannot cross the Potomac, without subjecting himself to all the liabilities of "Lynch Law." He knows not how soon he may be tarred and feathered, rode upon a rail, or cowskinned.

If our Mayor were to go South, at this time, it is more likely that the avenging hand of some Southern aristocrat might fall upon him for the justice he meted out to Nash, the notorious negro-catcher. . . .

The facts are, our Southern Planters, in education and habits, are aristocrats of the worst kind. They have no respect whatever for northerners and are determined to trample on them and their rights, whenever they come in contact with their own interests.

We are lynched and bullied out of everything by them. The north can propose no measures, nor claim no right in our National Congress that in the least clashes with, even an individual interest of the South, without subjecting herself to a tirade of threatenings and abuse.

It is time we had taken a stand on this subject, if we sleep much longer we shall be shorn of the last remnant of our liberty, and reduced to a bondage far less tolerable than the British yoke.

But let the South annex Texas to the Union, and divide it into States, and our NATIONAL SENATE is immediately A SOUTHERN HOUSE OF DICTATION: and the *liberties of the north, or the blessed Union, one of the two, are gone.*

Our only hope for the existence of liberty, with the Union of the States, is in the yeomanry and labouring classes of the north. THEY MUST SPEAK OUT on this subject. They have trusted these matters to others long enough. Half their rights are already bartered away, by other hands.

Half the States of the Union are now closed against them. For no man who has not the means and the conscience, to purchase and drive slaves, can live in a slave State. If he do, he will be of no repute, not eligible to any place of profit or honor.

How much longer northern freemen will sleep over their dying liberties, and suffer demagogues, newspaper editors, and southern traders, and speculators to rule the country we cannot tell.

This much we know, however, that Southern aristocrats, and northern office seeking demagogues, should no longer dictate the terms of our Union, nor the measure of our prosperity. . . .

The Colored American, New York, May 6, 1837

Despite constant setbacks, such as the convention of 1821, which gave suffrage to whites but disfranchised blacks, the black press took a keen interest in the possibilities of reform through the legislative process.

Next Monday, the Congress of the nation meets in extra session, to commence legislation under the Van Buren administration. What policy the "Party in power" may pursue, we cannot tell. This much we know, however, that there never was a period before, in the history of *our* Republic, in which so much depended on national legislation, as at the present. And perhaps there never was a time in which the chair of government, and the interests of the national departments, were committed to such feeble hands. Everything now depends on the wisdom, prudence, and decision of our Senators and Representatives.

We have always felt favorable to the politics of the present administration, but our preference has been for *principles* and not for *men*. How much principle we have at the head of our government, at present, is not for us to say; nor would we judge from the hasty, unwitting committal of our Chief Magistrate, at his inaugural. He was then in the flush of *glutted ambition,* and *unmanned* by the glare of human glory. What was to be expected of a political demagogue, at such a time? He has had sufficient time since, for cool, considerate reflection, and for deep repentance, which we hope have not been neglected.

The commerce and currency of the country should occupy a prominent place in the business of the pending session, if not the *chief place,* and the exclusive deliberations of this extra Congress of the nation. That our Senators and Representatives will be willing, at this extra meeting, to take up the more important measures of governmental policy, we cannot yet believe. They are too wise to suffer the Chief Magistrate, or any designing Southern politician, to bring them into foreign negotiations, or boundary legislation. They will wait for the voice of the sovereign people, before they meddle with these delicate matters. . . .

. . . And should Texas be thus hastily admitted into the Union, at the expense of our nation's honor, and the sacrifice of national faith— farewell to the union of the States. Ten thousand discordant clashing elements and interests stirred up, that will only subside with a division of the Union.

Should our national sin result in such a division, what consequences may not be experienced? We shall confine our answers to the South, for in our opinion, the North has nothing to fear from such a result. She would then look far better *to the age of God,* than in union with the slaveholding enormities of our guilty Republic. But with the South it would be otherwise.

Already blinded with self-interest, and given up to idleness and dissipation, the Southern regions of our country, if separated from the North, would retrograde to barbarous licentiousness, and mental and physical imbecility. From the Potomac to the extreme Southern boundaries of our government, throughout these regions of oppression and lawless aristocracy, where the slave and the honest white laborer alike, are oppressed and brutalized, would anarchy, bloodshed and rapine *delve* and *deluge* the country.

The very day in which the South, in any of her high-handed measures, succeeds in separating herself from the North, she casts her NATIONAL DIE, and may sing her FUNERAL DIRGE. Nothing but her connection with the North shields her from HIGH HEAVEN'S CURSE, and from the REVENGE OF BLOOD GUILTINESS. Leave the South to herself, and her *patriotic slave system* would soon work out its own redemption through *rivers of blood*. . . .

The Colored American, New York, September 2, 1837

The Presidential election of 1840 presented a dilemma for black and white abolitionists: Both Presidential candidates (the incumbent Martin Van Buren and William Henry Harrison) were opposed to abolition, and both Vice Presidential candidates (Richard M. Johnson and John Tyler) were slaveholders.

. . . Can, then, any abolitionist, consistently vote for the election of either of these candidates? It appears to us impossible. They are enemies of free discussion—are opposed to the exercise of political power in behalf of the slave, and to all legislative action of the government for the abolition of slavery. It is said, by refusing to vote for the candidates of one political party, you in fact vote for the opposite candidate?—that there are other questions, beside slavery of great importance, and men should vote for those candidates, who all things considered, will do most for the welfare of the people? Such reasoning befits those who are wedded to a party—or who believe that those *other questions* are paramount to the anti-slavery question—but abolitionists, who profess to believe that the cause of liberty is paramount to all other questions now before the country for discussion, and that on its success depends the perpetuity of our civil and religious institutions, cannot consistently aid in elevating men to the two highest offices in the nation, who, whatever may be their merits, pretensions or principles in other respects, set their faces like a flint against the abolition of American slavery. When we see distinguished politicians of the North truckling to Southern policy, reiterating their contempt of the Anti-Slavery cause in a way not to be misunderstood, and giving in their adhesion to the support of Southern institutions—in order to preserve or gain the support of slaveholding voters—we have just reason to fear, nay, to believe, that the same men, if their party succeeds, will continue to be northern men with southern principles, in order to preserve the ascendancy. They cannot be trusted and the guilt of elevating them to office should not rest in any degree upon abolition electors . . . all we have to say is, it is better to have the government administered by avowed political enemies, than by treacherous friends; it is better that opponents should have a temporary triumph than that the cause of impartial liberty should be trampled into the dust, and men bear sway who, to promote party policy, or even great financial or commercial interests, will postpone the claims of humanity and the rights of one-fifth of the American people to liberty.

The Colored American, New York, September 12, 1840

As objectionable as Van Buren was to abolitionists, Harrison (who became the ninth President) was even worse. His actions represent the depth of acceptance the society gave to the institutionalization of racism.

. . . With regard to Wm. Henry Harrison, the opposing candidate for the Presidency, he is generally less known than Mr. Van Buren, having for some time lived in retirement. But so far as his public acts are known, few of them will be found to have been on the side of liberty to all, or in favor of the rights of colored men. On the contrary, his famous Vincennes speech, his denial of his ever having belonged to any anti-slavery society—his signing a petition to Congress, praying that the ordinance prohibiting slavery N.W. of the Ohio river, might be suspended, and thus opening the gap to make Ohio, Indiana and Illinois slave states. His framing a law in conjunction with two judges, compelling slaves brought into Indiana to remain so during life—his signing a law authorizing slaveholders to bring slaves into the same territory under 15 years of age, and hold them until 55 years of age the males—and females until 32. His voting while a member of Congress in 1818, for the introduction of slavery into Illinois, in opposition to the ordinance against it. The following year in Congress, voting in favor of introducing slavery in Missouri—his vote the same day against emancipation in Missouri at the age of 25 years—his vote for the introduction of slavery into Arkansas—same day voted against emancipation of slaves born in Arkansas, and many other acts previous to 1820, all showing Gen. Harrison to be in feeling decidedly pro-slavery. His famous Cheviot speech also in July of 1833 against abolition. Many of these are old acts, but his readoption of them in 1840 in the correspondence between himself and the south, show him to have undergone no change in opinion or feeling. . . .

. . . For the same reason that we ought not, and cannot vote for either candidate for the Vice Presidency; in fine if we vote for one, we at the same time vote for the other. Both candidates for the Vice Presidency are slaveholders, while, then, we vote either of the two Presidential tickets, we are really voting for slaveholders and slave breeders. If then, the candidates for the Presidency were neither objectionable, having associated with them two slaveholders to be also voted for in voting for them, would render the ticket such an one, as no man claiming to be an abolitionist could possibly vote for, especially any colored man, many of whose relations are still writhing under the cruel system, and from which arises nearly all the evils we have to contend with. We cannot, then, if we vote right, vote either of the two Presidential tickets.

For whom shall we vote, then, is the question? It is taken for granted that we must vote for someone. All of our people who have the right to vote, believe it both right and duty to exercise that right, so do most abolitionists. An *anti-slavery* ticket is then provided of men, suitable for any office in the gift of the people, a ticket, based on principles which, if carried out, would advance the highest prosperity of the nation. We ought then and must vote the *Liberty Ticket,* with James G. Birney* at the head, who as a scholar has no superior among either of the other candidates, and to whom as a gentleman, a philanthropist and a Christian, all the others bear no comparison.

. . . If, however, on your state and county tickets, with the candidates or which you will be more familiar, there are men for any office with whom, or whose course you are satisfied with, and would like to see them in office, or continued in office, substitute them upon the *anti-slavery ticket* instead of someone already there, of whom you are persuaded to be no better man. But in doing which be careful.

The Colored American, New York, October 3, 1840

* A prominent abolitionist and editor, Birney was the Liberty Party's candidate for President in 1840 and 1844.

As the major political parties proved unresponsive to demands for the abolition of slavery, there was increased pressure to form a new party in the struggle for self-determination.

. . . Political action is a necessary fruit of our abolition principles, one of the necessary measures; and an *independent political abolition party* is a necessary fruit of political action. The one grows directly out of the other, and is to voting men, unavoidable. It is a concentration of power also, and an exhibition of sincerity and devotion to our principles, in all our duties, political as well as moral.

. . . Our paper is devoted, as well as to our social, moral and religious improvement, also, to our civil and political rights. It ought, therefore, and must, concern itself about those politics calculated, in our judgment, to secure those rights. Now, to talk about elevation, social or moral, without civil and political rights; is to talk about an elevation which never did, and in the nature of things, never can exist. No man is either socially, or morally elevated, in the proper sense of the term, who is proscribed and oppressed; who has not civil rights— who is half way between slavery and liberty.

Civil and political rights, equally distributed, brings men thus enjoying them, at least in the exercise of those rights, upon a social equality, together in social life. Thus bringing them into this social equality, tends to destroy caste, unite them together, and elevate them in all the other duties and relations in life. The possession of political rights, is the power necessarily moving on to this condition in life. The reason the colored population of this country are not socially and morally elevated is, because they are almost universally, as they ever have been, disarmed of this power, to wield for their own, and the good of others. . . .

The Colored American, New York, October 10, 1840

The author of the following letter, Thomas Van Rensselaer, became the editor of the Ram's Horn *in 1846 and was active in the convention movement. Like many blacks, he appreciated the efforts of white abolitionists but was critical of prejudice within the movement.*

A THIRD POLITICAL PARTY

I perceive this new organization has started a *daily* paper in which I find published an independent electoral ticket for the states of Vermont, Massachusetts, Connecticut, New York, New Jersey, Pennsylvania, Ohio, Illinois, and Michigan. The professed object of this party is to secure the rights of the *colored men* in THIS country; and in examining this list, so far as I can discover, they have given no opportunity to the poor colored man to speak for himself, by placing him in the Legislature where he *ought* to be heard with themselves. But it may be said that it would be contrary to the usages of civilized society to place colored men on a ticket with white men. Take the state of New York to test this movement; the number of colored people in this state is somewhere about 40,000, that of the professed *abolitionists* about 5,000; and yet not a single colored man's voice is to be heard in this new anti-slavery Legislature. In view of this state of things what better is this third abolition *party* for us than either of the other parties, and what colored man can give his vote to sustain it; and we call upon the true friends of the colored people not to sanction this exclusive movement. The leaders in the Revolution of this country set forth correct principles, but never carried them out in *practice*. And in conclusion we call upon every citizen that is in favor of human rights to withhold his influence from this Abolition Political Party.

The Colored American, New York, October 10, 1840

The first Southern black paper prior to the Civil War was the Daily Creole, *published by J. M. Weymouth. Actually, because of the pressure of the white community, it was more Southern in orientation than a true representative of the black community and was against the abolitionist movement.*

THE UNION MUST BE PRESERVED

We speculate in the disturbances and revolutions of the old world without a thought that a revolution is in progress at home. We stand on the verge of a civil strife which is pregnant with horrors and fail to realize our danger. Men are arrayed against each other, not merely differing on abstract questions of civil policy, or political economy, but with eternal hatred rankling in their hearts. The elements which constitute civil war are even now involved. . . .

The Daily Creole, New Orleans, August 14, 1856

The importance of self-determination in the struggle for political equality is reflected by this anonymous author.

"What do you colored people want?.," is a question that is very frequently asked by the politicians of the present day. "What would you have us do for you?" "Do you wish us to take you into our social circles, and there introduce you to our wives and daughters?" No, we want nothing of the kind, and you well know it too. Our being introduced into your fine parlors and keeping the company of your beautiful wives and daughters will not remedy the evils we complain of; no, not for a moment. All that we ask of you is what Diogenes asked of the monarch Alexander, styled the Great, that was to get out of his sunshine. So we say to those who pretend to be so much interested in our behalf: "Get out of our sunshine!" That is all we want from you. The laws that you would enact for yourselves are plenty good enough for us; we ask no better. The churches that you build to worship God in are just the size we need for such purposes. The common schools and colleges which you build and so richly endow for the purpose of educating your sons and daughters are plenty good enough for our children. We are firmly in the belief that all the trouble you put yourself to in order to get colored schools and churches for us is wholly useless, money thrown away, which might be expended in some other direction to great advantage. Likewise, we think the foolish Black Laws that you enact making invidious distinctions among men on account of their complexions are very much out of place and quite unnecessary in a country like this. We are of the opinion that we can get along with all the provisions made by our government, and think them just what we want on that score and nothing more. We want our rights as men, and shall never cease agitation until we attain them. When our political rights are acquired, the social will take care of themselves.

"T"

The Weekly Anglo-African, New York, August 20, 1859

The elements of political independence in the black political experience were the result of racism that permeated every aspect of society.

. . . We feel . . . that in striking *us* down, liberty and justice are also stricken down in the land. . . . With us it is not parties, but principles. Our intense opposition is not against true Abolitionism, nor yet true Republicanism, but against oppression and party corruption and wrong. Parties as such, be they of whatever name, are to us as the mere scaffolding to the building. If in examining the platform of the party, or in looking through the antecedents of men, we find either void of sound principles, we shall utterly reject the one and cast the other forth as a branch that is withered. To this have we, the intelligent people of New York, come. . . .

The Weekly Anglo-African, New York, October 15, 1859

Neither political party was willing to stand for equality in any form for black people. The persistence of this condition tested the utility of the system and the depth of white racism.

The two great political parties separate at an angle of two roads that they may meet eventually at the same goal. They both entertain the same ideas and both carry the same burdens. They differ only in regard to the way they shall go and the method of procedure. We, the colored people of this country, free and enslaved, who constitute the burden that so heavily bears down on both these parties—we, who constitute their chief concern, their chief thought, we who cause all their discord and all their dissentions, and all their hates, and all their bitter prejudices—we say both of these religious political parties, we, the blacks, must in some form or another, be sacrificed to save themselves and the country—to save the country intact for the white race.

The Democratic party would make the white man the master, and the black man the slave, and have them thus together occupying every foot of the American soil. Believing in the potency of what they term the superior race, they hold that no detriment can come to the Republic by the spread of the blacks in a state of servitude on this continent; that with proper treatment and shackles upon him, proper terrors over him, and vigorous operations for the obliteration of his mind, if he have any—that with these, and whatever else brutify him, he can be kept in sufficient subjection to be wholly out of the pale of danger to the Republic; that he can never be so much as a consideration in any calculation of imminence to the Government, on the contrary, it is held by this party that his presence, under these restrictions, is of incalculable benefit to the nation—the chief instrument of the development of her resources, and the cornerstone of her liberties. What the Democratic party complains of, is that the Republican party—not for the negro's, but for their own political advancement—advocate the necessity for a check upon the spread of the blacks—not as a free, but in chain, not as men, but as slaves; for in this—that the blacks as free men, shall have neither rights, footing, nor anything else, in common with the whites in the land—both parties are agreed; and in looking at matters as they present themselves to us at this moment, we are not sure that if any of the many withheld rights were to be secured to us, that they would not come from the Democratic side after all, notwithstanding the great excesses their leaders frequently carry them into. We mean the great body, acting as it will someday, independent from the party leaders. The great masses, if left to themselves to act up to their true instincts would always do much better in matters involving right and wrong, than they do when operated upon by what are generally supposed to be intelligent leaders. These are generally great demagogues, or great conservatives, neither of which have done the world any positive good . . .

The Republican party today, though we believe in the minority, being the most intelligent, contains by far the greatest number of these two classes of men, and hence, though with larger professions for humanity, is by far its more dangerous enemy. Under the guise of humanity, they do and say many things—thus for example, they oppose the re-opening of the slave trade. They would fain make the world believe it to be a movement of humanity; and yet the world too plainly sees that it is but a stroke of policy to check the spread, growth, and strength of the masses on this continent. They oppose the progress of slavery in the territories, and would cry humanity to the world; but the world has already seen that it is but the same black masses looming up, huge, grim, and threatening, before this Republican party, and hence their opposition. Their opposition to slavery means opposition to the black man—nothing else. Where it is clearly in their power to do anything for the oppressed colored man, why then they are too nice, too conservative, to do it. They find, too often, a way to slip round it, find a method how not to do it. If too hard pressed or fairly cornered by the opposite party, then it is they who go beyond said opposite party, in their manifestation of hatred and contempt for the black man and his rights.

Such is the position of the two parties today, and it is yet to be seen whether they will drive in the political storm they are creating, and which is now raging around them. In their desire to "hem in" and crush out the black man, they form a perfect equation. They differ only in the method. We have no hope from either as political parties. We must rely on ourselves, the righteousness of our cause, and the advance of just sentiments among the great masses of the Republican people, be they Republicans or Democrats. These masses we must teach that it will not do for them to believe, nor yet act upon the declarations of their party leaders, that we are a naturally low and degraded race, and unfit to have or enjoy liberty and the rights of men as citizens, and hence must be crushed out of the land. We must teach these masses that all this fabrication is a great political lie, an abominable injustice to an outraged but determined people who cannot be crushed out—a people outraged by overpowering brute force, and then declared unfit to come within the pale of civilization. All this is our work, and rising by all the forces within our grasp, high above the chicanery and vulgar policies of the day, we must perform, and well, our duty in these respects.

The Weekly Anglo-African, New York, March 17, 1860

In reply to many black leaders who called for a "colored state," this editor saw the possibilities of this development in the event of secession.

Those of our brethren who are excitedly anxious to found and endow a "Negro nationality" in some part of the habitable globe, may possibly be relieved in mind by persuing the following considerations. Some of us are so keen sighted that a hundred yards distant, and without seeing his face, we can tell a colored man by his walk. Others have such quick ears, without seeing him at all, we can tell a colored man by his voice, and especially by his laugh.

Now, as able editors ought to be, we are as keen sighted and as sharp-eared as the rest; and our ears and eyes have discovered, in one of these United States, nothing short of a "colored state" which during seventy odd years, has successfully "passed for white," but cannot do so much longer.

Our suspicions were aroused a winter or two ago when the representatives of this State in Congress were characterized in the Washington correspondence of the "Tribune" as gentlemen distinguished by "Africanized oratory." That phrase sank deeply into our mind and brain. It did not lie idly, but it turned itself over, and germinated, and led us to keep a watch on the State aforesaid. By and bye we discovered that the people of the State aforesaid were very fond of dress; that they lived in shabby houses, but loved music and dancing; that they had an eye to art; that their voices had a sweet, musical quality; that their young ladies were the veriest witches in the land; that their old men were—rooty; and that they did not support their own newspapers. Still, these varied facts did not assume definite form until we further reflected that this State—doubtless shy, as colored people will be in the matter of entering white people's meetings, came very reluctantly into the Union. Moreover, it has always been distinguished for "passing first rate resolutions" and then forgetting all about them.

But the crowning fact, which flashed the whole truth upon us like a burst of sunshine, did not occur until last week, when we read the proceedings of the Legislature of the State, full of fire and zeal and patriotism, and carrying everything before them, *until the hat was handed around for a million dollars.* Then—they behaved so that we incontinently exclaimed *"Thunder! That's a colored people's meeting."*

Need we say what State this is? Certainly not, for everybody will recognize it. Being matter of fact, we will give the figures of its progress in population since 1790:

year	white % inc.	free colored % inc.	slave % inc.
1800	40.00	76.84	36.46
1810	0.14	42.98	34.85
1820	10.85	49.89	31.62
1830	8.6	16.04	22.02
1840	0.47	4.48	3.68
1850	5.97	8.26	17.71
	75.03	198.49	145.82

entire population in 1850:

	274,568	8,960	384,984

population of its largest city in 1850:

	24,500	3,849	44,376

The colored people in this State, and in its principal city, are as two to one white. They increase more rapidly than the whites and have stamped in their impress upon the State so thoroughly that, in the event of secession, no earthly power can prevent them from becoming its absolute, as they are now its virtual masters! And what better way is there to account for the desperate energy with which this State struggles to veer from its moorings, than to say that her feeble legislators are magnetized by the terrible energies of their black superiors to do that act—secession—which will forever consecrate it to God and liberty!

The Weekly Anglo-African, New York, November 24, 1860

Black citizens in New Orleans were especially insistent on their political rights, since these derived from historical rights of emancipation under the French.

. . . We have denied time and again that the right of suffrage was confined—among whites—to those distinguished by a high degree of civilization. But we assert that the sons and grandsons of the colored men who were recognized as French citizens under the French rule, and whose rights were reserved in the treaty of cession, taken away from them since 1803, are not savages and uncivilized inhabitants of the wild swamps of Louisiana. We contend that the freedmen who proved intelligent enough to shed their blood in defense of freedom and the National Flag, are competent to cast their votes into the ballot box. . . .

We have been declared aliens in the land of our birth; we have been assimilated to unnaturalized foreigners. And although we are liable to draft and to be taken away from our families and avocations—which the true aliens are not—we have no voice in the State to defend our interests and no representatives to take part in the taxation of our people and our properties. . . .

The Tribune, New Orleans, January 17, 1865

The following "song" was printed only in the Black Republican, *though it may have been more widely adopted. It represents the unique attempt to develop a separate ethnic identification of black voters with the Republican Party.*

THE SONG OF THE BLACK REPUBLICANS.

I.

Now rally, Black Republicans,
        Wherever you may be,
Brave soldier's on the battle-field,
        And sailors on the sea.
Now rally, Black Republicans—
        Aye, rally! we are free!
            We've waited long long
            To sing the song—
        The song of liberty.

II.

Free workmen in the cotton-field,
        And in the sugar cane;
Free children in the common school,
        With nevermore a chain.
Then rally, Black Republicans—
        Aye, rally! we are free!
            We've waited long
            To sing the song—
        The song of liberty.

III.

We are the Black Republicans,
        We glory in the name;
Oppression made it one of ill,
        We'll make it one of fame.

Then rally, Black Republicans—
   Aye, rally! we are free!
    And sing the song,
    We've waited long—
The song of liberty!

IV.

We get our color from the Lord,
   He made it so to be;
He gave us freedom by the sword,
   His grace will make us free.
Then rally, Black Republicans—
   Aye, rally! we are free!
    We've waited long,
    To sing the song—
The song of liberty!

V.

Now grandly, Abraham Lincoln stands
   Beneath the Flag of all:
He flung us Freedom through its stars,
   From them our "Rights" will fall,
Then rally, Black Republicans,
   Aye, rally, we are free!
    We've waited long,
    To sing the song—
The song of Liberty.

VI.

Then rally, Black Republicans,
   Wherever you may be;
Brave soldiers on the battle-field,
   And sailors on the sea:

Come rally, Black Republicans—
Aye, rally! we are free!
And sing the song—
We've waited long,
The song of liberty!

The Black Republican, New Orleans, April 29, 1865

While President Andrew Johnson supported Southern attempts to reimpose the virtual enslavement of black people, through the Black Codes, the black press demanded equality.

Now that the life of the nation is saved, the accursed slaveholders' rebellion crushed, and the foul blot of slavery wiped from off the escutcheon of our beloved country, it becomes the imperative duty of every loyal man in the nation, but more especially those of the South —as by the nature of our institutions the responsibility of what is done by the Government is shared to some extent by the humblest individual—to let their opinions be known and their influence felt on the question of the reconstruction and readmission of the seceding States back into the Union. One of the principal reasons assigned by the founders of our Government as a just cause of separation from the mother country was that they were taxed without the privilege of representation. In the establishment of this Government taxation and representation was adopted as an inviolable principle; yet, strange and glaringly inconsistent as it may appear, this great fundamental principle of our Government from its very existence has been entirely ignored, so far as the colored men of the country are concerned. Taxed for the support of the National and State Governments in every particular as white men are taxed, they are denied all participation in the election of those by whom the tax is imposed. Amenable to the laws of the country, they have no voice in the selection of those who make or administer the laws. This monstrous wrong, this long and shameful violation of one of the cardinal principles of the Government, has been urged upon the attention of the American people in the Northern States, with but little success, owing to the fact that the leaders and masses of the political parties were but too willing to "crook the supple hinges of their knees" to the slave power, "that thrift might follow fawning." But in the South, where the great majority of our people have had no right to possess their own bodies, and the infamous Taney* *ex parte* judicial sentiment "that the black man had no rights that a white man was bound to respect" obtained universality, no attention has been given to this violation of the dearest rights of freemen. But now that slavery has been destroyed, and the loyal black population of the South are destined to become to some extent the owners of the soil in part, and almost exclusively the producers of the South; and are likewise making rapid improvement intellectually; they will not long tamely submit to be deprived of the right to a vote in the selection of those who are to tax their lands and impose burdens on their industry; and if in the restoration of the seceding States back into the Union, this cardinal principle of the Government is ignored in regard to them; if this grievous wrong is sought to be perpetuated; if the loyal black men, if the scarred veterans who have freely shed their blood to save the nation from destruction, are denied equality before the law; we shall have no permanent peace, for the reason that it will be not a peace founded on the eternal principles of right and justice.

The Black Republican, New Orleans, April 29, 1865

The reply to the suggestion by a white editor (in the San Francisco Morning Call) *that black people should cease demands for political equality, the editor of the San Francisco* Elevator, *P. A. Bell (who co-edited the* Colored American *1839–41), justified such agitation.*

. . . The rights which the negro has obtained are his by nature—he was endowed with them at his birth . . . and however much oppression may wrest them from him, they belong to him as a man. These alone will not suffice. They have been restored to us unwillingly and not until we had proven our claim to them by our prowess on the bloody field, and our ability to enjoy them.

The country, i.e. the Government lasted 85 years; all that time oppressing the negro, and depriving him of his God-given rights; and then came war, with all its horrid accessories—not by the negro, nor for his defense, nor for his protection, but to perpetuate the slavery and degradation which 250 years of oppression had entailed upon

* Chief Justice of the Supreme Court Roger B. Taney handed down the Dred Scott decision, from which the quotation is taken.

him. Then the "country" rose in her own defense, not to free the negro, but to prevent the white man from being enslaved, for to that end was things fast approaching.

It is an axiom in philosophy "that like causes produce like effects" and the spirit which would deprive us of our civil rights is akin to that which for two centuries and a half deprived us of our natural rights and they who would do so, could they succeed, would ere long attempt to deprive the next weaker class of their civil rights. . . .

Nothing "has been accomplished for the negro during the past four years," but for what the exigencies of the times imperatively called for and the God-scourged people demanded. We are not content with what you were willing to grant, and what was grudgingly given, or else the nation would have been rent in twain. . . .

The Elevator, San Francisco, May 5, 1865

The enfranchisement of black people was recognized as much a neces-sary step to securing the end of the Southern rebellion as arming the black man had been to winning the war.

. . . The Northern men were ashamed to ask the black man, whom they have helped to oppress, to fight side by side with them against the common enemy. However it was not long before the question, "Shall we arm the Negro?" headed the loyal journals of the country and it was finally determined that he would fight.

Congress voted him with the right of becoming an American soldier, and with alacrity he enlisted in the army. He understood he was fighting to proclaim Liberty and Equality to all the inhabitants of the land, and, after a severe struggle, in which the black men in solid columns marched up and took many a rebel battery, and displayed as much heroic virtue as the other soldiers of the Republic, armed rebellion was defeated.

The black man was admitted in the army, as a military necessity first, as a cook, teamster, etc., and then as a soldier.

The great questions now agitating the country are these: "Is the rebellion entirely subjugated, and will the black man be of any use?" We say armed rebellion is subjugated only for the time being; the rebels want to recuperate their strength and get into power in order to accomplish by stratagem what they could not by force of arms, and the loyal people will have, under *political necessity,* to arm the black man with the ballot, as they armed them with the musket by *military necessity.* . . .

The Tribune, New Orleans, July 25, 1865

The demand by freedmen at the close of the Civil War for hard-won political rights was in line with their insistence on being Americans and the need to offset discrimination.

. . . It seems to have become a mania. One set of people declare we won't work and must be made. Another is afraid that a war of races will arise. Another thinks we will abandon our Southern homes, and go North, to a land where they occasionally have negro riots. Another thinks we must be made to emigrate, leave the country, clear out incontinently. . . .

. . . We are not exceptional beings, we are human. In these dark bodies run the same red running blood. Beneath, beat hearts as warm and true as ever awoke to the glance of love, or throbbed with honor's high emprize.

Deal with us justly. Tell us not that we will not work, when it was our toil that enriched the South. Talk not to us of a war of races, for that is to say that *you* intend commencing to butcher us whenever you can do so with impunity. All we want is the right of men. Give us that and we shall not molest you. We do *not* intend leaving this country. No land can be fairer in our eyes, than the sunny one beneath whose skies we have lived. We were born here. Most of us will die here. We are Americans, and prouder of the fact than ever.

Deal justly with us. That's all we want. That we mean to have, come what may!

The Colored Tennessean, Nashville, August 12, 1865

The enthusiasm of black people which accompanied Reconstruction is typified in the following article.

ZION CHURCH ROCKED AS THE CRADLE OF THE FREE.
RECONSTRUCTION BEGUN. LIBERTY AND UNION.
NOW AND FOREVER.

The colored people of the State have been holding a Convention in this city. Delegates have been present from all parts of the State. Resolutions of importance have been presented and discussed with calmness and candor. . . . The evening sessions have been crowded with spectators and great enthusiasm prevailed. . . . The prosperity and future perpetuity of the nation has been considered as identified with the interests of the people. The "negro code" of the Legislature has been repudiated and equality before the law demanded.

The Leader, Charleston, November 25, 1865

Black conventions and meetings were held throughout the South to decide the political future of the newly Reconstructed states.

FREEDMEN'S CONVENTION

As the time is rapidly approaching when the delegates from the different cities and counties for this Convention will take their seats in solemn conclave, it may not be out of place in us to throw out a few suggestions that may aid them in their future deliberations. There will be some of the most important questions brought before the consideration of that body, that has ever been brought before any such a like constituted body of men; questions, the proper decisions of which will make an indelible impression upon the future of our race. Let these questions be considered and debated with the spirit of men, not with the high swelling tones of the braggart, nor with the sneveling, mercy-beseeching language of the menial, but with the dignified energy of men determined to show to both friend and foe that Freedom has yet some sons worthy of her benefits. And in our judgment the most important of these questions is that of *Our Rights.* First, What are our rights? and second; 'How are they to be obtained?'

The first question may be easily answered, and soon disposed of, from the fact that *our* rights are the rights of all freedman, whatever these may be. We may not have them all accorded to us by those who have it in their power to do so but that in no way effaces the fact, that they *are* our rights. But let us not, in the broad glare of new-born freedom, be led away by its resplendent glories into extravagant ideas as in what they really do consist. Man generally, in opposing wrong or maintaining right sees it magnify in proportion as his mind lingers in the contemplation of the wrong perpretrated or the right demanded, until he finds himself combating or defending what in calmer moments he might acknowledge was far from his original intention. Let us learn from the experience of others so that we might escape the quagmires of honest delusion. The second question, 'How to obtain our rights?' will be the most difficult to manage and the most important of the two. But let us not be afraid of its importance nor its difficulties. Let us meet them like men prepared, and willing to overcome. Consider well the source from whence they are to be obtained; deliberate calmly upon the relationship that source now holds to us and what it held so lately, and let our demands be in accordance with the most reasonable expectations. We council no fawning nor bowing because of former associations, neither do we call for bluster nor bragg, because of *new* relations, but let us remember that the firm, bold, conscientious and just demand, has the willing ear of every brave and honest heart. We have many warm, true heartened friends in this city and State, let them not be appalled at our extravagance nor pained at our slavishness. Let the manly expression of our sister State, be our expressions, and we feel certain that good shall follow in the footsteps of our formly asserted rights. In the Convention lately held in South Carolina our brethren asked for the establishment of law and order; the securing of life and property; and freedom to sell labor as a merchant to dispose of any of his comodities; for a fair and impartial construction of the pledges of the government on the land question, that the school, the pulpit and the press be as secure in that State as in Massachusetts, that equal suffrage be conferred in common with white men as a protection from hostility by their known faithfulness to their country's flag during the rebellion and because all free governments derive their power from the consent of the governed; they being in majority in the State, bearing for a long time the burden of an odious taxation without a just representation; that colored men shall not in every instance be tried by white men; and that neither by custom or enactment shall they be excluded from the jury-box.

Such as this let us demand, and let the righteousness of the demand come home to hearts of those whose prerogatives it is to say, *yes* or *no* to our just request.

The Colored American, Augusta, Georgia, January 6, 1866

❁

In response to attempts by legislators to enact "special" laws which would discriminate against black people, the following editorial appeared in the Loyal Georgian, *which succeeded the* Augusta Colored American.

. . . What necessity is there for a "negro code"? It is claimed that the freedmen required different laws from the white men. This depends upon the intention of the lawmakers. If they desire to keep the freedmen always in an inferior position and prevent their improvement, it can be most effectually accomplished by a system of laws like those prepared by the Commission.* But if it is their intention to give the freedmen fair play and an opportunity to improve their condition, they have, we believe, acted unwisely, for they must be aware that the effect of such legislation will be injurious to all persons of color by denying to them rights which white men enjoy. We object to all such distinctions.

It may be claimed with some reason, that because the freedmen are ignorant and but recently emancipated, the right of suffrage should be denied them, but upon no principle of justice, can men claim that for these reasons, civil rights should be denied them. In the name of 500,000 colored persons in this State, we demand that no distinction should be made before the law. We demand this because it is right, and because being citizens, they are entitled to the rights granted to other citizens.

The admission of a colored lawyer to practice before the Supreme Court of the United States, was virtually a decision that he was a citizen of the United States. If colored men are citizens, they are entitled to all the privileges and immunities of citizens in the several States. Therefore, laws that are not applicable alike to all citizens, are unconstitutional and void, unless the Constitution itself concede the right to make such distinction. But it does nowhere give the right to deprive citizens of their natural right, 'except as punishment for crime where the parties shall have been duly convicted.'

Therefore, no citizen can be deprived of the right to sue and testify, except as a punishment for a crime. In a word, all laws, which make such distinction are null and void.

We notice that a bill is before the Legislature of this State 'to exclude freedmen from other states from this State.' Such a law would be clearly unconstitutional and void; for, being citizens, they are 'entitled to all privileges and immunities of citizens in the several States,'

* A state commission recommending laws that would restrict blacks.

or in other words, they shall have the same privileges, exemptions, and freedom granted to other citizens; and all rules and regulations which apply to one citizen shall apply to all.

We are surprised that men, as able and as learned in the law as the committee, would have prepared the system of laws, mentioned above, should have fallen into the error of supposing, that one system of laws can be enacted for one class of citizens, and a different system for another class. We can account for it only upon the hypothesis that they hold "persons of color" are not citizens. The same rule must now apply to all persons of color for all are free . . .

The Loyal Georgian, Augusta, February 3, 1866

While the Congress was torn between those who favored Confederate and Radical plans for Reconstruction, the black press continued to argue for full citizenship rights. Opposed by the President, the Radicals in Congress were finally able to consolidate their position in July, 1866, when they passed the Freedmen's Bill over President Johnson's veto.

. . . It cannot be expected that a complete and final reconstruction of the lately seceded states can be effected, until all classes irrespective of condition and color, are made equal before the law. President Lincoln in his memorable proclamation declared the slaves free. Congress and the States acting upon what was so nobly begun, and accepting it as a declaration that neither law nor policy would allow them to retreat from, completed the work by passing and adopting the constitutional amendment, which declared slavery forever abolished. It is our duty to accept this as the highest law of the land. It is a decision pronounced from the tribunal of the people of this country from which there is no appeal. . . . Slavery has not only been abolished, but the emancipated race has been declared free. Is not freedom alike to all before the law, save where it is taken away for the punishment of a crime? . . .

The Loyal Georgian, Augusta, February 17, 1866

Black newspapers were centers of organizing, as the following example testifies. All across the South black people met in conventions and called upon the federal government for assistance and protection.

THE GEORGIA EQUAL RIGHTS ASSOCIATION

This is an Association organized by the Convention that recently assembled in this city. It is unlike any society that has heretofore existed in this State. Its object is to secure for every citizen without regard to race, or color, equal rights; hence its name. Unlike other societies laboring to secure the same object, it is not a secret organization. We are living in a state that has been a slave state and is not now free from choice, but from necessity. Most of the white citizens believe that the institution of slavery was right, and the best condition for colored men and women. Believing that slavery was right, of course they believed that the condition, which comes nearest to slavery, that can now be established, would be the best. We think otherwise. We believe that the best interest of the State demands that every man shall be equal before the law. We wish every citizen thought as we do. They do not, and what shall be done? We answer, discuss the subject and the right will prevail. Therefore, we say, organize your Associations; have public meetings; call out your best men be they Northern, or Southern men, white or colored, let us have a full and free discussion leaving the result to God and the enlightened judgment of the American people.

Our friends who wish to form Associations, can have a Constitution by applying at this office.

The Loyal Georgian, Augusta, March 3, 1866

Though the President vetoed the Civil Rights Act, the Radicals were able to pass it through Congress over his veto on March 27, 1866.

The question before the American people today is shall this be a free country? Freedmen of Georgia! You are free; yes, *citizens* of the United States. Show the world that you will be good citizens, industrious, honest, peaceable; also show by the interest which you manifest in public officers that you are worthy of being citizens.

One of the rights of free men is the rights of peacefully assembling together and deliberating concerning their common interests. In every county in the State you should assemble and form Subordinate Associations, and associate yourselves with the State Association. Let your meetings be public. Show by your acts that you intend nothing wrong; that you love your State and will labor for its interests; that, as freemen, you can assist in making this State one of the most wealthy and powerful States in the Union, and that you will try; but to enable you to do this, you must be free, free in *reality* as well as in name. Already the wisest men in the State admit that in your changed relation, you should enjoy the same civil rights that other citizens enjoy. . . . Again we say, form your societies; assemble together; discuss the questions which now agitate the public mind, and ask that the rights belonging to freemen shall be given to you . . .

The Loyal Georgian, Augusta, March 3, 1866

The black press, in the early years of Reconstruction, urged a policy of reconciliation and cooperation in rebuilding the country.

In a recent editorial of a paper edited by colored men we find the following sentence: "Black men are more interested in the well-being of their race than any white man can be. . . .

We want true representation. Let the whites be represented according to their numbers and the blacks according to theirs also."

If the white man cannot fully appreciate the interests of the colored man, then we infer that it must be equally impossible for the colored man to feel for the interests of the whites. Hence the demand is made that in legislation, each class should be duly represented, that whites may act for whites, and colored for colored.

The same principle is inculcated by blacks who say they love those of their own color better than whites, and by whites who claim that they can feel more deeply for the wrongs inflicted on their own, than on the colored race. If it be true that our affections, for humanity, should be varied by the color of the skin, then class legislation and representation are to be justified. . . .

It might as well be contended that persons with blue eyes cannot identify themselves with the interests of those of black eyes, as that a man with a light cannot feel full sympathy with his brother of a darker hue. . . .

In the great work of reconstruction we should scorn the idea of the white or black man's party. The broad basis on which we are to predicate our legislation, should be that of principle and not complexion. Man should be regarded as man entitled to all the sacred rights of humanity without any distinction on the account of race or color. . . . It is as repugnant to the great principle of the brotherhood of man, to organize a church on the basis of a dark, as white skin, and just as antirepublican to encourage political organizations and special legislation for the *black* as the *white* man. All should be admitted to equal rights and privileges in church and state whatever may be their race and color. . . . We should all live together in peace and harmony. . . .

The Advocate, Charleston, May 11, 1867

The following is a speech given on June 22, 1867, by Bishop Henry M. Turner* to the black citizens of Macon, Savannah, Augusta, Atlanta, Columbus, Georgia, etc. The office of the paper provided constitutions for those wishing to form proposed associations.

. . . Many of our fellow citizens in the country, and even in the towns and villages, are far from being awake to their own interests and to the interests of prosperity; not because they are disinterested at all, but because many cherish the foolish idea that they had better not have anything to do with political matters; thus leaving it, as they say, to their white friends and colored leaders to manage—misapprehending as you see, that they are individually responsible and connected to the weal or woe of our future civil and political status. The result is that hundreds declare they will not register; others say, they do not care to either register or vote until things are more settled; others, again, say they cannot lose the time just now, crops are being laid by, and for every day they lose, from three to five dollars are deducted from their wages; while still others declare it is useless to register, for they have already been told that if they ever vote in harmony with Congress, or old Joe Brown, their throats will be cut from ear to ear,

---

* Turner, a bishop in the AME Church, was a member of the Georgia legislature. Though disliked by white Georgians, he worked for the mutual advancement of both races. He became an ardent exponent of African emigration in the 1880's.

consequently, they are determined not to register, or vote, in the face of such events; especially, when they would be sure to vote to sustain the power that gave them freedom. . . .

The question then resolves itself into some plan by which the foregoing evils may be remedied, and the liberties of our race preserved. This can only be done by organizing associations in the above named cities, where a weekly or monthly fee can be collected for the purpose of salarying intelligent men to traverse the rural regions of our State, and deliver such lectures to them as will inform them that their inactivity now is an unpardonable crime. . . .

Let the people of our cities rise in the majesty of their strength and the more correct knowledge and send the true alarm like thunder crashes through the country, towns and hamlets, until every man shall see his duty, and be forced to do it. If the country districts vote wrong, our cities will be no more than a drop in the bucket. If the men are too indifferent to take action on this matter, I must respectfully appeal to the ladies. Ladies! form yourselves into societies; gather all the funds you can, and employ as many colored speakers (or white either) as you can, and send them in the field to teach our people what to do, and how to do it. Your destiny is ours; ours is yours. We rise and fall together. . . .

The Loyal Georgian, Augusta, July 6, 1867

Despite intimidations, the black press continually urged its readers to exercise their right to vote. The following article was written in response to the discharge of 78 black men in Washington.

. . . What holocausts of lives have been offered up to confirm liberty to the *formerly oppressed* in our land! The life of every man, if devoted to the end made legitimate with its creation, will be one of resistance *"unto blood"* if need be, against wrong and in the faithful support of the right.

The colored men of the South understand the meaning of patient endurance in suffering. They are released from this form of oppression—let them thank God!

They must not, however, understand that because of their deliverance they are therefore necessarily released from further endurance in behalf of the right. It may be that in the Providence of God some of the colored men of today may be called up to *lay down their lives* in protection of the principles of our Government. The man is to be envied who may be permitted to grasp such a distinction.

The colored men of the South will be—they are already being—attacked by threats that if they vote this Fall it will not be well with them, etc. We wish simply to say as an inference from what we have already said that *the colored man should vote this Fall.* He owes it to the martyrs who have fallen to procure his right, to, upon their graves reared to liberty, *vote* and vote *right.* He owes it to the great Union Republican Party of the land, that would enshrine the principles of truth and liberty, re-purchased and re-consecrated in the late war, to vote, and to vote to a man for that party. He owes it to his God, who has wrought his freedom, to vote as his enlightened, enfranchised conscience must teach.

The Republican Party has a sacred claim upon every colored voter, and that to this Fall.

Let every man who may get registered, resolve that as for himself *he shall* vote and get all others whom he may influence to vote. Let the Republicans of the North know the strength and character of the colored vote in the South. Vote—vote *in spite of every threat.* You shall be taken care of if you vote *right!*

The Loyal Georgian, Augusta, July 6, 1867

Compensation was an integral part of the design of Black Reconstruction and the concept of self-help. Black leaders concerned with present conditions and the necessity of building internally cohesive units within the black community warned of subversion. The author of this letter signed his initials "W.H.H." which probably stands for Wm. H. Harper, the Sacramento agent for the paper.

. . . If the African, like the Caucasian, had been trained for century after century amid the labyrinth of science and arts, and had their spirit been infused with the adventure of commerce and the developments of agriculture, their descendants would not be today contending for the ordinary rights of humanity. But even in this land of caste and prejudice, the test of their endurance and capacity to equal the highest development of human perfection had to pass a crucible of tyranny without a parallel on the American continent. . . .

All the contact the dominant race has met, through clash and triumph of arms, the power of Constitutional law, the advancement of political economy, and the impartial lessons of history, will, at some future time, be imitated and reflected with equal beneficial consequences by the struggling race who are now just beginning to see the light of their political glory beam forth in its full refulgence. No amount of suffering will ever erase this fond hope from their minds. . . .

There can be no misapprehension of the policy the Republican administration intends to pursue upon the subject of impartial suffrage. The Negroes who have rendered them signal service in the conflict on the field and at the ballot box, expect the simple recognition of their political rights in every portion of the land. They will be seriously disappointed if the weak-kneed conservative wing of the Republican party shall be permitted to dictate a course to that great element of freedom which has just triumphed in the second battle with the serried flanks of the rebellion. . . .

The Elevator, San Francisco, October 30, 1868

With the opening of public lands to settlement after the Civil War, a substantial black landowning community was established in Arkansas. Black people were denied access to representation through the party system by exclusion from primaries or elections. In the face of such overt racism, Tabbs Gross, the editor of the Arkansas Freeman, *suggested independent action.*

. . . The colored voters of this city are largely in the majority, and they have heretofore allowed themselves to be used only for the purpose of putting a certain class of white men in office who have no better claims to the offices than the colored men who do most all the voting.

Let the colored voters of this city reflect for a moment how *unfairly* they have been dealt with by the party in the bestowal of office. Although they constitute 9/10 or more of the *voting* population of the party, they have not received as much as 1/10 of the offices which have been controlled by the party.

It has been calculated . . . that in this city alone there are over 200 officials employed in the United States, State, County, and City service, with salaries and perquisites, amounting in the whole to over $350,000! Of this great number of paying offices, the colored voters hold less than *ten;* some of whom get no salaries at all, and the rest but mere pittances. Besides the office of City Collector, held by Mr. Rector, there is not an office in the city or county, held by a colored man, that pays more than ordinary day labor wages while 200 white men are filling offices worth $350,000!

Now is this just and fair and right? No! It is not; and every intelligent colored man knows very well it is not right. Well, if it is not right, why do you submit to it? You have certainly got the *power* to prevent it, if you dare exercise that power; and if you do not prevent it in the future, it is your own fault. The colored voters hold the *power* and they should exercise it for their own benefit. They have been pack-horses for a few greedy Radical leaders long enough. It is high time the colored men were beginning to look out for their own interests. We have been helping a few white men to make fortunes long enough. It is high time that some of us should begin to live in fine houses and drive fast horses, and fare sumptuously every day. We have got plenty of men among us capable of holding all these fat offices. . . . We can put forward honest, faithful and capable men who would command the confidence and respect of the whole community.

Let the colored voters, then, strike out for themselves, and help themselves to some of these rich and fat offices which they can easily get by just simply *demanding* them. All that the colored voters have to do is simply to *demand* their rights to get all they want. Let the colored voters make up their minds right now and at once, that they *will* have all the good paying offices of this city, and if they have any white friends to serve, put them in offices that don't pay so well.

We urge the colored men to take this matter in hand, right now. Don't allow a few trifling white men to cheat you out of these offices, through their little mean packed-up Conventions. If the Nominating Convention doesn't nominate you to a *fair proportion* of the paying offices, kick out of the Convention and run your own hook. We warrant, if the colored voters will try this game *once* they won't be bothered any more. . . .

We know very well that it has long since been cut and dried who was to be Mayor, and who was to fill all the other best paying offices.

The men have all been selected . . . the best paying offices will be reserved for a few white Radical leaders. Colored voters of Little Rock,
will you submit to this? We hope you will have manhood enough to
protest against such injustice; and that you will have independence
enough to repudiate any Convention that will so attempt to cheat and
defraud you out of your rights. If we can't get fair play through the
Nominating Convention, let us run an independent ticket, and if the
colored voters will promptly back such a move, we will guarantee success.

The Arkansas Freeman, Little Rock, October 5, 1869

*In the fight for equality, black men frequently appealed to the federal
government for protection, especially in the District of Columbia.*

The progress of the national arms and the national sentiment struck
down slavery in this district by statute, but left the element of slavery
predominantly in our local government still crippling enterprise, withholding education, and sneering at loyalty. It was felt that a solid
foundation for liberty and justice had not yet been reached. It was
seen that in a Republic all must be citizens on the basis of equality,
enjoying like protection and like privileges. To ensure these, the citizen must be endowed with the power to enforce his rights. Yielding to
these principles and to the popular demand of the loyal masses, the
national legislature wisely placed the ballot in the hands of every citizen and what has been the result?

The effect is apparent on every side. The city has assumed a new aspect. Improvement is advancing; public and private enterprise have
received a new impetus; population has largely increased; the cause of
education has advanced more within the last three years than it had
before for a quarter of a century. The ideas of progress, of self-de-
pendence and self-government have taken root and are flourishing
among our people. Each feels that he is a part of and has an interest in
the welfare of the city, the District, and the nation.

. . . The old fogies are opposed to Negro suffrage; and as they cannot withdraw it they seek to diminish if not destroy the opportunities
for its exercise. Here is the whole secret of the recently inaugurated
movement to take away our municipal government. . . . We ask that

body [Congress] to retain its Constitutional power of this District, to give us just laws, a perfect and appropriate municipal government, and proper representation on its floor and leave the people to conduct that government. . . .

The New Era, Washington, D.C., January 27, 1870

William J. Whipper, the author of the following two letters, was a lawyer in South Carolina, and a frequent correspondent to the New Era *(which changed its name to the* New National Era *in 1872).*

. . . We have been oppressed as a class and we must rise as such. Class interests have always been recognized in one form or another in our government and will continue to be. It has been asserted that as a class our votes decided the great political battle, and made the Republican party triumphant. As citizens we claim a right to share in the administration of the government, the emoluments of office as well as the right of voting to sustain it, pay our taxes for its support, and bear arms in its defense. When we rest our claims on educational fitness, we forget that we were black men before we were American citizens.

The New National Era, Washington, D.C., November 23, 1872

. . . I want class legislation in favor of liberty, justice and equality as a remedy for the evils of the past. It was class legislation that has changed our whole civil condition; it was to secure this blessing of liberty and enfranchisement that we petitioned Congress for that class legislation that has secured our citizenship and that we still continue to petition for the purpose of perfecting the "civil rights" bill. It was class legislation that placed us outside of the Constitution, and it is class legislation that must bring us back again. Therefore, I am for class legislation wherever it is needful, right, and in conformity with the principles of justice and humanity. . . .

The white race have had the benefit of class legislation ever since the founding of our Government, and it is full time we had, according to our representative capacities, possessed a just share of its blessings and rewards. When Congress erased from the national statutes the crime of slavery, the nation in a spirit of repentance demanded that indemnity should be given to the freedman, and the passage of the "civil rights" bill with other reconstruction measures followed, which was a species of class legislation, endorsed by every friend of freedom, justice and humanity. . . .

. . . We may justly anticipate the period when some black representative from the South, himself a former slave, or the son of a freedman, inspired by his love of race, and fired with patriotism, will rise up in Congress, and with his bold and native eloquence demand, in behalf of his poverty-stricken section, an appropriation of five million dollars, to be loaned to the freedmen for the improvement of their lands, and to aid them in acquiring agricultural implements. . . . Such a subsidy would take its rank with those that have already been given to railroads, steamships, and the Chicago fire. . . .

The New National Era, Washington, D.C., December 12, 1872

Because of their frontier experiences, black Republicans in Texas were more independent in their position, as indicated by the following letter written by "Olympus" from Galveston, Texas. One often finds the use of historical pseudonyms in letters to the editor.

. . . There is not a federal official in our town who can get elected to a city convention. They always drop us until election time, and at election time find out we will drop them. This is the game of "tit for tat." I don't know how you do it up in North Carolina, but that's the way we do it down here. We paddle our own canoe. There is nothing like a stiff upper lip. There will be more "Presidential elections" and municipal elections will never end, and fawning politicians will ever court our strength. We will never enter into the field of complete freedom and manhood, until we cease to be slaves of unscrupulous politicians. Let us be brave and fearless. . . .

The New National Era, Washington, D.C., June 5, 1873

The question of recognition as black Americans became a crucial one in the quest for a national identity. Then, as now, the demand for reparations became a central issue.

As the debris of American slavery is cleared away and colored Americans begin to make their appearance in the public and private walks of life, many difficulties overturn them in their demands for fair recognition. The burdens of oppression and prejudice, as a rule, have deprived them not only of the results of their own toil, but in large measure of all educational opportunities and social advantages. They have been excluded almost wholly from assuming high and honorable public responsibilities together with accompanying emoluments.

In considering the question of recognition, the wrong thus perpetuated must be acknowledged first, last, and at all times, until proper reparation is made. The Anglo-Saxon, having secured the start by unfair means, must either return and begin anew, or at once give to the new citizen an impartial chance in order to make the journey in life fair. . . .

But how is this demand for just recognition to be settled? . . . As color, or race, supplemented by injustice, has been the cause of exclusion, so let color, or race, reasonable fitness conceded, be the ground of recognition until the scales are once more balanced. The Negro respectfully demands a fair proportion of the powers, responsibilities and duties of life . . . Cool is the suggestion that the colored American, after enduring over two centuries of wrong and exclusion from the results of his own efforts and submitting to every deprivation of just public benefaction refrain from referring to his wrongs and his color (his identity) as at least one of the bases for recognition. . . .

The New National Era, Washington, D.C., August 28, 1873

William E. Walker, the author of the following letter, was a Virginia minister and active in the Republican Party.

. . . Equality of rights is the only true and just basis of Republican form of government. Whenever the rights of one class are denied, abridged, or destroyed, it is usurpation and tyranny and not law and justice. The theory, genius, and policy of the American government is to preserve the most friendly relations with all its inhabitants of every color, race, and clime. This can only be effected by abolishing all invidious distinctions and placing all its citizens upon one common platform. This proscription is one of the fouled lots and relics of slavery which still rests upon the escutcheon of the nation, and which impairs the character of the government, both at home and abroad, by all levels of freedom and equal rights. Let no such thing as one class legislating in behalf of another class any longer exist. This at once gives the lie to our professions, and stamps us as hypocritical and inconsistent. The perpetuity and life of the nation are dependent upon our adhering to the great principles that lay at the foundation of this Republic—liberty and equality.

The New National Era, Washington, D.C., January 22, 1874

The following correspondent, signed Red Cloud, Baltimore, was not sanguine about the political prospects of dependence on the goodwill of the Republican Party.

The civil rights and political liberties of five million of people may have to be, but ought not to be, trusted to the keeping and direction of any political trimmer, in this hour of their transition, who espouse to the Presidency simply on the ground of availability; neither can the Negro, without some heart-burnings, vote for any man who for his own political advancement has discriminated and palliated in favor of wrong or injustice to him as a controversy in law.

The People's Advocate, Alexandria, Virginia, May 27, 1876

Now that the pistol and bowie knife has begun again their murderous work in Mississippi and Louisiana we may expect again to see the independent press crammed with sensational and unreliable stories about the general uprising of Negroes to exterminate the whites. These outrageous lies in the beginning of each election year are manufactured in order to conceal their murderous outrages. . . .

"G. W. A."
The People's Advocate, Alexandria, Virginia, May 27, 1876

. . . To advise colored Republicans to form exclusive political organizations is to surrender to conservatism; is to practice what they openly avow as one of the fundamental principles of their party organization, and is the most effective step to retard the progress of Republicanism in the South.

The Peoples Advocate, Alexandria, Virginia, June 17, 1876

The black press stressed internal unity with loyalty to the Republican Party as the mainstay of political organization. Such a position, however, was made increasingly difficult as the Republican Party turned away from black demands for justice.

The colored men who have sought refuge and hope in the Democratic conservative ranks occupy a peculiar position. There is enough evidence of the temper of the Republican party toward them. It demands free speech, but not for the colored Democrats; it demands a fair election, provided the colored vote goes solid for Hayes and Wheeler; it orders out the troops to protect citizens at the polls, but only to protect Republican citizens. Upon colored Democrats and their friends devolves the nice, arduous duty of so deporting themselves as to give no shadow of an excuse to visit upon them the vengeance of the Administration. They must keep out of the way of the jackals who are lying in wait to rend them. The day is near at hand when the colored man will no longer be held in duress by the Republican managers. Let him do his duty as a citizen and patiently bide his time.

The Republican, Maryville, Tennessee, October 7, 1876

. . . it is well that our people should organize themselves and prepare for the coming contest. There are enough colored votes in the State of Kansas, if they were properly organized and held together to accomplish a great deal of good for the colored race. Our people need education, we need schoolhouses, competent teachers, and a common share in the school fund of the State. The time has come when we must act for ourselves. We have drifted around from place to place long enough and have got to make a bold stand sometime. . . .

The Colored Citizen, Fort Scott, Kansas, May 3, 1878

That strong efforts are being made to alienate the colored people of the republican party is too well understood to need any argument whatever to prove it, and that in many instances success is attending their efforts is too apparent to be doubted. We must be candid and say that these attempts to destroy the republican party by taking from it its strongest prop is to be regretted. . . .

The Colored Citizen, Fort Scott, Kansas, September 27, 1878

The following article was orginally printed in the Broadside *and is an example of the common practice of refusing voting rights to blacks in the South.*

The Negroes were not allowed to vote freely in any ward in this city, except the ninth. They were met with all sorts of frivolous questions by the democracy, and large numbers of them turned away illegally without voting. In the seventh ward seven Negroes had made three attempts to vote the Republican ticket and had been refused. They then stepped aside, took some of the democratic tickets which were on fancy red paper, and scratched off the name of the Democrats on them and wrote on the names of the Republican candidates, folded them up, went in on the Democratic side, presented their votes, and they were received without question, the democratic judges supposing they were voting the Democratic ticket.

The People's Advocate, Washington, D.C., September 11, 1880

Though the Republican Party granted some concessions to blacks, it refused to recognize them as equals.

. . . The question is, will the [Republican] party now turn its back upon its sentiments as expressed in its platform and on the stump, and gain a greater reputation for duplicity and demagogism than that of its political opponent for stupidity and corruption? This is the practical question which will be settled by recognizing on *common* grounds the claims of colored men for promotion to meritorious and trustworthy appointments in the civil service. If the Party fails to show its fidelity to its principles by continuing to annex the word *white* to every condition for high appointment, then the Bourbon Democracy can laugh our high-sounding professions to scorn; but if, on the other hand, the native and acquired qualifications of colored men are recognized in the line of promotion, as a general custom, and there are *more* exceptional postmasters, collectors of the internal revenue and of the port, special agents, postal inspectors than necessary to prove the rule which now obtains, the "solid South" and its Northern allies will be compelled to give their political opponents at least credit for sincerity and honesty of purpose.

The People's Advocate, Washington, D.C., December 18, 1880

Following the withdrawal of federal troops from the South in 1876, black people were subject to a reign of terror and at the mercy of white mobs. Deprived of every means of self-defense, jailed on the slightest pretext, and lynched for less, blacks turned to their party and government for protection.

. . . The Democrats of the South are determined that the colored voter shall either be Democrats, or not vote at all. Hayes refuses to give any protection whatever to the Republicans of the South and in almost every instance where colored people attempt to organize as Republicans, they pay for it with their lives. . . .

The Colored Citizen, Fort Scott, Kansas, October 26, 1878

Political independence in Kansas became a significant lever to win concessions from the Republican Party.

We address the colored voters of Kansas. We think the time for unity of action has arrived, and if there ever was a time in the history of this country when the colored voters should be united, it is now. The coming political contest promises to be the most exciting ever witnessed in this country . . .

The colored voters of this State compose no insignificant portion of the Republican party, and we think it nothing more than a wise and expedient measure for the colored State Convention to take some steps toward obtaining for the colored voters of this State more representation. . . . It is an undeniable fact that the colored voters of this State have been used as mere tools, and allowed others to talk and think for them long enough, and it is high time that the colored man commenced to think and act for himself in all matters pertaining to his welfare. . . .

The Kansas Herald, Topeka, April 9, 1880

T. Thomas Fortune, the editor of the New York Globe, *was one of the most outspoken advocates of the need for federal protection for the black community.*

. . . We fully understand the law of the United States—we know that it has the power to make citizens, and we know that it has no power to protect them. Thus the Negroes of the South were made citizens of the United States, but the states say they shall not enjoy the privileges of citizenship and the National Government has shown in a thousand instances that it had no power to coerce the states. That is, we have had, since the close of the war, every possible species of rebellion, usurpation, violence and down-right anarchy in some states, but the federal government has at no time interfered effectually in the interest of good government. This non-interference was based upon the powers vested in the federal government and those reserved to the states—the which vested and reserved rights have always made the central government the helpless foot ball of belicose states and placed the citizens of the United States more at the mercy of the state than at the mercy of the sisterhood of states. While the tyranny which has always flowed from centralized government is obviated, no check is placed upon the tyranny of the individual state. . . .

. . . We maintain that this is a government of the people—not white or black people but of the people. It is against this very arrogance that we protest. In a commonwealth of equals such as ours claims to be, no race, class or party has the right to claim to be the "governing class." Ours is supposed to be a government in which classes and distinctions melt into a harmonious whole. Until we reach this ideal of government, we will be a distracted, contentious people. . . .

The Globe, New York, February 17, 1883

In the face of disfranchisement, black editors urged consolidation and, in response to discrimination, counseled racial pride.

. . . As far as political unity of action is concerned, the colored man will preserve his clannishness until all parties teach him that they neither desire to use him as a tool, nor to degrade him as a man. The common instinct of man and brute is to concentration when danger is apprehended. The colored people are resolving themselves out of the habits of slavery into the habits of free men as fast as it is possible for them to do so, and the time is at hand when the colored man will be proud of the black skin which is the index of his African extraction, and the honorable political, social, and religious status which he will have made in this country under disadvantages which the white man is absolutely incapable of appreciating.

The Globe, New York, June 2, 1883

Despite federal legislation, the refusal of the government to intervene effectively nullified the law. Even these hypothetical protections were eliminated when the Supreme Court declared them unconstitutional.

The Civil Rights bill farce has again received a blow. Judge McCoy of the United States Circuit Court in Savannah, Ga., has just dismissed an indictment against defendants charged with "beating, wounding, and murdering Jerry Hamilton, colored, with intent to deprive him of full and equal protection of the laws." The indictment was remitted to the State courts of Georgia. The State courts of the South are the safety, the cloak, of the lawless cutthroats who live by intimidation and murder of black men. Not one white man in a million has ever been hung for deliberately murdering a black man. The United States, which makes the citizen, has no power to protect him in his rights. When the black man is outraged the United States turns its back upon him and the state adds insult to injury by sending the black man to the chain gang. They do not punish white villains who shoot white villains. What are we to do in an extreme of this nature? You can't expect blacks to receive a decent idea of the majesty of the law in a community where law is made the pliant tool to shield villains from justice and to severely punish honest men.

The Globe, New York, June 2, 1883

T. Thomas Fortune continued to urge agitation for reform along with self-improvement as blacks.

We believe in dissatisfaction; we believe in the manifold virtues of agitation. . . . In our own country the conflict of wrong and right has been long and bloody. Around the battlefield of Bunker's Hill and Yorktown and Manassas and Appomattox the masses contended and conquered and so they were always if they felt on the side of right. Agitation does not always lead to an appeal to arms. Peace has its triumphs and often they are more substantial that follow the victorious car of Napoleon or Wellington. Our history in this country dates from the moment that restless men among us became restless under oppression and rose against it. From Denmark Vesey to Nat Turner, from the flight of Frederick Douglass and Henry Highland Garnet from the bloodhounds of Maryland to the present time the voice of the race has been heard on the lecture platform and on the field of battle protesting against the injustice heaped upon the race. It has had its effect. Agitation, contentions, ceaseless unrest, constant aspiring— a race so moved must prevail. There is no half-way ground between right and wrong. This one or the other must obtain and prevail.

Mental inertia is death. Indifferent acquiescence in wrong is death. Tame submission to outrage is death. Agitation, constant protesting, all these standing up to be counted to be heard, or to be knocked down, this spirit breeds respect and dulls the edge of tyranny. We should learn that the aggressive man, the man who is always ready to contend for what is his, is the man who gets what is his.

In politics, in business, in social intercourse, we want to show more manhood, a deep appreciation of the philosophy of life. We must learn to lean upon ourselves; we must learn to plan and execute business enterprises of our own; we must learn to venture our pennies if we would gain dollars. We must wake up. We spend too much time in frivolity. Fortunes and reputation are not made in that way.

The Globe, New York, August 18, 1883

Many blacks were reluctant to participate in a political process by which they were effectively denied their rights. In spite of this, T. Thomas Fortune urged his readers to work within the political system to create needed changes.

We should vote, even if we have to fight to do it, for the ballot is an American freeman's guarantee of citizenship, and the man who attempts to deny him the right to vote says "You are not an American citizen—stand back!" The answer to this should always be "I am an American citizen—and I stand back for no man!" And upon this declaration the American citizen should stand or fall, vote or die! . . .

The Globe, New York, September 9, 1883

From the age of fifteen to seventeen, W. E. B. DuBois sent occasional letters to the New York Globe *and sold the paper in his hometown, Great Barrington, Massachusetts. The following is one of these letters, written when DuBois was fifteen.*

The political contest is near at hand, and the colored men of the town should prepare themselves accordingly. They should acquaint themselves with the political status and attitude of the candidates toward them, particularly their representatives. The choice of governor should demand a good show of their attention. Those who voted for Gen. Butler last year "just to see what he would do" have found it a pretty costly experiment. They will see that while preaching economy and refusing the necessary apportions to charitable institutions, he has spent an immense sum of money on needless investigations, such as Tewksbury, and the like. The colored men may well ask themselves how they have been benefited by his administration, although he professes to be their friend. A political office should not be the goal of one's ambition, but still if anyone wishes an office and is worthy of it, it should not be denied him on account of his color. We had an example of this here a short time ago, when a colored man, along with a number of white men applied for the position of night watchman. After an examination the applicants melted down to one white man, a strong Democrat, and the colored man, a Republican. A committee composed wholly of Republicans was chosen to decide between the two candidates and they selected the white man. The colored men of Great Barrington hold the balance of power and have decided the election of many officers for a number of years. If they would only act in concert they may become a power not to be despised. It would be a good plan if they should meet and decide which way would be most advantageous for them to cast their votes. . . .

The Globe, New York, September 29, 1883

The hypocrisy of the government in refusing to protect black people against terrorism of the Ku Klux Klan led many to doubt the practicability of working through the political system.

The colored people of the U.S. feel today as if they had been baptized in ice-water. From Maine to Florida they are earnestly discussing the decision of the Supreme Court declaring the Civil Rights Law to be unconstitutional. Public meetings are being projected far and wide to give expression to the common feeling of disappointment and apprehension for the future.

The Republican Party has carried the war into Africa, and Africa is accordingly stirred to its centre. . . .

It was only a few months ago that the Supreme Court declared that the Ku Klux law was unconstitutional—that the U.S. was powerless to protect its citizens in the enjoyment of life, liberty and the pursuit of happiness. What sort of Government is that which openly declares that it has no power to protect its citizens from ruffianism, intimidation, and murder? Is such a Government worthy the respect and loyalty of honest men? It certainly does not enjoy our respect and our loyalty to it is the cheapest possession we have.

Having declared that colored men have no protection from the government in their political rights, the Supreme Court now declares that we have no civil rights—declares that railroad corporations are free to force us into smoking cars or cattle cars; that hotel keepers are free to make us walk the streets at night; that theatre managers can refuse us admittance to their exhibitions for the amusement of the public . . .

We have the ballot without any law to protect us in the enjoyment of it. . . . We are aliens in our native land; we are denied an equal measure of that protection which flows from citizenship and which is denied to no other class of American citizens. . . . the Democratic party is a fraud—a narrowminded, corrupt bloody fraud; the Republican party has grown to be little better. . . .

The Globe, New York, October 20, 1883

The basic contradictions in American society became glaringly apparent as black people were effectively disfranchised.

. . . We are not to be browbeaten into servile compliance by adverse decisions on our common and inalienable rights as men and citizens, nor are we to be awed into submission and complacent acquiescence by the malignant exaltation of our foes. We are men; we are citizens. . . .

We do not ask the American government or people for charity—we leave that boon to be conferred upon aliens fleeing from the tyranny of European governments; we do not ask any special favor from the American government or people—we leave that to be conferred upon the cringing, sulking boozers who assassinate and rob in the broad glare of the noonday. But we do demand that impartial justice, which is the standard of reciprocity between equals. We are not Chinese peons knocking at the door of Congress for the privilege of sharing in the putative liberties of this hidebound government, with a mob of Sand Lot vermin dogging our heels; not at all! We are free men; we are American citizens; we are as equal before the law as the whitest man that was ever bleached by the snows of Caucasus, and we demand that the equity shall have ample and unequivocal and impartial hearing before the laws of the land, and the august bar of public opinion.

The honor of citizenship was not conferred upon us because men loved us; it was conferred upon us because our conduct in the war, when men's nerves and souls were tried, earned it. . . .

In 1876, in order to enjoy a temporary triumph, in order to place a prating, vainglorious, nerveless (wo)man in the White House, the Republican party sacrificed the black vote of the South, and it has reaped disaster and infamy ever since. It cut itself loose from the issues upon which the war was fought and won; it threw the black vote overboard, and it has not enjoyed one single triumph since, and it never will again, unless it takes up the thread of its political vitality where it left off in 1876.

Without our vote, the Republican party is doomed. It is doomed to destruction, because it has sacrificed principle on the altar of expediency, because it has called in the assistance of the Devil to fight the battles of the Lord. And now it talks about giving us sympathy! It may keep its sympathy; we want none of it. The party has lived out its usefulness, because it has betrayed the people and joined hands with the greedy cormorants of society—because it has grown wealthy and arrogant and indifferent. The people demand that it reform itself—or it must go.

The Globe, New York, October 27, 1883

As watchmen upon the political wall, as defenders of the people's rights, we have declared our intention to stand by the defenseless under any and all circumstances. Politically, we are Republican, pure and simple. But when the rights or interest of the colored race are involved, we become more Negro than anything else. . . .

The Grit, Washington, D.C., December 21, 1883

The call for an independent black vote was echoed at conventions held during this period. Such a position, however, was more popular in the Northern press rather than in that of the South and West, which tended to remain Republican.

. . . We are not the subsidized champion of the Democratic hag or the Republican nightmare. We are the advocate of equal and exact justice to each and every citizen in each and every State of the Union. Our idea of justice and liberty is broader than the Federal Constitution which has always been, and is today, a huge piece of jugglery drawn in the interest of slavery, caste and oppression, not to say open robbery. . . . In 1856, the Constitution was the bulwark of slavery; in 1884 it is the temple of narrowness and subterfuge. And the Republican Party and the Democratic Party fly to the Constitution for apology for crime and injustice.

The Globe, New York, February 9, 1884

For the most part black papers remained loyal to the Republican Party as the lesser of evils.

The colored man in this country is an important factor. There is no class of citizens more honorable and sincere to a government and more industrious. He has proved himself to be a strict adherent to the principles of the republican party, and a friend to his former master. He has sustained the republican party in power, and all he asks is protection. The democratic party will cut every Negro's throat to keep a white republican from getting control of the State, or National Government. The time has come that we demand, not only protection, but recognition according to merit. . . .

The Bee, Washington, D.C., March 8, 1884

. . . Let the colored people of the State, not feel discouraged or despondent. Their friends are not dead, nor do they even sleep. *Civil Rights* is still the great *heart platform* of North Carolina Republicanism, and, by the help of God and the eternal edicts of right and justice, this platform shall yet prevail.

The N.C. Republican and Civil Rights Advocate, Weldon, May 22, 1884

In Precinct "A," Fourth ward, Cincinnati, the judges, all Democrats, returned only 48 Republican votes cast at the recent election and gave the Democrats nearly 1,000, the total vote being somewhere about 300 more than was registered. To show beyond all doubt that the ballot box was stuffed, the *Commercial Gazette* published the names of 112 voters in that precinct who have made oath that they voted the straight Republican ticket. . . .

The Gazette, Cleveland, November 28, 1885

The development of racial identity was seen here as the prerequisite for national identity and political unity.

One of the strongest drawbacks to concert of any kind with us is that we are thoroughly American in sentiment and instinct. Our race identity is almost wholly lost in our identity and sympathy with American institutions. While we are largely regarded as aliens, we are most thoroughly indigenous. We have no other Fatherland than America, because here we were born, and here we must die. Africa to us is a sentiment, pure and simple. Slavery made us enemies one to the other, wrong and outrage made us blind, unreasoning partisans. But we are learning that race discord is a drawback; we are learning that blind partisan allegiance is a delusion and a snare. A few more years and the race will stand shoulder to shoulder and blind devotion to Party will be one of the things of the past.

The Globe, New York, February 16, 1884

The editor of the Gazette, *H. C. Smith, a leader of black Democrats, sought to shift the traditional allegiances of black voters away from the Republican Party.*

The time has come when the colored man must use to advantage that agency, his vote, which makes him the pivot upon which turns the success or defeat of any one of the great political parties. It has been demonstrated that the colored man is only courted for his vote. He only exists in the political world when his vote is to be cast, and after election he becomes a thing of the past. . . . But it is with us to say whether he will use this power to our own advantage, or use it in behalf of those who will give us no credit, no recognition for doing so. Don't let us blame any party for our political condition. A people who have the power to dictate terms and don't do it must not censure anyone but themselves if they don't get a goodly share of the spoils. But let us become united, let us become organized. . . .

The Gazette, Cleveland, March 8, 1884

*Paraphrasing a motto used by many including the New York Painters'
Union ("Peacefully if we can, forcibly if we must; When peaceful efforts
fail, then the Revolution!"—New York* Times, *September 15, 1871),
many black leaders saw political reform tied to racial solidarity and organization.*

It is our duty as citizens and especially the young men of this community to show to the country that we mean to have political reform.
. . . Let every young man and public spirited citizen be on guard and
protect our home interests. If we fail in this issue that is being made
by the respectable citizens of this community, don't despair, but work
with the same determination and will that have crowned all successful
revolutions. Be peaceable if we can, but forcible if we must. We ask
for fair play. . . . Now is the time to show to the American Congress
and the respectable people of this community that our politics are no
longer controlled by a mob; that the rum mill cannot buy the votes of
the colored citizens; that men of other States cannot have superior advantages and considerations in preference to our own people. Now is
the time to strike. Now is the time for citizens of the community to
show their powers and fidelity to a principle that we have fostered. We
mean freedom and independence to an oppressed race of people. . . .
The poor people of Rome were oppressed by an aristocracy and
where aristocracy reigns, it means slavery to the masses of poor people. The Plebians were no more than contrabands in America, and it
was not till the shackles were broken from the limbs of the Negro that
made him an American citizen. Today the once contraband is pioneer
of the black race. . . .

The Bee, Washington, D.C., April 5, 1884

*Although disillusioned with the prospects of inclusion within the Repub-
lican Party, many blacks who advocated an independent political course
were reluctant to break these traditional allegiances. The following letter,
written to the New York* Herald, *by T. Thomas Fortune, but unpublished,
was printed in the* Globe.

. . . What we need at this time are new principles and new parties.
The times are ripe for such. Old issues have become law, or eliminated

from politics; a new generation has come upon the scene and it is res-
tive under the fogyisms and the exploded theories now championed
by the two historic parties. When a new party comes forth as the
champion of equal civil and political rights to all men; of civil service
reform; of reduction of unnecessary taxation and a proper re-adjust-
ment of our disjointed tariff laws; of a national system of compulsory
education and of proper and needful restrictions upon the power and
extent of monopoly and corporate extortion—when such a new party
makes its appearance, I will make one of its partisans. Until that time,
I shall lean towards the Republican party and give it my support.

The Globe, New York, September 13, 1884

*As the federal government continued to ignore white terrorism in the
South, and refused to protect the rights of black citizens, meetings were
held to organize a response. One such meeting was held in Columbus,
Ohio, on December 22, 1883.*

A State Convention of colored men assembled here today in pur-
suance of a call issued some time since by a number of leading colored men of the State. The object of the convention is to take into
consideration the educational, moral, civil, and political interests of
the colored race, and particularly the question of the equal rights of
the colored people of the South. The recent decision of the Supreme
Court annulling the Civil Rights bill, as well as the murder of colored
men at Danville, Virginia, are the principal reasons for the assembling
of the convention at this time. . . .

The State Journal, Harrisburg, Pennsylvania, December 29, 1883

A few months after the Globe *was suspended, its editor, T. Thomas
Fortune, started the* Freeman.

. . . We venture to state that the colored man of character and intelligence who in any community of the South would today stand up
manfully for every civil and political right which is naturally and con-
stitutionally his—the right to vote and to speak and to counsel his

race in matters political, to take such fare on public carriers as his ticket entitled him, and to demand such equal portion of the school and other public benefits as his co-equal citizenship confers upon him —such a man we venture to say, would be shot dead in 24 hours, or strung up to a limb by a mob of "the best people of the place." . . .

The Freeman, New York, July 11, 1885

As the black man was used by the political system and deprived of every recourse from injustice and attack, many were inclined toward independent action.

The time has now arrived in the politics of this country for the Negro to think and act for himself. Too long, for his best interests, has he been the subservient tool of men who had no further use for him than to count on, in advance, his vote to serve their party interest. With no compensating results other than a few minor offices grudgingly given, the Negro has steadily and solidly for years, voted the republican ticket, without even availing himself of the privileges accorded the meanest, lowest, and most ignorant white man, viz. "to scratch a ticket." The reading and thinking portion of them were first aroused from their political apathy by the concerted action of the republican governors of several southern states, recommending to President Grant the disarming of the colored militia in the several states, thereby placing the Negro at the tender mercy of a bitter and unrelenting foe. . . .

The Bee, Washington, D.C., January 1, 1887

Calvin Chase, editor of the Bee, *was one of those editors who supported the independent political position advocated by Fortune.*

There is a great deal of work still left unfinished that ought to be done for the colored race in this country in the way of practical recognition of their citizenship. And as part and parcel of the great American community, under one common flag and one constitution. . . . The race does not ask for special privileges and favors, and only insists upon a free and fair chance in the race of life offered to other people in this country . . .

The Bee, Washington, D.C., January 15, 1887

When intimidation was insufficient to prevent blacks from voting, the ruling Southern Democracy often refused to accept Republican ballots.

With the suppression of opposition the larger portion of Southern democracy refrained from voting. It is only in sections largely Republican that the democracy find it necessary to take political action. This action was formerly violence and murder, but the more powerful method of not counting the Republican ballots is now generally adopted, being equally effective and less shocking to the nerves of Northern Independents, and those engaged in picturing the glories and advantages of the New South. . . .

The Weekly Pelican, New Orleans, April 16, 1887

Though men like Fortune urged an independent position, most black papers were opposed to such an action.

There seems to be three wings of the colored press. The most of the Negro editors are advocating Republicanism, and several are trying to show the advantages our people will have if they take an independent position in politics, while a very small majority pretend to show that the Negro's future salvation is in the arms of the Democratic party. The colored people are tired of traitors from any party; they are tired of being duped by the treacherous and speculative politicians, and they are tired of being petted for their vote alone. They want recognition, or at least the positions with money in them. Now the question is, who will supply this deficiency? But while the Republican party might have done more for the Negro, he had better hold his present political position until he is fully and thoroughly satisfied that some other party will give him a larger share of the spoils. [From the Marion *Headlight*]

The Negro's place is not in the front, nor in the rear of this political battle, but half-way. He has tried everything in politics, but the right thing, and that is a division of his vote as a mass. When he disclaims partyism and strikes for Negroism and its success, he will see the bright lights turned on. [From the Alabama *Cyclone*]

The Benevolent Banner, Topeka, Kansas, May 28, 1887

The following quotes are from papers of the town of Nicodemus, Kansas, founded by black settlers in 1877. The Western Cyclone *was succeeded by the* Nicodemus Cyclone, *which later became the* Nicodemus Enterprise.

. . . We shall always be found on the side of the people and against cliques, rings, and grinding corporations and shall endeavor to advance the interests of Nicodemus and Graham county regardless of any local strife that may exist, looking always to the interests of the majority.

Our interests are in Nicodemus, and for her welfare and advancement we shall put forth our best efforts.

In politics we have always been Republican and shall advocate the principles of that grand old party in the columns of this paper believing them to be just and right . . .

The Enterprise, Nicodemus, Kansas, August 17, 1887

Is the condition of the ballot box in the South changed? . . . We will answer by saying emphatically no. In many states of the South, the Republicans are at least six to one; and from these selfsame states, overwhelmingly Democratic majorities are counted. The colored men as a rule and especially in the South are naturally Republicans and would so vote if they dared to risk their lives to do so. . . . Lead and powder are successful intimidators and men for years who have been oppressed by unmerciful tyrants, cannot in a day turn aside such influences and successfully meet their antagonists. . . . Give each man life, liberty and the pursuits of happiness is an American idea of running a government.

The Western Cyclone, Nicodemus, Kansas, September 9, 1887

There is a movement afoot to call a convention of the Colored Republicans of Kansas to demand representation and palpably further the chance of certain professional politicians. We are opposed to any such move on general principles and look to see it die a "bornin." There are at present two great political parties and one side show in the country and if any person cannot find refuge in one of these let him go to Gallagher. The colored Convention would meet, pass a mountain of self-laudatory resolutions, and meet the regular Republican Convention to be treated as eloquent divine. . . .

The Nicodemus Cyclone, Kansas, March 9, 1888

As black voters became increasingly disaffected with the Republican Party, black editors, largely in the West, insisted that party loyalty was the only hope of achieving political goals.

Haunted by the suspicion that they are political slaves, and actuated by the financial inducements held out by the Democratic party, a number of Negroes have identified themselves with the infamous party of Negro slavery. True, they tell us that times and issues have changed and that the sentiment of the Democratic party has kept pace with the advancing public sentiment.

Notwithstanding that this be true, and we most sincerely hope that it is, yet the fundamental principles of the party are just the same, and the issues of today are simply a cloak that covers the real attitude of the Democracy . . .

The American Citizen, Topeka, Kansas, July 13, 1888

The organization of more than 1,000,000 black people in the Colored Farmers' Alliance represented the most serious threat of an independent black vote.

The Farmer's Alliance is making great efforts to get the colored people to vote their ticket in the coming election. . . . Is it not plain to every colored man that this alliance intends to plot the oppression of colored farmers? . . . But the Alliancemen are now saying they are going to organize a "nigger alliance." This was never thought of until this election when they need our votes. It is too late to fool us in this way. [From the Selma, Alabama, *Independent*]

We hope the colored people of Alabama will stand by their colors and exercise their rights as citizens. Let them contend for a *free ballot* and a fair count, in such a manner that all who prize and wish to preserve the liberties of the people will come to their rescue.

The American Citizen, Topeka, Kansas, August 3, 1888

American capitalism depended on the preservation of a cheap labor force and thus allied itself with those elements in the South which kept the black people in virtual slavery.

The Southern Democracy are depending on Northern capital invested in southern enterprises, to bring about such a conservative state of mind, as to prevent the enforcement of the Constitution guaranteeing every American in his rights. They know that wherever American capital is, there his heart will be, hence, they are building up their hopes that nothing will be done by the incoming administration that will interfere with their methods of cheating the colored citizen out of the exercise of the elective franchise. We have stood by the Republican party in season and out of season. We have taken our lives in our hands to perpetuate the life of the party of the Union. We have suffered untold wrongs at the hands of those who struggled long and hard to tear this country to atoms; and we will not believe until we are compelled to, that the Republican party can be longer influenced by the Southern Democracy, to longer allow us to suffer. We warn the Republican party of the danger of future delay in meting out equal and exact justice to all American citizens. The craftiness of the Southern Democracy, is only equaled by its barbarism and hatred of the negro, who has always been loyal to this Government. . . .

The National Leader, Washington, D.C., December 8, 1888

Carpetbaggers (Northern whites who went to the South) were accused of taking over government and businesses for their own personal gain—

sometimes with justification, but often to discredit and undermine attempts at fundamental changes.

. . . That class of the population which has made the South run with the blood of innocent citizens because of their faithfulness to the Union and their loyalty to the party that saved the Nation ought to be made to fear the just execution of the laws. Not only should the murderers and ballot-box stuffers be made to fear the law, but they should be compelled to obey and respect all laws giving equal and exact justice to all men. Who are the people of the South? Are they not every man, woman, and child, black or white, living in that section? Are the Constitution and the laws to be suspended as to one class of citizens and enforced as to another? . . .

The talk about negroes and carpetbaggers controlling the South is all nonsense. If the carpetbaggers and negroes in strict accordance with the laws, place in office men of their choice who under the Constitution has the right to prohibit it? What gives the South any more immunity from the carpetbaggers than has the West, which is being filled with carpetbaggers from all over the world? Enterprising, intelligent carpetbaggers will help the South. The lawless, Constitution-hating element now dominating that section is its worst enemy. The toiling, eager for education negro population is the strength of the South. That population, faithful when all others were faithless, should be protected in every right guaranteed by the Constitution of the country they have always upheld and never betrayed.

It is well for the loyal people of this country to remember that there are two classes of citizens in the South. One is a large class that had to be pardoned for treason against the Nation. The other is the class that aided in saving the Nation from the attempt to kill it by its treasonable foes. To both classes is the elective franchise given by the Constitution of the U.S. The treasonable class has succeeded through disobedience of the law in depriving the ever-loyal class of the exercise of the right given by the Constitution of their country. . . .

The National Leader, Washington, D.C., December 22, 1888

The time is near at hand when every American citizen must demand equal and exact justice in everything that goes to make up American citizenship. If the colored citizen accepts anything less, he acknowledges his inferiority to his white fellow citizen. We must contend for full and complete rights such as are enjoyed by all other classes of Americans.

It must be borne in mind by those who counsel patience to the blacks when they are seeking recognition that these black men fought for the salvation of this glorious union while those who fought *against* it, now enjoy all rights of an American citizen.

If the American people could be brought to such a sense of justice as to cause them to treat the negro as well as they do ex-rebels, instead of putting him at their mercy, there would be a show of gratitude that would be appreciated by those who fought to save this country.

The National Leader, Washington, D.C., January 26, 1889

Continual compromises with Southern Democrats eroded whatever progress black people had made in gaining their citizenship rights.

We think the President of the United States should pursue a wise policy towards the south, but not a conciliatory one, for in a conciliatory policy, the white citizen only, comes under that head for consideration. . . . The policy of the north from the first to last has been of a conciliatory nature towards the south, and the more it is tried, the less respect they of the south have for law, justice, and those that practice conciliation towards them.

There is but one way to remedy this evil, and that is the right way; enforce the laws at all hazards, in any and all parts of this great country; this has never been seriously attempted. Why should the South be further exempt from submitting to law and order? The attempt of ex-President Hayes to conciliate the South helped them to disregard law and hastened their solidarity. . . .

The National Leader, Washington, D.C., March 30, 1889

White and black politicians were well aware of the potential power of a united black vote. With power in the hands of whites, disfranchisement of blacks became almost inevitable.

. . . The Negro instituted and protected the Republican party in the South when all others ran away from it! In short we have always followed in the wake of whatever idea the Republican party has seen fit to espouse, whether it was prohibition, protection, or anything else. But very recently we have been informed that because we are black we are not protectionist. Be that as it may, we think we see something good in that mass of badness after all. It is this: according to the last census, that in 10 years, eight of the southern states the Negro will have the majority vote; very well then, let the whites exclude you from their organizations and there will be two white parties, evenly divided in the South, with one great large, solid Negro party—the result can be easily guessed.

The Advocate, Leavenworth, Kansas, April 20, 1889

Following some particularly racist remarks by President Benjamin Harrison, the black press responded, first editorially and second by a correspondent who signed his article "Argus."

. . . That Mr. Harrison and his forefathers enforced upon the Negro his ignorance, and that the wealth that is now used against him is his own, but was stolen from him by the men whom Mr. Harrison takes kindly by the hand and sympathizes with, because the Negro dares aspire to be voted for, or asks an office from the party that he has lifted into power.

Is it to be supposed that the southern white man will take more compassion on the Negro than Mr. Harrison? Will they allow the Negro to become a full citizen (including the right to hold office) when Mr. Harrison makes a distinction and refuses to appoint him on account of color? Will the southern deal more kindly by the Negro because Mr. Harrison says he would not live beside one? . . .

The latest reports show that there is to be a Southern policy adopted by the Republican party; and these reports are borne out by the fact that Mr. Harrison has not appointed colored men to any office. . . .

Now in view of the above circumstances, will not every Negro who votes the republican ticket endorse the acts of the administration, and the policy outlined by the leaders of the party? The answer must be yes!

And if 50% of the Negro vote in this Congressional District should stay away from the polls, and by their absence reduce the majority of the republican candidate to that extent would not this be taken as an expression of dissatisfaction with the policy above referred to? The answer must be yes!

As the congressman may be solely elected in this district without a single Negro vote, what necessity is there for the Negro to swell a majority that would be taken as an endorsement of the policy that the Negro must be eliminated from politics.

Let us think and then act; let 3000 Negro voters in this district stay home and by their absence condemn a policy that sacrifices the Negro. . . .

The American Citizen, Topeka, Kansas, April 26, 1889

For such staunchly Republican papers as the American Citizen *and the Leavenworth* Advocate *to counsel withholding votes indicated the seriousness of the situation, as well as an increasing resistance by black people to being used as pawns by the political parties.*

. . . Why will you put yourselves in bondage by voting and giving your lives for the election of the republican party, when they are the great hindrance to your success? They are the very ones who are now watering the roots of prejudice in this country, so that it cannot die, but grow in abundance. You may ask who should you vote for as both parties near and about on election day clothe their wolfish selves in lamb's clothing. Vote for neither party and watch the tide of times for its results.

The American Citizen, Topeka, Kansas, May 3, 1889

THE FREEMAN'S POLITICAL HOROSCOPE

A Prospective View of the Political Situation in '92. The Negro in Every Procession but the Republican, which has metamorphosed into a White Man's Procession.

The Freeman, Indianapolis, August 3, 1889

The Black Man
and Labor

O NE *of the most pressing problems in the field of labor today is the racial conflict within unions. Unions, particularly those in the skilled trades, have often been barriers to black workingmen and have continued a pattern of segregation, discrimination, and exclusion. Innovations such as the "quota system" in the hiring practices of the construction industry have been directed toward overcoming a form of racism that has existed in this country since the beginning of the union movement. No single issue has so threatened unions in this country as has the exclusion of black men.*

The polarization between black and white workingmen which resulted from the use, by employers, of black men to break strikes contributed to the refusal of unions to integrate. Tacit agreements between union and management to exclude black labor and formal and informal measures within the union structures effectively denied black people the opportunity to work or learn a trade. It is for this reason that unemployment among blacks is consistently three and four times greater than that of whites. This phenomenon, in part, explains the origin of black unions.

The second aspect of black labor organizing is focused on the direct exploitation of black people through such institutions as the convict-lease system and sharecropping—basically extensions of the plantation system. The preservation of such forms of institutionalized racism in the South and more subtle and sophisticated forms in the North substantiates the theory that black people stand in a colonial relationship to white society.

The black press was keenly aware of this dilemma and, as exponents of the philosophy of self-help, constantly stressed the necessity for industrial education. Generally supportive of integrated unions, the papers expressed pride in such black unions as the Negro Labor Union and were often spokesmen for black workingmen who were discriminated against. They saw the American labor movement as one of the most powerful means for achieving equality.

The following article was written by "Peter Paez" and expresses the interest of many, including Samuel Cornish, co-editor of the paper, in building black agricultural communities.

AGRICULTURE

Experience has taught us that agriculture of all other pursuits stands pre-eminent. Equally so, from the dependence in which it holds the other arts of civilized life, as from Divine appointment, whereby it is evident that man is destined to derive his support directly or indirectly from this never failing source. So that whether we be engaged in manufactures, or commerce, or science, still we must look back to the "parent art" agriculture, which holds precedence of all, and from which they necessarily sprang.

. . . Who then is more independent than the consistent farmer? who the bulwark of his nation more than he? and from whom must the essentials for prosecuting a war, the supply of the army and navy be derived, if it be not derived from him?

First, then, let those of our brethren who are located upon farms, allowing that they have no immediate interest in the property, continue in their present employment. They will escape contagion of the vices, and temptations to the luxuries of cities; they will command a more respectable standing in society than the mass of their brethren, rushing into the already too populous towns, to indulge in idleness and dissipation; to lengthen the catalogue of vagrants, to fill the mouths of their enemies with arguments against them, to wound the feelings of their more discreet brethren, and every way shamefully to abuse their "young freedom" as a certain editor would express it.

Secondly, Let those who are now in these city, destitute of trades, professions, or pursuits by which an honorable subsistance might be obtained, retire from the scene of commerce. Of these, many have been bred farmers, but have abandoned the artless toil of a rural life, for the more ungrateful tumults of the metropolis.

Suppose a few families, possessing each some means, were to embark in the measure I have been considering: that they purchase a parcel of cleared land, in a fertile region and convenient to some market town: that they devote their time to the culture of this land; and that they are enabled by diligence and skill, to appear at market with provisions as good and as cheap as their white neighbors: would they not meet with a ready sale?

This example would have its influence to entice others to engage in the same pursuit; and by this means the city would be cleared of numbers to whom employment could be given by men of their own colour, but who are now scarcely able to find means adequate to sustain them. And in process of time, the whole would be convinced of the superior advantages derived to the agriculturalists, over those continuing in cities; at least so far as it regards securing the comforts of life, respectability of character, and ability to educate their children.

Were our poor to become so far convinced of the truth of these remarks, as immediately to embrace the object recommended, I feel assured, that the result would be highly beneficial to many thousands of our race.

I am in hopes that some experienced agriculturalists, will cast such light upon the subject, as will render it clear to the minds of those interested.

Freedom's Journal, New York, August 31, 1827

When the Reverend Samuel T. Cornish left Freedom's Journal, *he moved to Bellville, New Jersey. Though he was a business agent for the paper, his connection with it was tenuous, and no articles with his name appear, except for the following advertisement which appeared regularly until the paper ceased publication in 1829.*

LAND FOR SALE.

THE subscriber is authorised to offer to his coloured brethren, 2,000 Acres of excellent Land, at less than one half its value, provided they will take measures to settle, or have it settled, by coloured farmers. The land is in the state of New-York, within 70 miles of the city: its location is delightful, being on the banks of the Delaware river, with an open navigation to the city of Philadelphia. The canal leading from the Delaware to the Hudson river passes through the tract, opening a direct navigation to New-York city. The passage to either city may be made in one day or less. The land is of the best quality, and well timbered.

The subscriber hopes that some of his brethren, who are capitalists, will at least invest 500 or 1,000 dollars, in these lands. To such he will take the liberty to say, this land can be purchased for 5 dollars the acre, (by coloured men), though it has been selling for $25. He also takes the liberty to observe that the purchase will be safe and advantageous, and he thinks such a settlement, formed by coloured families, would be conducive of much good: With this object in view he will invest 500 dollars in the purchase.

SAMUEL E. CORNISH

Freedom's Journal, New York, March, 20, 1827

Aided by Freedom's Journal, *abolitionists were encouraged to stop buying slave-produced products, a boycott which had been going on for some time.*

. . . We abominate slavery, and all its advocates. We consider it as the most iniquitous system of injustice ever set in operation; which must sooner or later meet its due reward. God is just; and though divine justice may slumber awhile, it will certainly overtake the oppressor. We think it highly becomes *each of us,* more especially, to manifest to mankind our decided disapprobation of slavery and all its concomitant evils; and how can we show that we are really in earnest on this subject, than by the adoption of such measures as will at once convince the public of the sincerity of our professions. The idea, that others would use the produce of slave-labour, if we did not, should weigh but little with us: that is a subject between them and their own consciences.

We ought ever to bear in mind this important fact, that every *25 individuals who use slave sugar* require the labor of one poor slave; and according to this ratio, which we believe to be correct, the consumption of slave sugar by the coloured population alone of this city would require at least the labours of 50 of our enslaved brethren, and the whole free population of the United States the labours of 2000! This is the mere article of sugar. If we take into view others, such as coffee, rice, etc. how much more striking will the number be! This is a subject worthy the candid consideration of every man of colour. Shall we, when our friends and patrons in Europe and America, have set us the example, purchase and use the produce of slave labour, when articles, the produce of free labour, equally as good, and equally as cheap, can be purchased in the different cities. Would it not be preferable to proscribe the use of such, than by our system be the means of strengthening the hand of the slave-dealer, by the purchase of *slave sugar* and *coffee*? Shall the free coloured population of the United States be the means of finding employment—of *adding to the labours and groans and stripes of 2000 of their enslaved brethren*? All the divine precepts—all the ties of nature and humanity—all the rules of equity and justice—labour is certainly a great evil, which ought to be remedied immediately, and which, we trust, our brethren will take into deep consideration.

Freedom's Journal, New York, October 19, 1827

ADVANTAGEOUS NOTICE

The Subscriber will undertake to furnish colored apprentices, gratis, to the different Mechanical business. *Philanthropists,* on application to him, at his dwelling, in the evening, at No. 272 Spring Street, up stairs, or through the day at No. 118 Anthony, near Elm St., will be attended to.

Colored parents and guardians of our youths, are respectfully requested to give in the names, residence, and age of their boys, in season, so as to secure a place, that will be to their future advantage.

JAMES FRASER
The Colored American, New York, April 15, 1837

In 1837 New York City denied licenses to black cart drivers and porters. The editor of the Colored American *took up the challenge.*

. . . Is it not an OUTRAGE upon revelation and reason, and even a violation of the laws of instinct, by which birds and beast are governed? We have seen some species of the animal creation, who would wait until the weaker caught their prey, and then seize upon and take it from them: but it was left for the Municipality of a christian city, to prevent the hungry poor from pursuing an honest calling, by which they might get bread for themselves and their children.

It may be said on the part of those in authority that they have made no enactments, especially prohibiting colored men from driving carts or rolling wheelbarrows. This is true: but they have made incorporate laws prohibiting all men from pursuing these occupations without *special license,* and they withhold these licenses from colored men, while they give them freely to white men, without respect to name or nation, and too frequently without respect to character.

It is further pleaded on the part of the authorities, that it is IN MERCY to the colored man, that they deny him license. Were they, it is said, to license colored carmen and porters, it would bring them into collusion with white men of the same calling, and they would get their horses and carts "dumped" into the dock, and themselves abused and beaten. We confess this is mercy on the part of our authorities, with A VENGEANCE TO IT!! And it is a compliment indeed to our worthy carmen and porters.

Who are the carmen of New York, and who the porters? Are they *illiterate, savage barbarians?* NO, READER—many of them are among our very best citizens, men who for moral worth and industrious enterprise, are the pride of our city, and whose names will ever be united with all that is glorious in our nation. They are, some of them, leaders in the HOLY CAUSE of equal rights, and are laboring to do away, FOREVER, those monopolies and distinctions which are the curse of the nation.

We do not believe, should the authorities license colored men as carmen and porters, there would be any serious difficulties whatever. But were the case otherwise, are not the authorities bound to see every citizen protected in his rights, and sustained in his honest efforts to get bread?—Surely they are. Any colored citizen, who with a respectful petition and recommendation in his hand, applies for license as a carman or porter, is entitled to them: and the authority which withholds them, alike violates the laws of the land, of humanity, and of God.

This illegal proscription of colored men is not practiced in the dark. It is an open violation of law and of conscience. We know an instance in which a worthy citizen, fully convinced of the injustice and cruelty of withholding from colored men THEIR LEGAL RIGHTS, and prohibiting them from pursuing lawful callings, got up and *signed himself,* a petition to the Mayor in behalf of an industrious, worthy man. This same gentleman afterwards *himself* became Mayor of the city, and actually denied the same man a license as a porter?

The spirit of injustice and slavery apparent in this inhuman measure of taking from the colored man the means of getting his bread, is disgraceful to our Corporation, and should *immediately* be put away and repented of. It is disgraceful to oppress in this manner, any of our citizens— Deny a man any other privilege, rather than the privilege of honestly getting his bread. It is also disgraceful to indulge in such feelings of slavery, and resort to, as an apology, the fear of public sentiment. THE CARMEN WILL NOT SUBMIT TO IT!!! . . .

The Colored American, New York, September 16, 1837

With the war at an end, the Southern black community saw the end of slave labor in Louisiana as the beginning of a new age.

In former years slave labor was a very profitable institution in this state, so much so that almost everyone who could procure means enough of obtaining slaves, had them without fail. This became the custom so much, in this section, that there were but few of any standing whatever that owned slaves. Very often the poorest among us who could only by the greatest exertion procure a few hundred dollars, expended even that in the purchase of a Negro. After a short time his so-called property enhanced so much in value that this poor fellow was conveyed to the market, sold at private sale or bid off under the hammer of the auctioneer. Two young ones were then purchased and brought home by the owner who fattened them up and prepared them for market. In the meantime if the owner had nothing to occupy their time, they were hired out at so much per month; the owner received the money as regularly as the month came around and very often this monthly accumulation was received more regularly then the rent of a public dwelling. By this means the slave owners became rich, and indolence took the place of industry. Today the scene is somewhat changed. Slave labor is no longer recognized in Louisiana, and that man or woman as the case may be, that was but a short time since held down by the yoke of oppression, is now at liberty to breathe the pure air of heaven. . . .

The liberty of this persecuted race has, it is true, been purchased at a dear rate. The blood of untold thousands has been poured out freely for the restoration of the Union, the liberty of the bondsmen and the promulgation of the privileges of Jefferson, while our brave defenders march along fighting for a destroyed Union, the slaves are buckling on their armor, and take up their line of march in the same direction shouting for national liberty. . . .

The Tribune, New Orleans, August 13, 1864

Political philosophy, it would seem, did not interfere with one of the cruelest forms of reinstituted slavery, the convict-lease system.

. . . There is Mr. Hodges, who made the $70,000 out of the Penitentiary Contract, who is mighty loud in his professions of friendship for the colored people, but he has had one of them sent to the Penitentiary for a little petty theft, that would not have been noticed by a real true friend of the poor colored boy, whose ignorance, perhaps, was his only crime. But that is not all that Mr. Hodges is doing. He is working the Penitentiary convicts on good fat outside jobs, for which he gets well paid, on which the honest colored laborers of the city ought to be employed. And he is now trying to use his influence with the colored people to have officers elected in the city government that will give him the contracts for building bridges, and other public works, on which he will employ convict labor—to the great injury and prejudice of the honest colored laborers of the city. So far does Mr. Hodges carry his love for the "nigger" that instead of employing a good, honest colored girl as a house servant, we are credibly informed that he appropriates the services of one of the colored convicts for that purpose. And Mr. Hodges is the very King of the Radicals in this town! We wonder when our colored countrymen will have their eyes opened to the false professions of the Radical friends!

If our colored friends would turn their faces against these bad Radical demagogues, and vote for good honest true Republicans, as their leaders, we would soon have a good respectable party of whose doings we would not be ashamed, but until that is done we can expect nothing for our party that will reflect honor upon it or credit upon the state.

The Arkansas Freeman, Little Rock, October 5, 1869

Following the Civil War, labor organizing took on new forms among the newly freed black labor force, who envisioned a different role in the changing Reconstruction society. They saw in labor unions the possibility of overcoming the tradition of slavery and bettering their condition.

RADICALISM

. . . The organization of Labor; the Association of Laborers; the union of hearts and hands; these are the indispensable means for progress. These form the only practical Radicalism. Before these, the mists of Prejudice, both of color and of class, will vanish; and the "New Era" containing in it "both good hap and sorrow" will down upon our favored State. Let us move forward patiently and steadily to meet it.

The Tribune, New Orleans, October 4, 1864

As the country and the South particularly moved away from more radical forms of Reconstruction and favored Southern compromises, the black worker saw clearly that his own strength and unity were the bases of equality. Reflecting this combination of a new social structure with the philosophy of self-help is the following.

. . . We urge the colored laborer to organize his labor, to do it wisely, universally and consistently. We shall seek to illustrate the wisdom of the maxim that labor and capital is one when the laborer is not coerced and when capital is respected, and that therefore all profits should be mutually shared. . . . The pressing need of the hour is education. Seven generations of enforced ignorance and systematic robbery, together with moral degradation to which we have been subjected, make it necessary for we citizens to cast aside all scruples as to the use of public money for the support of non-proscriptive [integrated] schools and to overcome all personal prejudices, insuring the benefits of education. . . .

The New Era, Washington, D.C., January 13, 1870

As a result of discrimination against black workers by the National Labor Union (established in 1866), a separate black National Labor Union was formed in 1869 with Isaac Myers at its head. When the white union began to decline in the early 1870's, a Labor Reform Party was promoted, and an appeal was made to black workers for support. In the following letter to the state presidents of his union, Myers stated the reasons against such support.

In reply to the several communications addressed to us in relation to giving support to the Labor Reform party, we take the occasion to say that it is well understood by you that the Colored National Labor Union is not a political organization. The object for which it is organized, is to develop the intellectual and improve the material condition of its members. No political test is applied as a qualification to membership, yet we feel morally bound to give our support to that party whose principles and legislation conform to the interest of American labor.

The Labor Reform party has no connections whatever with our organization. It is not a national organization, nor indeed, can it be. If, by the organization of our Government, or the customs of society, there were established a permanent laboring class, then there would be a reasonable pretext; but no such condition of society exists. . . .

Never before in the history of the country have the working people received so large a remuneration for their labor, and been so prosperous and happy, for which we are especially indebted to the legislation of a Republican Congress in its policy of protection to American industry. By this policy there has been a steady and unprecedented development of the resources of the country, an increased demand for all kinds of labor, native and foreign, and better wages that is paid in any other part of the inhabited globe.

Nothing could be more disastrous, especially to the workingmen of the United States, than the financial and tariff dogma of the Democratic party. Whilst professing great friendship for the laboring classes, its legislation, when in power, has invariably been in the interest of a privileged few, against the development of home productions, but in aid of foreign manufacturers and workshops.

Under the policy of the National Administration of the Government, three-fourths of the workshops in the United States must be

closed and their million of honest, skillful workmen seek less remunerative employment or be forced back to the overcrowded workshops of
Europe. The prices of all labor, which would be thus placed in an unequal competition with foreign labor, would be reduced fifty percent,
while there could be no visible reduction in the prices of the necessar-
ies of life, house, rents, etc. Therefore your duty is plain. Cast our fortunes with the party whose record and aim is to make labor abundant
and remunerative, education universal and cheap, and to secure equal
and exact justice and equal rights to all the citizens of the United
States without distinction of race or color. That party is the Union
Republican party.

The New National Era, Washington, D.C., April 11, 1872

*Efforts to organize collective or cooperative farms among the freedmen
were part of the attempt at self-help, often against great obstacles. An
early example occurred in Colleton County, South Carolina, where thirteen years later the Knights of Labor were to find fertile ground for organizing. The information originally appeared in a paper published by them,
the Waterboro* News, *and was reprinted in several papers.*

. . . In this country the colored people own, and are successfully
conducting some of the largest plantations. This is done under a sort
of communism. A number of them, in some cases so many as fifty,
form themselves into a society, elect their officers and adopt by-laws.
They have regular meetings, at which the officers report, and a spe-
cified amount is paid into the treasury by each member. When sufficient is accumulated into the treasury, a suitable plantation is selected and the purchase made; usually the payments are in one, two,
and three years, a good portion being at the time of purchase. The
land is equally distributed by the officers elected for that purpose
among the members of the society, or so much as they wish to cultivate. Each is free to work as suits him, and each can dispose of his
crops as he deems proper. The only thing required is honesty and a
prompt payment of all dues, which are usually light. Anyone failing to
meet his dues, or convicted of dishonesty, has all amounts previously
paid by him for the purchase of the place to refund, and is required to
move off the plantation, all his rights and claims having been for-

feited. If, however, any one desires to leave the society he is paid all amounts paid by him toward the purchase and for all permanent improvements erected by him. No new member is admitted except by the consent of the whole society.

All sick are cared for by the society, if unable to care for themselves, officers being elected to look after such cases and report their wants to the society at its weekly meeting, or at special meetings, if the exigency of the case requires it. All disputes arising between members are brought before the society, a certain number of the officers being designated to hear and endeavor to amicably arrange all dissensions, and very seldom, if ever, they fail. Petty litigation—that is the great bane of the colored people in any section—is in this way avoided. These societies are principally formed from people who work for hire, fifty cents per day being the sum generally; the plantation is instantly bought as soon as sufficient funds are in the treasury to make the first payment; but few, if any, own animals in that time, their small resources being expended in the purchase, money and erection of houses. Still they have, in all cases where an exorbitant price was not paid for the land, proved successful, failures for a time occasionally arising where incompetent or unfaithful officers had been selected, but with their usual shrewdness, these incompetent officers were soon detected, and others more capable were selected in their place. Upon those that have been in operation three or four years the land has been paid for, and the members have acquired considerable personal property, and are generally prosperous. A sort of rivalry seems to spring up between them, which is productive of economy and thrift. These societies are located in the country east of the Savannah and Charleston Railroad. We do not presume to say that only the colored people who have formed themselves into these societies show thrift and the accumulation of property, for a number who, six or seven years ago, were not worth a dollar, now carry on successfully large rice and cotton plantations, and are becoming heavy taxpayers. But in the particular section in which these societies are formed more property exists among their members than among those who are fighting the battle of the life and death on their own account, while from the formation of these societies they are enabled to purchase more valuable property and secure greater privileges than they could if each laid his money out in a separate purchase, in which case ten or twenty acres or more of poor land would be all he would be able to buy, as no planter would consent to cut off and sell small tracts of his best land and retain himself the poorer portion. This is undoubtedly one of the reasons of their success, as on nearly all the plantations in this section a large portion of the land is almost valueless. By securing the whole plantation they obtain sufficient good land for their purposes, while he who purchases for himself generally gets such land that it is impossible to make more than a poor subsistence from.

The New National Era, Washington, D.C., September 25, 1873

Prejudice and discrimination faced the black worker in every aspect of American life, and one of its more effective forms was denying access to the apprentice system as a method of excluding black people from learning trades and professions.

. . . There is something in America, commonly called *prejudice* that so opposes the progress of the colored people, as to render it well nigh impossible for them to make any headway at all. . . .

We have a great number of young men that would like to become skilled workmen; but hardly can there be a locality picked out in the whole country where it is possible for the colored parent to get a mechanic on any terms whatever, to take his boy and learn him a trade. If you go to the brick mason or plasterer and try to get your boy in, he will tell you, yes we will take him to make mortar or carry brick; but we can't take and learn him the trade. And so, if he would learn any other trade he is refused—and the boy dispirited, comes to the conclusion that every avenue for his advancement is blocked. Yes, blocked by caste prejudice, and so with our young ladies. If an advertisement is read in our daily papers, that apprentices are wanted to learn dressmaking, or bonnet-making, or trimming, and a young colored lady makes application for the place, she is told that the *kitchen* is supplied with a cook and the main shop is only to be filled with white girls. If a clerk is wanted in a grocery house, or a dry goods store, and a young colored man of good education and pleasant address makes application for the place, he is told that they have a man on their delivery wagon now, and that behind the counter they have only white boys, not that their qualifications are not all sufficient, but their faces are not white enough, that's all. So there is in every avocation, except the lower ones in life. If we look at the educational advantages offered in most localities, we will find the same prejudice exists. . . .

The Colored Citizen, Fort Scott, Kansas, November 23, 1878

The following letter by Isaac Myers originally appeared in the Christian Recorder *of Philadelphia, the official organ of the AME Church. The* People's Advocate *moved from Alexandria, Virginia, to Washington, D.C., in 1877.*

A good deal has been said about the colored man having a "fair chance in the race of life," and it is very true that in everything and everywhere he has not a "fair chance." In all of the large cities there is a prejudice by the white mechanics against giving the colored mechanics a "fair chance." All branches of the trades are governed by rules and regulations which are so framed as to exclude the colored man. . . . Very few colored apprentices can be seen anywhere except as bootblacks or newsboys, and this makes us apprehensive of the future. . . . This prejudice against the colored man's "fair chance" in the trades, is confined exclusively to the middle and lower classes, and is of foreign birth. The Southern cities were built by colored mechanical labor. In this city 20 years before the late war, it was no unusual thing to find a majority of colored mechanics engaged in all the leading trades, and even where white men were employed it was generally under colored foremen. In cities further North, colored mechanics were in fair demand, and all who chose could get work at current wages, and in many instances were given them. But Irish emigration was destined to strike a blow at the colored mechanic from which it will take years for him to recover and regain his lost ground. Not because opportunity has not presented itself, but because of his lack of energy, and want of confidence and pluck. There are hundreds of mechanics scattered around in the different cities in the middle and northern states and we may say in nearly every prominent city in the Union working at common laborer work, at wages from $1.00 to $1.50 per day but should be at work as carpenters, bricklayers, plasterers, painters, etc. receiving wages from $3 to $4 per day. It cannot be said that "as a rule they are not good workmen" nor can it be truthfully said that their labor is not in demand. What is wanted is for them to

put themselves into a position where they can be got at by capitalists.
. . . Everywhere the white trades unions prohibit the admission of
colored men as members and white contractors, no matter how favorable, are prohibited from employing colored mechanics except under
rules laid down by these societies and as long as these organizations
prove effective, they will remain. No colored boys to take their place,
until finally the trades will pass out of their hand altogether and no
conditions of political parties can or will change this inevitable state
of affairs one whit. . . .

The People's Advocate, Washington, D.C., September 24, 1881

The colored laborers of Newberne, N.C. including stevedores,
dockhands, draymen, washerwomen, cooks, and nurses have formed
a Laborer's Union and agreed upon a regular scale of prices for work.
This is a good move. The shoemakers, painters, bricklayers, carpenters, plasterers, etc. of our own city would be wise to follow the example of our hod carriers. If they don't do it now, the time will come
when they are compelled to do it or go to the wall. Remember this!

The People's Advocate, Washington, D.C., October 1, 1881

*One of the earliest black cooperative movements is discussed in the fol-
lowing article. The company was formed by Isaac Myers as a result of the
exclusion of black laborers from work in the Baltimore shipyards in 1865.*

We take great pleasure in acknowledging the receipt of the annual
statement of the Chesapeake and Marine Railroad and Drydock
Company of Baltimore. The above named company was organized,
we believe in 1865—a time when the white caulkers and other dock-
yard hands organized against the colored men of like occupation—
and was the direct result of prejudice and hatred. The organization
has been conducted on wise and economical business principles, until
now it can show figures somewhat astounding to the colored people in
other cities. . . .

Now, the very class who opposed Negro labor are glad to be employed by the company . . . and we hope and predict that it soon will
be a great power in the matter of encouraging business enterprise

among the colored people and of great substantial benefit to its stock-holders. . . .

The People's Advocate, Washington, D.C., January 21, 1882

Perhaps the most exploited of the black working class were farm labor-ers, who were the subject of this observation.

. . . The colored men of South Carolina are not only defrauded of their right to vote, but they are only allowed 40–60¢ for a day's hard labor. They are taxed without representation and robbed of their hon-est toil without power of recourse in law or equity for redress. . . .

The Globe, New York, January 20, 1883

The sharecropping system was one of the many ways blacks were tied to the land in new forms of servitude. In the following article by "Le Duke," we observe the standard procedures.

. . . The *modus operandi* of the Tennessee Grangers is something like this; A colored farm hand or small farmer is hired by one of the Grangers* to cultivate said Granger's farm, say of 75 acres. The la-borer is furnished with stock and utensils necessary together with a sufficient quantity of provisions to run him from seed-time to harvest, *provided* said laborer will agree to give the Granger two-thirds of the entire yield. . . . The laborer is supplied with provisions but he is in-formed by the Granger that he, the Granger, is forced to pay 15% in advance of the usual cost on account of the great length of time be-tween purchase and settlement. In addition to this the colored laborer is informed that the Granger *ought* to have some little *consideration* for his zealous friendship in securing the above provisions at such a rea-sonable advance . . . which will amount to an advance of between 30 and 40% on provisions. Besides this, the Granger does all the figuring. The colored man is charged with everything and credited with noth-ing. If a pig dies or the wind blows the barn down and kills a sheep,

---

* The Grangers (1870–77) were one of the early farmers' associations (exclusively white) which emerged after the Civil War.

the colored man must pay for it, and if he dare question the farmers of the charge he is ordered off the farm, and the Justice of the Peace says he has violated the contract and cannot have his share of the crop. . . .

The People's Advocate, Washington, D.C., December 1, 1883

John Swinton, a Socialist editor in New York, had a great impact on T. T. Fortune. Swinton had fought alongside John Brown in Kansas and worked with Fortune when he went to the New York Sun.

In looking over the solemn collocation of labor strikes and the distresses of laboring men all over the country in the columns of *John Swinton's Paper* we find the following item:

> "The colored coal-wheelers of New Orleans struck for an advance of from $3.50 to $4.00 a day. White men are said to be willing to fill their places at $2.50, at least that is what the Associated Press says."

We have no doubt that the Associated Press is correct in its statement. There are, doubtless, an army of white laborers in New Orleans who would take the place of colored coal-wheelers, whether they were on strike or not at $2.50 per day. There is perhaps more unadulterated sycophancy and prejudice in labor unions than anywhere else in the country, not only between whites and blacks, but whites and whites as well. No other class on earth are so industrious as laboring men in making profession of undying devotion and fraternity to each other, and yet losing no opportunity to cripple any movement put on foot by their unions for the betterment of the condition of the whole member. Nor is it possible in any one branch of labor to get all the men to join and abide the dictation of a central head.

That there should be so much dissension and irresolution on the part of laboring men is natural. When a man is compelled to look to the day's labor for bread for his family as well as for himself he can't very well be expected to take sides with any movement which makes more hazardous the precarious means of his subsistence. Hence the failure of so many organizations in their efforts to force corporations like telegraph companies to make an honest division of the surplus of capital and labor. To this source can also be traced the inability of labor organizations to decide upon and pursue a given political program. Being dependent upon the labor of the day for fuel and food the laboring man is as absolutely the slave of his employer as was formerly the black slave of the South. Concert of action is utterly out of the case.

But the pretentions to harmony and mutual sympathy put forth by laboring men are worthy of remark only because they are never, because impossible to be, fulfilled. Take the demagogic agitation on the Pacific Coast which shut the industrious Chinaman out; take the labor organizations which prohibit by stringent rules the admission of colored men, principally of these the United Engineers Association, which declares in so many words that none but white men shall enjoy membership or benefit of the association; take the hostility to colored printers which exists in this city, and of the viciousness of which we were at one time made to feel the full force—all this goes to show how hopelessly the laboring men are disunited. It is almost an impossibility to find a colored carpenter or mason in this city, and we venture to state that the employment of one on any building in course of construction here would produce instantly a strike of all the white laborers. Thus labor is hopelessly arrayed against itself.

We remember a conversation we had with John Swinton, in the course of which the striking coal miners of West Virginia and Ohio were referred to, and the question of colored men taking the places of white miners was strongly condemned. That, too, when the white miners refuse to accept colored miners into their labor associations. Of course Mr. Swinton, who is intensely loyal to the laboring man's interest (and we claim also to be loyal to their interest) will condemn in proper spirit any such underbidding on the part of white laborers as is indicated in the item of news which we take from the columns of his excellent paper. If unanimity is necessary to the success of any movement, surely labor unions stand most in need of it. If corporations are to be kept within an honest division of the net proceeds of capital and labor it can only be done by a thorough union of all labor forces honestly directed.

The Globe, New York, January 26, 1884

Against the background of increased labor organization and unrest sweeping the country (including farm labor in the South) and the failure of the political parties to include black citizens in a significant role, T. Thomas Fortune was one of the earliest (and few) black editors to recommend the formation of a new political party. He saw the possibility of such a party, organized along class lines and based on the interests of workingmen and women, as the vehicle of reform. This radical departure from traditional allegiances of black people to the Republican Party, however, met with opposition, and a few years later, Fortune advocated the formation of a self-protective pressure group, the Afro-American League.

. . . There are "new forces" in our politics which cry aloud for organized action and agitation. The oppression by the money power of the masses; the denial of rights which lie at the roots of our institutions; the venality of legislators, and the pliability of the interpreters of the laws—all of these things imperatively show the necessity of organized resistance.

The time is fast approaching when something must be done to stay the onward march of organized robbery and general misgovernment, or we will fall to the horrors of irretrievable ruin and misery which afflict the people of the old world.

The colored people of the United States have a peculiar interest in the creation of a new party which shall champion the rights of all—in the granting of more of the immunities of a civil government, and in the easement of the enormous burdens placed upon labor by onerous taxation and unjust laws enacted in the special interest of capital, to defraud labor of its just proportion of its production of wealth. The future warfare in this country will be based upon resistance to landed aristocracy and money sharks to whom the servants of the people have granted unjust franchises.

The laboring men of the South, the North, and the West, have a common cause, and they will yet present a solid front to the masterful forces which press them down, will yet stand in solemn array against the men who revel in luxury while labor, the wealth creating power, shivers in the March winds and dies by the wayside. . . .

The Globe, New York, April 5, 1884

A meeting in Louisville, Kentucky, was perhaps indicative of some tentative forms of alliances that were forming. The Hod Carriers, a predomi-

*nantly black union, was to form a strong basis for black union organiz-
ing.**

. . . The white laborers' union came to their milk at last. Sunday
August 9th. they held a joint session at Beck's Hall. At that meeting
there was a resolution adopted, with but a few dissenting votes to
admit colored mechanics of all trades to join them. This enables them
in the case that there were a general strike to command respectable
wages for their wives and children, who have heretofore suffered on
account of disorganization and obnoxious color line that has for so
many years impeded both the white and colored man's progress in the
past. The motto of the labor's union in the future, will be united we
stand, divided we fall. The most important business transaction was
the adoption of a resolution giving representation to all organized
bodies of working men regardless of color, creed, or previous condition of servitude. The object of this was to secure the admittance of
the Hod Carriers Union, an organization which is necessarily a part of
the Brick Layers Union. The Hod Carriers Union has between 200
and 300 members. . . .

The Freeman, New York, August 22, 1885

*The Knights of Labor represent a turning point in the history of labor
organization in their attempt to include black people and their outspoken
advocacy of equality. They were the first to aid in the organization of
rural Southern blacks, and though failing in this because of white opposition, they laid the groundwork for the Colored Farmers' Alliance which
was to soon follow. Their idealism and militancy, however, may have
aroused some apprehensions.*

The agitators who have been over-officious in their attempts to
commit the Knights of Labor to a socialistic policy and who have attempted to use the Order for purposes outside of labor reform have
evidently gone too far. All class movements attract great attention for
a time and the hope of the rank and file, the ambition of the leaders,

---

* In order to capitalize on racial tensions, employers hired blacks (or used black convicts) when whites struck and used whites (often immigrants) to break strikes by blacks.
Black workingmen realized this and called for a united labor movement, but whites
were unable to overcome their prejudices.

and the scheming talent of the hangers-on, contribute to make the interests something like enthusiasm. But in a country where independent thinking is encouraged, and where independent action is regarded as an adjunct of manliness, it is almost impossible to bring the uneducated under autocratic rule.

Some of the leaders in the Knights of Labor organizations have read the signs of the time aright, and have spoken their warning. These are the real friends of the organization and of labor reform, but there are other men, heartless as to the interests of the laborer and eminently selfish in the use that is to be made of the machinery of the organization. These men hope to use the Knights of Labor in a campaign, well-knowing that after the Order has been so used it will be greatly injured. They care nothing however for the interests of the order, but are wrapped up in the objects which they hope to accomplish by using it boldly and unscrupulously.

The Weekly Pelican, New Orleans, January 22, 1887

An example of the kind of equality that seemed to exist within the Knights of Labor is related by a correspondent from Monongahela City, B. W. Grinage.

. . . The Order has many colored members and the white members seem to be proud of their dark-skinned brothers and take particular pains to show them that they are welcome to that high and honorable body. For they have recognized the undoubted fact that without the aid of the colored man it would be a hard thing indeed for the miner, the mechanic, and laborer to offset the power of capitalists. The colored man has also become cognizant of the fact that he has an equal right with his white brother to demand and receive proper and just remuneration for his labor. There seems to be a tendency among some men of our race to look at everything pertaining to union of the two races with a prejudicial gaze, thereby making the color line stronger; and by talking and writing about things that they know little or nothing about, are helping to build up instead of tearing down that black line, Prejudice, that has been the bain of our race for years. And until such men learn that it is by our own grand efforts to a great extent that this line is gradually being eradicated, it will be much better for them to let their tongues rest and their pens rust. The Knights of Labor of this place has 18, or 20 members of color, none of which have been treated with anything but the greatest respect by their white brother members, and the number is increasing rapidly. . . .

The Gazette, Cleveland, February 20, 1886

In a letter originally written for the Detroit Plaindealer, *Jere Brown, a member of the Carpenters and Joiners Union of Cleveland and represent- ative in the Ohio legislature, defended the Knights.*

. . . In this organization which is subordinate to the National or- ganization, there are several colored members and no distinction has ever been shown in the election to offices, obtaining employment, sick and death benefits, etc. There are in Cleveland many colored men who are mechanics, and with a very few exceptions they are members of the particular organization formed in the interest of their trade. Bricklayers, plasterers, blacksmiths, cigarmakers, machinists, molders, etc., have as members in each of their unions colored men. In the Knights of Labor there are colored men also; and to my certain knowledge in one local assembly, organized a few years ago, a colored man was a charter member. For years I have been importuned to enter into the formation of an assembly to be composed exclusively of colored men, but have persistently refused, believing as I do in mixing and not in isolating and ostracizing ourselves, thereby fostering and perpetuating the prejudice as existing today. At no time since my resi- dence in our "Forest City" over 16 years, do I recall one instance where white laborers have refused to work with the colored co-labor- ers, while I do not say that such instances have not occurred, its hap- pening in labor organizations, certainly they would have come to my knowledge. On the 26th. day of January, there convened in the city of Columbus, the "State Trades and Labor Assembly of Ohio." A dele- gate to that assembly was a colored man, Robert Gray, Esq., a resi- dent of Akron, O., by occupation a bricklayer and a member of the union in that city. There was no doubt as to his genuineness as his dis- tinctive color precluded that. In a conversation with the gentleman I learned that he had occupied every station in the local organization, from the lowest to the highest, and that no distinction was or ever had been shown him on account of his color. . . . That there were no such distinctions either thought, or sanctioned by these organizations in any manner; that if they did exist it was of a local nature and totally at variance with the principles of labor unions. . . . In my immediate vicinity no trouble exists as to gaining admission into shops, factories, and other branches of the trades a young man desires to enter. If our youths prefer to enter into the professions in preference to the trades, we can not shape their course otherwise but by teaching them the folly of it. . . . There is no influence that will be a greater lever to eradicate all prejudices that may exist than the influence of *education, organization and agitation.* But no separate organizations can effect what we desire to accomplish; for as we are a component part of this great government, we *must* have accorded to us such treatment as other citizens have, which can only be attained by persistent agitation and intermingling. If one applies for admission either as a member of an organization or for an apprenticeship in a workshop, let him not be discouraged by one refusal, but continue, and his aim will eventually be accomplished. . . .

. . . my advice is summed up in a few words: Educate the children; teach them their duties as citizens; that they are inferior to no other race on the face of the globe; to always assert their manhood at all times and places; that all labor is honorable, and that it is far more preferable to be a mechanic than to occupy any menial position.

The Gazette, Cleveland, February 20, 1886

The demand for land and the stress on labor unity and organization are reflected in these three letters, originally published in the Detroit Plaindealer.

. . . The colored laborers should not allow themselves to be placed in an antagonistic position towards the laboring classes of other races, unless the hostility and opposition of those classes make such a course on their part, a necessity.

We all know it to be a fact that labor oganizations, in many parts of the country, among the whites, do not recognize the meritorious claims of colored people. Why? That race prejudice has something to do with it cannot be truthfully denied, but this, in my opinion, is not the principle reason. Less than a quarter of a century ago the colored people of this country had no political, social or industrial status. The laboring people of that race represented, at that time, contrary to their own wishes, it is true, opposition to free, intelligent and remunerative labor. This was one of the principal causes of the late civil war—the war between free and slave labor. The colored laborers were justly looked upon, at that time, and consequently unjustly looked upon in many localities now, as a degraded and servile class. It is the present duty of the colored people to do whatever is necessary to eradicate this erroneous impression. Let them impress the white laborers with the fact that while they are not disposed to antagonize their interests, and are determined not to do so, unless it becomes a necessity, yet they insist upon justice for themselves—a right to an equal participation in the enjoyment of the fruits of honest and well paid labor.

I do not wish to be understood as endorsing all the means that are employed by some labor organizations to secure a recognition of the justice of their claims. Lawlessness should never be countenanced or encouraged. The laboring people of the country can, in my opinion, through organization and cooperation, secure for themselves the just rewards of labor without resorting to any methods that cannot be sanctioned by the most law abiding people of the community. . . .

JOHN R. LYNCH, [Speaker of House, Mississippi, 1872; Congressman from Mississippi, 1873–1877, 1882–1883] Washington, D.C.

In discussing the labor problem and the Negro's connection therewith we must first confess in the question of labor as with politics we rail against abstractionists in the way of our advancement, while the fault is largely our own; do we take instant hold of our advantages?

We are the unskilled labor of the country, and unskilled labor is a close ally to pauperism; pauperism is a communist, and it is into this condition that the customs, discriminations and injustice of the white race is forcing us. It has been the unwritten law of the land that color disqualifies a man for positions that involve master minds and trained hands, and it is as absurd as the principles of prejudice which debar the Negro from acquiring that sort of protection and education; it is tyrannous and barbaric, as well as injurious to the economies, political and moral.

In the South the Negro will first find a general sympathy for his legitimate advancement, and a personal interest in his prosperity and well being. The Negro question in the North is merely a theoretical one, which cannot be appreciated by those of the South where the same is practical. In the North the Negro is a sentiment, and illegitimate political agitation has been the bane of the race. In the South, he is the most important part of the daily life and labor of the country; having interests in common with the white race and bound to it by many ties of friendship, obligation and consanguinity. The educated Southern people almost as a whole feel the heartiest desire for the moral and industrial elevation of the Negro, and are doing all they can to promote the same. They have studied carefully the moral of the census of 1880.

. . . We by our votes make at least three congressmen, hold the balance of power in this State. Why not use it? And taking the whole country through what can we not do? We could force a recognition of all our wants. Let an organization patterned after the Knights of Labor be formed, and every colored man North and South join it and give it the full weight of his confidence and labor, and if this combination be true to each other force each of the great political parties to accede us our rights.

Although we may not at first come up to the highest standard as political and labor revolutionists, it will open the way for more advanced positions in the future, this may not be all we desire, but it is in the right direction, and if such a movement is supported by us solidly it will eventually lead us to all which we desire. As a means of enforcing recognition of us politically and industrially it is perhaps all that is necessary. . . .

C. Fare Martin, Dowagiac, Michigan

The industrial destiny of the Negro in America is a question of vast moment. Compared with it his position as regards politics appears as nothing. In fact the political importance of any class of citizens in a republic is but an exponent of their intellectual, material and, I had almost said, moral condition. Like all great questions this presents many phases. To one of these not yet touched upon, I wish to call attention. I refer to the Negro's relation to the land. Whatever I may say, the importance of this division of the question will be at once perceived.

Land is that from which all labor finally draws support. It is, moreover, as indispensable to our existence itself as the air we breathe. It follows, then, that whatever renders the acquisition of land by all men difficult, or whatever makes the condition of life hard for the producer who tills the land, is a manifest injustice. America with her millions of broad acres has not yet felt the need of offering a solution for the land problem—the problem of the age. But today not a small part of our race is groaning under a system of rent which allows the products of labor to be appropriated almost as effectually as did slavery itself. So long as this continues the race as a whole can make no permanent advancement.

The Negro's position in the United States has always been, and still is, anomalous. His being received as a slave was a satire upon the love of freedom of those who early sought these shores; his continued bondage gave the lie to the Declaration of Independence; his unredressed wrongs today make a mockery of the governments' boasted strength to enforce its laws. In short, of all the many ingredients that enter into this nondescript broth of humanity called the American people, the Negro alone seems to be indissoluble.

But despite the fact that the black race appears now like an excrescence on the body politic, it is nevertheless an integral part. Here in America the Negro is; here he will remain, to be an honor or disgrace as he puts forth his own efforts, and as wholesome aid in everything that pertains to good citizenship is rendered or withheld. Furthermore, the South is the stage on which his destiny is to be accomplished. An individual influence of schools, of journals, and of men may flow out from the North; but in the South the development of the race as a whole is to be wrought out. This idea of a separate nationality many good men among us, I know, hold we must discard. And, indeed, there exists no physical cause that prevents the free intercourse between, and the amalgamation of the African and Caucasian races. But the Negro bears on his face "clear, instantaneous and irrefragible evidence" of his servile origin, which alone is the cause of all the prejudice against him. And it will take generations before such evidence shall be dissociated from this degrading circumstance. So that we do well to keep in view the special needs of our distinct existence.

Nor can it be said that all legislative acts directed to the sole benefit of the Negro should be regarded by us with disfavor. There is one race in the United States for whose good special legislation is enacted.

Now, I hold that the Negro's claim to governmental aid is juster than that of the indian. The latter, it is true, has been robbed of his country, to develop which he had done comparatively nothing; but the former still remains unrequited for generations of ceaseless toiling. More than this, the Nation itself was responsible for the existence of slavery; and when the freed slave was endowed with the rights of citizenship, the Nation assumed the grave responsibility of making him a good citizen. How is the nation discharging it?

Whether the ills of the land-toilers here are to be remedied, as some suggest, by giving to each "three acres and a cow," or, according to the plan of others, by having the government purchase land and resell it on easy terms to the laborer, matters little. That the necessity of applying some adequate remedy is seen in all. So if "the mule and forty acres" are not secured, a chance of acquiring the ownership of the soil ought to be given the Negro. Is such a scheme Utopian? Could it find lodgement only in the brain of a visionary? I believe not. "The great soul of the world is just" says Carlyle. In spite of their greed a high sense of justice exists among the American people. Nor do I believe that they will perpetuate the shame of a "Century of Dishonor" in their treatment of the Indian by another in their treatment of the Negro.

John F. Jackson, Ripley, Ohio
The Freeman, New York, March 13, 1886

The use of convict-lease labor presented problems to both black and white workers. The author of this letter, W. A. Pledger, was the editor of the Atlanta Defiance.

Nearly all of our bricks are made by convicts; the coal we use is dug out by convicts; our railroads are built by convicts, and now that the demand for convicts for building railroads, digging out coal and making brick is not up to the ability of the jail to supply, lessees are running large farms. So you see, it is not probable that it is necessary to trump up charges now to get convicts since we have plenty from the back stock. . . . The ante-bellum landlord has not forgot his hatred for manual labor, nor has he forgotten his love for money and he is not slow to acquiesce in anything that turns in any manner to re-establish the prior-to-the-war customs and usages, and especially so when the privilege of lording it over a few Negroes is involved. . . . The poor white man is joining his brother in black in the organization of labor societies—such as the Knights of Labor—and great changes may be expected. While I regret that the Negro should be in organizations that antagonize capital, yet if capital has not the foresight after admonition to look for itself it is no fault of mine and yours.

The Freeman, New York, March 13, 1886

The Knights of Labor were increasingly viewed by black workers, especially urban workers, as the realization of their own strength and as a vehicle for achieving equality. In this editorial, T. Thomas Fortune reflects the enthusiasm shared by many.

All the world as far as this country is concerned appears to have gone mad after the Knights of Labor. . . . The Knights have sprung into power like a young giant. Only a few years ago and the wailings of the toilers of the land were poopoohed by the press and unheeded by the politicians while the lords of capital smiled in their sleeves at complaints and demands which seemed so utterly absurd as to warrant no serious reflection. In the last Presidential election the vote of the labor party was such a very small thing as actually to have been lost in the great stack of votes polled by the two national parties. How will it be in the future? The power of the leaders of the labor unions as demonstrated during the past six months puts an entirely new phase on this aspect of the matter. Labor has heretofore been powerless simply because it was a disorganized leaderless mass. Now it is organized; now it has masterful leadership. At the nod of an authorized person, thousands of men in every line of industry desert their posts of duty and simply paralyze the productive and carrying agencies of the country. Before this organized power capital, even the great body of the people, is as powerless as labor once was.

Political economists have for years snarled at the proposition that labor was the productive and capital the nonproductive force in our sociology, and that when labor ceased to produce capital would wither into the elements out of which it was delved. But the events of the past few months have gone very far towards vindicating the tenability of the proposition. The political economist of the future will have largely to reconstruct this glaring heresy before he has a correct premise upon which to predict his deductions and conclusions.

To become an invincible power the Knights of Labor have wisely concluded to enlist the support of all grades of labor, barring out no nationality except that of the Chinese. Hence colored men all over the Union are rapidly becoming affiliated with the organization. For instance the colored waiters of New York have formed a strong assembly of the Knights of Labor, and meet Thursday every week at Garnet Hall, and some of the ablest speakers of the Central organization are present to instruct them in the requirements of the parent Union. In most other branches of labor colored men are affiliated with white organizations, not being strong enough to form a separate assembly. We predicted this result a year ago in the book we published under the title of "Black and White," but we did not expect so speedy a consummation of the prediction then made.

We do not hesitate to say that we fear the conflict which must result from organized capital on the one hand, and organized labor on the other. The gravity of such conflict is correctly estimated by those more directly interested pro and con. We believe in that absolute justice which it is so very difficult to secure in either the social or political relations of men. Tyranny in some one of its multiform variations, seems far more natural in the practice than equity. It therefore almost reduces itself to a choice between the tyrants we shall have, and of which of them is the safer. For centuries we have had the tyranny of capital, and an odious and unjust tyranny it has been, and if we are to have the tyranny of labor we shall after awhile be in position to judge which of them is the more odious, which the more conducive to the happiness of the greatest number and to the general progress of the race.

After all it is a matter of how far forth the masses shall share with the capitalistic oligarchs and sharks the interest of the fruits of labor— whether the fellow who develops the gold mine shall sleep on a board and eat pone cake and hog, while the fellow who claims to own the mine, but does not work it, shall sleep in a palace and fill his stomach with caramels and ice cream.

The revolution is upon us and since we are largely of the laboring population it is very natural that we should take sides with the labor forces in their fight for juster distribution of the results of labor. We cannot afford to stand off from or to antagonize the army under whose banners we labor in the common lot of toil. We do not make conditions. All we can do is to fall into line on the right or left, and which side it shall be will depend entirely upon whether we are a capitalist or a laborer.

The Freeman, New York, March 20, 1886

The most serious problem threatening a black-white coalition was the use of black workingmen as strikebreakers. The call for a strike always raised the possibility that blacks, often denied the opportunity to work under any other conditions, would take the openings and confront white workers. In reply to an editorial in a white paper urging blacks to take the jobs of white strikers, the editor warned against such action.

. . . We lay down dogmatically that the colored laborers cannot afford to antagonize the interests of white laborers, for the interests of the one and the other are identical in every particular. They are inseparably yoked together by a common lot of toil. We venture to say that no class of our population has been more systematically wronged, outraged, and robbed than the colored laborer. Capital from the earliest period of American history has crushed out his life and thrown his mutilated carcass to the vulture crows. . . .

. . . Attempting to persuade colored men to place themselves in direct antagonism to organized labor as against organized capital would hurry the race into untold misfortunes, not the least of which would be the few broken bones that would follow an attempt of colored men to take the places of white strikers.

The fact of the matter is that trades unions in every department of industry are holding out the olive branch to colored men. The invitation to affiliate with these has gone forth far and wide, and is being accepted on every hand, as it should be. The hour is at hand when the wage workers of all races are organizing for the purpose of forcing a more reasonable distribution of the products of labor. Can we afford anywhere to antagonize such effort? Are we to spurn the offers to cooperate being held out to us? Are our interests with those of labor or with those of capital?

We must not get on the wrong side of this labor fight, just now begun in earnest, and which promises to be the absorbing question during the next ten years. We repeat, we cannot afford to get on the wrong side of the fight. The black man who arrays himself on the side of capital as against labor would be like a black man before the war taking sides with the pro-slavery as against the anti-slavery advocates.

In the North, we grant, we are largely barred out of the industrial pursuits of the character now striking for justice and fair play, but every year the way is becoming smoother for us. Prejudice on the part of white workmen is steadily softening; so that if we pursue the proper policy in the present complications, a few years hence we will have but little to complain of on this score. But the condition in the South is altogether different. We do the bulk of the skilled and manual labor of that section . . . nothing short of a potentiality like the Knights of Labor can ever force Southern capitalists to give their wage workers a fair percentage on the results of their labor. If there is any power on earth which can make the white Southern employers of labor face the music it is organized white and black labor, with the labor power of the Nation to sustain it. The Knights of Labor should "carry the war into Africa," so to speak, for nowhere else in the Union is labor more systematically shorn of its dignity and just remuneration than in the South.

We do not here enter into a discussion of trades unionism and its inevitable tendency; nor the injustice of the boycott, nor the absurdity of the claim of trades unions that employers shall employ only such men as belong to their organizations. These questions are not lawful weapons, and encroach disastrously upon the freedom of the citizen. But that labor has as much right to organize for its protection and advantage as has capital admits of no discussion. It is for the people to see that organized labor does not encroach upon the liberty of the citizen in its efforts to protect itself and secure such advantage as it is justly entitled to. These are purely incidental questions. The main question for colored laborers to consider is: Can they afford to array themselves against organized labor as in favor of organized capital? We maintain that they cannot.

The Freeman, New York, May 1, 1886

Mistrust toward blacks who were forced to break strikes and the refusal of white workers to work alongside them put black workmen in a "heads I win, tails you lose" dilemma. Many saw the only hope in separate black unions as strikes increased during this period and white unions resisted integration.

. . . There is one striking feature, however, of these strikes. . . . It is the utter dependence of our colored union men upon the disposition of the whites. For instance, the hod carriers, who are for the most part colored, by reason of the dissatisfaction of the bricklayers, were forced, by their dependence, to join the strike, notwithstanding the wages they were receiving was quite satisfactory. As for colored bricklayers, plasterers, and the like, they have not taken any considerable part in the strikes. This grows out of the fact that they have not been invited. These colored bricklayers and plasterers, in order to insure the proper performance of their labor, must depend entirely upon colored hod carriers. But these hod carriers, by reason of their regulations and their dependence upon the whites, are forced to ignore the demands of colored mechanics, and the consequence is a corresponding disadvantage to the colored mechanic. Moreover, were the colored hod carriers less allied with the whites and were there a stronger attachment on their part to the colored journeymen and mechanic, should the whites strike for unreasonable demands, an opportunity would be offered to colored mechanics whereby they could monopolize the trade which would greatly benefit to both, mechanic and unskilled laborer. But as it is, the colored mechanic and colored common laborer must suffer together, notwithstanding the one is not entitled to the benefits, while from the other is withheld wages which he deems satisfactory. As we said before, our sympathies are with the working classes; but they are first of all with the colored laborer which is being discriminated against and crushed wherever it is possible and made dependent when it can be treated no worse.

Now the question which occurs to us is, cannot something be done which will unite all colored labor into one strong fraternity with the view to establishing an importance and a power which will either force the white Unions to open wide their doors, or enable sub-fraternities to stand independently of the white striker? The attitude of the colored laborer in this country is simply humiliating. Trained mechanics and willing workers are told that they cannot join a Union formed ostensibly for the purpose of protecting labor and for defending itself against the impositions and tyranny of capital. Would it not be wiser to stand aloof and attract attention and sympathy by filling up the breaks which these strikes occasion, rather than manifest undue sympathy for a movement which in practice operates against the interests of colored labor? The time has come when the colored laborer must look to himself for protection. It is unreasonable in the view of past history, to suppose that the whites will show any very great interest in our material welfare and unless we begin to form counter forces to those which the whites are forming against us, we will find ourselves gradually growing weaker and weaker until, having no power to defend, we will succumb and be forced to occupy those grades of labor which are unremunerative and which the whites decline to perform. When we consider our dependence upon our labor, we cannot fail to see the importance of striving to protect it, and of encouraging alliances which will tend to strengthen and develop it. Let us have a consolidated Colored Craftsmen's Protective Union and see what by earnest effort wisdom and fraternal co-operation can be accomplished.

Strikes are good things for the whites because they are benefited; they will become beneficial to us only when we manifest a disposition to oppose discrimination and determine to protect ourselves.

The Bee, Washington, D.C., May 8, 1886

There are numerous instances when black unions did take independent action as part of the labor movement in demanding equality, as indicated by the following report from Louisville, Kentucky.

Mr. J. S. Woods, president of the Hod Carrier's Union, told me that I was misinformed about the hod carriers taking part in the parade of May 1. Said he: "There were only four of our members in the procession, out of 275, and they are the only four of our Union who belong to the Knights of Labor. The Knights of Labor sent a committee to wait upon our Union asking us to adopt their charter as our own. We inquired if they would concede the right of apprenticeship to our children and admit those of us who are mechanics to full membership in all of their different lodges, allow us to work upon the same scaffold together as their brother?"

Said he: "What reply do you think that committee gave us? The chairman of that committee told our Union that these questions would be an after consideration. Isn't that proof that the Knights of Labor intend to use the colored man as a tool? Suppose our Union had accepted the proposition, without asking them for equal rights?

We would have been duped into a second slavery. Further than that the Negroes are barred out of the machine shops, the factories, off of railroad engine and all other mechanical doors are closed against him controlled by the Knights of Labor."

I asked Mr. Woods if the Hod Carriers' Union was a secret organization? "No, sir," was his answer, "but the Knights of Labor and trade unions are. I have no objections to any secret orders that do justice to all nationalities alike."

He asked me if I had ever heard of a colored society being boisterous in the strikes of 1877 and 1878. The few colored men who took part were hunted down, arrested, tried, punished in the courts and kept out of employment by the same white working men who inaugurated the strikes. There were several colored unions that did not turn out May 1. Among them the Teamster's Union, which number 200 and over; the Coachman's Union, 160 strong; Hotel Waiters, Butlers and a number of others that would have added a thousand more to the procession.

The Trades Unions or the Knights of Labor cannot succeed as long as the color line exists. Mr. Wood said: "We are well aware of that and there is an agreement among all the colored Unions of this city to stand aloof from all white labor organizations that refuse to recognize us as their brother. These white organizations must concede all rights to the colored man themselves. When they do this then the Hod Carriers' Union will unite with them."

The Freeman, New York, May 15, 1886

It would appear that the Knights of Labor (at least in the South) had other activities, as indicated by one of the most militant prophetic black spokesmen, Bishop Henry M. Turner, the author of the following letter.*

For a generation or more the battle over the centralization of the power of the Government has raged with unabated vigor. . . . The

* Henry McNeal Turner was born on February 1, 1834. He learned to read at the age of fifteen. He worked in a law office, studied Greek, Latin, and Hebrew, and in 1860 was ordained in the AME Church. He was the first black man appointed a chaplain in the Army (by Lincoln in 1863). He was a delegate to the Georgia Constitutional Convention in 1867 and a member of the state legislature in 1868. From 1880 to 1892 he was bishop of his church for Georgia and chancellor of Morris Brown College in Atlanta. He visited Africa a number of times and introduced Methodism there. He died on May 8, 1915.

ghosts of State rights, State sovereignty and State commonwealth, with all the hair splitting theories with which fancy and imagination would environ them, have been harked up from the tombs again and again, lest the rising generations should come to a conclusion that we had a government able to protect itself and citizens, and not a mere social States union which did not amount to a farce or a hill of beans. They have whittled in one way and another at our Government until it is not a decent sham. Then to crown the farce, that conclave of human asses in Washington City, known as the United States Supreme Court, have decided that protection of life, liberty and property is beyond the province of the General Government. Hence bands of night "marauders," cavalcades of bloody banded roughs, to shoot down innocent men in the temple of justice. Knights of Labor with torch aflame in hand, to fire the houses and scatter ruin and destruction broadcast in the land, are allowed to stride the Nation and leave hell itself in their wake, while no one by the authority of the General Government can say, "what doest thou?" Such is the state of things existing in our country. Thus revolution, anarchy, blight stare us in the face every day we live. It is only a question of time when this Nation will tumble to pieces and be rent into fragments. I have seen it coming for 10 years. No nation can long exist, that is held together by a mere rope of sand. The blood of thousands which cries to Heaven for vengeance upon an impotent Government, will surely be answered as there is a God in Heaven to answer. This may appear to some as ephemeral, or visionary, but it's coming, yes it's coming. But the question may be asked, why have the legislators and judiciary of the country been so foolish as to whittle the power of the Nation down to such a condition? I can answer. It has been done to put the Negro out of the protection of the General Government, so that the States would have supreme control of his life and person. Done in their efforts to prevent or destroy centralization or power in the General Government, the whites have placed it beyond their own reach. The Knights of Labor have the right to shoot down every Government officer in the land who dares meddle or interfere with them in the least. . . . There is no power that can reach them but the States, and it does not matter what they do, the General Government is powerless to interfere. Let them fire cities, kill men by the hundreds, pillage and do whatever they please, only the States can say stop. And if the Knights submit to anything else, they are fools. If I were a Knight, and an offi officer of the General Government were to get in my way, I would have him to one side so fast he would think that lightning had struck him. Who ever heard of a Nation that could not protect its own inhabitants before; yet such a Government or national conglomeration is the so-called United States. All brought about, too, just to defect the possibility of recognizing rights and giving some protection to them while the subject was black. . . .

The Gazette, Cleveland, June 5, 1886

Organizing black workers in the South was, at best, a dangerous task —but necessary and highly successful. The source for the following article is listed simply from the Leader, *which probably (but not necessarily) refers to the* National Leader, *published in Washington, D.C.*

Early in the progress of the strike last spring upon the Texas and Pacific Railroad, the Knights of Labor in the southwest discovered that many Negroes were obtained without much difficulty to do the work which they had supposed must be done by themselves if at all. Soon afterward a dispatch from some point on the Gould system [Union Pacific] Texarkana, we think it was, stated that the colored men of Western Arkansas were being organized as Knights of Labor. It was added that the movement was exciting "grave apprehension." Now it appears that the landowning class of whites are in a painful state of excitement in that region, owing to the turbulent strike of certain colored Knights working on two or three plantations. In the end, this strike may amount to much or little, probably the latter judging by yesterday's dispatches, but it is still an extremely interesting suggestion. It needs only a passing glance at the possibilities of the organization of the colored laborers of the South as Knights of Labor to convince any intelligent person that the most tempestuous industrial disturbances of the last 6 months in the North may be totally cast in the shade before long by greater disturbances in the former slave states. First of all, the grievances of the colored laborers of the south, especially those who work on plantations, are much greater than any of which northern working men complain. The truck system of payment, the renting out of convicts, and the ingenious devices whereby the tiller of the soil is kept always in debt to its owner, make the condition of a large part of the southern Negroes, little better than slavery, and their social and political oppression adds its weight to their crushing burdens. Desperate diseases are often met by a resort to desperate remedies, and in that fact lies one reason why the Knights of Labor movement among the colored laborers of the South may cause startling results. Another very significant point is the intolerance with which any organized effort on the part of the Negroes to coerce or resist the employing class will surely be met. The guilty conscience of the South told its dominant class before slavery fell, and tells them still, that there are crimes against the colored race which the wildest carnival of rapine and slaughter will hardly avenge. This alone is enough to make the white capitalists recoil in terror and rage from any organization which may embolden and strengthen the Negro race. The authors of political, social and industrial oppression are never inclined to deal quietly and reasonably with anything which seems likely to make an end to that oppression and possibly punish it besides. And it must be admitted, on the other hand, that the Negro laborers of the South are possibly very unfit as yet to use the power of an organization like the Knights of Labor prudently, wisely and justly. During the existence of slavery they were without any semblance of organization, a fact which was largely the cause of their quiet submission to great wrongs. . . . If the Southern Negroes, finding themselves for the first time in a powerful organization which promised them the pecuniary support of hundreds of thousands of white men, besides that of their own race, and should be intoxicated to the point of serious mistakes and wrongs, it would not be at all surprising, and herein lies another highly significant feature of the situation in Arkansas. At every turn the natural friction between employers and labor organizations is sure to be so complicated and intensified by race feelings, old fears and hates and by the differences both social and political which do not exist in the North, that the Southern whites may well look with apprehension upon the spread of the Order of the Knights of Labor among the colored people of the section, and yet it may prove in the end the long-sought wedge which shall split the solid South industrially, socially, and politically.

The Gazette, Cleveland, July 17, 1886

But the editor of the Gazette, *a staunch supporter of labor organization, urged greater alliance to the Knights within integrated unions.*

. . . We especially call the attention of our southern exchanges to it and request them to advise our brethren to organize lodges of Knights of Labor *at once.* . . . Those in the North, where there is a possibility as in Northern Ohio should unite with the white lodges and thereby refrain from drawing a color line. . . . Then the one great boon so desirable among our people, UNISON, is obtained in such organization. With the assistance of the thousands of colored educators scattered throughout the South the standard of the lodges of colored Knights of Labor of the South will, to say the least, compare most favorably with that of the white Knights of Labor of our western country. . . .

The Gazette, Cleveland, July 17, 1886

A different view of the strike was taken by T. T. Fortune, who saw in the organized struggle of black workers the possibility of an end to oppression and real social transformation.

Last week there was an uprising of colored men (who are Knights of Labor) on a large plantation in Arkansas, and for some time very serious trouble was feared. These colored farm laborers struck for higher wages.

There were only a few hundred of these colored men, and yet they threw the entire country into a state of nervous excitement. A large number of planters immediately removed their families without the vicinity of the trouble; and frantic appeals were made to the county and State authorities to put down the strikers, before any violence was shown, and to protect the lives of innocent planters and their vested rights, when it does not appear that these were in any great danger.

. . . The industrial condition is more vital at all times than the political since the former hinges upon the latter. And we may henceforth expect to hear of more trouble arising out of the industrial than out of the political relations of the whites and blacks of the South; for we assert, without fear of successful contradiction, that nowhere else in the world can be found a more odious, unjust, and tyrannical landlord system than that which obtains in the South. It is a virtual continuation of the slave system, with the landlord relieved of the obligations and responsibilities to the laborer imposed upon him by the laws of the slave system and his right in the person as well as the labor of the slave.

All the laws of the South are made in favor of the planters, and it is notorious that the wages paid by them to their employees are simply pauper wages; and this is aggravated by the store account and order system by which the laborer seldom ever sees a dime of cash and is frequently allowed to overdraw his account, or is overcharged, for the purpose of being held at the pleasure of the planter. There is more direct and indirect robbery of the colored laborers of the South than is practiced anywhere else on earth. The thing is simply infamous and will cause infinite trouble in the future.

The Freeman, New York, July 17, 1886

At the Knights of Labor Convention held in Richmond, Virginia, District Assembly 49 of New York, which was integrated, was refused accommodations at a local hotel because of a black delegate, Frank Ferrell. The assembly decided that it would board only with colored families—"they would only go where their colored brother was admitted on the same footing."

The Knights of Labor in session at Richmond [Va.] at their opening session last Monday took Southern prejudice, arrogance and intolerance by the throat and gave it the most furious shaking it has had since the war. The occasion was the action of New York Assembly 49 in refusing to sanction the discrimination made against their colored fellow member Ferrell by a Richmond hotel keeper. The honor of introducing Grand Master Workman Powderly to the Convention and the people of Richmond was assigned to delegate Ferrell, who, in doing this, followed Gov. Lee in a very neat speech. Mr. Powderly said the honor had been conferred upon Mr. Ferrell to show that the Knights of Labor recognized neither the race nor the color of its membership, but that all were brothers, possessing equal rights and privileges. The Bourbons of the South may rage to their hearts' content, but the fact remains that there is one great organization in the land which recognizes the brotherhood of all men and has the courage to practice what it teaches. . . .

The Freeman, New York, October 9, 1886

It was among the sugar workers that the Knights were particularly effective.

Ten thousand laborers throughout the sugar district of Louisiana are on strike. Fully nine-tenths of these laborers are colored men, and all are members of the Knights of Labor. . . .

The Weekly Pelican, New Orleans, November 3, 1886

Reaction in the white community to black organizing was highly antagonistic, and there was no hesitation at applying any measures to repress the black worker.

[Columbia, South Carolina] The efforts of some of the organizers of the Knights of Labor in this State to enroll the colored people in the order has caused much bitter feeling against the order by the farmers. Some papers advised the farmers to "spot" all white men like "Russell" endeavoring to organize colored Knights of Labor, and drive them from the neighborhood. These journals have advised that "the Legislature should appropriate money for the maintenance of the militia, as well-equipped soldiers may be needed of this organization goes on." This the Legislature has done and to further protect the farmers against the organization of the colored people living on their plantations, the Senate passed by a large majority, and the House will doubtless make it a law, a bill making it a conspiracy, punishable by fine and imprisonment, to interfere between employer and employee in any contract, whether written or verbal. The possibility of a strike at cotton picking time when the whole crop of the State would be lost if not properly gathered, was the principal argument used, together with a declaration that if a strike occurred among the colored people, much more blood would be spilled than last summer at Chicago and St. Louis.

[Charleston, South Carolina] The bill now before the Legislature to prevent the organization of colored laborers in the agricultural sections in Knights of Labor is causing a great commotion among the leaders of the colored people of this State. Rev. J. Wooford White, one of the most intelligent colored preachers of the State has issued an address in which he says that this bill has for its aim the grinding down and driving to the wall of the Negro laborers. In closing his address, Mr. White says: "From the point of equity considering the circumstances surrounding all laborers, the Negro is the most excusable in forming organizations of a legal kind to better his condition. Do the white people imagine that by threats they can keep away the Negro's agents or organizers and in this way by force keep them in this State or prevent them from being organized for mutual protection! If so, they reckon without their host. The great drawback to the Negroes lies in the fact of their being too easily satisfied. The Shylocks of this State today are the farmers who want the crops made and gathered without paying a reasonable price for labor. They can reduce wages to the lowest point, and if they are asked for justice it is refused, and when the Negroes organize for mutual protection this is to be pronounced illegal and who dares to resist is to be incarcerated in prison. . . ."

The Gazette, Cleveland, December 25, 1886

Despite some advances in the North, conditions in the South worsened, and it was clear to T. Thomas Fortune that the exploitive capitalist system would only be broken through confrontation with a powerful and organized working class. The following represents a distillation of some of his views he had developed in Black and White: Land, Labor and Politics in the South, *published in 1884.*

The present problem in the South is purely industrial. The condition of things produced by the results of the war is most natural in its every phase. It should have been the easiest thing in the world to have foreseen that upon the lines laid down by the moulders of the Reconstruction policy chattel slavery would certainly be followed by industrial slavery, no less galling and degrading to the enfranchised class and far more profitable to the employers of labor. The fetters were no sooner removed from the limbs of the black slave than the fetters of condition took their place; so that today it is a painful and notorious fact that the last condition of the common laborers of the South is, in many respects, much more degrading and demoralizing than the first.

When the war came to a close the whites owned all the intelligence, all the capital, all the land. They had been educated as the dominant class. To rule and tyrannize was bone of their bone and flesh of their flesh. The war had despoiled them of their property in slaves and largely of their accumulated capital capital; but it did not despoil them of their superiority of education and their control of the land. The accumulated increment of labor had been swept away, but the primal agencies of accumulation had been left intact. As a consequence, recovery from the exhaustion and prostration of the war was only a question of time. The black laborer must produce in order to subsist, and this very necessity resounded to the enrichment of those who controlled the agencies of production and who in consequence held a lien upon the surplus earnings of the laborer. In the very effort put forth by the laborer to sublet he enriched those who controlled those agencies of production without which labor cannot reproduce.

In nearly every Southern State the white capitalists have managed to have placed upon the statute books laws intended to protect and enrich the employer of labor at the expense of the laborer. The legislatures of those States have not needed any outside influence to pass such laws. They have passed them to benefit largely those who composed such assemblies—men who had vaulted into power over majorities contemplation of which staggers the mind.

No state in the South is more completely ruled by the unscrupulous arm of usurpation than that of South Carolina, because no Southern State has such a preponderating black majority. Since 1876, when the treachery and cupidity of the managers of the Republican party gave the State Government over to the Hamptons and the Butlers [Senator M. C. Butler of South Carolina],* the whole end and aim of the white rulers have been to make voiceless the black vote of the State and to chain the black toilers to the car of the capitalists and landowners.

When it became known that the Knights of Labor were going to organize the black laborers of the South the most serious apprehensions were aroused throughout that section. . . . The time is now when the laboring classes all over the country must take up the question of Southern labor and the methods by which it is defrauded, pauperized and tyrannized over before they can hope to accomplish the ends they

* Wade Hampton was governor of South Carolina from 1877 to 1890.

have in view. The colored people of the South are gradually, as a class, sinking deeper and deeper into the cesspool of industrial slavery, and selfishness and greed are hedging themselves about by statutory enactments of the most unjust and iron-clad nature. What the end will be no man can safely say, but it is a comparatively easy matter to predict that the pathway thereto will be honeycombed with fraud, cruelty, and bloodshed. Capitalists and landowners, in all times and all countries . . . have been unscrupulous and cruel, yielding no inch to the sentiments of justice or humanity. The capitalists and landowners of the South of today will be found to be as stubborn and unjust as the ante-bellum slave holders. What they yield of justice and fair play will be at the command of organized and irresistible power; and none but knows just what this means in the last resort.

The Freeman, New York, December 25, 1886

Semisecret organizations of black farmers and sharecroppers in the South were not uncommon. Aided by black unions and especially by the Knights of Labor, this movement grew in strength during the 1880's and was beginning to resist attempts at exploitation and oppression.

The colored people of Cass County, Texas, are excited over a Ku Klux raid that was made upon certain members of the race at Douglassville recently. The trouble arose from the recent organization of a secret society, the aims and objects of which are a profound mystery to the white population. It seems that several ignorant, burly white brutes, claimed that it was organized for the assassination of obnoxious white planters, and driving them out of the country by burning their property and worrying them until they are willing to sell out at a heavy sacrifice. Consequently, about twenty masked horsemen entered Douglassville during a church meeting in the evening, and at the point of their shot guns, marched four of the leading officers of the new secret society to a house, where an iron box was kept which was thought to contain a list of the marked men . . . Although four colored men, leaders, were kicked, cuffed and beaten with gun-barrels, they persistently refused to tell the objects of the society. The papers were all returned to the iron box and the masked raiders left the village, baffled in their raid. The decent white citizens at Douglassville, Queen City, Atlanta, and Linden have since held meetings and denounced the outrage, which has served somewhat to allay the excitement among the colored people, who vowed vengeance if any further attempt to pry into their affairs is made. As Cass County has a population of 20,000, nearly two-thirds of which is colored, any trouble between blacks and whites in that section would result seriously for the latter.

The Gazette, Cleveland, November 6, 1886

Although instances of black and white unity were uncommon, they did occur, as indicated by the following report from Pensacola, Florida.

COLORED AND WHITE WORKMEN UNITE AGAINST OPPRESSION

. . . The scene of Palafox's Wharf was not a pleasant one, owing to the rage the major part of the men were in. Some of the offending parties were badly used, getting several severe blows, and having to leap into the bay, or seek refuge in the boat houses. On the 2nd. the "guano men" (or the men that work in guano; all quit work and marched to Sunday's Hall, held a meeting, elected officers, and formed a society to be known as the Guano Association. . . . On the 3rd. they called to get the pay due them. Their employers paid them, but refused to give them the wages they asked. Tuesday was a laughable day indeed. The Escambia Rifles (white) marched out with glittering muskets and bayonets to make the poor and oppressed colored and white men fall in submission; but they were badly mistaken for as soon as they got as far as the workmen dared to have them come they were surrounded. The workmen politely pointed out the way, and they willingly went back to their armory. . . . Yesterday the officials of the railroad brought in from along the line about 160 men to take the places of the guano strikers. They were met on the wharf by the strikers, who told them what would be the consequences if they went to work. After hearing the wrath that would befall them, they told the officials that they would not risk their lives. . . .

The Freeman, New York, February 12, 1887

The Louisiana sugar strike was one of the most impressive displays of black unity and strength. It was brutally repressed, culminating in the lynching of the black organizers, George and Henry Cox.

The killing of 12 colored men at Thibodeaux last week, also the murder of the two Cox brothers who were arrested on Tuesday as agitators charged with making incendiary speeches, and taken from the jail by the whites and shot to death, are reported as growing out of the Louisiana sugar strike. The Coxes were leaders in the strike and prominent in the labor organizations. . . . Do the whites of the south suppose that colored people are going to continue to submit without a practical protest against their inhuman treatment? If they do, they are basing their supposition upon a frail foundation. They may as well make up their minds at once that the colored people will not in the future be led as lambs to the slaughter. Education is enabling them to know and appreciate their rights as American citizens, and in the future they will not be backward in claiming these rights and insisting upon a fair and impartial interpretation of the laws which govern this country.

Power is a dangerous weapon, especially when it is possessed by unscrupulous men. The oppressed always sooner or later arise and shake off the galling chains of oppression, and they do this even if they cause rivers of blood to follow in their wake. Unscrupulous men who possess power which has been obtained by usurpation and fraud should be careful how they exercise it. The whites in the South should take warning in time, or they may have to repent when repentence will avail them naught.

The Age, New York, December 3, 1887

Though black papers were, in the main, sympathetic to labor organizing, they were uncertain of the benefit of striking when black men were still discriminated against by fellow workmen. Some were hostile because of their antagonism to Socialistic ideas.

There seems to be trouble in the camp among the Knights of Labor. Thousands of innocent working men were decoyed into joining this order by evil designing men who had, for their object, the sapping of the laboring class money. Men who were well satisfied with their employers were forced to surrender their jobs and go out on a strike to favor a few figureheads who called themselves bosses. Now it is that the working class see that the purpose of these men were bad and injurious to them and they are withdrawing as fast as they joined. We believe in seeing that all men unite for their mutual good, but not for their detriment. Although Mr. Powderly is doing everything for the good of the organization, still these figureheads and money ringsters are clammering for a change. Henry George's absurd and ridiculous land ideas are being agitated among local organizations of anarchal inclinations. We want to see every man attain as much wealth as possible and not because one man has worked hard and accumulated a handsome fortune shall it be taken and distributed out among Europe's criminals and paupers.

The Western Cyclone, Nicodemus, Kansas, October 7, 1887

T. Thomas Fortune, an ardent supporter of the Knights of Labor, was nevertheless critical of an ill-planned, unsuccessful strike which weakened the organization.

It is apparent to the most hearty sympathizer of the labor organization known as the Knights of Labor, that in their conflict with the Gould system of railroads they were all wrong in the question at issue, and that the outcome of the strike has been a deplorable failure all along the line. It is plainly apparent that the organization was seduced into ordering the strike by short-sighted leaders of a local organization, and that those persistently refused to listen to the wiser and maturer counsels of better informed men of the National organization. . . .

The Freeman, New York, April 10, 1886

Militancy among black cotton pickers appears not to have been unusual by the second decade after the Civil War. The situation in Mississippi was perhaps the most volatile and indicates early strategies and tactics.

NEGRO COTTON PICKERS THREATENING

Coffyville, Miss.

The white people all along the line of the Illinois Central railroad and in every county of the delta are actively preparing for an anticipated general attack by the blacks. Prominent men with whom interviews have been had are seriously considering the outbreak, and arms are being bought on both sides. At Water Valley, ten miles north of here, 200 men have organized for protection. At Grenada, ten miles south of here, it is supposed that negro cotton hands have organized and will demand an increase in their wages or guard the fields with shotguns and prevent others from gathering the crops. . . .

The Advocate, Leavenworth, Kansas, September 28, 1889

The Colored Farmers' Alliance was apparently connected with this series of outbreaks in the fall of 1889. The planters, in response, quarantined the alliance store and wiped out the local black newspaper in the area of Greenwood, Mississippi, which had been a center of resistance.

. . . It has been discovered that the Durant Commercial Co. of the Farmer's Alliance store at Durant, Mississippi has been furnishing the money to Negroes by which they procured their guns. They, of course, did this as a regular commercial transaction, but they have been resolved upon. The Vaiden Negro newspaper has been ordered discontinued.

The number of guns captured amount to 220. They are the improved Winchester and Spencer rifles. The plan of the Negroes becomes more diabolical as each tale is unfolded. Last Sunday, four Negro excursion trains from Greenville, Jackson, Durant, and Winona were to have arrived here early in the morning. The alarm given on last Saturday caused the railroads to cancel the excursion trains. It is estimated that 1,000 Negroes were to come. . . .

The Bee, Washington, D.C., September 21, 1889

One of the rare firsthand descriptions of the cooperative effort in the Colored Farmers' Alliance is provided by E [Emanuel] Fortune, Jr., T. Thomas Fortune's elder brother.

. . . I gained some information about the colored Farmers Alliance in the western part of the state (Florida) while there. I am indebted for this information to Mr. R. B. Martin, who says he was one of the victims of this now very little appreciated organization in that section. It is said that an agent came there from Texas for the purpose of organizing branch organizations and that he proceeded to do so and also establish an exchange store. To establish this store each farmer was taxed so much. The store was started with a capital of $1,200. The object of the store was that the colored farmers might exchange their produce there for groceries, and when buying for cash obtain groceries cheaper than at other stores. The store was established by the agent sent out and run more in the line of a personal affair than for what it was intended. Colored farmers were charged as high prices for goods at this store as at others, and in some cases where produce was left to be disposed of, no returns were ever made for it. The store is now closed and the Alliance is said to owe the store $161 and the firm, or store, although said to be run on a cash basis, comes to $600 debt. . . .

The Age, New York, November 2, 1889

The following is a biography of Isaac Myers, organizer of the first national black union and numerous black cooperatives. Myers died on January 26, 1891.

Mr. Isaac Myers of Baltimore, Md. The founder and President of the Aged Ministers Home of the AME Church is in every sense of the word a self-made man. Born of poor parents in a slave state, that afforded no school privileges for colored youths, his success in life is a noble example of what push and pluck can accomplish under the most adverse circumstances. He received a common school education in the private day school of Rev. John Fortie and at the age of 16 was apprenticed to James Jackson, a prominent colored man in his day to learn the trade of ship caulking; how thoroughly he mastered the business may be inferred from the fact that at the age of 20 he was superintending the caulking of some of the largest clipper ships that were then being built in that once famous ship-building city.

In the year 1860 he entered the wholesale grocery of Woods, Bridges, and Co. which became, during the war, the largest establishment of its kind south of Mason and Dixon's line. He acted here in the double capacity of chief porter and shipping clerk and acquired a knowledge of the grocery business in all its branches that subsequently served a good purpose.

Leaving the above establishment in 1864 he organized and successfully conducted a company grocery store, which if left to the control of his judgment would have been today one of the great institutions of Baltimore.

In 1865 he resigned the management of the above institution, and returned to the shipyard. In this year the great strike against colored mechanics and long-shoremen was inaugurated under the leadership of the notorious "Joe" Edwards. The city was under the control of "Know Nothing" influence, and in sympathy with the strikers, and notwithstanding the bold fight made under the leadership of Mr. Myers, Wm. F. Taylor and Charles O. Fisher, every colored mechanic in the shipyards and longshoreman, over 1,000 were driven from their employment. It was at this juncture that the executive and great organizing abilities of Mr. Myers were first demonstrated. In December of this year he conceived the idea of the colored people buying a shipyard and marine railway. The proposition was submitted to a number of merchants who promised their work. He called meetings in all the colored churches of Baltimore; organized a company, and within four months raised $10,000 cash in shares of five dollars each, exclusively from colored people; purchased of James N. Muller his yard and railway for $40,000, and 300 colored caulkers and carpenters found immediate employment. For a while they enjoyed almost a monopoly of the business of the city, also giving employment to a large number of white mechanics. He secured a government contract of $50,000, against the combined competition of ship builders of Wilmington, Philadelphia, Baltimore, and Alexandria. The moral influence of this organization restored the longshoremen, but the stevedores, taking the advantage of the situation, and condition of the men, cut their pay. He organized the workmen, prepared a protest and submitted it to the merchants, who ordered the pay restored to $2.50 per day, upon the penalty of giving their work to Philadelphia stevedores. The entire debt of the shipyard was paid off in five years from the profits of the business, after which he left it to enter the political arena. The same year he was appointed a messenger to the Hon. John L. Thomas, collector of customs of Baltimore, being the second colored man appointed to a position under the Federal Government in Maryland.

In January 1870, at the suggestion of George T. Downing of Rhode Island, Fred G. Barbadoes and the late Rev. J. Sella Martin, a conference of the leading Republicans of the country, white and colored, was held at the residence of U.S. Senator Pomeroy in Washington, D.C. and it was desired to petition Hon. John A. J. Cresswell, Postmaster General, to appoint Mr. Myers a special agent of the Postoffice Department. The application received the endorsement of the Committees on Postoffice and Postroad of the U.S. Senate and House of Representatives, the only endorsement of the kind on record, and on March 7, 1870, Mr. Myers received his commission, and was assigned to the supervision of the mail service in the Southern States with headquarters at Washington, D.C. About this time the Labor Question, under the leadership of the great champion of labor, Trevellick*, was seriously agitating the mind of the country, it being their purpose to put in nomination a national ticket, and as a condition precedent, to divide the colored vote in the Southern States by the organization of labor clubs. Mr. Myers grasping the situation, and to offset Trevellick scheme, issued a call for a National Labor Convention of Colored Men, which met in the City of Washington, January 10, 1871. It is a historical fact that this was the largest and best representative convention of colored men ever held in the United States. The convention remained in session five days, and formed a national plan for the educational and industrial organization of colored people and elected Mr. Myers president. Within six months a State organization was formed in nearly all of the Southern States, as well as in some of the Eastern and Western States. In August of the same year, Mr. Myers appointed Mr. Isiah C. Wears, of Philadelphia, and Peter H. Clark, of Ohio, as delegates representing the Colored National Union and the three met the great National Labor Congress at Cincinnati, August 14th. the

* Richard Trevellick (1830–1895) was an important leader of the National Labor Union, one of the organizers of the National Greenback Labor Party in 1876, and later an active member of the Knights of Labor.

largest gathering of white labor men ever assembled in this country, their purpose being the organization of the Labor Reform party. The position taken by Myers, Wears, and Clark was against the amalgamation of politics with labor. After a careful summing up of the plans and purposes of the congress, on the fifth day Myers made a very characteristic speech in defense of General Grant's administration, and in support of the Republican party as the friend of labor, the only speech of the kind made in the convention; it produced considerable excitement and threw the convention into a tumult. It was with the greatest difficulty that he was protected from personal assault on the floor of that convention. He was forced back over the railing into the space occupied by newspaper correspondent, by the pressure of the excited delegates. The speech was published in most of the leading newspapers of the country, August 18, 1871. In the state campaign of North Carolina, 1872, he rendered invaluable service, and the success of the National ticket, owes more to any of the political managers of that campaign, of which evidence in his possession will show. In the following year the Hon. Fred Douglass was elected president, since which time the National Labor Union has ceased to exist. . . .

In 1879 he retired from the service and opened a coal yard in Baltimore. He was in 1882 editor and proprietor of the Colored Citizen, a weekly campaign newspaper, published in Baltimore. In the same year he was appointed a United States gauger, and became one of the most proficient and popular men on the force. He resigned the position of United States gauger Feb. 2, 1887, the day the Democratic collector took charge of the office, and was the only man in the State who made a voluntary resignation. In the Presidential campaign of 1888 he was Secretary of the Republican Campaign Committee, of Maryland; also rendered valuable service on the stump. In 1888 he organized the Maryland Colored State Industrial Fair Association. Their first fair held in that year, eclipsed any similar one ever held by colored associations in the United States. He organized and is President of the Colored Business Men's Association, of Baltimore; he also organized the first Building and Loan Association of that city. He has been 15 years superintendent of Bethel A.M.E. School of Baltimore. It is generally regarded as the leading Sabbath School of that denomination, and is pronounced by Secretary Smith "the banner S.S. of the world." He is also a trustee of said church, and Secretary of the Board. He is past grand master of Masons of Maryland, and author of a Masons' Digest, favorably commented on by Masonic writers, is also a prominent Odd Fellow and Good Samaritan.

He is the author of a drama in three acts, entitled "The Missionary."

The Freeman, Indianapolis, October 12, 1889

THE RACE PROBLEM
The Different Methods of Solving it as Observed by *The Freeman's* Artist.

The Freeman, Indianapolis, March 30, 1889

The Black Exodus

THE *subject of colonization and migration is divided into two major periods, separated by the Civil War. Prior to the war, black people had nearly unanimously rejected colonization schemes, primarily because they saw themselves as black Americans. Since the plans of the American Colonization Society included only free blacks, the black press correctly saw this as an attempt to preserve the institution of slavery by removing a very active abolitionist group. Although black people had deep cultural ties to Africa, they did not wish to expatriate themselves.*

During the 1850's with an increasing attempt by the government to officially sanction slavery, to maintain the position of black people as inferior, there was increased interest in emigration to Canada and the Caribbean Islands. It is clear that such a direction was determined by the desire to establish a black liberation movement which could attack the slave states.

Following the Civil War, blacks turned to achieving equality in a "Reconstructed South." When these efforts failed, they moved westward and established black colonies across the Mississippi. The black exodus in 1879, which was largely responsible for bringing thousands of black settlers to Kansas, was carried on throughout the 1880's, culminating in efforts to establish an autonomous black community in Oklahoma.

The black press (with the notable exception of Frederick Douglass) supported this westward migration. They saw such a move as an effective way of combating racism and of building black communities where they would be able to develop without the destructive effects of prejudice and oppression. Here they could build their communities not in spite of racism, but as a result of the positive expressions of a free people.

The response by the black community to the proposals of the African Colonization Society was overwhelmingly negative, as indicated by the following letters. They demanded, not removal, but inclusion as American citizens with full equality.

. . . It should be a matter of no small concern to the free people of color to perceive the rapid progress of the Colonization Society: its increase cannot be viewed in any other light, than a desire to get effectually rid of the free people. . . . I am aware that many philanthropists have become converts to the colonization scheme; many, I doubt not, who have at all times espoused the cause of the oppressed, and imagine that it will ultimately prove beneficial to them; others think that it is the only means by which Africa can become civilized, and "Ethopia stretch forth her hands to God," but they do not penetrate the real views of the Colonization Society, who have carefully disguised their intentions; which have since the formation of this society been aimed at the liberty of the free people; many of the Southern States have the same object in view, witness their severe laws against those people: for instance, they are prohibited from returning to the state of South Carolina, on any pretext whatever. The colonizing plan . . . is intended indirectly to force the free people to emigrate, particularly those in the Southern States, where they are so much oppressed by prohibitions and taxation. It cannot but be warmly patronized by slaveholders. . . .

Mr. Clay's proposal is to remove annually six thousand of those persons, and thus he says keep down their alarming increase; this he avows to be the grand object of the Society. The Baltimore Memorial, to which he adverts, was not the unanimous sentiments of the colored people; for I am credibly informed, that at least two-thirds of the meeting dissented from it. At a meeting lately held in Philadelphia, of the most respectable people of color, consisting of nearly three thousand persons, to take this subject into consideration, there was not one who was in favor of leaving this country; but they were all opposed to colonization in any foreign country whatever. . . .

A MAN OF COLOUR
Freedom's Journal, New York, May 18, 1827

The author of this letter, William Watkins, was one of the black abolitionists instrumental in converting Garrison from his procolonization views prior to his publishing the Liberator.

. . . For, in the first place, it appears very strange to me that those benevolent men [abolitionists] should feel so much for the condition of the free coloured people, and, at the same time, cannot sympathize in the least degree, with those whose condition appeals so much louder to their humanity and benevolence.—Nor, is this all: we are apprized that some of the *most distinguished* of that society, are themselves SLAVEHOLDERS! Now, how those men can desire so ardently, and labor so abundantly, for the exaltation of the free people, thousands of whom they have never seen, and feel so little concern for those who are held in bondage by themselves; whose degraded condition is directly under their observation, and, immediately within the sphere of their benevolence to ameliorate, is a philanthropy, I confess, unaccountable to me. Indeed, I have thought that a philanthropic slaveholder is as great a solecism as a sober drunkard. If these gentlemen disavow being actuated by interested motives, and would have us to think favorably of them and their proceedings, they must commence their labor of love by striking at the root of the great and growing evil;—they must commence by proclaiming deliverance to their own captives;—they must open (to the extent of their power and influence) the prison doors of those that are bound, and set at liberty those that are bruised. Until this shall have been done, or at least commenced, we shall continue to question the genuineness of their benevolence.

But there is another objectionable feature in the plan of this society, well calculated, as we think, to corroborate our suspicions of the motives of its founders. Its members hold out the anti-christian doctrine, that justice cannot be done to us while we remain in this land of civilization and gospel light. They tell us, we can never enjoy the unalienable rights of man in this "land of the free and home of the brave"— that if we desire the privileges of freemen, we must seek them elsewhere; not in Hayti, on account of its proximity to this country, but on the burning sands of Africa, where say they, "being permanently fixed, a mighty ocean will forever intervene as a barrier between us and them." Now, permit me to ask, why this strong aversion to being united to us, even by soil and climate? Why this desire to be so remotely alienated from us? Is it to extend to us in the hour of danger, the friendly hand of assistance? Or rather is it not to get effectually and for ever rid of that heterogeneous, or supposed "dangerous element in the general mass of the free blacks," who, it is said, "are a greater nuisance than the slaves themselves?" Thus the members of the African Colonization Society frequently speak; and I think we may learn from such, as well as many other observations of like import, what is the life-giving principle of the African Colonization system. We are, say they, "an inferior race—repugnant to their republican feelings"; in short, "a nuisance." Not indeed, that we have made ourselves so by our crimes,—no: but we are a "nuisance," because the Creator of all things, the Sovereign Ruler of the Universe has thought proper, in his infinite wisdom, to tincture us with a darker hue than that of our white brethren. Or, if you please, because the lot of our ancestors happened to be cast in the torrid zone, beneath the scorching beams of a vertical sun. This is our crime; and for this alone we are told that we can never be men, unless we abandon the land of our birth, "our veritable home," and people an uncongenial clime, the barbarous regions of Africa. O that men would learn that knowledge and virtue, not color, constitute the sign of human dignity. With these we are *white,* without them *black.*

Again, were the members of that distinguished institution actuated by the motives so generally ascribed to them, why is it, permit me to ask, that they dread, or become offended at an investigation of the principles upon which the society is based? Why is it that they would have us yield with implicit credulity, without the exercise of our own judgment, to whatever they propose for our happiness? Does not the dread of liberal enquiry indicate something radically wrong in their principles? They should ever bear in mind, that if it is their prerogative to devise, it is ours to investigate. We are all interested. Some of the benevolent societies of our land, have proceeded on principles widely different from those which we have just noticed. They, so far from dreading a liberal investigation of their views and motives, are making every possible effort to attract public attention. It would appear, that they are never so sanguine in their expectations of success, as when the public are disposed to scrutinize their pretensions. They do not dread, but court investigation. . . .

. . . They most pitiably deplore the ignorance, barbarity, and moral corruption that have for so many centuries maintained an unbroken sway over her unfortunate sons. But what have they done, or what are they doing to effectuate a destruction of this deplorable state of things among them? Their speeches will, in some sort, furnish an answer. They tell us that we, who are "of all classes of the population of this country, the most vicious, who being contaminated ourselves, extend our vices to all around us; to the slaves and to the whites"; are to be the pioneers of this great work of regeneration and reform. Fine materials indeed to accomplish so glorious a work! . . .

A COLORED BALTIMOREAN

Freedom's Journal, New York, July 6, 1827

The appearance of a paper from the North, edited by persons of our own color, and devoted to the interests of our long oppressed and stigmatized race, cannot fail to awaken the liveliest joy and gratitude in every bosom, that is not callous to humanity and virtue. We, at the south, are peculiarly interested in its welfare, for we are those on whom its effects may operate most beneficially. . . .

Instead of expending money in colonizing free people in Africa, who are free at home, and who if not satisfied here have the world before them to go where they may think best; expend this same money in liberating from bondage such slaves as philanthropic owners might wish to liberate, but whose poverty may prevent from so generous an action. This would be paving the way for a general emancipation. It would be gradual, it is true, but at the same time more politic. For although as a man of color, I am greatly interested in this subject, yet I am certain, many disadvantages would be experienced from a sudden and general emancipation; if indeed it was possible. . . .

. . . What is to become of this colony when it becomes sufficiently rich to tempt the rapacity of foreign governments? What to protect it from piratical desperadoes? What are they to do if having to contend, not only with external, but internal foes? For to suppose that the natives will ever consider them in any other light than as intruders, and consequently as enemies, is as fanciful as false. It will be impossible for private societies in the United States to protect them, and can we rationally entertain a hope that the General Government will interpose, after what occurred last winter in Congress? We confess our inability to see anything cheering in the prospect of this society; and we deem it a christian duty to tell our colored brethren so. . . .

A FREE COLORED VIRGINIAN

Freedom's Journal, New York, July 6, 1827

In reply to an editorial in the Georgetown Columbian and District Advertiser, Freedom's Journal *stated its position.*

. . . That we have made any effort, through this Journal, to prejudice the minds of our brethren against the Society, or render them suspicious of its motives, we positively deny: but that we are opposed to colonization in PRINCIPLE, OBJECT, AND TENDENCY, we, as unhesitatingly affirm. We have never desired to conceal our sentiments. In soliciting patronage to our Journal among Colonizationists, we expressed ourselves to many of them as opposed to colonization in any shape, unless it be merely considered as a missionary establishment; yet, if we were wrong our minds were open to conviction, and we wished to see the subject discussed; they were generally pleased with the idea. . . .

Freedom's Journal, New York, June 8, 1827

The subject of colonization evoked many series of articles, both from white (usually in favor) and black (usually against) readers of Freedom's Journal. *The following series is signed with the pseudonym "Investigator," which may have reference to the refusal of the Colonization Society to allow thorough investigations of their organization.*

. . . I have ever found the advocate for colonization actuated by the same popular motives, and when opposed, resort to the same arguments. Your correspondent advances the following. First, That some of the best men in the country have been, and are still engaged in the plan. All this may be, and yet a correctness of principle does not necessarily imply a correctness of judgment. Secondly, That colonization is necessary, in order to convince the enemies of emancipation that Africans possess capacities equal with the whites, under the same circumstances, to maintain Republican institutions, to govern and provide for themselves. The contrary idea is advanced by very few at the present day, and when advanced, argues wilful obstinacy, or self interest, and betrays a mind, the change of which unworthy a sacrifice on the part of our friends. Thirdly, He suggests the unsuitability of the man of colour, ever being raised to his proper standing in this country, an idea wholly unworthy the enlightened members of the Colonization Society. The spirit of the times as well as the movements of Providence strongly indicate the contrary. Such a view of the subject is dishonorable to the Supreme, and contrary to reason and scripture. As well may the christian relinquish all efforts to christianize the world, believing it useless to attack confirmed habits of obstinacy and rebellion against God and his Christ. . . . I cannot here refrain from saying to the Advocates of colonization that any plan which implies in our brethren or their descendants inferiority, or carries with it the idea that they cannot be raised to a respectable standing in this country; but must be accommodated to some other place and circumstance is wholly at war with our best interests. . . . Fourthly, Your correspondent claims for the Colonization Society, the honor of having changed public sentiment in Maryland and Virginia in respect to slavery. Is he not doing injustice to the "Genius of Universal Emancipation" and the several Abolition Societies?

Fifthly, He censures you for opposing the society, because comparatively few of its members are slaveholders, and consequently inconsistent in their conduct. It is not comparatively few, but a majority of the parent institution that come under that class. None of the public orators, before that Honorable Body, have on any occasion represented that society as contemplating the final Abolition of Slavery; but the contrary, as having nothing to do with slavery.

As to discouraging your friends, they are friends from principle, and when their principles are changed, cannot abandon your cause; except it be in their rights in behalf of the Colonization Society, in which particular we would say, "save us from our friends."

Finally, Your correspondent observes that our enemies at the South would gladly join with us in opposing colonization and thereby prevent the necessity of emancipating their slaves. This is not a fact. Perhaps your correspondent is not aware that slaveholding states make use of the colony as an apology for enacting the most oppressive laws, and grinding out the free population from among the slaves, believing their slaves will thereby not only become more profitable but more content. Colonizing the free people of color in Africa is never going to facilitate emancipation but rather to retard its progress. Let the friends of the people of colour endeavor to make an intelligent and respectable community of colour in this country, if they wish to facilitate emancipation; this will appeal to the hearts of slaveholders and do more in breaking the bands of slavery than a thousand colonization schemes.

We hope the Advocates for colonizing the free people of Africa will cease substituting their own imagination and wishes for facts, and submit to a fair and thorough investigation of the subject. . . .

Freedom's Journal, New York, August 31, 1827

According to the plan I suggested in my last, I proceed to expose the injustice of the Colonization scheme. If the colony be considered as a Missionary station, a home for recaptured Africans, or an Asylum for such slaves as their masters may see proper to emancipate, in those states where emancipation is prohibited without removal, or any such like purposes, we give it our decided approbation. But if it be considered as an Asylum for the free coloured population of this country, we protest against it, as being unrighteous in its motive and movements, and as an unwarrantable meddling with the rights and interests of a large portion of our citizens. That it is not a Missionary station is plain, from the fact that no missionary society have ever considered it as such; neither have there ever been any efforts made by its patrons, to procure qualified missionaries for the colony. If the objects of the Society were emancipation, and the establishment of an asylum for the emancipated, why not Judge Washington, and a host of its slaveholding worthies that they may abandon it at once? It is not fair that they should be deceived, and kept ignorant of its true motives. There is no doubt but the Society, as Mr. Clay, its monthly publication, and its agents have said, contemplates the removal of the free population of colour to the coasts of Africa; in which particular we pronounce it as unrighteous and meddling. This Republic, first in science, religion, wealth, and politics, is composed of the descendants of the pilgrims, emigrants from every nation, not excluding African, the kidnapped Africans and their descendants, and we believe the descendants of German redemptioners and transported criminals. All these the Constitution recognizes as constituting our Republic, and as being free and equal, and while unrighteous usages, deprive the slave of agency in his person and actions, they have no right to meddle with the free men of colour, many of whom emigrated to the country as other freemen, and never have been most distantly connected with any of its slaves; and who are as truly Americans as the President of the United States, and as much entitled to the protection, rights and privileges of the country as he, while they behave themselves.

Such are the people for whom the Colonization Society have taken it upon themselves (without making them a party in their deliberations, or consulting their wishes at all) to devise and prosecute plans for their total removal to the coasts of Africa. Is not this a gross encroachment upon the rights of from four to five hundred thousand coloured citizens? Is it not reasonable that we should suspect the motives of any body of men, who indulge in such an astonishing usurpation of our rights? We cannot tell how the Society could expect anything else, but opposition from the enlightened of our brethren.

Whatever the Colonization Society may have said to the contrary, there is not one out of every ten thousand from Maine to the Gulf of Mexico, that wishes or is willing to be colonized in Africa. This is a truth that should not be disguised. Wrong impressions have gone abroad, and efforts have been made, and still are making, to impose them on the Congress of the United States.

The measures of the Colonization Society, have not only been contrary to the wishes of our brethren, but against their repeated remonstrances.

This is a true picture of the Society; still its agents and advocates are pushing its concerns by all the zeal and influence they can possibly command, and are ready to denounce the enlightened and interested man of color who dares suspect or oppose them. It is true they tell us we need not go contrary to our will, yet they use all the means in their power to seduce the ignorant and uninformed to their wishes. We unhesitatingly assert, by resorting to the same measures, with their influence and talents, they could have as easily persuaded such as have gone, and such as may go, to emigrate to Botany Bay, as to Liberia.

In this way do the Colonization Society trifle with the liberties of five hundred thousand freemen of color, whose rights to the country are equally as good as theirs, or any other citizens, and many of whose fathers fought and bled for the liberty we enjoy. Where is the justice of their conduct as a Society? By what law or example are they guided? Surely not by the sacred Scriptures, nor the example of the primitive Christians. Surely not by equity or reason, and we should say not by an unbiased conscience. Were there a shadow of justice in the colonization scheme, or a single argument in its favor, we might have been carried by its plans; simply from the consideration that there are many ministers, officers, and members of churches engaged in its concerns: but as it is, our population will have increased five hundred thousand before that Society will have removed five thousand. The free people of colour will never go to Africa. . . .

Freedom's Journal, New York, September 7, 1827

. . . It is said by colonizationists, that such is the state of prejudice against our colour, and relative situation, that we never can be materially advanced in the scale of being, or possess any political advantages in this country; therefore it is necessary to colonize us that we may be raised to our rightful standing. Is not this deifying prejudice and paying homage at the shrine of one of the grossest sins that ever disgraced the human family? Who are the propagators of such sentiments? Who is it that possesses the hardihood, at this enlightened age of the world, to oppose this dark monster to the progress of light and christianity? Certainly not the eagle-eyed politician: he can penetrate too far into years of futurity, he is too conversant with the "signs of the times." . . . We but wish to be treated according to our merits, and respected as virtuous citizens—Give us the same facilities to education and competence as others possess and we are satisfied. But by the by, if our sable sires could bequeath us millions, avarice, the Goddess of America, would soon wink at our dark faces . . .

Freedom's Journal, New York, October 5, 1827

The author of the following letter was Bishop Richard Allen, founder of the African Methodist Episcopal Church and staunch opponent of the Colonization Society.

I have for several years been striving to reconcile my mind to the colonization of Africans in Liberia, but there have always been, and there still remain great and insurmountable objections against the scheme. We are an unlettered people, brought up in ignorance, not one in a hundred can read or write; not one in a thousand has a liberal education. Is there any fitness for such to be sent into a far country, among Heathens, to convert or civilize them; when they themselves are neither *civilized* nor *christianized?* See the great bulk of the poor ignorant Africans in this country; exposed to every temptation before them; all for the want of their morals being refined by education, and proper attendance paid unto them by their owners, or those who had the charge of them. It is said by the southern slaveholders, that the more ignorant they can bring up the Africans, the *better slaves* they make. It is enough for them to know the words, "*go* and *come.*" Is there any *fitness* for such people to be colonized in a far country, to be their *own rulers?* Can we not discern the *project* of sending the free people of colour away from this country? Is it not for the *interest* of the slave holder, to select the free people of colour out of the different states, and send them to Liberia? Will it not make their slaves uneasy to see free men of colour enjoying *liberty?* It is against the law in some of the southern states, that a person of colour should receive an education under a severe penalty. Colonizationists speak of America being first colonized, but is there any comparison between the two? America was colonized by as *wise, judicious,* and *educated* men as the world afforded. William Penn did not want for *learning, wisdom,* or *intelligence.* If all the people in Europe and America were as ignorant, and in the same situation as our brethren, what would become of the world; where would be the principle or piety that would govern the people? We were *stolen* from our mother country and brought *here.* We have *tilled* the ground and made fortunes for thousands, and still they are not weary of our services. *But they who stay to till the ground must be slaves.* Is there not land enough in America, or "corn enough in Egypt?" Why would they send us into a far country to die? See the thousands of foreigners emigrating to America every year: and if there be ground sufficient for them to cultivate, and bread for them to eat; why would they wish to send the first tillers of the land away? Africans have made fortunes for thousands, who are yet unwilling to part with their services, but the free must be sent away, and those who remain must be *slaves?* I have no doubt that there are many good men who do not see as I do and who are for sending us to Liberia, but they have not duly considered the subject—they are not men of colour. This land which we have watered with our *tears* and our *blood,* is now our *mother country* and we are well satisfied to stay where wisdom abounds and the gospel is free.

Freedom's Journal, New York, November 2, 1827

WANTED IMMEDIATELY

THIRTY able bodied men well acquainted with farming to go out to Hayti, as cultivators. For terms enquire of the subscriber.

JNO. B. RUSSWURM

Freedom's Journal, New York, May 30, 1828

Although Freedom's Journal *was begun initially as a forum opposed to the Colonization Society, its editor, John Russwurm, was persuaded to change his position.*

OUR VINDICATION

The change in our views on colonization seems to be a "seven days wonder" to many of our readers. But why, we do not perceive; like others, we are mortal; like them, we are liable to changes, and like them, we should be allowed the privilege of expressing our sentiments, a boon which is not denied to the most abject being in this country. We are sorry there are those who are unwilling to grant us this liberty, but as Freedom's Journal has ever been an independent paper, we shall continue to express ourselves on colonization, and on all other subjects which we may deem proper. It is not our object to injure the feelings of any—we feel towards them that charity which it becomes every man to exercise to his fellow. Our columns have ever been open to a free discussion of this important subject and they are still open; but is it reasonable to suppose that we should grant freedom of enquiry to others and deprive ourselves of it? We live in a day of general illumination, and it is our happiness to be among those, who believe in the feasibility of establishing a flourishing colony in Africa, which in progress of time, may be the means of disseminating civilization and christianity throughout the whole of that vast continent.

It is our happiness to be among those, who believe it to be far preferable, for the man of colour, aspiring after wealth and respectability, to emigrate to Liberia, where every incentive to virtuous action, is before him continually, than to remain here, where the mere name of colour, blocks up every avenue—where if he have the feelings of a man, he must be sensible of the degraded station he holds in society, and from which it is impossible to rise, unless he can change the Ethiopian hue of his complexion. He may possess wealth; he may be respected; he may be learned, still all united will avail him little; after all, he is considered a being of inferior order; and always will be, as no opportunity will ever be afforded him to cultivate or call into action the talents with which an All-wise Creator may have endowed him. . . .

Freedom's Journal, New York, March 7, 1829

From the following editorial, it is clear that Russwurm's support oj colonization was largely a response to American racism.

COLONIZATION

We feel proud in announcing to our distant readers, that many of our brethren in this city, who have lately taken this subject into consideration, have like ourselves, come out from the examination warm advocates of the Colony, and ready to embrace the first convenient opportunity to embark for the shores of Africa. This we may say looks like coming to the point—as if they had examined for themselves and satisfied of the practicability of the plan, are not afraid the world should know it.

The subject of Colonization is certainly important, as having a great bearing on that of slavery: for it must be evident that the universal emancipation so ardently desired by *us* & by all our friends can never take place unless some door is opened whereby the emancipated may be removed, as fast as they drop their galling chains, to some other land besides the free states; for it is a fact, that prejudices now in our part of the country, are so high, that it is often the remark of liberal men from the south, that their free people are treated better than we are, in the boasted free states of the north. If the free states have passed no laws as yet forbidding the emigration of free persons of colour into their limits; it is no reason that they will not, as soon as they find themselves a little more burdened. We will suppose that a general law of emancipation should be promulgated in the state of Virginia, under the existing statutes which require every emancipated slave to leave the state, would not the other states, in order to shield themselves from the evils of having so many thousands of ignorant beings thrown upon them, be obliged in self-defense to pass prohibitory laws? Much as we may deplore the evils of slavery—much as we *may* desire the freedom of the enslaved; who could reproach the free states for enacting such laws? so, that if no good whatever arose from the establishment of colonies, the fact that they remove all obstacles in the way of emancipation should gain for them the support and good wishes of every friend of humanity, & of every enlightened man of colour. It is true, that no such laws at present are in force to our knowledge, but who can foretell how soon before they may, without waiting for the period of a general emancipation in any of the slave-holding states.

Our wiseacres may talk as much as they please upon amalgama-
tions, and our future standing in society, but it does not alter the case
in the least; it does not improve our situation in the least; but it is calculated rather to stay the exertions of those who are really willing to
make some efforts to improve their own present conditions. We are
considered a distinct people, in the midst of the millions around us,
and in the most favorable parts of the country; and it matters not
from what causes this sentence has been passed upon us; the fiat has
gone forth and should each of us live to the age of Methuselah, at the
end of the thousand years, we should be exactly in our present situation: a proscribed race, however unjustly—a degraded people, deprived of all the rights of freemen and in the eyes of the community, a
race who had no lot nor portion with them.

We hope none of our readers will from our remarks think that we
approve in the least of the present prejudices in the way of the man of
colour; far from it, we deplore them as much as any man; but they are
not of our creating, and they are not in our power to remove. They at
present exist against us—and from the length of their existence—from
the degraded light in which we have ever been held—we are bold in
saying, that it will never be in our power to remove or overcome them.
So easily are these prejudices imbibed that we have often noticed the
effects on young children who could hardly speak plainly, and were
we a believer in dreams, charms, etc., we should believe they imbibed
them with their mother's milk.

Sensible then, as all are of the disadvantages under which we at
present labour, can any consider it a mark of folly, for us to cast our
eyes upon some other portion of the globe where all these inconven-
iences are removed—where the Man of Colour freed from the fetters
and prejudice and degradation, under which he labours in this land,
may walk forth in all the majesty of his creation—a new born creature—a Free Man! It was, we believe, the remark of Sir James Yeo,
while on the African coast, that the natives whom he saw were a fine
athletic race, walking fearlessly as if sensible of their important station
as men, and quite different from the thousands of their brethren
whom he had seen in the West Indies and the United States; and
never was a truer remark made, if we are to credit all other travellers
on that Continent, who have likewise borne testimony to the same
fact.

While some of our friends have wondered at our change, others
have been bold enough to call them in question and to accuse us of

improper motives; of such, we ask, who has made half the sacrifice we have to oppose the Colonization society? who has labored half so much by night and by day for the same end? who has had to bear the brunt of the battle while those who led us into action were sitting quietly at home? who has suffered much for conscience sake? Let none consider these as vain boastings. We merely insert them to refresh the memories of those who are now loud in denouncing our change.

We have said so much lately on the subject of colonization that we expect some will begin to think it high time that some other subject should occupy our attention, but we entreat them to bear with us a while only, our time is but short, and the more we investigate the subject, the more important it appears. . . .

Freedom's Journal, New York, March 14, 1829

There seems to be little doubt that Russwurm's position on the Colonization Society led to the break between him and Cornish. The Rights of All *began publishing just after* Freedom's Journal *ceased and wasted no time in attacking the colonizationists.*

. . . That the establishment of a colony on the coasts of Africa should be considered a christian charity, and that it will be a powerful engine in spreading civilization and religion throughout that vast continent, I have no doubt, and that it should from the commencement have been considered a missionary colony, and wore a aspect, I am equally bold in asserting. But that it is ever going to meet the object many contemplate, or ameliorate the condition of the vast body of our coloured population, I never shall believe. Nothing appears to me more trifling than to talk of repaying to Africa, the debt we owe her, by returning her sons to her coasts. I consider that the shortest way to accomplish this grand object is, to do her sons justice where ever we find them, if the world be too unrighteous to do this, the church of God should not—let the same powers, the same efforts and the same prayers, be resorted to in this particular, as are resorted to, in the correction of other abuses, and the Bible for a guarantee, that they shall be successful—educate this oppressed and afflicted people, encourage them in agricultural and mechanical pursuits, and there will be no difficulty in making them good and happy citizens. *But make the mas-*

ter Christ's servant, and the slave Christ's freeman, and even the southern sections of our country, shall become a home for the oppressed,
slavery will be but a name in our dictionaries. However successful,
and prosperous the colony at Liberia may be, it will never reduce the
coloured population of this country. Send 20 thousand annually to the
colony, and yet this population will increase from 40 to 50 thousand
yearly in the United States, and shall this vast body of our neighbours
and our household be forgotten in our zeal for the interests of a small
colony? That the interest of the christian public, in behalf of the coloured people of this country, has diminished, in proportion to their
zeal, in behalf of the Liberian colony, is evident to every enlightened
man of colour, and also to every unprejudiced white man, and it is not
our duty to call back, or at least to call for a division of the public attention, the public effort, and the public prayers in behalf of our
brethren in this country? . . .

The Rights of All, New York, June 12, 1829

*Many laws which in practice favored the interests of colonizationists
and slaveowners were proposed; some in fact were enacted. The following
article was written in response to such oppressive legislation.*

BARBARISM IN AMERICA

The powers that be in Ohio, in whom invested we know not, some
few years ago passed an act, certainly not a law, by which the coloured population were required individually to give Bonds, and I
think freehold security to the amount of 500 Dollars for their good be-
havior, and as an indemnity in case of their becoming an expense to
the public—An act unparalleled for illegality and barbarism in the
history of the world. Certainly its cruel authors never could have seen
the Declaration of Independence, nor the Constitution of the United
States, or they would have perceived it equally illegal to have made
such demands on the coloured settlers as it would be on the whites.
But at this we are not so much astonished, Ohio was originally settled
by the illiterate lower class from the New England states. The subject
of surprise is that at this advanced period of that state's history, and in
this enlightened age of the world, when principles of liberality and humanity are pervading and characterizing every nation, the Supreme

Court, shall I say of that enlightened state, declare the law (act, for there is no law in it) constitutional. I appeal to the statesmen, the christian, and to the common sense of the public, and ask for the legality, the humanity or even common sense manifested in such barbarous policy? . . . *The powers* that be, complete the human tragedy, by ordering the coloured population forthwith to leave the state in thirty days, or comply individually with this abominable 500 dollar bond act, which is utterly impossible, and which must have been intended as an impossible requisition. *Pharaoh like make brick without straw!!!* . . .

If the principles of our Union, by which life and the possession of property are and should be secured to every individual, are suffered to be so shamefully and so unconstitutionally invaded, I tremble for our happy Republic. Our extended Union, exalted happiness and boasted strength, will very soon be, but as so many spider webs. We shall soon have nation rising up against nation, in our midst. One unchecked violation of law, and of right, especially when done officially, leads to another—crime is productive of crime, until the perpetrator who has exhausted himself in tyrannizing over others, becomes his own tyrant, and in this way, the capturer becomes captured. . . . Our individual advice to the coloured people of Ohio is, conduct yourselves well, obey the *law* of your state, be industrious and economical, let your prudent conduct, and exemplary life, prove you to be worthy citizens of our favoured Republic, but do not *remove one step from your native state and mother country, rather become martyrs to the injustice, you have but once to die.* But if you should be otherwise disposed, and do emigrate from a home that has treated you so badly, we recommend you settle in upper Canada, there are lands sufficient for you all—The climate is salubrious and healthy, the country fertile and of easy cultivation, the government equitable and generous. If you go to upper Canada, you will not have farther to emigrate, and the facilities will be as great or greater, than to any other place. Another advantage you will possess, that you would not anywhere else is, that you will there be near neighbors to your friends in Ohio, and when the occasion may require, you can reciprocate their civilities. Already there is a settlement of coloured people from the United States in upper Canada, exceedingly flourishing they have introduced the cultivation of tobacco with success into that country, and besides supplying a vast portion of the home consumption, exported 800 hogsheads last year, to the mother country. They are encouraged, and respected, and patronized in every respect, as much as emigrants from any other country. The colony at Liberia, every thing considered, will bear no comparison with this settlement.

A word on another subject and we are done, *by no means go to Africa,* we but perform what we conceive conscientiously to be our duty in giving this warning, if we are wrong, God forgive us, for we conceive of no enemy to the coloured people of this country so formidable as the "Colonization Society". . . .

The Rights of All, New York, August 14, 1829

The Reverend Nathaniel Paul, the author of the following address, had been an agent for Freedom's Journal *in Albany and pastor of the African Baptist Society in that city.*

You are aware that the idea has been suggested and the sentiment has become popular to a considerable extent, that such are the prejudices existing between the white and coloured population, or rather in the white against the coloured people, that it will be impossible to improve our condition while we live in this country, and that the only possible means by which we can be benefited is a total emigration to the land of our forefathers.

That prejudices do exist is too obvious to be denied, and that these prejudices are extensive and deeply rooted is equally true: but that they are so universal as is pretended, or so deeply rooted that they cannot be eradicated is to me at least doubtful. I mean not to raise my voice against all the operations of the colonization society whatever may have been the motives of its founders, or present supporters. I would wish to give it an impartial investigation, and award to it all the merit to which it can justly lay claim. I am free to admit that a well regulated colony upon the western coast of Africa will be productive of great good; it will do much toward exterminating the foreign slave trade, and open an asylum for those slaves that may be manumitted in this country; and above all, be instrumental of introducing the light of science and religion into a portion of that vast and benighted continent; and this in process of time may probably be effected. But the idea of an entire emigration to that country, we denounce as utterly chimerical and absurd. . . .

. . . We claim this as *our country,* as the land of our nativity, and to achieve its independence our fathers faced her enemies on the field of battle, and contended even unto death . . .

The Rights of All, New York, September 18, 1829

At a meeting of the Colonization Society, Francis Scott Key, composer of the national anthem, delivered a speech in support of the society, to which Samuel Cornish responded.

. . . He of the Capital divulged the secret, in a speech of more than an hour, which tired every body, and almost emptied the house. The speech was characterized by repetitions and cunning, without logic, or good sense. His premises were all false, and consequently his reasoning the same. He began by stating the degraded situation of the free coloured people, of the free and slave states, and asserted the impossibility, in the very nature of things, while prejudice dwelt in his little heart, which cannot be bigger than a cherry, of their ever having any privileges in this country—*they must always be degraded and oppressed, free but in name, impossible that they can be otherwise*—CONSCIENCE, RELIGION, GOD nor the BIBLE cannot make this nation do them justice—*Satan is stronger than the Deity, the prejudices of our little souls are more than proof against the progress of light, of liberal principles, or of religion.* Is it not hypocrisy for such men to profess a belief in the bible? Is not F. S. Key a Pagan, and his God a bat, or a mole, who should he dare name the rights of the oppressed, would be driven by the poisonous affluvia of his prejudice into Capt. Symes' hole? How dare such a man to speak of the triumphs of the Cross, or the progress of light. His next absurdity, was, that the slaveholders were willing to emancipate their slaves could they but be removed to Liberia. One argument which he made use of in the establishment of this position, was the unprofitableness of slave labor, and the deterioration of slave states and slave counties. This argument, if followed up, would prove too much for the man of the Capital. It would prove the certainty of universal emancipation, without colonization. Slaveholders, will yet have to starve, or set their slaves free, even should it be with the view of giving them their own lands, and suffering them to be their own neighbors. One idea more, and I am done with this orator, remarkable for his cunning. He dared to underrate the labours and influence of the Hon. Abolition Societies of our country, by strongly impeaching their wisdom and prudence. He repeatedly asked, what good they had done, and answered by asserting that they had done harm. Does not the worthy gentleman know, this very hon. body of men, have been the means of emancipating more than half the States in the Union, and by turning them from sin to righteousness, saved our national fabrick? It may be, that he is indebted to these very men for his existence. . . . Does not Mr. Key know that the Abolition Societies have, and are educating their thousands of coloured youth. This mode of slandering the Abolitionists is very ungenerous in the worthy gentleman. . . .

The Rights of Man, New York, October 16, 1829

From the very outset, the Colored American *was dedicated to opposing any colonizationist movements.*

We have frequently been told by our white brethren, *professors too,* that were they in our place they would do as the pilgrim fathers did, leave the country. *They would go to Africa.* We should never remain in a country where we could not enjoy ourselves, and where our way was blocked up. (By the way, this is very generous on the part of our brethren, first to trample on us, and then persuade us, it is too intolerable to be borne.)

Such views of the feelings and duty of pious, intelligent colored citizens are very erroneous. Our happiness does not consist in the estimation in which we are held by our oppressors. It rather consists in enlightened and enlarged views of our relations, and in the discharge of our duties.

When community persecute and insult us, and when we are denied the privilege of men, because God has made our color to differ from others, our consciousness of intrinsic worth, and virtuous equality, buoy us up, and we look down, with commiseration and holy contempt, on such narrow minded detractors.

We always, as Christians, have tenderness and pity in our hearts, for the American people, who so cruelly rob us of ourselves, and of our rights. This is the only spirit we desire or mean to cherish towards our white fellow citizens. We are aware that it is far better to be the oppressed, than to be the oppressors, and that we have far less to envy, than to pity.

The discharge of duty also, renders our situation, in this country, *even desirable*. Much better that we suffer affliction with our brethren, than that we flee our country, and "enjoy the pleasures of sin for a season." Let no man, therefore, endeavor to seduce any of us to forsake the land of our birth, and the graves of our fathers. For high and holy purposes we have determined to remain here.

The few of us that have qualifications for, and the means of leaving the country, should act the part of *base traitors* were we to do so, and leave behind the millions of our brethren, who are in bondage, and cannot go. We will never do it! God hath placed beneath a colored skin a soul too noble to be guilty of such conduct. We have suffered sore affliction, and we know how to suffer still. Our tribulation has worked in us patience, and patience experience, and experience hope —such as maketh not ashamed.

We will never swerve from our purposes—universal emancipation, and universal enfranchisement—should we die in the pursuit, we will die *virtuous martyrs* in a holy cause.

The Colored American, New York, April 15, 1837

The Colored American *consistently presented arguments against the American Colonization Society and in support of abolitionists.*

It is often triumphantly, and with a sneer of self-gratification, and affected disdain, by colonization agents . . . asked, what have Abolitionists ever done for the colored people?

We will here answer the question, and in a very few words. They have created A CONSCIENCE on the subject of Slavery, and prejudice against color, throughout the length and breadth of our land.

1. It pervades the slave-holding regions, and restrains the whip. It prevails in the free States, and throws open the churches and colleges to colored people, and their youth. It enters the seminaries of learning and organizes the young men, consecrating them to the interests and improvement of the colored free-man, and the slave.

2. In a word, this CONSCIENCE has seized fast hold of some thousands of the most devoted Colonizationists, and converted them from the error of their way, making them truer patriots, and more holy men.

They now find room for the exercise of more enlarged benevolence at home, and are spending annually their thousands in building up the waste places of our country, instead of wasting their substances, and gratifying their pride and prejudice, by sending their poor and illiterate brethren to perish on the benighted, pestilential shores of Africa.

3. This CONSCIENCE has banished Esquire Findlay [leader in American Colonization Society] from the city of New York, with all his traps and snares, by which he deceived the unwary. He could not abide its heart-searching influences, its pungent appeals. He had either to go, or become an honest man—he chose the former instead of the latter. . . .

The Colored American, New York, May 6, 1837

The attack on colonization was based primarily on the inclusion of black people as American citizens.

When we reflect seriously upon the treatment which the colored citizens of the United States have received at the hands of their white brethren, for fifty years, our soul is filled with amazement. We often, in view of this subject, find ourselves involuntarily exclaiming, how can it be? Do not our white brethren know, that at least some of us, have as keen sensibilities, as refined taste, and as good education as they have? That some of us were bred and born as respectably as they? That we have used the same industry and enterprise, and accumulated as much wealth as most of our fellow-citizens, and yet have they no respect for our character or feelings?

Why should a colored man, who is equal in wealth, in education, in refinement and in taste, be subjected to legal disabilities—debarred the institutions of the country—crowded into negro pews in the church, and into dog-cars on the Railroad, or pantries on board the Steam-boats? Can anyone answer these inquiries? . . .

Some say, let the colored people leave the country! We reply NO BRETHREN. We would rather die a thousand deaths, in *honestly* and *legally* contending for our rights *in this our native country.* We cannot act in this respect so IGNOBLY as our Pilgrim fathers did. We will stay and seek the purification of the whole lump. With the character of the country we are identified, and with its character we intend to sink or swim. If the country sink in disgrace, we will perish amidst its ruins—yet seeking its regeneration and salvation. . . .

The Colored American, New York, September 30, 1837

Charles B. Ray, the author of the following letter, was a general agent of the Colored American *until he became a co-editor in 1838. Canada, a terminal of the Underground Railroad, had also drawn thousands of black settlers.*

The great error amongst our people in reference to Emigration is that there is not enough of the spirit of it among them. They are too fond of old places, as well as of old habits and customs; they seem to be more strongly attached to old locations than people generally—they adhere to them, father and son, mother and daughter, as though away from them there could be neither rest nor hope to body or mind.

In most cases, where there has been any disposition to emigrate, the attention of the persons has most invariably been turned to Canada; nothing short of entirely leaving the States would answer.

It appears to me, that this selection has been wrong; especially is it now, at these times of disaffection there. The attention of colored persons to Canada, as the place of their destination, has been because of the equal laws existing there. The laws of Canada, render colored men residing there eligible to office, the same as white men, but those offices which, in most cases, men of color emigrating there, are mentally qualified to fill, were so far from having much honor attached to them, or being lucrative, that they are, in view of their circumstances, rather a burden and not at all desirable. A friend in Rochester, who had resided in Canada and told me that one year during his residence there, the offices of the township are pretty equally distributed among the colored citizens, as well as white—himself was appointed township clerk, an office as good as any in the town; yet by no means lucrative. Many other colored persons were induced into office, but they were all so much of a burden that they refused to receive them another year.

Some of the disadvantages of Canada, which more than counteract the equal laws are, the few internal improvements, and the consequent lack of labor. Wages are also much less than in the States, the provisions, some kinds, are fewer, not sufficiently, however, to make up for the reduction of wages.

Some persons go to Canada, because land is cheap, only just as cheap as in the States. Others go to get rid of prejudice; in this they are defeated. Prejudice is just as strong there as here, and rather worse. Canadians borrow their prejudice, and do not know how to use it, and they consequently abuse it, and it bears more heavy upon the colored men. The people of Canada are afraid of emancipation, and dread it; they think because of the fugitive escapes there for a refuge, if emancipation takes place, the current will set them all northerly, and empty them into Canada, and they will be overrun with colored people. Hence, they are prejudiced to Emancipation, and the emancipated. I was informed of this by a person having lived there, as well as by those living in the vicinity. If our people would know, whether there is as little prejudice in the States, as in Canada, under the same circumstances, let them settle about, indiscriminately, among the white people, in farming communities, and become cultivators of the soil, and they will not have occasion to think or know, much about prejudice against them.

In my tour I visited two colored farmers, in the western part of this State. One of them owned two hundred acres of land and upwards, in the farm, in a beautiful part of the State, and another smaller some fifteen miles distant cultivated by his son. The old gentleman lives among an intelligent farming community; he nor his children know very little about prejudice; and suffer nothing on account of it. He is consulted in town matters, and church matters, as they consult each other. If we would run away from prejudice, it is not necessary that we should run out of the U. States, but scatter thousands of us all over the country, and buy up the soil and become cultivators of it. In this way, better than any other, can we get rid of prejudice.

Some infer, that Prejudice in our country, is the same every where, and under all circumstances, from the laws which exist in some of the States, disfranchising colored men, and from the power of it felt in large cities, where there are ten thousand of us proscribed together, but not so, circumstances, in this case, after case.

The Territory of Wisconsin, in my view, holds out greater inducements to colored men to emigrate to, than any spot on earth. It is an immense tract of country, west of the State of Michigan, one inch of which has not yet been sold, nor has it been brought into the market for sale. Yet it is fast being peopled, by honest and industrious farmers. It has an excellent soil for producing, and a climate not colder, if as cold as Oneida County of this State.

People from the eastern states are pouring in there constantly, selecting their plots of ground, and settling upon them without money and without price, clearing up their land and cultivating it, and raising wheat and other produce in abundance, and colored men have the same privileges equally with white men.

I travelled on the canal, a short distance, some weeks since, with men and their families bound to Wisconsin. The men had been there, selected their plots of ground, got in their crop, prepared for their families, returned for them, and were then going back to take up their permanent residence.

Men of color, with a very small amount of money can do the same and in a few years be independent men—for who is so independent as the farmer. They may go ahead of their families, 14 months, select their plot of ground, clear up some, get in their crop, build their log house, and return with their families, and arrive there sufficiently early in the season, to gather in their crops, and will not want ten dollars in money when they arrive.

They may continue to cultivate and improve their selected lands, until Government shall bring them into the market for sale, when they will have an opportunity of buying it at Government price, one dollar and twenty-five cents the acre; and during the interim in which they may have resided upon it, they may raise enough, over and above wants, to pay for it.

Another advantage in emigrating to Wisconsin is that it is yet a territory; there is, therefore, no state constitution, nor corrupt statute laws. If colored men emigrate there, and become settlers and citizens, when it shall be proposed to make a state of it, and to draw up a constitution for it, they will have a right to a voice in saying what shall be the character of that instrument, and of those laws by which themselves, and the citizens generally, are to be governed; and by their influence, they may have them just and equal.

It may be said, it is a great way off. It is just as far for colored men as for white men. Besides, persons can step on board a steamer at the foot of Barclay street in this city, and they need not step on land again until they arrive at Green Bay, in Wisconsin, unless they choose.

I hope our readers among our people, (and I would more of our

people were readers of our paper,) will give the subject a little attention, especially before they determine to settle in Canada.

Brethren, it is time we were up and doing, and awake to every good
thing, to every enterprise, interest and improvement.

The Colored American, New York, November 18, 1837

As the country moved closer to Civil War, the Weekly Anglo-African
*displayed an increased interest in colonization, reflecting a general mood
of black people.*

Of all the despicable meanness, of all the coldblooded treatment
that of the American Government towards the Government of Liberia
surpasses anything that has yet come within the range of our observation. If it was a matter between two private individuals, we should
have no hesitancy in pronouncing it an act of double-distilled villainy;
but as it is, we must run no such risk, but simply state the main features of the case, and let the community judge for themselves. The Liberian Colony, be it known, the American people claim as a vine of its
own right hand planting; a vine planted and nurtured for the especial
benefit of the colored man; an asylum reared to enable him to escape
from degradation; a place in which he may rise from his low and dependent condition to one of respectability and honor. In a word, by
being freed from the shackles that hamper him here, and a removal
from the inequalities and prejudices that meet him on every hand, to
this land of promise, he may become a man.

All this is claimed by the promoters of *African* colonization here.
Yea, more! they say in Liberia of all his mutual relations with that
Government, he (the colored man) has "our well-wishes and our sympathies, and even our pecuniary aid." Well, this colony of Blacks has
become a real regular government, acknowledged by England, France
and other European governments, as such. But does the American
Government in common with the rest so acknowledge it? Oh, no! This
very Government and people who have the welfare of the Blacks in
that land, would not so much as listen to a proposal to form a treaty
or even receive an agent from that Government for such purpose. Let
us look a little further in this matter. Mr. E. J. Roy, a man of color,
emigrated a few years ago from Ohio to Liberia and by enterprise, in-

dustry, and much perseverance, became a successful merchant there. Well, Mr. Roy, not willing to confine his mercantile operations to one or two continents arrived the other day at our ports in his own brig Eusibia N. Roy, a first sailer of over 300 tons, carrying Liberian register and colors, and with a cargo of African produce valued at $30,000. On this cargo, Mr. Roy was compelled to pay duty and a tonnage duty of 80¢ per ton upon his vessel. Why was this? Simply because he was a colored man, hailing from a colored government. Who planted that Liberian colony, new government? Why, this same American people, whose government now thus ruthlessly robs her sable sons of their hard earned and honest gain without even the shadow of justice.

But says our American Government, there is no reciprocity treaty between us and Liberia. And why not? Simply because we Americans refuse to form one with them, and then force our goods upon the Liberian people on the same terms as other governments, who have formed just and equitable treaties; taking care, at the same time, to impose the heaviest possible duties that the absence of a treaty will allow. The American Government has never paid the first cent to Liberia in the way of tonnage duties since she has been a colony.

If we could, with as little expense, manufacture a few hundred more black merchants, like Mr. Roy, having them arrive in port every day or so, freighted with African produce, Uncle Sam might derive quite a handsome revenue—one sufficient certainly to grease the wheels of not only that part of the political machinery in the New York Custom House, but even in *Washington*.

The Press that have at all ventured to mention the subject, have with characteristic meanness, spoken not one word of the injustice of the act, but with reference only to the probable pecuniary losses likely to ensue if such a course be insisted on by our Government. Verily, we are a magnanimous people—a model for the rest of the world!

The Weekly Anglo-African, New York, July 23, 1859

At this time, emigration to Haiti, led by the Reverend James Theodore Holly and James Redpath (a white abolitionist and a friend of John Brown) had begun to attract the interest of the black community. The debate over Haitian emigration played a most important role in engendering a discussion of the condition and future of black people in this country.

The following letter was written by the Reverend Henry Highland Garnet, who supported Haitian emigration.

. . . Hayti needs population to develop her agricultural and mineral resources and to fortify and defend her against the invasion of a slave power of the Western world. She is capable of containing ten millions of inhabitants, and has only a little over one million in her borders. She needs men and labor, and labor will be amply rewarded. . . .

But with regard with Africa the case is far different. She does not need population, for that she already has in abundance. *She needs but a few to direct the labor,* the elements of which are on her soil and to call them forth into systematic, productive, and economical activity. It is the power of the colored men of America to supply the wants of both countries, and thus give the death blow to slavery, and bless our scattered race throughout the world. These are my views in brief, and I trust no one will trouble himself further about the probability of a change in my views. Both of these grand and stupendous schemes have entered so deeply into my heart and thought that they have become a part of my existence, and hence, while I live, there can be no change in my principles and opinions on this subject. . . .

The Weekly Anglo-African, New York, December 22, 1860

The following is a letter by James McCune Smith (1813–1865) a prominent black doctor in New York City, educated in Glasgow and one of the leading intellectuals of his day. It was written in reply to Garnet.

. . . The Haytian emigration scheme is an attempt at an experiment which was made and failed thirty years ago. At that time the Haytian Government sent to the United States one of its most honored citizens—M. Granville—who laid before the colored people proposals for their emigration. Between two and four thousand of our people migrated to Hayti and within six or ten months, nearly all who survived or could get away from Hayti returned to the United States. . . .

Your duty to our people is to tell them to aim higher. In advising them to go to Hayti, you direct them to sink lower. You and those with whom you are immediately identified—nay the most if not all of our people in the free States—believe themselves of equal force and ability with the whites, come whence they may. We affirm by our lives and conduct that if degraded, it is not by our innate inferiority but by the active oppression of those who outnumber us. The Haytians have a proverb, universal among the masses "Aprez bon Jo-blanc"—"Next to God is the white man." The Haytians too, like the Liberians, further admit their inferiority by making it an article of their constitution that "no white man can become a Haytian (or Liberian) citizen."

No, my dear sir, the free blacks of the United States are wanted in the United States. The people of Maryland said so the other day when they voted that they should not be reduced to slavery. Even the people of Charleston S.C. say they cannot spare them as free men, even to be converted into slaves. And our people want to stay, and will stay at home: we are in for the fight and will fight it out here. Shake yourself free from these migrating phantasms, and join us with your might and main. You belong to us, and we want your whole soul. . . .

The Weekly Anglo-African, New York, January 12, 1861

The following week, Garnet replied to Smith's attack on the Haitian emigration movement.

. . . What are you doing for the young people of New York, and for those of the whole country? You are not an inch in advance of the emigrationists in this matter. You saw us struggling last winter in this city to establish a reading room for our sons, and you, and your whole tribe refuse to contribute a cent to keep it open, and when it failed, your standing army laughed. . . . You anti-emigrationists seem to desire to see the hundreds of colored men and women who have good trades to stay here and be the drudges and menials of white men, who will not employ or work with them. . . . And you anti-emigrationists, Dr. Smith, are no better in this respect, than your hard-hearted white brethren. You likewise "do not employ niggers." You pass by the black tailor, mantua-maker, milliner, and shoemaker, and carpenter, and employ white people who curse you to your teeth. Why, your own party will not even employ a black doctor as a general thing. A few weeks ago, an Irish gentleman showed me a beautiful mansion on the thriving Sixth Avenue, which to your great credit, belongs to you. I looked upon it, and felt proud of the success of my early friend. . . . I looked in vain to discover a dark face at work. There was not one there—no, not even a hod-carrier. By the side of your property, another equally imposing was going up, owned by the Rev. James M. Gloucester, and I saw there also an entire absence of the practical application of your professed principles. Mr. Gloucester is the largest real estate and house owner in the State of New York among the colored people. But who builds and repairs these buildings? I mean the property of Dr. Smith, and the Rev. Mr. Gloucester. Tell me, do you even go so far as to hire your houses to black people? There is one colored tradesman whom you patronize, that is the black "barber" for no one else will shave you!

The Weekly Anglo-African, New York, January 19, 1861

From March 16, 1861, to August 10, 1861, the Weekly Anglo-African *was under the editorship of George Lawrence, Jr., a strong supporter of Haitian emigration.*

. . . We are not in favor of an indiscriminate emigration anywhere —to Canada, the Far West, Africa, Central America, or Haiti. Those of us who are content with our present condition and prospects, who feel that *here* we can work the most efficiently for the Anti-Slavery cause will not and ought not to emigrate anywhere, for to leave what we believe to be our post of duty would be criminal and cowardly. But neither do we hold, on the other hand, that it is our duty *because* we are colored men, to remain in the United States; and we have no sympathy with the theory occasionally advanced that to leave this country is in all cases a desertion of our brethren in bonds. It is a majority of the whites alone, not the colored men or abolitionists in any degree, who are guilty of slavery in the United States; and on that majority, therefore, devolves the responsibility of the crime, and on them will the penalty for continuing the iniquity be afflicted. . . .

. . . Hayti cannot but command the most lively sympathies of all men of African descent. It is the only nationality of our race in the Western Continent; it is the only land in which we have conquered our liberty by the sword against the bravest white warriors of the world. It has a history of extraordinary interest, abounding in incidents that none of us can read without a glow of pride of race. . . .

The Weekly Anglo-African, Washington, D.C., March 16, 1861

We wish to inform such of our colored friends as are interested in Haytian emigration that a large number of colored people now in this city, exiles from South Carolina, in view of accepting the generous offer of the Haytian government, have formed themselves into an emigration association, adopting a constitution, so as to go out to Hayti in an efficient manner. . . .

The Weekly Anglo-African, New York, February 2, 1861

The Haitian emigration movement was viewed not as an escape from American racism, but as the means of building a base from which the émigrés could attack the slave states.

Listen! We want our rights! No one is going to *give* them to us, so perforce we must take them. In order to do this, we must have a strong nationality somewhere—respected, feared. We require a government that can not only catch slave-dealers and slave holders, but *will* hang them so surely as they are caught. . . . We can make of Hayti the nucleus of a power that shall be to the black, what England has been to the white races, the hope of progress and the guarantee of permanent civilization. Look at her position; she is at the center of a circle in whose plane lie Cuba, Central America, and the Southern Slave States. From that centre let but the fire of Freedom radiate until it shall enkindle, in the whole of that vast area the sacred flame of Liberty upon the altar of every black man's heart, and you effect at once the abolition of slavery and the regeneration of our race.

Let us prepare, then, to aid Hayti in the coming struggle, with our sympathies, our fortunes, and our lives. Contribute arms and hands to bear them.

VOLUNTEER

The Weekly Anglo-African, New York, April 13, 1861

HAYTIAN BUREAU OF EMIGRATION
Boston April 23, 1861

A sailing vessel will leave New York City on May 17, for Hayti. Fifty-one emigrants are already engaged for this vessel. Any others intending to go, under the terms announced by the Agents of the Government of Hayti are earnestly requested to give immediate notice to this Bureau.

A. E. NEWTON, Corresponding Secretary

The Weekly Anglo-African, New York, May 4, 1861

AFRICAN EMIGRATION

Persons disposed to Emigrate to the Yoruba country, Africa, and desiring aid in effecting the purpose, can receive full information as to how such aid might be procured by forwarding their name and address to Robert Campbell, 661 N. 13th. Philadelphia.

The Weekly Anglo-African, New York, May 4, 1861

The following editorial demonstrates the importance of Haitian emigration to those concerned about "black nationality."

The nineteenth century having devoted itself to the reform of long-existing abuses, the spread of civilization, the enlightenment and elevation of the entire human race, and finding its operations somewhat retarded by the depressed condition of the negro race and their descendants, desires to establish a Nationality for the purpose of lifting the race to the level of civilization, and enabling it to contribute its share to the progress of the age. The nineteenth century wants a Black Nationality, because it is an instrumentality that cannot be dispensed with in the rehabilitation of the black race, and it looks to us to furnish the energy, the enterprise, the men to aid in its development. . . .

To him who desires the elevation of our people, as such, this, then, is the question. How can we make ourselves a distinct people and a homogeneous nation? . . . We hold that all measures for our advancement as a race, must contemplate the preservation of our identity, and the ennoblement of our hue. We consider it one of the worst features of our exceptional social position, that we are come to look upon our color as a badge of degradation, and are anxious to remove it.

. . . In the overshadowing presence and constantly increasing bulk of the white population, there is no prospect for us, but subordination and absorption. The idea of retaining our present social attitude, in the hope of ameliorating its conditions, involves, not the elevation, but the extinction of the most enlightened portion of our race. Surely this is not the result which any true lover of his race, who desires to wipe off the stigma which civilization has attached to the word *negro* wishes to attain? Our perfect development and consequent preparation for the work we have to do, requires our separation from the influences which draw us apart and cause us in our prurient desire for recognition as Americans to lose sight of our duty to ourselves. . . .

If, then, we can carve out a separate existence here, either under the American flag, or over it, be it so. But if we cannot, then migration is our only policy, and sacred duty. Indeed, were we fully alive to our true interests and the destiny of our race, migration would have been the preference of our past, not the *dernier resort* of today. Standing in the light of history, especially the history of our Continent—conversant as the better educated among us are with the influences that have molded American society and its institutions, and continue to dominate its policy toward our race—our abject clinging to the skirts of a people who seek to cast us off, illustrates at once our degradation and the emasculating power of slavery.

The Weekly Anglo-African, New York, May 11, 1861

During 1865 and 1866, Southern legislators enacted the Black Codes in an effort to continue the institution of slavery. Such measures became especially important in the wake of large-scale migrations to the North.

It is ascertained that 3,200 freedmen have emigrated from this State during the last three months, to Mass., Conn., and other New England States on contracts to work at $20 a month; and they are still going. Thousands are going from Virginia, and yet the supply is inadequate to the demand. . . .

The South Carolina Leader, Charleston, December 31, 1865

We advise the colored men to buy their land, and then buy their own gins; buy the land this fall; now is the time to make the bargains.

The Weekly Free Man's Press, Galveston, Texas, October 24, 1868

Though conditions began to improve somewhat under Radical Reconstruction, the basic dependency of black labor on white landowners remained as a source of exploitation.

. . . Statesmen and friends of the latter races urge emigration to the fertile fields of the West, where cheap lands and good climate await the earnest toil of enterprising laborers to return wealth aplenty. We say to the colored people of the South, though you may be able to obtain employment at home, the time seems to be far distant when you can become owners of the soil, and consequently independent of the will of land-owners. Until you are independent of those who own the land and who can dictate the terms upon which you will be employed, you will be but little better than slaves. . . .

The New National Era, Washington, D.C., December 12, 1872

. . . not the land agents, not the attractions for a colder though more invigorating climate, but in the action of the planters themselves must the causes for the exodus be found. . . .

The People's Advocate, Washington, D.C., April 19, 1879

By the late 1870's substantial black communities had been built in Kansas. Emigration reached a high point in the exodus of 1879, led by Benjamin "Old Pap" Singleton, Henry Adams, and others.

. . . For colored men to stay in the rebel-ridden South and be treated like brutes is a disgrace to themselves and to the race to which they belong. The only way then that lies open to our people is to leave the South and come to the West. While we don't favor the colony idea very much, believing that the best course is to get as near other people as you can, yet, we would prefer that to being cheated and abused by the whites. When the South begins to lose her laborers in great numbers, then she will begin to see the folly of her course towards them, and her own necessities will force her to change her policies. . . .

The American Citizen, Baltimore, July 26, 1878

Regarding the movement that is depopulating the South of its best laborers, some have asserted that the idea of a life of ease and trifling-ness has had much to do with prompting the people to join the great Exodus. Such talk to us seems the height of great nonsense. The people are leaving the South because they can't stay there without submitting to a slavery worse than that from which the war lifted them. They know that they will have to work for a living in Kansas, but the thought that they will get the living after they do work for and earn it is the great moving cause today that is propelling them forward.

The American Citizen, Baltimore, April 26, 1879

The loss of a significant portion of Southern black laborers owing to emigration presented serious economic problems to white planters.

The one great thought in the minds of nearly all the people of the South and also of many of the people of the North is how to stop the exodus of the colored people. . . . The only possible way to put an end to that movement from the South is for the Southern white people to change their cruel course of treatment toward them.

The American Citizen, Baltimore, July 19, 1879

Domestic colonization increased in popularity as Southern society became more repressive, and an alternative had to be found for achieving self-determination.

What is to be the final destiny of the colored race of this country is a problem, the solving of which has long engaged the best attention of every thoughtful colored man and every friendly white man and is as yet unsolved. Almost every thinker has expressed his opinion upon the subject, and the opinions have been as various as the thinkers themselves. . . . I boldly assert that the only practical plan for ever settling the question is for the black men of this country to select one of the territories of this government and to gain by legal means possession of it, and then go into it, and settle it up and go to work and build towns, cities, railroads, manufacturing establishments, schools, colleges, churches, and everything else necessary, and thus form a state of their own. In this way, and in this way only, can the Negroes make of themselves a happy and prosperous people. No thinking black man, who deserves the name of such, can doubt for a moment his ability to build up a powerful and prosperous State. We have the bone and the muscle to do the hard work, and we have among us the talent and the statesmanship to regulate the political machinery, and we have educated men to run the schools and colleges, the ministers to manage the churches, and the mechanical skill to run all business of that character, and capitalists to build railroads through our State will not be lacking. . . .

The Colored Visitor, Logansport, Indiana, August 1, 1879

The political impact of the migrations from the South were not lost on black leaders, who saw in it a lever against the oppression of their people. The following is a report of the Committee on a Permanent Form of Organization established by one of the many conferences to bring together the black community and encourage migration.

We the colored people of the United States of America in Conference assembled at Nashville, Tennessee, this 6th. day of May, 1879 do declare the first principle of a republican form of government to be equality of its citizens before the law, and the obligation of the government to protect all classes of citizens by its laws; that we recognize with profound regret the existence of a race distinction having caste and prejudice as its principles, and directed toward the colored people of this country with such a force of discrimination as to nullify the Constitution and render the law inactive or inoperative; that the civil, political and intellectual advancement of our race was thereby seriously impaired and the life and property of our people are unjustly abused, therefore,

Be it resolved That we do hereby form ourselves into a national society to be duly incorporated under the laws of the United States, and to be called the American Protective Society to Prevent Injustice to the Colored People.

Section I. The objects of the society shall be 1. to foster a national union. 2. to protect civil and political rights. 3. to facilitate educational and moral improvement. 4. to encourage the purchase of agricultural land and the removal thereon from all states where colored people are unjustly treated. 5. to encourage agricultural and business capacity. 6. to improve the sanitary relations among the colored people. . . .

Whereas the political and civil rights of the colored people from the Ohio River to the Gulf of Mexico are abridged and curtailed in every conceivable manner; whereas there seems to be no disposition on the part of the great majority of the southern whites to better this condition of affairs, or to grant the colored people their full rights of citizenship, and whereas a further acquiescence in the abrogation of our rights and privileges would prove us unfit for citizenship, devoid of manhood and unworthy the respect of men;

Resolved that it is the sense of this conference that the great current migration which has for the past few months taken so many of our people from their homes in the South, and which is still carrying hundreds to the free and fertile West, should be encouraged and kept in motion until those who remain are accorded every right and privilege guaranteed by the Constitution and laws. . . .

The People's Advocate, Washington, D.C., May 17, 1879

Abandoned by their Northern friends in Congress and threatened with Southern repression, black farmers turned toward the Western territories.

. . . All concede that it would be more desirable if the Negro could in the present generation get a recognition of his manhood at the South, but to do it the Negro must be put on his own land. Old abolitionists ever since the war have been appealed to in behalf of the Negro's landless condition to furnish the capital required to secure homesteads for the freedmen, but in vain. Only when it became evident that the friends of the freedmen would not furnish this aid required does the Exodus furnish the only practicable alternative. . . .

The People's Advocate, Washington, D.C., September 20, 1879

Though conditions were hard for the black settlers in Kansas, black editors continued their highly effective promotion of emigration throughout the black communities in the South.

Many good people in the East have probably heard of a "Kansas dugout" and have thought of it as a sort of human habitation peculiar to partial civilization and frontier barbarity. This is by no means a fair conclusion. "Dugouts" are not simply holes in the ground. They are generally dug into a side hill. They have two or more sides, with windows and doors. The floor and the roof are of earth. They are warmer than most of the more pretentious dwellings. They are as comfortable as they are cheap, and in nearly every place they protect a happy and prosperous family. Though comparatively few in number at the present time, they are still foremost among the best devices for building a fortune from the ground up. "Despise not the day of small things" is the motto of those who dwell in the dugouts.

The Kansas Herald, Topeka, February 6, 1880

Although favoring the exodus, the Herald *was apprehensive about the ability of the black community to absorb the thousands that were arriving.*

The exodus from the South continues and while we favor people coming from that section, we must be allowed to say that we do not favor the idea that they should all come to Topeka before seeking homes in this State. . . . The crowded conditions of the barracks at times render that institution anything but comfortable and parties arriving here who can possibly do so should give that establishment a wide berth. . . . We are in favor and would be glad to welcome every colored man from the South to the growing West. We think some good might derive from a move to get some of our people from the South to go elsewhere than Kansas; not that this State is too crowded, but because other western states hold out as great inducements as Kansas.

Another and prominent reason why we favor the exodus is because affairs in the South have undergone such a change that it is simply impossible for the colored man to remain there with any degree of safety to either life or property; because he is not allowed to exercise the rights guaranteed by the laws of the very State in which he resides; because he is cheated, robbed, and even murdered by his professed best friends; because he has no redress for wrongs before the courts of his native State, and in fact is not looked upon by the chivalrous Southerner as constituting a part of the body politic; because he is not allowed representation in the councils of his State when it is generally known that the colored voters are in the majority. . . .

The Kansas Herald, Topeka, February 6, 1880

A letter from the Journal of Progress *indicates the enthusiasm of the would-be settlers. To aid and encourage them, immigration societies were established throughout the South.*

A few days ago a note was received asking information in regards to Immigration Aid Societies. The enquirer seemed to represent quite a number of colored farmers in Monroe County, Georgia, who are anxious to leave for some more genial clime. There are hundreds of colored farmers in Georgia dissatisfied with their present condition. So deep-rooted is their discontent that many will leave for the northwest at no distant future.

The Kansas Herald, Topeka, February 6, 1880

The heavy influx of people continued, and serious problems arose, not only in caring for them, but in its total effect on the already established community.

From the present indications it appears that the influx of colored immigration will be larger this spring and summer than ever before. The Southern states generally, and notably Mississippi, seemed determined to stamp out the exodus by the enactment of laws as oppressive and anti-Republican as the Russian despotic government in its war against Nihilism. The effort must prove abortive since the colored man will leave in spite of all that can be done to retain him forceably, simply because life under existing conditions is unbearable.

The Relief Board, whether intentional or otherwise, does not seem to comprehend the scope of the movement they are supposed to guide and direct.

The Kansas Herald, Topeka, February 13, 1880

. . . We think it is an outrage on the working men of this city, both black and white, to allow these refugees to compete with them in the manner of cheap labor. Of late we have heard a great deal of complaint among the working classes in regard to the refugees being the direct cause of the reduction of wages that have been made in this city, and give as a reason that the pauper labor from the barracks is met at every turn.

The Kansas Herald, Topeka, March 26, 1880

Deteriorating conditions among the newly arrived "exodusters" led to the following letter by "Old Pap" Singleton, the man who had led thousands to Kansas.

I have received a letter from Tennessee. There are a thousand people that have sent here for me to come after them. . . . They have sent for "Old Pap" but I find that the city is overrun with exodusters at this time and I think it would be inexpedient to bring more here at present. But still they want to come here and nowhere else; and there is no way of getting around it as Kansas is their destiny and they are bound to come. I am now getting too old and I think it would be better to send someone more competent, and identified with the immigration and has the interest of his race at heart and not his own pocket; someone that has heretofore directed and established colonies in the State and is known in the South. They should be sent to turn the tide of immigration . . .

The Kansas Herald, Topeka, March 12, 1880

Pap Singleton was called the Moses of the exodus of '79 for good reason.

The friends of Pap Singleton, the father of the great exodus, have decided to celebrate his next birthday, the 15th. of August. Pap was born in 1809. . . . He was the prime mover of the Real Estate Association formed in Nashville, Tenn. in 1868. In this association was inaugurated the movement which resulted in the great hegira. Pap led out a colony and located them at Baxter Springs, Kansas in 1875. All the party have done well. Several other colonies were subsequently located by him, among which are Singleton colony in Morris and Lyons county. Between 1875 and 1880, Pap travelled back and forth repeatedly between Tennessee and Kansas, until he had conducted hither, according to statistics gathered from railroad and steamboat officials, 7,432 exodusters. On the 19th. of May, 1876, Pap and others called the first Emigration Convention ever assembled in America, in Nashville, Tennessee.

The Colored Patriot, Topeka, Kansas, May 4, 1882

The railroads had a great interest and role in settling the territories, coincidental with the black settlers. It is significant that Oklahoma was being discussed as the site for an exclusive black colony at this time.

The M.K. and T.R.R. [Missouri, Kansas and Texas Railroad] traverses the Indian Territory from the line of Kansas to Denver, Texas. This may be deemed a sort of exclusive right in as much as the government has not seen fit to grant a single right of way to other railroads. To this extent it is a monopoly. Now this franchise, valuable as it is, cannot be successfully utilized until this vast country through which this road passes has been settled and its agricultural resources developed, in other words, what this road most needs now, is "way freight," which is always more profitable than "through freight." The Indians are not good railroad patrons and hence the desire of the railroads to seize what is known as the Oklahoma Territory and settle it up by such persons as would bring grist to their mill. Capt. Payne, under railroad inspiration, attempted to invade the territory, but with poor success; since that time the railroads have been casting about for new agencies; and they believe they have found the agencies in the cooperation of the members of the A.M.E. [African Methodist Episcopal] Conference. I say A.M.E. Conference because 5, or 6 ministers who belong to that Conference are here as delegates asking Congress to do precisely for them what it declined to do for Payne. The question may be asked—Why should not this territory be set apart exclusively for the colored people? The moment these people are eliminated from the American people they will require for their protection class legislation; legislation which has always proved destructive to the interest of those whom it was designed to protect. . . .

The Colored Patriot, Topeka, Kansas, June 22, 1882

Henry Simkens, the editor of the Arkansas Mansion, *left his native state, South Carolina, in 1860. Apparently the family moved to Haiti, where they owned a business. In 1877 he moved to Little Rock. Like most black pioneer editors, he was a staunch advocate of domestic colonization.*

. . . Now the colored people as a mass are enjoying nearly every right here that they can enjoy in Canada, and if we continue to qualify ourselves and not stop to force ourselves on anybody who are not willing to receive us. The caste prejudice will in time die of itself sooner than it could be killed by any special legislation. Had it not been for the special legislation, the whites of the south would have respected colored men of distinction, also colored ladies and gentlemen on travel, and treat ill-bred blacks as they did, and do ill-bred whites, but the Civil Rights Bill took away all the superior virtues of colored people and formed them into one class, and that the lower class.

Hence, we believe that annuling the farcical civil rights bill by the Supreme Court will not militate against the interests of the colored people, and it is better that the bills be defined by the present judges than left to a subsequent bench, who may decide that they are unconstitutional and absolutely void, which would throw us back where we were 23 years ago. A political revolution is imminent, and we should be prepared to make our interest paramount to any other party, or sect, and we think our leading men will see it in that light, just as soon as they allow their excited passions to be cooled down.

It should be remembered that at the National Convention at Louisville we pronounced the civil rights amendments a dead letter in which the supreme court has only concured. Let us be patient; if we can't stay in the states, let us go to the United States territories, not to Africa.

The Arkansas Mansion, *Little Rock, October 27, 1883*

The author of the following article, signed "Le Duke," was a frequent correspondent and shows the interrelationship between cooperative movements and black colonization.

. . . It is high time we were organizing. It is high time we were reaping the results of co-operation. We possess all the necessary elements and incentives. We have a cause; we have numbers and we have all the means necessary to form a grand organization looking to the alleviation of the sufferings of our people by the securement of our full political, civil and social rights. Just now we have a peculiar cause. Our brethren in all parts of the south are being massacred because they dared to express their political opinion. Their lives, their property and their prospects are being taken from them. Their condition is but little less deplorable than in the dark days of slavery. . . .

We should form associations for the purpose of removing such families as desire to go to the West where they will find lands and friends. Let the colored people hold a meeting, and form a committee composing men whose reputation for honesty and earnestness is unquestioned, whose duty it will be to accept contributions from the colored people for the purpose of defraying the travelling expenses of emigrants and securing to them such comforts as shall be necessary.

The People's Advocate, Washington, D.C., November 17, 1883

Emigration to the Indian Territory as a place where black people could obtain land and exercise self-determination was a continuation of earlier colonization efforts in Kansas.

There is some prospect of a new field being opened to the Negro of the South, who may seek to better his condition by removal to some other part of the country. In the Indian Territory, which lies south of the state of Kansas, there is situated a fertile tract of land, almost entirely occupied by the Cherokee Indians and Negroes. The latter were slaves of the Indians before the war and have lived with them ever since the emancipation. They are believed to be entitled to a considerable portion of the land in the Indian Territory, and application has been made to the government for an investigation and decision upon their claims. The Secretary of the Interior gave a delegation of colored men who called upon him the assurance that inquiry shall be made into the matter. The Territory is now in the exclusive possession of the Indians, who have not succeeded as agriculturalists and the resources of the country have not yet been made available. But if the claims of the colored people to some of the land should be allowed, a vast field would be opened for them to become producers of wealth. Those who have struggled on in the various States of the South, unable to do more than make a bare living, owing to the better part of their earnings going to the storekeeper, would find an opportunity to settle and make homes for themselves.

The Globe, New York, April 14, 1883

Interest in African emigration was revived with the efforts of Dr. Edward W. Blyden of Liberia and Bishop Henry M. Turner of the AME Church. Dr. Benjamin F. Tanner, editor of the AME Christian Recorder, opposed this idea. Fortune, while agreeing basically with Tanner, argued for greater interest by blacks in Africa.

. . . Emigration may play a very important part in the solution of the question of our position in this country. Whatever may be the wishes of the thoughtful men of the race, the mass of our people in the South are growing fearfully restless under the wrongs and outrages to which they are subjected daily, and they will certainly attempt, in the near future, to seek in emigration, or otherwise, that protection and immunity which the lying Constitution of the United States denies, and has always denied them. . . .

The Globe, New York, January 13, 1883

Kansas and Oklahoma were not the only territories that drew black settlers, as this letter by John Jones, from Chicago, indicates.

The rapid development of the Dakota territory in the last four years has been the wonder of the whole American people. . . . In the year of 1882, a colony of quite a number of colored men of Chicago was organized. The colony was named after Mr. Watkins, who was the prime mover of the enterprise. . . . They have taken up several thousand acres of land at Villiard, the County seat of McHenry County.

The Gazette, Cleveland, Ohio, December 29, 1883

*Though colonization in the Western states was accepted enthusiasti-
cally, African colonization, at this time, was not.*

The resolution recently introduced in the Virginia Senate by Mr.
Kerner, inquiring into the expediency of establishing an experimental
colony for colored people, has attracted very general attention. Mr.
Kerner has received letters from many parts of the country, especially
from the North, approving the subject. Among the correspondents are
one or two gentlemen who have been long engaged in missionary
work in Africa. One of them expressed the opinion that, if Mr. Kerner's project is carried out, the colony ought to be established in Africa, where he thinks the colored people would not only develop the
country, but would in time make such a colony profitable at the commercial interests of the country. This correspondent claims that the establishment of such a colony meets the approval of many of the most
intelligent men of this country. The plan, however, does not meet with
interest among the colored race in this section. . . .

The State Journal, Harrisburg, Pennsylvania, March 8, 1884

*In a letter from Monrovia, Liberia, dated January 31, 1885, the author
warns of some of the problems encountered by black settlers and the corruption of the Colonization Society.*

. . . my advice to those who desire to come now is to stop for the
present until they are definitely informed that the Colonization Society has made some changes in their agency here; or, come out at their
own expense. The emigrants that come to the country are said to receive six months rations from the Society, but rarely ever get three full
months rations. Half-starved, they soon become discouraged and
leave the country in disgust. Without proper medical attention, and
having most of the time some inexperienced old woman to attend
them during the fever, some die for the mere want of attention; but
worse of all, the agent of the Society is an Englishman, who is opposed to the American emigrants, and uses their provisions for his
family; dines sumptuously like an English Lord, while the poor emigrants die from starvation.

The Freeman, New York, March 7, 1885

I. B. Burton, the author of the following letter, wrote encouragingly from Crete, Nebraska, where a small group of black settlers had bought land, and suggested cooperative ventures.

. . . A large company can emigrate and purchase railroad lands for about half of what it would cost single persons, or single families, and the fact is, single persons are by no means as desirable as families or large settlements. . . . Wholesale goods and machinery can be shipped the same way in large lots for the colony with wide-awake agents. Windmills are indispensable in the far west, and one windmill could be made to answer four or five farmers—each having an interest in it. . . .

The People's Advocate, Washington, D.C., January 19, 1884

The following is a description of a black settlement in Iowa and is a good example of early social history.

Muchachinock is a town five miles south of Oskaloosa, Iowa in a rich coal region. The output is about 120 cars daily. The population is about 20,000 of which 1,500 are colored, mostly from Virginia. They have two churches, one Methodist, the other Baptist; two frame school houses attended by about 200 children. There is one large dry goods store, quite a number of ice cream and eating saloons, and confectionaries and boarding houses kept by colored men. They have a colored brass band, an Odd Fellows hall, a goodly number of Masons, and a Mutual Benefit association. None have ever been buried by the county. There is no Justice of the Peace, no constable, or police force to support. All offences, according to mutual agreement, are tried before a committee, and fines enforced thereunder go to the Mutual Benefit association. There are but three billiard halls in the town.

These colored miners average $70 per month, and many as much as $80.

The People's Advocate, Washington, D.C., February 23, 1884

Mexico at various times was a terminus for black settlers. It was not until 1895, with a formal offer of land from the Mexican government and

*money appropriated by Congress, that a few thousand went to Mexico.
This project, however, was not successful.*

. . . In every war waged by the American people for Independence
or self-preservation, the colored people of this country are inseparably
associated. And no other race of people on the continent has added
more than they to the development of our resources. Then why should
they go to Mexico, or any other territory? Simply to gratify the hate
and the venom of a few men who are more a hindrance than a help to
the progress of their country.

The Southern portion of the United States is the natural home of
the colored people of this country. They thrive better nowhere else in
the world. The conditions of climate suit them perfectly. They have
lived there so long they have become a portion of the soil they cultivate. Then why should they leave?

. . . The colored people of this country came here not because they
wanted to, but because the white men wanted them to; now that they
are here, they have no intention, present or remote, of leaving. They
are citizens with co-equal rights; they are a portion, a very important
portion, of our industrial force; they have acquired interests here
which are rooted in American civilization—then why should they
leave? . . .

The Globe, New York, September 6, 1884

The following article was obtained from an exchange paper.

The termination of the Presidential election in favor of the Democracy has had an unhappy effect upon the colored population of the
South. It has begotten a feeling of dread and a spirit of unrest which
no assurances of the Bourbons can allay. Southern dispatches all go to
show that the Negroes of that section are anxious to place themselves
beyond the reach of harm and therefore are leaving with their household goods to a place of refuge. A dispatch from Chattanooga says
that for a number of days, many colored people have been passing
through that place enroute from South Carolina to Kansas and Arkansas. They move in squads, half a dozen or more, and carry with

them such of their personal effects as will be serviceable in their new homes. When it is possible, they migrate in larger numbers. . . .

The Gazette, Cleveland, December 13, 1884

The following articles indicate the extent of the migrations and their impact on Southern society, both black and white.

The daily papers report the existence of an extensive exodus of colored people from North and South Carolina; so extensive indeed that a serious disarrangement of the labor supply of those States is threatened. . . . Denied any voice in the making or enforcement of the laws; denied all civil rights, and supplied with inadequate school facilities; and given a pittance as wages of labor and robbed of the greater portion of this by contractors, shopkeepers, and others with whom they have money dealings—why should not this people be restless? Why should not they seek in other sections to better their social, material and civil conditions? The colored man must, in the future, be his own master and thinker, and he is beginning to understand this.

The Freeman, New York, January 16, 1886

Our colored exchanges mostly look favorably upon the so-called hegira of colored laborers from North and South Carolina to the West. It is urged that there is a glut of colored labor in the South, and that those who remain will be benefitted by those who go, by equalizing somewhat the supply to the demand. . . .

It should be remembered here that the Republic of Mexico offers splendid inducements to settlers. . . .

The Freeman, New York, January 23, 1886

The following letter was written by John L. Davis, from Salina, Kansas, on April 16, 1886.

With the coming of Spring time comes also commencement when

forth from university, normal school, and colleges there go many out into the broad paths of practical life. Perhaps among the number there may be some who do not know where they shall go, and to them I wish to say a word. Several good colored lawyers, especially graduates from the Law Department of Howard, could find lucrative practice in some of the cities in Kansas, inhabited as they are by Southern exodusters, and who as buyers of little homes pay for legal advice to white lawyers, and would as soon, if not rather, pay it to one of their own color. I can cite three cities where good lawyers could succeed. Several good physicians could find a living practice in some of these little towns in Western Kansas. A lady in Junction City, Kansas, a town of some 3,000 inhabitants and perhaps between 500 & 700 colored people told me that if a good doctor of color were to come there in a year he would have nearly the whole town, because there were so many quacks. Merit not color would win. This is true of the city from which I write, and also of other little but lively growing places in Western Kansas. A number of business men, with a small capital could make money out here in the commission, real estate, grocery, or general agency business, and if any young man wants a place to settle down and build up a firm business on a profitable basis, he could find no better field than here in Western Kansas. In my travels as a minister I find that the people in this State are willing to help a worthy and struggling man irrespective of race, or color. The ignorance of many of the colored people stands as a check to their more rapid progress. The fiendish brutality of Mississippi and the tyrannical injustice of Kentucky are forcing many from those hot beds of Southern deviltry to the free soil and air of Kansas. They are coming in every day on every train on the U.P. [Union Pacific] and other railroads. They want leaders, helpers, guides, temporal as well as spiritual. Young man, if you are about to finish at Howard, Fisk, Wilberforce, or Hampton, do not hang around Washington waiting for a chance to feed on government pop, or go to Boston to wait in a hotel, and thus sink what little manhood you had at first, but come this way—come to bear trials, come to work and wait, come to wait and win, come determined to be or die trying. You are wanted, come.

The Freeman, New York, May 15, 1886

TO THE FRONT

NICODEMUS LAND CO.

Officers

President — S. Garland
Vice President — J. T. Young
Treasurer — D. Williamson

Secretary — Wm. H. Cotton
Corresp. Sec. — A. G. Tallman

Locators

Z. T. Fletcher
J. T. Young

General Office, Nicodemus, Graham County, Kansas

CHEAP HOMES!

CHEAP LANDS!

Lands For The Millions
In The Solomon Valley in the
Vicinity of Nicodemus

The best lands in all Kansas, is in Graham county, in the Beautiful Solomon Valley—come and see for yourself.
Come one and all and settle in the garden of

THE NORTHWEST

Thousands of acres of Wild Lands, Improved Farms and Stock Ranches for sale in Graham and Rooks Counties.
If you want to get land cheap, call on us soon, as the land is

RAPIDLY INCREASING IN VALUE

If you want to get a home, cheap, come to us—we can make

YOU HAPPY

The Western Cyclone, Nicodemus, Kansas, July 15, 1886

The following article, written by Will M. Clemens of Jacksonville, Florida, explains reasons for the sweeping migrations to Southern oppression.

. . . There is going on an exodus of Negroes to the Western States. Over 3000 have already left North Carolina alone. It is not an organized movement but there is a manifest method in it. I can but see one valid reason for this exodus. The Negro is not virtually a lazy, shiftless individual. He will work, and work hard, if paid for his labor. All about him here in the South the lack of thriftliness and industry. He has little to inspire him to labor for a home when his white brother is an indolent creature, who prefers to wander idly about the streets rather than work. The Negro wants an air of prosperity all about him. He seeks it in the West, and thus I can readily see a reason for the Western exodus. The condition of white labor in the South is largely the cause of the depressing condition of all classes in the South. The Negro is poorly paid for his labor, as compared with the laborer in the North. And the white laborers and mechanics in the South are the ones to blame.

There are other reasons why the colored man should seek pastures new, notwithstanding that he is more prosperous here than his shiftless white brother. In every southern state there are laws on the statute books which give the white landlord almost absolute control of the interests of the colored renter or laborer. The "crop mortgage" system is only a legalized form of confiscation. A colored man is compelled to pay an exorbitant price for the use of land to begin with—often as much per acre as it could be bought for by a white man. In order to get provisions for his family while his cotton is being raised he must pledge his whole crop in advance, and pay for everything he buys at rates two or three times as those which are asked in the regular channels of trade. At the end of the year he is indeed fortunate if he can settle with his landlord and storekeeper by turning over to them all the proceeds of his labor, and more frequently he finds himself still in debt after such a transfer. . . . The Negro is not a free agent in the transaction. He is entirely at the mercy of those who fix the contract. His absolute necessities deprive him of all liberty of choice. He must have land to cultivate and must pay an exorbitant price for it. He must have food and clothing for his wife and children, and he must pay the merchant a double price for the same. This is the prevailing rule throughout the South. I do not speak of any special case. The law is on the side of the white man. The courts are with the white man and so is public sentiment to a certain extent. The Negro is a slave still in a certain sense. He is not treated as the white men, and here lies the secret of success and prosperity in the great South. Her whole labor system is liable to pull to pieces for want of wise and timely action in the direction of assuring the colored people that the wrongs under which they are suffering shall be removed. This is the cause of the immigration to the West. The Negro mechanics and laborers in the towns and cities are prosperous and contented as I have stated. The agricultural class, those who raise cotton and till the soil, are the dissatisfied ones. . . . Without the Negro, the South is doomed a failure. She will never be prosperous without his aid, and if the South were wise she would hasten to correct her laws and look upon the Negro as her salvation.

The Freeman, New York, January 22, 1887

The origins and early history of Nicodemus, the all-black community in Kansas, were presented in the town's paper.

Nicodemus was first plotted as a government townsite June 8, 1877, by the Nicodemus Colony, an organization formed at Topeka that year with W. H. Smith as president; S. P. Rountree, secretary; Z. T. Fletcher, corresponding secretary and postmaster. In 1878, J. W. Niles was chosen president and Ex-State Auditor McCabe secretary. . . .

The first free-to-all fight in the town was between Rev. John Anderson and Deacon Joseph Jones in an argument over scripture.

In '78 there were between 600 and 700 people on the town site being the year of the heavy immigration to northwest Kansas, here was made general headquarters and Nicodemus then contained more inhabitants than any town north of the K.P. [Kansas Pacific] railroad and west of Beloit . . .

The first school was held in Z. T. Fletcher's dugout with Mrs. Fletcher as teacher, the average daily attendence being about 45.

Z. T. Fletcher was the first postmaster, serving from '77 to '86, the first post office being kept in a dugout in the south east corner of the town. The mail was kept in a tea chest with a partition in it and for two years only two newspapers were regularly received at the office. The mail was carried from Ellis once a week by W. H. Smith, president of the colony and father of Mrs. Z. T. Fletcher. It was carried on foot. . . .

The Western Cyclone, Nicodemus, Kansas, April 21, 1887

During the first settlement of the Nicodemus Colony it was very hard times. Coming from the states of Kentucky, Tennessee, and Mississippi, the people were poor at best and it was hard work to open up a new country without money, but the majority of them have withstood the hard times of drought and hot winds and most of them are prospering today, and among the original colonists you will find some of the best farmers in the country, men that are now fairly well fixed financially, seven years ago had only parched corn and very little of that to eat. . . .

The first election ever held in the country was at Nicodemus in June, 1880 to locate the temporary county seat which was decided in favor of Millbrook and Gettysburg; people from all over the county voted here that day. . . .

The Western Cyclone, Nicodemus, Kansas, April 28, 1887

As Kansas began to reach the saturation point in emigrants and as new plans were projected for making the Oklahoma Territory an all-black state, the black press urged its readers to consider the move.

Let every colored man who wants 160 acres of land get ready to occupy some of the best lands in Oklahoma, and should it be opened up, there is no reason why at least 100,000 colored men and women should not settle on 160 acres of land each and thus establish themselves so firmly in that territory that they will be able to hold their own from the start.

The discontented and oppressed Europeans have heard of the intended opening of this country and they are now falling over each other, so to speak, to reach America in time to enter the best of these lands. Let the colored American keep his eye on Oklahoma and when the opening alarm shall have been sounded, move forward and take it. We shall keep our readers posted on whatever Congress does on this matter, to the end that they may be prepared to act unitedly and at the proper time.

The American Citizen, Topeka, Kansas, March 1, 1888

By the spring of 1889, black settlers had established themselves in the new territory led by John Young and D. B. Garrett.

. . . the Young and Garrett colony from this city which was organized by the First Colored Real Estate Homestead and Emigration Association of Kansas has located in township seventeen . . . each man has secured 160 acres and 2/3 of the lands are timbered. . . .

The American Citizen, Topeka, Kansas, May 3, 1889

❀

By the fall of that year there was something of a colonization fever, with several different organizations and plans offered.

An immigration society which has been recently established here [Topeka] to provide for an exodus of negroes to Oklahoma has received letters from Tennessee, Georgia, Alabama, Louisiana and the Carolinas saying there would be 20,000 immigrants from those states as soon as they could gather their crops and get ready to leave.

The Advocate, Leavenworth, Kansas, October 12, 1889

W. H. Ellis of this city, [San Antonio] who, with Ferguson of Fort Bend, County, is engaged in a gigantic scheme to colonize the Negroes of Texas in Mexico. . . . The Mexicans had made them a concession of $2,000,000 in money and 450,000 acres of land in Vera Cruz. . . .

The Plaindealer, Detroit, October 11, 1889

The scheme to move several hundred Afro-American families to Mexico was looked upon as visionary and impractical, but recent developments look toward its successful realization. A Mexican company has been formed with a son-in-law of President Diaz as one of the directors to furnish lands for all the families that come—50 acres free and 100 on time. A measure has already passed the Senate with but one dissenting vote for appropriation of $2,000,000 together with a grant of 450,000 acres of land. Although a few papers oppose, the majority are in favor of it. It is calculated that 20,000 families from Texas will avail themselves of this opportunity and move into Mexico this winter under the guidance of Mr. Ferguson. . . . The land of the *Montezumas* is again to become the home of the dark race, for if these first colonists succeed, others will follow. This movement, together with the number who are constantly moving to the West and North-west, will soon give those who favor emigration a chance to see the workings of their pet schemes. No sooner will the rural districts of Texas be depopulated than immigrant agents from that state will be in Georgia, Mississippi and Alabama inducing black laborers to come and fill their places.

The Plaindealer, Detroit, October 18, 1889

But it was to the West, the Promised Land, that most emigration flowed.

We learned that there is a great exodus going on of the Negroes from North Carolina to Mississippi, Louisiana, and Arkansas. Knowing as we do the brutality of southern bulldozers, the depravity of the midnight assassin, and the ballot box thief, the heartlessness and cruelty of the southern planter and taskmaster, we do not wonder that the Negroes are up in arms to leave the seemingly justice-forgotten and God-forsaken section of the country; but why they should flee from one den of ravenous and beastly thieves to seek refuge in meshes of another. . . . We feel what a great wrong is being perpetrated upon these people in inducing them to break up and leave miserable homes for those which can only be more miserable in a short time. If the leaders of this movement would lead these people to the north and west, where their condition would be at least slightly improved, there would be at least, an appearance of good faith on their part. But under the circumstances, it seems that these people are being dragged about from pillar to post to satisfy the avarice and cupidity of a few designing southern planters, aided by some of the would-be leaders of the race, for a few paltry dollars. . . . Come West, friends, come west, and grow up with God's country.

The American Citizen, Topeka, March 22, 1889

The following item from Greenwood, Mississippi, shows the interest in emigration and also that such threats to the labor supply had induced some changes in the delta.

. . . a conference was held at W. H. Smith's Law Office to consider the matter of Emigration and to inaugurate such organized efforts as may be deemed necessary to practically corroborate with the committee in selecting homes and securing employment for their friends. In case the committee should feel justified in recommending this tide of emigration from their state in this direction. . . .

They are outspoken in their expressions at surprise at the favorable condition of the labor system and the future prospects of the race in the Delta. They seem to regard the opening of these rich lands and the advantageous condition which are offered their people in this section as a Providential means which will contribute largely toward the solution of the race problem. The members of the committee disclaim any purpose of moving their people in large and irresponsible bodies as is sometimes indicated through the press. They say that their committee is the outcome of a restraining influence on the part of the more intelligent of their race who oppose the system of removing their people in large and ill-directed bodies, or under the auspices of irresponsible labor agents who have no interest in their future welfare.

Their purpose is to secure homes and employment under favorable conditions before they recommend the migration of their people, and then only under judicious and well-matured plans. The committee proposes extending their trip down to Vicksburg, from thence they will visit other points in the Delta and extend their observations through Kansas, Arkansas and Texas. They think that many thousands of their people will find homes under favorable conditions and good wages in the section covered by their observations during the approaching season.

The Freeman, Indianapolis, August 24, 1889

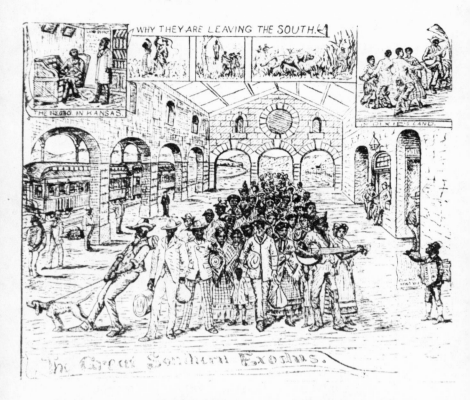

THE GREAT SOUTHERN EXODUS

The Freeman, Indianapolis, April 13, 1889

Creating a Black Community

PERHAPS *the most important function of the black press was in building self-confidence and self-respect as a foundation for black self-determination and black unity. Such efforts were based primarily on various forms of self-help, which involved a concerted attempt to resolve the problem presented to black people by a racist society. In meeting these issues directly, black journalists were often confronted by the paternalism of white abolitionists. It was largely through the efforts of black journalists that Garrison, for instance, prior to the publication of his newspaper the* Liberator, *shifted his support away from the American Colonization Society. Later, Garrison opposed Frederick Douglass' desire to publish his own paper. Although most white abolitionists were opposed to slavery, few regarded the black man as an equal.*

In rejecting slavery and injustice, black people rejected the history of degradation—that essentially dehumanizing process. Clearly, the black press saw this development in spite of the experience of slavery, and that view of progress was coordinate—not with a servile assimilation into the white world, but with the clear demand for acceptance as equals.

The following is a list of the African Free Schools, and some reflections on the importance of education. The author is most likely Samuel Cornish, who was an agent for the schools. The first of these schools was founded in 1787 by the New York Manumission Society, a group of white abolitionists, but the system was expanded with the help of black abolitionists.

. . . *Portland, Me.* With a colored population of 900 provides one school for the education of their children under the care of a mistress. Better things are in progress.

Boston, Mass. With a colored population of 2000 provides, assisted by the liberal donations of the late Abel Smith Esq. three schools for the instruction of their children, viz. two primary under the care of African female teachers, and a Grammar School under a master . . .

Salem, Mass. With a colored population of 400, put a school into operation the last year, for the education of their children, but for causes unknown to us, it closed after six months.

New Haven, Conn. With a colored population of 800 provides two schools during three months during the year under the care of a master and a mistress.

Providence, R.I. With a colored population of 1500, and Hartford, Conn. with 500 provide *none.*

Philadelphia, With a colored population of 15,000 provides *three* schools for the instruction of their children, under the care of four teachers.

New York, With a colored population of 15,000 provides *two* schools for the instruction of their children under the care of a master and a mistress. Parents, we learn, who are able, are obliged to pay $1 per quarter for each child.

We need not mention the names of any other places as we know of none other schools. Seeing then that the schools now in operation for the education of our children are so few and imperfect; ought *others* to wonder that not many after arriving at manhood, are fitted to take a respectable stand in society. What are the advantages to be derived from an instruction in these schools, compared to those of a higher and more elevated nature? What are the incentives held out to a lad of colour? Are there higher schools to stimulate him to greater exertions? Is he placed, and considered, an equal with other boys in school of the same rank? Do the committees or trustees, expect him to be well grounded in the elementary branches? A little smattering, and a few words recommendatory from his teacher, are all they look for from a boy of colour. The very idea of his colour, is enough to elicit praise from his learned visitors, when the same exercise performed as well by another boy, would pass unnoticed, and be considered as a thing of course.

We suspect it is unnecessary to mention, that much depends upon the teacher, as well as the pupil. We are so skeptical, that we cannot believe, that almost *anyone* is qualified to keep a school for our children. Enemies may declaim upon their dullness and stupidity; but we would respectfully inquire, have they not had dull and stupid instructors; who, if placed in any other but a colored school, would hardly be considered as earning *their salt;* but we must be silent, as anyone who possesses a few qualifications (unnecessary to be here named) is, in the general estimation, fit to keep a school for us. We protest against such silence, and to show our sincerity, shall continually raise our feeble voices against the unequal advantages for education enjoyed by our children: and though, upon the community at large, this may have little effect; yet we trust, there will be found, some "unjust judges" who wearied with us may strive in real earnest to do something for their education.

. . . Writers, old and young are fond of exclaiming "there is a wide difference in point of intellect between the African and the European. It is in vain to plead the degraded condition of the Negro—had not nature dealt out her gifts to him with a sparing hand, we should not have remained so long without evidence of her liberality. There are some thousands of free blacks in America, that no one has ever given the least indications of an elevated mind." Taking it for granted, that the above refers more immediately to the United States, we call upon the advocates of the system to point us to one *individual* who has enjoyed to the full extent all the privileges of his fairer brethren. Though there are thousands of free people of colour in the country, yet, to them the seats of knowledge have been as the temple of Janus, in time of peace. We will not enumerate the causes of the exclusion. They are well known. In South America and Hayti, where the Man of Colour is seen in all the dignity of man, freed from the prejudices and endowed with the rights, and enjoying all the privileges of citizenship, we behold him not a whit inferior to any of his fairer brethren. Conscious of his dignity, he acts and feels himself a man. . . .

Freedom's Journal, New York, June 1, 1827

Lewis Tappan and his brother, Arthur, were white abolitionists who gave tremendous support to black people, especially in education.

REMOVAL OF SABBATH SCHOOL

The Sabbath School hitherto held at No. 165 Chapel street, (or West Broadway) is moved to a room under the Broadway Tabernacle.

—Entrance from Anthony St. This school is for scholars of all ages without distinction of color or denomination. New scholars can be accommodated and the services of an additional number of teachers would be gratefully accepted. School commences at 9 o'clock, A.M.

LEWIS TAPPAN, *Superintendent*

Freedom's Journal, New York, July 6, 1827

Although Freedom's Journal *was mainly concerned with the condition of the Northern black community, it did include occasional reports from the South, as the following of June 20, 1827, from Tuscaloosa, Alabama.*

Some time during the last week of one of those outrageous transactions—and we really think, disgraceful to the character of civilized man, took place adjoining Bibb and Autauga counties. The circumstances we are informed by a gentleman from that county are—That a Mr. McNeilly having lost some clothing or some other property of no great value, the slave of a neighboring planter was charged with the theft. McNeilly in company with his brother, found the negro driving his master's wagon, they seized him and either did or were about to chastise him, when the negro stabbed McNeilly, so that he died in an hour afterwards; the negro was taken before a Justice of the Peace, who after serious deliberation, waved his authority—perhaps through fear, as the crowd of persons from the above counties had collected to the number of 70 or 80 near Mr. People's (the justice's) house. He acted as president of the mob, and put the vote, when it was decided that he should be immediately executed by being *burnt to death*—the sable culprit was led to a tree and tied to it, and a large quantity of pine knots collected and placed around him, and the fatal torch was applied to the pile, even against the remonstrances of several gentlemen who were present; and the miserable being was in a short time burnt to ashes. An inquest was held over the remains and the Sheriff of Perry County, with a company of about 20 men repaired to the neighborhood where this barbarous act took place to secure those concerned, but with what success we have not heard, but we hope he will succeed in bringing the perpetrators of so high handed a measure to account to their country for their conduct in this affair. This is the second negro who has been thus put to death, without Judge or Jury in that county.

Freedom's Journal, New York, August 3, 1827

✧

One of the many examples of institutionalized racism which occurred so frequently and blatantly was a bill presented to the Senate of Pennsylvania requiring that every black person who came into the state had to register himself with a certificate of his freedom within twenty-four hours or be subject to arrest, imprisonment, and sale. This concept of a black man as property, embodied in law, was an accepted part of white society, both North and South. Such measures became necessary as more and more slaves escaped to freedom and were to culminate in the Fugitive Slave Law. In the winter of 1828, a series of letters were published in Freedom's Journal *attacking this law and its assumptions, signed only as "A Man of Colour" (probably James Forten, a wealthy black sailmaker and abolitionist in Philadelphia).*

. . . why are we not to be considered as men? Has the God who made the white man and the black, left any record declaring us a different species? Are we not sustained by the same power, supported by the same food, hurt by the same wounds, pleased with the same delights, and propagated by the same means. And should we not then enjoy the same liberty, and be protected by the same laws. . . . It cannot be that the authors of our Constitution intended to exclude us from its benefits, for just emerging from unjust and cruel emancipation their souls were too much affected with their own deprivations to commence the reign of terror over others. They knew we were deeper skinned than they were, but they acknowledged us as men, and found that many an honest heart beat beneath a dusky bosom. They felt that they had no more authority to enslave us, than England had to tyrannize over them. They were convinced that if amenable to the same laws in our actions, we should be protected by the same laws in our rights and privileges. Actuated by these sentiments, they adopted the glorious fabric of our liberty, and declaring "all men" free, they did not particularize white and black, because they never supposed it would be made a question whether *we were men or not.* . . .

February 29, 1828

. . . The man of colour receiving as a visitor any other person of colour, is bound to turn informer and rudely report to the Register, that a friend and a brother has come to visit him for a few days, whose name he must take within 24 hours, or forfeit a sum which the iron hand of the law is authorized to rend from him, partly for the benefit of the Register. Who is this Register? A man, and exercising an office, where ten dollars is the fee for each delinquent, will probably be a cruel man and find delinquents where they really do not exist. The poor black is left to the merciless gripe of an avaricious Register, without an appeal, in the event, from his tyranny or oppression! O miserable race, born to the same hopes, created with the same feeling, and destined for the same goal, you are reduced by your fellow creatures below the brute . . . what have the people of color been guilty of that they more than others should be compelled to register their houses, lands, servants, and children. Yes, ye rulers of the black man's destiny, reflect upon this; our children must be duly registered, and bear about them a certificate, or be subject to imprisonment and fine. . . .

March 7, 1828

I proceed again to the consideration of the bill of unalienable rights belonging to the black men, the passage of which will only tend to show that the advocates of emancipation can enact laws more degrading to the free man, and more injurious to his feelings, than all the tyranny of slavery, or the shackles of infatuated despotism. And let me remark, that this unfortunate race of humanity, although protected by our laws, are already subject to the fury and caprice of a certain set of men, who regard neither humanity, law, nor privilege. They are already considered as a different species, and little above the brute creation. . . .

There are men among us of reputation and property, as good citizens as any men can be, and who, for their property, pay as heavy taxes as any citizens are compelled to pay. . . . The villainous part of the community of all colors we wish to see punished and retrieved as much as any people can. Enact laws to punish them severely, but do not let them operate against the innocent as well as the guilty. . . .

March 14, 1828

. . . It is in vain that we are forming societies of different kinds to ameliorate the condition of our unfortunate brethren, to correct their morals and to render them not only honest but useful members to society. All our efforts, by this bill, are dispised and we are doomed to feel the lash of oppression:—As well may we be outlawed, as well may the glorious privilege of the Gospel be denied us and all endeavours used to cut us off from happiness. . . . An appeal to the heart is my intention. . . .

March 21, 1828

Although this inquiry was not answered, it is significant that such questions were being discussed.

NEGRO

Mr. Editor.—With the derivation of the word at the head of this article, I am well acquainted, but how it can, with any degree of propriety be applied to us, I am at a loss to discover. I have been, for years, endeavoring to ascertain the propriety of applying this term to us, but without effect. Knowing, dear sir, the very extensive circulation of your truly valuable paper, I send you this, hoping that it may meet the eye of some of your readers or correspondents, who will give some information respecting the application of the above to us; and, at the same time, I should like to ascertain whether we are negroes, or as those who are truly ignorant, or actuated by the principles of prejudice, call us negroes.

Yours Very Respectfully,

AN ENQUIRER

Boston, August 24, 1828

Freedom's Journal, New York, August 8, 1828

Perhaps the most important component of self-help was education, and it is interesting to note the broad implications of this concept—it included the entire black community.

1st. What shall the Christian public do for our free coloured population? We answer, unanimously join the several abolition societies, and unite with those honorable bodies, in educating and settling them as farmers in the country—such as are mechanics encouraged in their several branches of business, discountenance the mean and shameful associations of white mechanics who refuse to work in the same shops and offices with colored men, wherever a man colored is found possessed of more than ordinary virtue and talent, as an inducement to others, extend to him, more than ordinary patronage.

2nd. What is the duty and policy of the free population of color, under the existing state of things in this country?

To this enquiry, we shall answer as follows:—

1st. place, let there be associations formed in all the towns and cities of our country, comprising the whole colored inhabitants, let every male of health and employment, pay into one general fund, at least six-pence monthly and every female, half that sum, those in circumstances not to be governed by this rule, but to give according as "the Lord hath prospered them." . . .

2nd., let the monies raised in this way be placed in the hands of an executive committee, composed of one or two competent men, chosen from each religious society in the town or city as may be, who shall appropriate them to the establishment of libraries, reading rooms, schools, academies and one general college embracing all the mechanical arts, with a thorough classical education, the library and professorships be furnished from the general fund, students be taxed for nothing save their board.

3rd., let the executive committees employ one general agent, whose duty it shall be to continue traveling from one extremity of our country to the other, forming associations communicating with our people and the public generally, on all subjects of interest, collecting monies, and delivering stated lectures on industry, frugality, enterprise etc., thereby linking together, by one solid chain, the whole free population, so as to make them think, and feel, and act as one solid body, devoted to education and improvement.

4th., let there be no compromise, but as though "born free and equal" let us contend for all the rights guaranteed to us by the constitution of our native country.

5th., let there be no delay, but let us immediately, in our large towns and cities commence this necessary work. Philadelphia, New York, and Boston should break away. The result would be sufficient funds for all these purposes.

As a beginning, we will inform our readers that our subscription book is now open, and as soon as 60 subscribers are obtained at one dollar annually, our Reading Room and Infant Library will be opened for the benefit of the subscribers—young men are particularly requested to call and enter their names, and if we cannot obtain volumes let us commence with papers and pamphlets.

The Rights of All, New York, September 18, 1829

Black editors never lost the opportunity to instill in their readers the belief that through their own education they could help abolish prejudice. Samuel Cornish, the editor, was particularly interested in trade schools.

When we reflect upon the apathy of the coloured population of the middle and eastern States with respect to education and refinements —when we see the coloured people of large towns and cities, and throughout whole regions of highly improved country, perfectly dead to the importance of improving their own mind and securing to their children the benefits of an enlarged education; our heart sickens within us. I ask why have we not a system of education established among us, connecting by one strong chain, the common, the grammar, the collegiate and the professional school, where everything relating to a polished and useful education may be taught—why have we not mechanical institutions, where our children may obtain a thorough knowledge of all the useful arts—is it because we grasp after flowers and neglect solid and wholesome fruits! Is there scarcely a family of any respectability among us, who does not spend from ten to fifty dollars annually in unnecessary gratifications. Let us sacrifice or rather consecrate, the means of these unnecessary, and sometimes sinful indulgences, to the lid of a sealed box, for the purpose of education. It is truly said that knowledge is power, and let our coloured population once become as learned, as refined, and as wealthy as other classes of community, and prejudice will hide her face—the tyrants spell will be broken. To talk about prejudice against color is nonsense; but raise up sons learned and enterprising with offsets of 20 or 30 thousand dollars—but rear daughters intelligent and polished heiresses to their tens and hundreds of thousands, and the fair sons and daughters of Columbia will forget the law of lights and shades—it will be expunged from our system of philosophy. And as should be, merit will form the estimate of character and respectability. The term Africa, will no longer be synonymous with that of degradation. It may be said, by some, all this is very good, but how shall it be attained. I answer, cease to lurk about the large cities, no longer hold to occupations calculated to perpetrate your degradation. Be untiringly industrious, and frugal even to miserliness, and make the very oppression intended for your injury, the means of your wealth and improvement. This has been the case with the Jews in some parts of Europe, they have been oppressed until the wealth of whole towns and cities have been pressed into their hands. . . .

The Rights of All, New York, September 18, 1829

The open practice of buying and selling slaves and especially the kidnapping of free and escaped blacks were a source of deep resentment and consequent resistance. Under the leadership of David Ruggles, the Committee of Vigilance was formed in New York to protect blacks from slave hunters. Ruggles himself was the subject of harassment and intimidation for his attempts to stop these kidnappings. The following article was signed "B" and probably stands for Philip Bell.

"SLAVE IS ADVERTISED FOR SALE AT AUCTION IN WASHINGTON, TAKEN ON EXECUTION ON ACCOUNT OF THE UNITED STATES BANK!"

We copy the above text, on which we intend to preach a short sermon, from the *New Era,* of Jan. 2— What a reflection for every patriot and philanthropist. A slave in these United States—the land of the free, and the home of the brave! But how much better is the thought when we tell the public, that the number of slaves in the District of Columbia, is only seven thousand; regular slave traders reside at the seat of Government! Oh how inhuman and disgraceful! In the District of Columbia six thousand Slaves are computed to be sold every year, to go out to Virginia alone. We regard these Slave dealers as Cannibals, and we mention them with the same feelings as we would a gang of thieves or counterfeitors. Just read the following advertisement:—

"WE WILL GIVE CASH

For one hundred likely young negroes of both sexes between the ages of 8 and 25 years. Persons who wish to sell would do well to give us a call, as the negroes are wanted immediately. We will give more than any other purchasers that are in market, or may hereafter come into market.

Any letters addressed to the subscribers, through the post office at Alexandria, will be promptly attended to. For information, inquire at the subscribers, west end of Duke Street, Alexandria, D.C.

FRANKLIN AND ARMFIELD."

There are also Slave drivers at Washington, who make it a business to drive droves of Slaves, further South by land. The children are carried in wagons, but the rest are forced to walk. The miserable and wicked wretches who conduct the branch of the business are provided with thumb screws, as instruments of torture, to be applied to refractory slaves. These droves, as we may imagine, present a melancholy spectacle; but the worst remains to be told. Free persons of colour coming into the District are liable to arrest, imprisonment, and sold into Slavery for life, for jail fees, if unable from ignorance, misfortune or fraud, to prove their freedom: we could throw more light on this dark subject, did our limits permit us; we have however, several chapters on this head.

At present, we content ourselves with giving our readers the following extracts and if there be an edge to them it is caused by the *substantial truth* they tell:—

"Washington, the seat of government of a free people, is disgraced by slavery. The waiters in the hotels, the servants in private families, and many of the lower class of artisans are slaves. While the orators in Congress, are rounding periods about liberty in one part of the city, proclaiming *alto voce,* that all men are equal, 'resistance to tyrants is obedience to God,' the auctioneer is exposing human flesh for sale in another! I remember a gifted gentleman in the Representatives, who, in speaking of the Senate, pronounced it to be, 'the most enlightened; the most august and most imposing body in the world.' In regard to the extent of imposition, I shall not speak; but it so happened that the day was one of rain, and the effect of the eulogium was a good deal injured by recollecting that, an hour or two before the members of this enlightened and august body were driven to the Capitol by slave coachmen, who were at that very moment waiting to convey them back, when the RIGHTS OF MAN had been sufficiently disserted on for the day."

I trust I do not write on this painful subject in an insulting spirit but, that slavery should exist in the District of Columbia, that even the footprint of a slave should be suffered to contaminate the soil, peculiarly consecrated to Freedom, that the very shrine of the goddess should be polluted by the presence of chains and fetters is, perhaps, the most extraordinary and monstrous anomaly to which human inconsistency—a prolific mother—has given birth.

The man who would study the contradictions of individual and national character, and learn by how wide an interval, profession may be divided from performance should come to Washington. He will here read a new page in the volume of human nature; he will observe how comparable is the extreme physical liberty, with bondage of the understanding. He will hear the words of freedom, and he will see the practice of slavery. Men who sell their fellow creatures will discourse to him of indefensible rights; he will be taught the affinity between the democrat and the tyrant; he will look for charters, and find_____ [sic]; expect liberty, and be met by bigotry and prejudice.

READ THIS

Beware of Kidnappers.—The truth made known.—Annexed to this paragraph is a statement, a painful interesting narrative, from under the hand and seal of our old friend, Mr. David Ruggles: one of our most worthy and useful fellow-labourers in the common cause of Human Freedom. It is almost needless for us to say, that Mr. Ruggles is a person of most exemplary character; his enemies being judges well known to this community; and his various statements, in relation to KIDNAPPING, already made public from time to time, in the daily papers of this city, have, as well they may, attracted public attention, and universal surprise. Has not the reign of terror commenced! What year of the world do we live in! And under what government has our lot been cast! If the statements of our brother be true (and we have no reason to disbelieve them, nor have we ever yet seen his various allegations authoritatively denied) we may well ask the important question, without fear of offence to any set of men, what opinion are we to form of the manner in which our Laws are administered; and what language shall we adopt in portraying the *manly* conduct of such characters as reside among us? And from whence have these MEN derived that strange kind of power, which ought to be honestly resisted by all.

And when so much has now come to light, shall we not infer quite naturally, that much, very much remains unexposed? We hazard nothing when we boldly assert that there is no crime of greater magnitude—no enormity more foul, than that of making a *Slave of a Freeman* among us; and DEATH is too light a punishment for that wretch, (we allude now to every Kidnapper,) who should violate all laws both natural and civil. We say to one and all our friends, AWAKE! Beware of these Slave-catchers! and while you are freely allowed to differ among yourselves on other points, in this one matter be *united!* Imitate the conduct of a Ruggles, and be as one man in the firm and unalterable determination to maintain your just rights and defend your property and persons against all attacks of men, with *"roving commissions,"* or warrants pretending to be from Governor Marcy, or any one else authorizing them to arrest any free coloured man, against whom they may have some private spite, and pointed out by some notorious Slave-catcher. . . .

The Weekly Advocate, New York, January 14, 1837

Developing a sense of national identity depended on the establishment of responsibilities and rights as citizens.

Brethren, God hath laid on us great responsibility—we have to act an important part, and fill an important place, in the great cause of humanity and religion—and in the work of emancipation. On *our* conduct and exertions much, very much depend. It is our part, by virtue, prudence, and industry, to uphold the hands of our devoted and sacrificing friends—let us not be found wanting. Should we prove unworthy our few privileges, we shall furnish our enemies the strongest arguments with which to oppose the emancipation of the slave, and to hinder the elevation of the free.

On the other hand, should we establish for ourselves a character—should we as a people become more religious and moral, more industrious and prudent than other classes of community, it will be impossible to keep us down. This we should do, we are more oppressed and proscribed than others, therefore we should be more circumspect and more diligent than others.

We live in an age of reform, and if we lay not hold of every means of reformation and improvement, we shall be left in the background and the contrast between our condition and that of our white brethren will be widened—then let us as a whole people, avail ourselves of every measure calculated to cultivate the mind and elevate the morals. No oppressed COLORED AMERICAN, who wishes to occupy that elevation in society which God has designed he should occupy, should be intemperate or even touch, as a beverage, intoxicating drinks, none should be idle or extravagant, none profane the Sabbath nor neglect the sanctuary of God, but all should be up and doing, should work while it is day. We owe it to ourselves and we owe it to the poor slaves, who are our brethren.

On our conduct, in a great measure, *their* salvation depends. . . .

The Colored American, New York, March 4, 1837

Reports of the New York Committee of Vigilance and notices of its meetings were regularly printed in the black press.

Important Meeting of the New York Committee of Vigilance. An important meeting of this Committee will be held on Monday next the 13th. inst. at half past 7 o'clock at the Phoenix Hall, Chapel Street or West Broadway. Every member of the Executive Committee and the Friends of the cause of human liberty, are invited to attend. The friends and acquaintances of *Thomas Bryan,* a free boy from this city, who is now confined in prison at Vicksburg, Mississippi to be sold for his jail fees, are expected to attend without fail. Facts will also be stated in relation to the case of Thomas Oliver, who was lately sold as a slave in New Orleans. Any person who can give information in relation to John Robinson Welch, a mulatto boy, between eight and nine years of age, who was lost on Thursday afternoon, Feb. 25, will serve the cause of humanity, by disclosing such information to the meeting as may lead to the recovery or by leaving it with his distressed mother. . . .

D. RUGGLES, Sec. N.Y.C.V.

The Colored American, New York, March 11, 1837

Prejudice in the church was particularly galling to black ministers, like Samuel Cornish.

Never were any people more exposed to infidelity, than are the colored people of our country—nothing short of the immediate and special providence of God, could have kept them so long, from this damning and fatal error.

In other countries infidelity has probably a stronger hold than in this—yet such is the light of christianity, and such the benevolence and charity of God's people, in those countries, as to leave no one class of community more exposed than others. This is not the case in America. The churches in our land, notwithstanding their high profession—if they have the faith of our Lord Jesus Christ at all, have it with respect of person. Professed disciples of the impartial Jesus, select whom they will love, and whom they will not—hence it is, that our colored brethren, many of whom bear about in their bodies the mark of their Savior's dying, are the objects of their christian (I had like to have said, religious) hatred, and oppression. Last night I was sick *so much so* as to make it very inconvenient to prepare myself and walk two miles to church this morning, consequently, I am denied the privilege of my Master's house—deprived of those holy emotions which fill the soul and buoy it up to heaven, when christian brethren come in contact in the house of God. But why this deprivation? Are you so much of a bigot that you cannot enjoy yourself in other churches, such as are in your reach? Not at all—not at all, there are four or five churches of the same denomination, professing the same faith that I do, within four hundred yards of my dwelling. I could easily walk to either of them—I know and I love their ministers—I have been a brother Presbyter with them, for fifteen years—*but I am a colored man!*—God in his sovereignty, dyed my skin a darker hue, and they hate me for it—I may walk throughout their Sanctuary, and unless I sit against the wall or go into their *Negro pew,* they have not a seat for me—such, reader, is the situation of pious "colored Americans," in the United States. I ask, is it not to be expected that Satan will take the advantage of thousands, by presenting this crying sin of the church as an argument against the reality of the religion of THE CROSS. For if the principles of God's Bible are not sufficient to subdue the prejudice and hatred of the heart, to make a man love his brother as he loves himself, and do unto him as he would his brother should do in return, what is the Bible worth, more than the Koran and what is a Christian better than a Mohametan!

A few weeks since, it being too cold to send our little son two miles to church, we said to him, go to the Rev. Dr. —— church; he did so, and was handed to a pew near the altar and comfortably seated; he is fair and his hair rather straight. A sabbath or two afterwards, he concluded to take his brother with him, to hear the same Rev. Dr. —— [*sic*] very well my son, but take a seat back, be as modest as you can, he did so, and took his brother whose color and hair betray his origin with him—and one christian after another, who through mistake, got into the same pew—fled from *them,* as though the leprosy was upon *them.* My little sons discovered the prejudice and were grieved to the heart—and one of them said, "Mother, why do the white people hate *us* so?"

Are these things consistent?—should the disciples of the Bible, act in this way?—do the preachers of the Cross discharge their duty, in suffering this sin in the church? Certainly not. This evil must be done away, or judgment will "begin at the house of God." Infidelity, and Popery will fill the land, and overspread the ruins of the church. My brethren in the ministry, I beseech you, see to it. You are verily guilty —you are *Slaves* to a wicked public sentiment—you dare not warn the people—God will hold you responsible, and did I not fear, you and your father's house, (the church) would be destroyed, *I would not dare,* give you this warning.

The Colored American, New York, March 18, 1837

Self-help was an important part of racial pride, and black leaders often referred to Africa and that heritage for cultural resources. Encouraging and assisting various forms of self-help were an important aspect of the black press.

The position we hold in community is a prominent one—all eyes are upon us. Many philanthropic minds are waiting the result of the measures of our improvement before they enlist in the holy cause of the slave. And many tyrants are waiting and praying for our deeper degradation as an opiate for their consciences and an extenuation for their guilt.

How then ought we to occupy this important and responsible position. "What manner of people ought we to be?" Feelings of this kind should abide in every breast; for vain will be all our theories about respectability and elevation, unless it becomes a practical subject with us. It is a lamentable thought, that for a number of years we have held the improvement and elevation of our injured people, merely in the abstract—we have not taken it home to ourselves, in our relations and responsibilities to community at large. This was more excusable in the time of ignorance, but now God and providence, our own interests and the suffering condition of the slave, all combine in calling on us to amend our ways. Each one for himself, must commence the improvement of his condition. It is not in mass, but in individual effort and character, that we are to move onward to a higher elevation. I cannot do the essentials for my neighbor, nor he for me—but each can do them for himself.

. . . We verily believe that God's set time has come for restoring Africa and her descendants to their former elevation in the scale of being. And making her a great and holy nation. And should any of our brethren be found in the way, or be as dead branches, God will remove them, that their place will be filled with fit materials.

The Colored American, New York, April 22, 1837

Many blacks, though appreciative of efforts made by white abolitionists, were unhappy about their paternalism and sometimes with their dual standard with respect to blacks in the North.

The colored man who does not hold the person, the character and the doings of American Abolitionists in the highest estimation, is unworthy the form he wears, and the standing he holds among the reputable of his race.

The Abolitionists of the present day, unlike all others, have adopted God's standard as the guide of their lives and the rule of their actions. They have willingly made themselves of no repute, and counted their lives not dear unto themselves, so that they might finish their work, and in its accomplishment, testify the purity of the Gospel of the grace of God.

Upon the Altar of conscience and of God, they have placed their lives, their property, and their sacred honor—willing to sink or swim, live or die, by their principles. We concede to them everything which constitutes purity of motive, and zeal in prosecution. They are, emphatically, our best friends; we love and honor them as such, and we would commend them to the confidence and affection of our *brethren everywhere.* Yet, with the wise and good Reformers of every age, they have much to investigate, and much to learn, before they are fully furnished to the work in which they are engaged.

Our object at this time is, and we trust ever will be, both in public and private, from the pulpit and through the press, to throw the little light we have, or may possess, on the subject of Abolition. . . . The success of our cause depends much on the nature of its basis, and the materials of its super-structure. Our friends should judge of us as they do of other men, or they never can succeed.

If we ever occupy a level, and we surely shall, with our white brethren, we must possess the same cardinal virtues, the same intrinsic worth which they possess. We would have our friends and brethren know, unless our moral and intellectual attainments be *measured by the same rule, and brought to the same standard* by which our white brethren are tried and estimated, we cannot occupy the same place in society, nor be held in the same repute.

We want NO FAVOURS in this matter—we wish not to be carried forward with any of our imperfections. We feel ourselves under the same obligations, and capable of the same moral and intellectual responsibilities.

If we have not the same culture, appoint us not to the same posts. If we have not the same moral worth, repose not in us the same confidence. If we have not the same social capacities, bring us not into the same associations.

We hope we shall not be misunderstood, though we have written these paragraphs obscurely—let him that can *understand, read.* We hold Abolition doctrine, and well directed Abolition effort, as we do Bible doctrine, and Christian effort. To them, we would say, *"God speed."*

The Colored American, New York, May 27, 1837

One of the most important functions of the black press was to warn black people of dangerous situations.

On Monday, John Davis, who was arrested a few weeks since by the Negro Catchers, *Boudinot* and *Nash* was liberated by the payment of the sum demanded (we believe about $300). The amount was made up by contributions and collections, in several churches. In the present instance we rejoice. Mr. Davis is an aged man and a respectable citizen; bearing an irreproachable moral and religious character, and he also has a family who are dependent on him for their support. But we are, as a general rule, opposed to making N.Y. a market where the slave trader and his infamous agents can procure their price for the souls and bodies of our brethren. We are ready, at all times, to contribute our might towards resisting, through a course of law, the claims of the *men-stealers* upon the life and liberty of any of our unfortunate brethren. And we will also when they have escaped from bondage, assist them to elude their pursuers and flee to lands where slavery is unknown but we cannot conscientiously lend our aid and influence (except in extraordinary cases, like the present) to fostering such a barbarous traffic and supporting such wretches as Nash and Boudinot. It is contrary to our principles as Abolitionists and as Christians. . . .

CAUTION

Our colored friends, and others in this city, and elsewhere, are cautioned against trusting a man by the name of C. V. Caples, late from Boston. He is a mulatto and sometimes passes for a Spaniard. Beware of him!

The Colored American, New York, May 27, 1837

The black community in New York and other large urban centers was forced to provide their own schools and teachers when the public school system would not admit their children.

. . . There is no people who need education more than we do, and no people who have less call for the services of their children. Yet out of four thousand children, of the right age, in this city, there are not more, if so many, as one thousand in regular attendance at school.

This ought not to be the case—we have the best of teachers; men of our own color, who take a national pride in bringing forward their scholars. They study themselves, *night and day,* that they may be more thoroughly furnished with knowledge, to impart to our children. And shall we forgo the privilege of sending our youth to such men, and to such institutions? We hope not.

Would it not be well for us to establish committees in every ward, for a similar purpose with that of our Philadelphia friends?

The subject calls for immediate action. There are three thousand children among us, out of school; not only losing the advantages of a good education, but growing up in idleness, and without that moral restraint which a good school exercises over its scholars.

The trustees of our public schools are our friends. Many of them are noble minded men, who deeply sympathize with us in our disabilities and oppression. They would willingly destroy the cord of caste, which disgraces our nation, and is eating out the vitals of our institutions, religious and civil.

Let us do our part, fill up the schools, and effect a punctual attendance, and the trustees will spare no pains nor expenses in furnishing all the means of a useful and finished education.

We ought to feel more interested on this subject, brethren—we owe it to posterity. We are not always to be a downtrodden people. Our infant sons, should we give them suitable advantages, will be as eligible to the Presidency of the United States, as any other portions of the community; and it is our wisdom, if possible, to give them as ample qualifications.

The Colored American, New York, July 1, 1837

The concept of black people as "a nation within a nation" was constantly reinforced by institutional racism and caste prejudice.

The colored people of these "United States" are the involuntary subjects of a social and political despotism, alike unrighteous and cruel; the guilt of which lies *wholly* at the white man's doors . . . Is the colored man degraded? Who degraded him? The white man—the church of Jesus Christ. Has she not organized all her institutions? Does she not perform all her holy services? and arrange all her sanctuaries and seats in obedience to the spirit of CASTE PREJUDICE AGAINST COLOR? Does she not take from and deny the colored man all the means of improvement, respectability and education? Truly she does.

The Colored American, New York, July 8, 1837

The growing refusal by blacks to accept any position on less than an equal basis was disconcerting to some abolitionists, who could not yet accept this.

The abolitionists are often accused by their dishonest opponents of having *increased* the prejudice of the "whites" against the "colored" citizens. This accusation is false, and we cannot believe that those who make it, are honest in doing so. The convictions of their *own minds* are against them. They know that with themselves, and with the community at large, prejudice against color has become a matter of CONSCIENCE. Men cannot now practice it with impunity, but five years ago they did so, without any difficulty, or compunction. In this ONE FACT, abolitionists have gained *ninety nine points* in every hundred.

The facts are these: ten years ago, our colored population were looked upon as *goods* and *chattels,* and every consideration conferred upon them was done as a FAVOR, and our best men took to themselves merit for every instance of the kind. In their contracted, narrow views and feelings, and in their false education, they thought themselves, *on account of their color,* infinitely elevated above their colored brethren, and therefore could treat them with *a little kindness,* without the danger of being thought on an equality with them. And they had kept the colored man's mind *so dark* on the subject of his rights, that *he himself,* did not presume to make any claims on the ground of equity of law, and of religion. No wonder that there was sometimes, under these circumstances, a little stooping on the part of our oppressors, towards the oppressed and *deeply injured* colored man; for who will not sometimes play with his dog?

But now the SCALE IS TURNED. Abolitionists have thrown off the veil. They have shown that God created all men EQUAL, and of the same blood, and that in equity and law, they are on a LEVEL. . . . Of all this, the colored man is *fully convinced;* hence he stands ERECT, with his eyes uplifted to heaven, and acknowledges NO SUPERIOR but God. Here is the RUB, and here is the *increased prejudice.* The colored man asks nothing as a FAVOR, nor will he have it as such. He demands it as a RIGHT, and he is bound in conscience, under God, to have it as such.

This is a *bitter pill* for his oppressors, who have always arrogated to themselves superiority, on account of their complexion. They cannot drink down the acrid drug at once, yet the CONSCIENCE which abolitionists, under God, have created, is pressing it down by degrees. Its application will be sure and *effectual,* for the antidote is taken from God's moral ethics.

It is then strange that in this state of things men who have been educated to tyrannize over others, and think themselves superior, should show their prejudices, and oppose the elevation to an equality with themselves, those whom they have considered inferior, and upon whom they have been accustomed to trample! . . .

The Colored American, New York, September 9, 1837

The following editorial was written in reply to a letter by William J. Whipper (a leading black advocate of passive resistance) in praise of the Moral Reform Convention, which Cornish opposed.

. . . As a public sentinel it was our business to see that none were deceived by sounding Titles nor vain pretenses. We were then, and still are unwilling to expose the ludicrous position in which the brethren have placed themselves. Their visionary views and fantastical dreams, we hope will never pass the precincts of Philadelphia, let them DIE THERE, where they originated, without contaminating the atmosphere of any other region.

. . . We positively never will, ourself, voluntarily expose through our paper, the ridiculous views and feelings of the leading members of the Moral Reform Society.* It would do incalculable *harm,* and no manner of *good.* We think too much of brother Whipper, as an individual and as a philanthropist to expose him so publicly.

He further suggests that there are contradictions in our strictures, we PRAISE and we CENSURE. We confess that we do both, AND WE MEANT TO DO BOTH. Good names nor good men are no security against terror. "To err is human." The General Assembly of the Presbyterian church last spring was made up of some of the wisest and

---

* The American Moral Reform Society for Improving the Condition of Mankind was originated by black followers of William Lloyd Garrison who emphasized the uplifting of "the whole human race," rather than concentrate on blacks. Whipper referred to himself as an "oppressed American" rather than a "colored American."

best men, of whom the nation or the world can boast, yet they spent TWO WEEKS in ecclesiastical lynchings.

The brother further says, "there are those to whose perception and judgment, you and I might bow with grateful humiliation, that will be unable to know what you mean by definite object, if the promotion of edification, temperance, economy, peace and universal liberty are not within the range of your vocabulary." We must tell the brother that however they may feel in Columbia [Pa.], in New York, in perception and judgment, in plain matter of fact WE BOW TO NO MAN, yet for his (brother Whipper's) information, we will tell what we mean. We mean that the "Moral Reform Society" should have definite OBJECTS, as well as definite actions. When we give our money to promote "education, temperance, economy, peace, and universal liberty," we want to know among whom these moral virtues are to be cultivated, and whether they have less or more means, whether they are less or more cultivated, and whether they are making less or more effort, than *we, ourselves*. Will the brother answer these questions, or shall we get the answers from the VAGUE Constitution of the Society? We mean that the society should spend its means and strength in efforts to improve and elevate, the poor, proscribed, downtrodden and helpless COLORED PEOPLE, of our country, and that its members should SAY SO, and give us a constitution guaranteeing that they will not waste themselves in BOMBASTIC, HUMBUG EFFORTS, to improve the WHOLE NATION!

Were we to take a bag of gold, and in imagined benevolence of heart, and fancied definiteness of action, throw it to the multitude, instead of seeking out and defining who are needy, and giving it to them, would not our benevolence be questionable?

Until the Moral Reform Society re-organizes and defines its OBJECTS, as well as its measures, it will do no good, and is UNWORTHY the *confidence and patronage* of the colored men and his friends.

We will now tell the brother what we mean by "baying the moon," as he asks an explanation of the subject. To bay the moon, is to leave the *great centre of light* which God has given, to follow the indefinite flitterings of *our own creation*. Morally—It is to leave *God's great moral lights*, REVELATION and REASON, and suffer ourselves to be governed by the VISIONS and NOTIONS of feeble, fallible men. We are now done with the Society. . . .

The Colored American, New York, September 9, 1837

David Ruggles often published information about kidnappings in the Colored American. *He himself published two papers, the* Mirror of Liberty *(1837–?) and the* Genius of Freedom *(1845–47). In the late 1840's he became a hydrotherapist, and advertisements for his "Northampton Water Cure" appeared in Frederick Douglass' paper* North Star *in 1853.*

August 14, 1837   *Office 36 Lispenard street*

Chairman of the N.Y. Committee of Vigilance:

Sir—It is with regret that I make this letter a substitute for my personal appearance at the regular monthly meeting of the New York Committee of Vigilance. Though declining health compelled me to retire from the city and take refuge in the country, my heart is with you in the cause of Freedom. As there is much anxiety in the public mind, in relation to the case of William Dixon, and his absence from the city. I will state he is not kidnapped by that gang of desperadoes, which infest our city, as has been reported, but owing to measures resorted to by a certain party, he has taken the advice of his friends and retired to the country for a little season.

Having labored under great embarrassment (as you are aware) during the past month, my report is not as complete as I wish it to be, the number of cases relieved by your committee during the past month are nineteen, the number of cases to be relieved are five, owing to the absence of the *effective means,* they cannot receive the benevolence of your committee.

Yours vigilantly,
DAVID RUGGLES

Receipts from last month $32.00
Expenses from last month $54.00
Balance against the Treasury . . . $22.00

The Colored American, New York, September 9, 1837

The author of the following item, David Ruggles, regularly brought such instances to the attention of the public.

A BOY KIDNAPPED

Shipped and regularly cleared at the Custom House.

A West Indian named Ayres, imported an apprentice from the

Island of Jamaica, named Edward Watson to this city, who shipped him on board the Brig. Buenos Ayres, Capt. Stewart, for South Carolina, where the boy-stealer declared his intention to sell him for cash, owing to his want of friends.

After ascertaining all the facts in the case, and collecting sufficient proof to convict the thief, application was made to Judge Irving for a writ of habeus corpus to liberate the boy; but His Honor declined issuing it upon the ground that he was sick, and should soon leave his office and go to bed.

Application was then made to Judge Ulshoeffer, who peremptorily refused to allow the writ, as he wanted his dinner and could not attend to it. When the counsel stated that the vessel was about to sail with the victim, and that delay was dangerous, the Judge with dignity, equalled only by the loftiness of the act, advanced to the door, opened it with all the authority of a Judge, and said "there's the door—this is my house." The applicants quit the premises, and could not succeed in obtaining the writ until the next day, when it was too late to rescue the writhing victim from the cruel fangs of slavery. Ayres, having left the vessel and decamped with the boy for the south by land.

The Colored American, New York, September 16, 1837

TAKE CARE OF NUMBER ONE!

Brethren, this doctrine, when abused is a dangerous doctrine. It is the Rock upon which we have always split. "Take care of No. ONE" carried Mr. Russwurm to Liberia; it made [Benedict] Arnold sell his country, and it has plunged the South into all the guilt and shame of a cruel system of slavery.

This principle has existed and operated too long and powerfully among colored Americans. But for this unholy principle, our population would have been twenty years in advance of what they now are. Take care of No. ONE made the prosperous part of our brethren in the South, *slaveholders,* and carried them to give sanction to the fiendish practice, as fast as they gained their own liberty. It made the more successful of our people, in times past, to hoard up every dollar they got hold of, regardless of the public good, and at the sacrifice of every principle of action, worth living for.

A few years ago . . . all the influence obtained, and the treasures possessed by individuals or bodies of men among us, was only valued in respect to their benefit. There was no community of interests felt by our brethren. If we wished each other success in business, and prosperity in moral and mental efforts, and it is doubtful whether we did or not, our wish only extended to "Be ye fed and be ye clothed." We did nothing for the general good, nor did we seem to care for it.

Is there not too much of the same spirit among us, at the present day! What are we doing, ourselves, for the elevation of our people, *as a body?* Are not too many of us satisfied with taking care of No. ONE?

Poor as the body of colored people in this country may be, yet there is a vast amount of property held by individuals, which should tell upon the condition and interests of the whole. But this is not the case. If philanthropists among our *white* fellow citizens, were to judge of the MEANS of colored Americans, from their contributions and actions, in their OWN BEHALF, they would set us all down as a parcel of poor tools, unworthy their sympathy and their efforts. . . .

Shame on our rich men, with their *two, three, four* and *five thousand dollars* annual income, besides a prosperous business! Some of them think so much of No. ONE, that with all their money, they have not soul enough to educate their children *liberally,* FOR THE PUBLIC GOOD. Tell them that it is important that we should have learned and accomplished men among us, and that they have the means to educate their children—and they will tell you, that they must learn their children to get a living *for themselves!*

The fact is, that the few educated and efficient young men we have, some who would be an honor to any people, are from our poorest families—the rich being too parsimonious to educate their sons, or too careful of No. ONE to be willing to sacrifice as they would say, the life of a son to the PUBLIC GOOD.

Brethren, what will become of us, if we do not learn to do better? We never can be a people until we maintain our own cause and support our own institutions. We must give more liberally, and act more efficiently, or *never claim to be freemen, nor expect to be elevated.*

The Colored American, New York, January 27, 1838

Some black leaders (like William J. Whipper, active in the Philadelphia Moral Reform Society) rejected the use of the term "colored" Americans and preferred "oppressed," which would broaden the concept to include anyone who was oppressed.

. . . To us, and we should think to any one of good sense, laboring under such persecutions as the colored citizens of Philadelphia are, to be called "Colored Americans" would be like a ray of Heavenly light, shining amidst the blackness of darkness.

Oppressed Americans! Who are they? Nonsense, brethren! You are COLORED AMERICANS. The Indians are RED AMERICANS and the white people are WHITE AMERICANS, and you are as good as they and they no better than you—God made all of the same blood. . . .

The Colored American, New York, March 15, 1838

Following are the minutes of a meeting of the New York Committee of Vigilance.

. . . After prayer by Rev. Theo. S. Wright,* Mr. David Ruggles introduced three native Africans which were imported to New York from Rio-Nonez by Capt. E. Farwell, with one other, whom the Captain cannot account for.

Mr. R. [Ruggles] said he did not introduce them to the meeting because he supposed that the audience had never seen native Africans, nor because it was an unusual practice for American vessels to bring them to this country; to his knowledge there had been twenty-two native Africans imported into the port of New York, within the last twelve months; a larger number of persons than the Colonization Society has succeeded in exporting from this state to Africa the last fifteen years. He believed that there had been more Africans brought into the United States in the last two years, than the society has succeeded in exporting to Africa since its existence.

As these men had been discharged by the Captain and owners of the Barque Transit, and found by the Committee of Vigilance in a very destitute and distressed condition, he wished that those who had contributed to their relief might see them and receive their thanks as they would probably return to their families in Africa in a few days.

* Theodore Wright, a leading black abolitionist during the 1830's and 1840's, was born in Providence, Rhode Island, in April, 1797. He attended Princeton from 1825 to 1828 and was the first black man to receive a degree from a theological seminary. He helped organize many literary and antislavery societies, and he took over the Reverend Cornish's church in 1829. He died on March 25, 1847.

The case of the three young men who were kidnapped was introduced. The meeting was addressed by Mr. William Johnson, and Rev. Theo. S. Wright.

After a collection was taken up a gentleman from the south, who was impressed with the truth of the statement relative to northern citizens being kidnapped and sold at the south, wished to bear testimony, corroborative of the fact that many free persons from the north were held at the south as slaves.

Extracts were read from some of the slanderous articles recently circulated in the newspapers against the Committee of Vigilance.

Resolutions were offered by Mr. N. Southard which were adopted.

Facts were stated by Mr. Jones who was attached to the steamboat Newcastle, but left her before the sale of the young men.

The meeting was further addressed by Mr. Ransom, F. Wake, N. Southard, and Rev. Enoch Smith. The Meeting then adjourned.

W. P. JOHNSON, Sec. protem.

The Colored American, New York, August 25, 1838

Throughout the late 1830's and early 1840's David Ruggles, secretary of the New York Vigilance Committee, wrote, spoke, and organized his black brethren in the dangerous task of thwarting slave hunters and vigorously combatting discrimination.

Mr. Editor—Permit me to say to your readers, that my trip to the East, after the notorious Thomas Lewis, who participated in kidnapping and selling three of our fellow citizens in slavery at the South, was attended with insults and outrage from New York to Providence, which I did not expect to meet on the route through "the land of steady habits" as is explained in the following article, which appeared in the *Providence Courier* of the 9th. inst.

CAUTION TO TRAVELLERS

I left New York on Tuesday evening for this city in the steamboat Rhode Island, on the route through Stonington, on which I was most egregiously defrauded and lynched.

The Clerk of the boat having received full fare, viz. $4.00 agreed to send me through in the enjoyment of the same privileges that all passengers (who had paid full fare) enjoyed. But from the statement I received from the railroad Conductor, I considered myself defrauded and lynched, from the consideration that I paid full fare to the Clerk of the boat, who furnished me with a deck ticket. After arriving at Stonington, and the Conductor of the cars failing to extort 50 cents more from me, insisted that I should not have that car, saying, "You are a d-d abolitionist." The three others forcibly ejected me from the car, and forced me into what they call the pauper or jim crow car.

DAVID RUGGLES

The following additional remarks were excluded by the editor of that paper, viz:

"Abolitionists are cautioned against taking the route over the Stonington Railroad."

I wish to state here, that Highway Robbery is a crime that used to be punishable with death in New England; but now *"forties"* are employed in steamboats, and on railroads, that will commit larceny upon men's pockets and rights, and lynch them with impunity. Travellers assent to the outrages committed on the defenseless and unprotected, by their neutrality in such cases of plunder.

I send it to your paper that your readers may understand that travellers are liable to be defrauded and lynched, on the route to Boston on the Stonington Railroad.

Yours respectfully,
DAVID RUGGLES

The Colored American, New York, August 25, 1838

One of the most difficult things for white Americans to understand is the demand for black self-determination. The black press sought to explain this to its readers.

. . . No people can be, essentially, benefitted by a system of favors. As a people, the colored citizens of this republic have been, already, almost ruined by the favor showing system. We hope abolitionists will never fall into the error. Colored men, to be as other men, must be left to combat the same vicissitudes, and by the same necessities of the case, be goaded on to the efforts and enterprise common to other men. What abolitionists have to do is to make the way level to them as to others, and leave them, individually, to seek place and elevation. As in the case of "Israel," for all these things, they should be left to inquire.

It is in the youth among us, we look to see our people brought forward and incorporated in all the ramifications of society. In them are our clerks, and merchants and mechanics, and farmers, and manufacturers, &c. Let abolitionists NOW, *this year,* as our correspondent would have them, in the selection of apprentices and journeymen—of clerks and partners—of mechanics and farmers—of laborers and servants—give our people an equal chance, and a preference, all things being equal, as they conscientiously may, ours being a neglected people (for it is Christ-like to remove disabilities and proscriptions) and we are satisfied.

Any organized, special effort, to get bread for us, as colored people, and then put it in our mouths, would do us *harm* rather than good. To cast up "the highway" and "gather out the stones" is the business of our friends, but to improve and elevate our condition, emphatically, the business of ourselves.

The Colored American, New York, September 1, 1838

The following overview of the abolitionist movement presents an interesting analysis of the divisions within the movement from the point of view of a black man, critical of discrimination against black abolitionists.

. . . Our organization is *national,* and embodies the principles of unity, which if carried out, must preserve it. It was, during the first four years of our existence, proverbial of us, that in our love of humanity, we lost sight of our *theological* differences, and religious peculiarities; that all *sectarian jealousies and sectarian bigotry,* that all party predilections, and every other extraneous thing, were lost sight of, in our devotion to the cause of the slave, as though they never had been. To be an abolitionist was to be a moral hero, and clothed the man with a kind of moral sublimity. In fine, we presented an unbroken front, impenetrable to the shafts of our enemies. Great similarity of views, harmony of feeling, and devotion to measures, were characteristic of us, so that it was also proverbially said of us, we were men of *one idea,* and we were accused of having withdrawn our charities from other benevolent associations, and devoted money and power to the

Anti-Slavery cause, which to some extent was true, because most men gave support to the former, while exceedingly few contributed to the latter, and our grand cause advanced, increasing in numbers and in strength, conquering and to conquer, amidst threats, mobs, gags, bonfires and pillage, as though wafted by the waters of life, and the breezes of heaven, toward her destined haven. *Colored* men were found there, co-operating and looking on, cheered in prospect, and full of hope of a change in their political and social condition. Such was *Anti-Slavery* up to the winter of 1838; but, alas, how changed! We have indeed fallen out by the way; many things are the occurrences of every day, by no means honorable to *Anti-Slavery principles,* or *Anti-Slavery men.*

In our own native Massachusetts, foremost always in moral reform, *sectarian jealousies* have arisen, and so provoked have they been, as to result in a division of their ranks. Two Anti-Slavery organizations exist, at great loggerheads and with each other a *newspaper war* is carried on, in too much bitterness of spirit, and the dead are raked up, as it were, to bury the living. In New Hampshire, few though they be, they are becoming sensitive about extraneous things, alienated in their feelings, and are well nigh a division among them. May they be saved from such a calamity. Maine and Vermont adhere to first principles and measures concerning themselves about little else but good old Anti-Slavery going on conquering and to conquer.

In our own Empire State, where we have as good Anti-Slavery capital as may be found anywhere, we are divided but about other things and attended with less of bad feeling than the divisions in the East. Ours is a political division, or about voting, but it is of bad tendency to the cause. It were better for us to be united upon all points, than to be divided upon any one. Some are for voting upon true Anti-Slavery principles, others are for compromising with their party. Some are forming a third party and cutting off all who do not rally around it. . . .

Ohio Anti-Slavery men have more harmony and unity among them. Small differences of opinion only exist but of little bad tendency to the cause, and well is it for the character of Ohio, for Anti-Slavery men, and principles with the colored population, and the abundance nature has done, are about all that is of reputable notoriety in the State. . . .

But while these things, painful as many of them are, exist, and while some of our people are discouraged, with hope sinking, and some

growing indifferent, and some taking sides, we remain with the same
love of Anti-Slavery principles and the same confidence in Anti-Slavery measures. We find, while from this state of things the cause of our
people advances slower, and no sooner, more for us to bend our enemies to, in contending for independence of thought and of principle
among our people, to defend their character, to urge their claims, and
to insist upon our doing our work with others most heartily when they
will, when they will not, not stopping to fall out by the way; this is no
time for *colored men* to pause a moment—everything is done, and
much of it is to be by *ourselves*. . . .

The Colored American, New York, March 21, 1840

"LOOK OUT FOR KIDNAPPERS!"

A woman had been "accosted" by two men from Georgia who tried
to abduct her as they believed she was an escaped slave. If there be
any such a woman in New York, this notice is to warn her to escape to
the mountains, and remain there until the Georgia and New York kidnappers shall have been consumed by the mighty spirit of liberty.

Am. Anti-Slavery Society: HENRY B. STANTON
SAMUEL CORNISH
JAMES GIBBONS.

The Colored American, New York, April 4, 1840

*Many black leaders became disillusioned with the sometime contradic-
tory stance of abolitionists who could not accept black people as equals.*

Modern abolition is with us, right in principle, and the measures we
believe, are the legitimate issue of those principles. We believe, all
things considered, they are the best that could have been devised, for
the disenthrallment of the slave. We do not pretend to say, however,
that by a long experience in them, they may not be improved and per-
fected. We have ever felt a strong attachment to them, and still feel, so
far as the slave's release is concerned, the same unshaken faith in
them. We believe, if they are carried forward consistently and perse-
veringly, that they will lead to the overthrow of the slave system and
the slave power in our country. Such a result may not be brought
about in the same way in which abolitionists might hope and desire,

neither may the slaveholders be moved to such a result by those motives best, in a long run, for themselves, the emancipated, and the country, and most to be desired by us. Nevertheless, that such will be the issue, we have no manner of doubt; therefore we are an abolitionist; also, because we believe the overthrow of the slave system will greatly be for the interest and advancement of the free colored population, inasmuch as all our obstacles to advancement in this country, and all our disabilities arise from that system; take this away, and those go with it; take them away, and we are in the best country in the world, and were as happy a people as live in it or any other. Upon this ground we have always thought it proper to urge upon our people to co-operate with anti-slavery men and measures, as having a tendency to promote our interest. We have never expected to derive much immediate benefit from the progress of these measures, only as they affected our moral condition, and changed the morbid public feeling, and the public principles toward us. In these views not a few of our intelligent brethren disagree with us; they expected more from abolitionists, and not having realized it, they are disappointed. We have thought, that abolitionists started with a view to the abolishment of slavery, and adopted measures to that effect, but in carrying forward those measures, they intended to advocate equal rights for the free colored man, and his moral elevation in the scale of human being. How faithful they have been in the latter, we leave their history and their works to testify. Doubtless, they have not all been so faithful as our condition and their duty would have demanded. They have not all of them stuck so close to their colored brother as they ought; this, with their opponents, is the greatest test to the insincerity of their principles. This class of our brethren think that abolitionists began at the wrong end, to do their work; we agree with them, if the elevation of the free colored man was their first and leading object; in which case their measures would have been ill-timed and out of place, but as this was a secondary, and the abolishment of slavery the primary, they in our opinion began at the right end.

One would have supposed, in any case, in view of all this, that if a body of men rose up to discuss slaveholding, with a view to its overthrow, and regarded the colored man as his brother, that they all would have co-operated most heartily and continually, and especially though silently, would the colored men of the South who hold their liberties with the slenderest thread, and with a vengeance, too. . . .

The Colored American, New York, April 25, 1840

One of the important and unique functions of the black press was to expose prejudice and racism in the various aspects of American society.

. . . There is a kind of aristocracy in our country, as in nearly all others. A looking down with disdain upon humble life, and a disregard of it. Still we hear little about prejudice against any class among us, excepting against color, or against the colored population of this Union; this so monopolizes this state of feeling in our country that we hear and see less of it in its operations upon others, than in other countries. It is the only sense in which there is equality; here the democratic principle is adopted, and all come together as equals, and unite together, the rich and the poor, the high and the low, in an equal right, to hate the colored man; and its operations upon the mind and character, is as cruel and disastrous, as it is murderous and wicked in itself. One needs to feel and wither under its effects, in order to know it; and the colored people of the United States, wherever found, and in whatever circumstances, are living epistles which may be read of all men, as to all that is paralyzing to enterprise, destructive to ambition, ruinous to character, crushing to mind and painful to the soul, in the monster prejudice.

For it is found equally malignant, active and strong, associated with the mechanic arts, in the work shop, in the mercantile house, in the commercial affairs of the country, in the halls of learning, the *Temple of God,* and in the highways and hedges, it possesses almost ubiquity, it is everywhere, where lives and moves one of the proscribed class, doing its deleterious work.

Yet prejudice against color, prevalent as it is in the minds of one of our community against another, is unnatural, and habitual. If it were natural it would prevail everywhere with the same class, but it does not, therefore is not natural. If it were, children would manifest it with the first signs of consciousness, but with them, all are alike affectionate and beloved, they have not the feeling because it is a creature of education and of habit. And while we write, there is now playing at our right a few steps, a colored man and a white child, with all the affection and harmony of feeling, as though prejudice had always been unknown.

Prejudice overlooks all that is noble and invaluable in man's being, it forgets that housed in a dark complexion is equally and alike, all that is lofty in mind and noble in soul; that there lies an equal immortality. It teaches to graduate mind and soul, either by the texture of the hair, the form of the features, or the color of the skin, and forgets that all that is noble in man and distinguishes him as an animal, consists in what is invisible, and not in what is external and visible.

This is an education fostered by prejudice, consequently an education almost universally prevalent in our country, an education, too, subverting the principles of our humanity, and turning away the dictates of nobler beings from what is invaluable to meaner things.

We have treated prejudice as hatred, as a sin, and criminal alike in all, one class of the community is equally guilty in fostering the principle as another. The white people of this country, strongly prejudiced against the colored people, have no grounds for their prejudice, unless having injured the latter, they hate them; for perhaps it is a principle in the corruption of our nature, to hate those whom we injure.

But the colored people have grounds, being the injured party, for a prejudiced state of mind, although it would be alike criminal in them, as in others, but not having inflicted injuries, they have less of prejudice.

It is often asserted that this spirit color-phobia, prejudice, exists among ourselves towards each other, and based on complexion. We know there are surmisings, jealousies, and envyings, foolish, groundless, and wicked in themselves, existing amongst us; but that the colored people hate each other, based on complexion, we do not believe; that hatred of humble life exists amongst us, we deny. Let them assert it who may, let them believe it who may, we have not and do not. Let those indulge such a feeling who may wish too, we envy not the head nor the heart of him who does, any more than we do him who lives, harboring in his bosom, that such a state of things actually exists among us.

We ask, finally, those who imagine this state of feeling among us, to examine well the grounds of prejudice, look at it as a principle of hatred, and see if it can or does exist among the colored people, and if it has not lived in imagination, more than reality.

The Colored American, New York, September 26, 1840

KIDNAPPING

Madison, Iowa, December 18, 1840

Sir: As I am actuated by a love for our race, with yourself and others, I take up my pen to inform you that you may transmit through your valuable paper to the public, the present condition of a small boy who has been decoyed away into bondage by a northern man with southern principles. The boy's name is Francis Jackson; he told me he also had two sisters, Sarah and Mary Jackson. He stated that his father was a seafaring man, whose name was also Francis, and to the best of his knowledge, he died at sea. He also says, they lived in Philadelphia, in Front between Shippen and Pine streets. He came out to Pittsburgh with his uncle, and lived some time in Pittsburgh with a Dr. Simmons, and was living with the same gentleman when, being on the levee one day, this villain asked if he did not want to go down to the river and learn to ride races; he says he went, and after staying at Louisville, Ky., a few days, he put the boy on another boat, and sent him down to Vicksburg. He told the boy at the time he wanted him to go down and ride races; but he had sold him to a man who had him in charge, whose name is Kenner, a planter, and lives six miles above Domsonville, in Louisiana.

JOHN CARTER

The Colored American, New York, January 16, 1841

IMMEDIATE INFORMATION WANTED

A colored man, named Rufus Kinsman, is now confined in the Calaboose in New Orleans as a fugitive slave. He affirms he is a free man, is a native of New Haven, Conn., has sailed as a seaman from Hartford and N.Y. Any information respecting him will be thankfully received.

WM. JOHNSON
Sec. Vigilance Committee
198 Hudson Street
New York

The Colored American, New York, February 6, 1841

White abolitionists were often inconsistent in their attitude toward free blacks in the North, as they were unaware of their own racism. Though

the following article is signed "M," it is most probably by the editor, Stephen Myers, a conductor on the Underground Railroad in Albany and an active conventionist and abolitionist.

For several years we have been astonished at the indifference manifested by abolitionists, in regard to the adoption of some effectual measures for advancing the welfare of free people of color. . . . They profess to possess the most generous and benevolent feelings towards us, and deeply lament the unhappy situation in which we are placed by unjust laws and a cruel and oppressive prejudice. They regret and acknowledge that we labor under a thousand disadvantages from which every other class of community are exempt, and wonder that with all the accumulated hindrances to our progress to become intelligent and respectable members of society, we possess moral fortitude sufficient to rise above the surges of persecution.

Twenty-two thousand abolition votes were polled during the last year in the States in favor of persons opposed to Southern slavery, and a large number of those opposed to political action withheld theirs. Large numbers in this and other States have also with us petitioned the legislatures for the repeal of those laws which were unjust, oppressive, anti-republican and inimical to the interests of the colored portion of the community. Now with all this array of sentiment and feeling, and political action before us, the natural inference would be that the united wisdom, wealth, influence, benevolence, and sympathy of so large a portion of our citizens, could and would have devised some efficient means for bettering the condition of at least a portion of the people of color. . . .

We never expected that abolitionists would place themselves upon a level even with the most intelligent and respectable of our people; neither did we desire their daughters in marriage. We did not expect to ride in their carriages, nor desire to mix in their parties of pleasure; but we did *HOPE* that they would do for us some things, which they have not only neglected but what appears to us to have been foreign from their intentions. We supposed that while they advocated the rights of man and the cause of suffering humanity, that they would have been foremost in opening every avenue, and destroying every barrier in their power that was closed against us, or that retarded our progression; and that by doing so they would be enabled to present those with whom they plead for the restoration of the inalienable rights of man. . . . Probably there are no less than 30,000 abolitionists in the states and doubtless among them there are mechanics of every description; who, instead of endeavoring to break down prejudice and make a powerful thrust at slavery, by taking our youth and instructing them in the various branches, content themselves and suppose that we also are contented, by having them disseminate what they call *their* principles from one end of the country to the other. They profess to be opposed to slavery, but with the greater portion of them we believe that it is that slavery only which exists at the south.

Now we ask if the prejudice which exists at the north is not akin to the slavery of the south? We firmly believe it to be so, and if the prejudice of the northern abolitionists will not permit them to take as apprentices colored boys, or if their regard for the prejudices of others will not allow them so to do, *we also believe* that the influence of their example is more injurious to colored people at large, than the disinclination of the slave holder to release the victims of his avarice. And until the abolitionists eradicate prejudice from their own hearts, they never can receive the unwavering confidence of the people of color. We do not ask for money, neither do we wish them to educate our children; these we will endeavor to provide for by the sweat of our brow, but we *do* ask that their workshops may be opened to our youth, and that those of us who are already in business may be patronized. . . .

The Northern Star and Freeman's Advocate,
Albany, New York, March 3, 1842

The colored man who is robbed of his liberty, and by the laws of the south is made "goods and chattel," in the north has granted him an equitable trial by jury. This law is now denounced as unconstitutional by the federal court of this session—while in the south when a vessel enters its ports if navigated by a colored freeman of the other states, as cook, steward, or seaman, he is taken from the vessel, lodged in prison and there detained until the vessel again leaves port. . . . Will the north take no steps to correct this evil so oppressive and so injurious to commerce, and so insulting to the free institutions of the north? . . .

The Northern Star and Freeman's Advocate, Albany
New York, March 10, 1842

The following is an editorial from the Mystery, *edited by Martin Robison Delany, and is a good example of his concern for the elevation of his people and his attempt to engender race pride.*

. . . The condition of our race, yes, our poor unfortunate race, we say poor unfortunate, because, unless we can be brought to see and feel and be made really sensible of our *true* condition, all that we may attempt towards the amelioration of our condition must fall as "pearl cast among swine." The condition then of our poor unfortunate race is such, that it implants degradation at once in the minds and bosoms of our youth—detracts from the graces and virtues of our tender maidens, and lamentable to reflect upon, it blights the fairest prospects of womanhood, disheartening and carrying desolation with it, almost totally plucking out and destroying the last remnant of those ennobling qualities so essential to a wife and mother, the first and true guardians of the rising generation, those indispensable propensities and qualities which distinguish woman and make her the evident superior of her race.

Situated as we are, as mere nonentities in the midst of others—the most deserving respectable and praiseworthy among us, in the eye of the law and its consequent enactments, being placed far beneath the most vile vagabond while being denied privileges granted to the pauper and vagrant—those by the laws, declared to be nuisance—while privileges which from their nature necessarily elevate the female, the wife, mother, sister and daughter, and stimulate the tender youth; we colored male citizens, are made the degraded vassals of the most insufferable servility, more intolerable than death itself.

Spurned the right of election as representatives, and peerage as jurors, denied and robbed of the elective franchise and consequently the right of representation; (in many of the states) deprived of the right of testimony even against a vagabond; though our hoary-headed father or mother may be maltreated, abused or murdered, our wives or sisters ravished before our eyes! Prohibited the right of bearing arms as patriots and soldiers in defense of our Country, thereby precluding us from those *claims* upon our country in common with other inhabitants or citizens; denied the right of *citizenship in toto,* in order thereby to exclude us from the protection of the laws, which of course we are prevented from having any part in making, thereby disdaining to make us the subjects of legislation, except it be for the object of stamping us with still deeper degradation.

This scheme of oppression being complete, as a matter of course it follows that the forfeiture of every claim to civil and decent respect is fully implied in the base surrender of our manhood, crouching in servility at the feet of insolence and usurpation.

The Mystery, Pittsburgh, Pennsylvania, December 16, 1846

The following letter by Martin R. Delany, co-editor at the time of the North Star, *is typical of his consistent attack upon white racism in American society.*

. . . It is time that the voice of outraged humanity—high time that it was raised against this intolerable crusade against our rights, and insufferable rioting against liberty—reckless trampling under foot our most delicate sensibility, and cherished sense of propriety. . . . The weight of a nation grind us in the dust, and we dare make the effort to cast it off. There appears to be a fixed determination on the part of our oppressors in this country, to destroy every vestige of self-respect, self-possession, and manly independence left in the coloured people. . . .

The North Star, Rochester, New York, March 30, 1849

The following letter by Mary Ann Shadd, from Wilmington, Delaware, stressed the necessity for black people to act independently.

. . . Do you not think, sir, that we should direct our attention more to the farming interest than hitherto? I suggest this, as concerning the entire people. The estimation in which we would be held by those in power, would be quite different, were we producers and not merely, as now, consumers. . . . We have been holding conventions for years—have been assembling together and whining over our difficulties and afflictions, passing resolutions on resolutions to any extent; but it does really seem that we have made but little progress, considering our resolves. We have put forth few practical efforts to an end. I, as one of the people, see no need for our distinctive meetings, if we do not do something. We should do more and talk less. What intellectually we most need, and the absence of which we most feel, is the knowledge of the white man, a great amount of which by, intercourse in public meetings, etc., we could glean, and no possible opportunity to seize upon which should be allowed to escape. Should not the importance of his literature upon us, and everything tending to add to his influence be forcibly impressed, and we be directed to that course? The great fault of our people, is in imitating his follies; individual enterprise and self-reliance are not sufficiently insisted upon. The influence of a corrupt clergy among us, sapping our every means, and as a compensation, inculcating ignorance as a duty, superstition as true religion—in short, hanging like millstones about our necks, should be faithfully proclaimed. I am willing to be convinced to the contrary, if possible, but it does really seem to me that our distinctive churches and the frightfully wretched instruction of our ministers—their gross ignorance and insolent bearing, together with the sanctimonious garb, and by virtue of their calling, a character for mystery they assume, is attributable more of the downright degradation of the free colored people of the North, than from the effect of corrupt public opinion; for sir, notwithstanding the cry of prejudice against color, some think it will vanish by a change in condition, and that we can, despite this prejudice, change that condition. The ministers assume to be instructors in every matter, a thing we would not object to, providing they taught, even in accordance with the age. . . . "Pay no attention to your perishing bodies, children, but get your souls converted; prepare for heaven. The elective franchise would not profit you; a desire for such things indicates worldly mindedness"—Thus any effort to a change of conditions by our people is replied to, and a shrinking, priest-ridden people, are prevented from seeing clearly. The possibility of final success, when using proper means, the means to be used the possibility of bringing about the desired end ourselves, and not waiting for the whites of the country to do so, should be impressed on the people by those teachers as they assume to be the only true ones; or at least there should be no hindrance to their seeing for themselves.

The North Star, Rochester, New York, March 23, 1849

Racial self-respect and self-help were interdependent; one without the other was meaningless, as the following letter by Thomas Duff indicates.

Let every Colored resident in the State . . . abandon such positions as boot-blacks, waiters, servants and carriers, and other servile employment, and if they cannot engage in trading, mechanical pursuits, or farming, let them pitch into mining from which they have not been debarred. . . . Money can be made if followed with industry, accompanied with strict economy. And money will purchase and stock farms, and certainly our people are as well, if not better qualified for that calling as any on the face of the earth.

I do not wish to be understood as despising any of the callings I have mentioned above, or as wishing to bring them into contempt. But I would recommend our people to abandon them, because so long as we follow such pursuits, so long we will be despised. The world may preach the dignity of labor, and the man who has attained a prominent and influential position may boast of having started in life as a boot-black, or any other menial calling. But however pretty this may be in theory, everyone is aware that it does not exist in reality. The man is judged and courted, not for his inherent qualities, but for his position and wealth. . . . Why cannot we have our preachers of the gospel in every town in California? Certainly we are able to support them, and the influence of 50 or 100 intelligent anti-political clergymen, of our own class and selection, would exercise a vast influence. Then we should establish debating and other literary societies in every place, by which information and intelligence would be diffused amongst those of us who are too far advanced in years to commence our education by ordinary means of schools.

The necessity of establishing schools for the education of our youth, would seem too evident to need urging. And yet there is scarcely a village or town in California that possesses a common school for the education of Colored children. It is true that we are compelled to pay taxes for the support of those already established, and from which our children are excluded; but that, of course, is only *just* and *right.* It is also true that we are denied our portion of the public school fund but as we are not possessed of any rights which the white man is bound to respect, it is perhaps only right and proper that we should continually give and never receive. . . .

Mirror of the Times, San Francisco, December 12, 1857

What are we doing to advance the cause of our rights at present in this state—comparatively nothing. We have settled down into a state of indifference and lethargy on this question. . . . . We are quarreling among ourselves instead of uniting on the subject of our rights, and devising some general plan of operation for the good of the whole people. . . .

Mirror of the Times, San Francisco, December 12, 1857

. . . The white man as a general thing thinks he has reason to look either contemptuously, or patronizingly down upon the black man. Why should the black man still continue to look fawningly, or cringingly up to the white man. The black man must learn to stand more firmly upon his feet—his own feet. To do this he must seek more independent employments and follow them with more success and make whatsoever he does follow more respectable.

The Weekly Anglo-African, New York, September 3, 1859

. . . Let us then cease to be longer a landless, floating people, but seek to find anchorage in the soil of our country. . . . It must be a part of our well understood policy to get good available real estate. Where such is to be had, and one cannot make the purchase, let two join and affect it, and sometimes a whole company. . . . Let enterprising colored men of small means who are not disposed to purchase city or town property lay their means out on good, small farms, paying what they can to properly secure them. . . . Let it become part and parcel of our policy to give and hold bonds and mortgages among ourselves. By such a means we shall gradually—we may say rapidly—get a vaster amount of real estate into our possession, and carry with it a vaster amount of real valuable influence of the right sort—a kind with more to us than all the ephemeral, political, and dreamy stuff that we can gather up from now until the end of time.

The Weekly Anglo-African, New York, February 10, 1860

The following is a letter by Martin Robison Delany to the Reverend J. T. Holly, rector of St. Luke's Church, New Haven, Connecticut, and leader of the Haitian emigration movement. The white man referred to in the second paragraph is James Redpath, who was also a leader of this movement.

. . . My duty and destiny are in Africa, a great and glorious (even in its defects) land of your and my ancestry. I cannot, I *will not* desert her for all things else in this world, save that of my "own household," and that does not require it, as it will thereby be enhanced.

. . . The black man should act and do for himself, just as the white man under like circumstances would be justified in doing—*self-reliance* on the principles of Black Nationality. . . . I object to a black government appointing over black men a white, when blacks are competent to act and no policy requires the appointment of a white. I object to white men in such cases, getting all the positions of *honor* and *emoluments* while the blacks receive only the *subordinate,* with little or no pay! I maintain this position as necessary to self-respect, and treat with contempt the idea that it makes no difference in such cases whether the person be white or black, while black men are still occupying inferior positions in the midst of a people who deny their equality in all the relations of life.

The Weekly Anglo-African, New York, February 2, 1861

To black Americans, the flag symbolized their oppression. As part of their resistance, a number of black men emigrated to Haiti, where they hoped to form a "Negro Nationality," as well as establish a strike force against the South. Although the Civil War had begun, black men at this time were not allowed to join the Army.

The American flag is our flag; for we are Americans. But the usual interpretation of it, now so popular, but so full of prejudice—"the Constitution and the Enforcement of the Laws"—is not ours alas! but that of our bitterest and most malignant enemies. Withered forever be the hand, and paralyzed the arm of the colored American who lifts up either in support of the Federal Flag; until its supporters, seeing the justice of our claims and the greatness of our sufferings, they shall inscribe upon it the glorious motto under which, as we hear, our brethren this week sailed forth to found a great Negro Nationality in the Antilles—the new watchword of the John Brown Abolitionists—terrible as the desolating breath of the volcano, but beneficient as the general sunshine of spring:

EMANCIPATION OR EXTERMINATION

The Weekly Anglo-African, New York, April 27, 1861

A party of colored men made their appearance on Broadway, a few days since, with drum and fife, and bearing the American flag, and attempted to march up the street. They were dispersed by the crowd, their drum and flag taken away, and were informed that "niggers could not be allowed to carry that flag!" Comment is unnecessary.

The Weekly Anglo-African, New York, May 4, 1861

The agricultural revolution occurred within the context of the transformation of the plantation system and attempts to retain it. The following articles reflect the various forces that existed and some of the alternatives.

For good or for evil, the plantation system inaugurated by the military commander of the Department of the Gulf seems to have resulted in a total failure. . . . The plantation abandoned by their rebel owners imperatively required to be cultivated under the penalty of relapsing into forests and of starvation to the former cultivators. Something had to be done. . . . The plantations were leased out to the government to the teeming swarm of avaricious adventurers . . . whose sole endeavor and object was not to enlighten, improve and elevate, but to make as much money as possible out of the labor of these colored proletaries. . . .

The Tribune, New Orleans, September 24, 1864

. . . So long as the freedmen will remain under the control of the former planters and overseers who had charge of them at the time that slavery existed, so long as the new lessees will follow in the old path, there will be no means of extending to the laborers the benefit of a true and practical liberty. We must at least set up in the several parishes some examples of plantations worked on a different and more liberal plan in order to gradually introduce the laborers to a different mode of life. . . .

The Tribune, New Orleans, January 28, 1865

. . . We proposed that a few "managers" possessed of some means and desirous of participating in the actual elevation of the African race should form associations and start the new system. . . . Laborers must be bound to the plantations by their interest only. In order to

foster this interest, they must not only receive monthly or weekly pay,
but ought to be made partners in the yield of the crops. . . .

The Tribune, New Orleans, January 28, 1865

THE COLORED SOLDIERS TO
TAKE THE PLACE OF PLANTERS

. . . Our basis for labor must now be put on a democratic footing.
There is no more room in the organization of our society for an oligarchy of slaveholders or property holders.

A Banking Association, calling into action the small contributions
of all friends of freedom, will strike a mortal blow upon the remnants
of slavery. . . .

The Tribune, New Orleans, March 1, 1865

*With the Civil War at an end, black people reflected a basic optimism
about their own prospects, as well as society in general.*

THE DUTY OF COLORED MEN IN LOUISIANA

The people who have just thrown off their chains, have now a high
duty before them. God has surely broken the bonds that bound us,
and man was made the instrument—his blood the price. We have
privileges now. Let us enjoy them rationally, and like men. We have
been outraged. Our intellects have been chained as well as our bodies.
Indeed, our very souls were not our own. It was a crime to teach us.
We dare not hold a book in our hands. We were dragged through the
streets and into the jails, without cause, and no chance at justice. The
chains were strong; they were heavy. The dark clouds that hung over
us; the chains that bound us; the prisons, whose very walls re-echoed
our lamentations as we sent them up to heaven—these have all passed
away; a river of blood has passed on with a mighty current, carrying
the accursed things out of the world.

Better times have come. We live in brighter days. The sun shines
and the blessed rain of heaven is falling. But are we yet in a safe
place? Are we standing on holy ground? Is all accomplished that can
be accomplished? Is there still in store any good that we, as men and
citizens, can attain?

We are hardly safe. The Government of God and of the United States make up the ground of the black man's safety. That, added to the honesty of purpose in his own heart, will bring him to permanent security.

The ground on which we stand is not holy. There are many remnants of the past guilt yet polluting the soil and the atmosphere. There are cruel and dangerous prejudices that must be outlived. The sting of the serpent of slavery is in the hearts of the people. They may die with it, but justice and righteousness will live for ever, and with them we must and shall succeed.

Much is accomplished. The main works are carried. The assault has been successful, but the enemy has only fled! He is weakened, but not captured or overcome. The heel must bruise his head and crush it. This will be done by us, not with the sword, not with words, newspapers or orations, but by our life, our conduct, our own very faithfulness to the freedom we have commenced to enjoy. Honesty, industry, temperance, religion, education, truthfulness—these will be the virtues that will make us strong; and then let us be strong by our unity, our harmony among ourselves. Let us gather to our help every white man who has a soul big enough to be bold and strong for the right. These are many; let us make them as many more, and not one less. With these, let us appeal to Heaven and to the conscience of the Christian world, and we will find ourselves ultimately strong enough to win.

There is yet much that we can attain. The United States Government has almost lost its glory on account of "its filthy garments." It has repented and thrown off its blood-stained mantle, and enrobed itself in righteousness to a commendable degree. We can expect much, but let us not be satisfied by merely expecting. We must ask, petition and strive. Above all, our devotion to our flag, and our manly conduct must be our loud appeal and the ground of our hope.

We offer these remarks with the belief that our thoughtful men will ponder them well. They bear in them the full aim and object of this journal.

The Black Republican, New Orleans, April 15, 1865

The following letter, written by J. J. Moore, indicates a common theme—the need for equality and self-development.

There are two conditions of things necessary to raise us to the social eminence of our favored neighbors; one of those conditions lays imperative obligations upon the Government, general and local, and the other upon ourselves.

The first true step or move towards our real elevation to political eminence, which is incumbent upon the Government, is to set us right before the law . . . to give us the common rights of citizens—in political franchise, in the general advantage of the free school system of our land, from its lowest to its highest advantages—without which we can never be educated as a mass. Also, give us in common with the other races, civil liberty; give us equal advantages with them in the development of the common resources of the country, in all its avenues to wealth. . . .

The second condition of things necessary to raise us to a level with the highest grade of society, is incumbent upon ourselves. This consists, on our part, in acquiring those social developments peculiar to the elevation of the other race—which constitutes their social condition. The first of these is the development of moral power; second, intellectual power; third, mechanical and manufacturing power; fourth, scientific and inventive power; fifth, we must create business enterprise among ourselves by combination of capital to lift us out of menial servitude to which condition, so long as we remain as a class, we can never be respected; sixth, we must cultivate unity in business and feeling—creating among ourselves a great moral, intellectual, and commercial center that will conduce to independence, wealth, happiness and respectability. . . .

The Elevator, San Francisco, May 5, 1865

At the war's end, Major General Samuel S. Cox, the Union candidate for governor of Ohio, proposed the separation of all black people into a selected area in the Gulf States. This was met by opposition among black freedmen, who believed American society could and would change. This attitude, however, changed a decade later, confirmed by the migrations westward.

. . . If four years of war against slavery, if the patient patriotism of the Negro, if all the many acts of personal devotion to the sick, suffering, imprisoned and escaping Unionists, if the constant and invaluable information received from the slaves everywhere by the Federal officers, if the blood which was shed at Fort Pillow, Honey Springs, Port Hudson, Petersburg, and within sight of where we write, has only tended to make the white soldiers and loyal citizens of the Republic bitterer haters and contemners of their black brothers-in-arms, then all we have to say, and we say it in sad sincerity, is that the war is a failure, the sacrifice a lie, and this boasted dominant race is totally unfit to be the guardians and maintainers of the great principles and demands of civilization. . . .

. . . We don't intend to separate. We are Americans, born on the soil; and with inherent rights, which we know full well this great Republic will yet grant and defend us in possession.

There are no such race-hatreds as General Cox so forcibly paints. We are bone of one bone, blood of one blood; we are part of this race, though our skins have darker hue. This may be unpalatable talk, but it is nonetheless true. . . . Why, does not the General know, that the best blood of the haughty South runs in the veins of her darker children. These white men have yet some natural affection left. If we remove to the territory mapped out for us by General Cox, our white relatives will follow us. . . .

This whole question of manhood suffrage is a simple one, and is, if men will look at it from the simple, and human standpoint of a wise equity, entirely disconnected with any question on the races being able to live together. We have done so for two hundred years, as master and slave. *We know we can live in harmony with the whites as freemen, if only allowed to. . . .*

. . . There is but one other word to add here. It is to warn the country of a fact borne out by all history. It is this. A people can be kept in complete bondage much easier than be retained in a partial bondage. The planters of the West Indies were glad to get shut of the apprenticeship system by which the transition was abridged. No danger need be apprehended if the national honor is redeemed, and we are placed where we can protect ourselves. Do this now while the power is given; the whites will acquiesce and the exuberant gratitude of the blacks will be mainly manifested in efforts to be worthy of their position. There will be no difficulty of importance. Delay it, let it be a bone of contention for years to come, something for demagogues to play with, and trouble will most likely result.

The Colored Tennessean, Nashville, August 12, 1865

In response to the demands by black people for education, denied to them in slavery, one of the great accomplishments of the Freedman's Bureau was to establish the foundations of public education in the South.

It is beginning to be recognized by the thinking men of the South, that is it a moral duty on their part to educate the colored population. It is impossible, in the present wants of the South, to do without the labor of its four millions of blacks. As they are part of the social system, the question arises, is it not better to so improve this class that the country may have the benefit of its virtues, and not be afflicted by its vices if left to ignorance and a mischievous self-indulgence which arises from it? . . .

The Colored Tennessean, Nashville, October 7, 1865

This letter by a newly freed man from Edisto Island, South Carolina, an island taken over by black people after the war, was a response to attempts by its former owner to reclaim it.

I hope soon to be called citizen of the U.S. and have the rights of a citizen. I am opposed myself to working under a contract. I am as much at liberty to hire a white man to work, as he has to hire me. I expect to stay in the South one year after I am mustered out of service, but not to hire myself to a planter. I have seen some men hired who were turned off without being paid. They try to pull us down faster than we can climb up. They have no reason to say that we will not work, for we raised them, and sent them to school, and bought their land, and now it is as little as they can do to give us some of their land, be it little, or much.

The South Carolina Leader, Charleston, December 31, 1865

The Southern planters, following the Civil War, tried to reassert their control over their former slaves by saying that freedmen would not work. The black press defended the freedmen and exposed incidents of corruption in the Freedman's Bureau, which had been established to help black people in the South.

But a few months ago nearly half of the inhabitants of this State were slaves—now they are free. Will this change be a benefit or an injury to the State? . . . The labor system of the State has been overturned, and a new system is to be established. . . . It is evident that the success of the free-labor system is alike for the interest of both parties, and we shall use our influence whatever it may be to this end. We shall strive to induce those laborers who receive fair compensation and kind treatment to be industrious and faithful and we shall labor to secure for all good wages and kind treatment. To make free labor successful, it is necessary that the laborer shall be fairly treated. . . . give the freedman justice, impartial justice, and we believe he will work better as a freeman than he did as a slave. If you do not do this, you ought not to expect him to be faithful. . . .

Two races inhabit this State, which have heretofore lived together as master and slave; in their changed relations, we shall not only do nothing to create a disturbance between them, but shall use our influence to settle any difficulty that may arise.

The Loyal Georgian, Augusta, January 20, 1866

Following the Civil War, many blacks, though free by law, were kept on the plantations and promised compensation for their work. But such promises were rarely fulfilled, as indicated by the necessity for intervention by the Freedmen's Bureau, a federal agency whose purpose was to aid newly freed slaves.

. . . the Freedman will work if the right spirit prevails, and they are fairly treated. They have received no compensation for the labor performed since that time, and very few have received fair compensation. Hundreds were poorly fed and clothed, and have been turned out upon the world almost naked, and without hardly food enough to prevent starvation because they refuse to make contracts this year for insufficient wages. . . .

Mr. Davis (Jacob R. Davis), Agent of the Freedmen's Bureau, for Richmond county, has, within a few days, collected for the Freedmen on one plantation $1,800. Daily large numbers of freedmen appear before his Court and complain that their employers have refused to pay the money due for work performed last year.

In Edgefield District, South Carolina, the condition of the freed people is heart rendering. They are not only in many cases driven from the plantation without pay, but no Court has been established that will give them justice, and they are unable to collect the money due them for labor performed since they were free. . . .

The Loyal Georgian, Augusta, January 27, 1866

The school referred to below was run by the American Missionary Association. It had one teacher and 167 students.

We had the pleasure of visiting the Trinity free school. . . . The ladies who teach these schools make sacrifices enough without requiring them to perform an amount of labor which will certainly ruin their health if they continue to perform it for many months. We suggest that the society which employs them engage one, or more colored teachers for each of the schools. . . . We would also suggest that if colored teachers are employed, a school should be established for their benefit. The expense will be much less than it is to send teachers from the North and we believe more good will result from this, or similar plan than to employ only white teachers; for they will be taught not only what to teach but how to teach, and many worthy young ladies will be benefited by giving them employment.

The Loyal Georgian, Augusta, January 27, 1866

In 1833, black people in New York formed the "Phoenix" societies to provide education, welfare, and other social services needed in the black community. This pattern was carried to other states, notably California.

There is no question among mankind as to the importance of mental cultivation as a lever of elevation. All agree if we, as a people, could or would become an intellectual people that prejudice would be destroyed. Slavery is dead; prejudice remains the barrier to political and social progress . . . The Phoenixonian Institute proposes a unity of action. We propose to undermine the tower of ignorance by establishing an institution for the education of children of the State of California. . . .

The Elevator, San Francisco, June 21, 1867

The concept "Buy Black" was an important one in developing the black community and its self-sustaining qualities. This was, however, difficult to promote.

It is admitted by all that we should now be a unit in action as well in business as in politics, and in every way we can strive to build each other up. . . . Does one of our own farmers want merchandise, and a colored man has it to sell, let him that wants give to his own color, that has it to sell, the preference. A plow made by a black man, tells us more than a hundred first-class speeches. . . .

"a mechanic"
The Arkansas Freeman, Little Rock, October 5, 1869

If indeed we have any capitalists at all amongst us, you will find them to be of that class who never invest in any enterprise amongst their own people.

The Virginia Star, Richmond, September 8, 1877

The importance of Africa as a cultural reference point in the development of racial pride underlies the semantic ambiguity and dispute that arose over the use of the word "Negro."

. . . The Negro. How long is this word to be tolerated by the people of African descent? To me it was distasteful even in early childhood, now it has become extremely obnoxious to me. . . . We all know that Ham and his posterity settled Africa. Yet, eminent historians tell us that the descendants of Ham were not all Negroes—simply,

I suppose because many of them rose to eminence and distinction. The Egyptians and Ethiopians were proud and prosperous nations, and it would shock the fastidious of today to have it said that the grand and stupendous pyramids were designed and built by Negroes, or that the great art of embalming belonged to them. . . . What their origin is, or in what part of Africa they reside I have never been able to ascertain. . . . If all the intelligent people of African descent in this land disdained the name as I do they would rise up and with pen and tongue protest against it, until it was clearly proven to them that they belonged to that race, if such a race exists. In my opinion it is nothing but a word of reproach and insult.

"G. G. P."

The New National Era, Washington, D.C., February 1, 1872

In the aftermath of the Civil War the black press sought to bring together poor white and black against the oligarchy of wealth. The most direct and obvious route was through education.

. . . Everything that will bring the poor white man and the colored man together should be done; they should be taught to make common cause against the rich landowners of the South who never regarded a poor white man of as much importance as they did slaves. Educate the poor white children and the colored children together; let them grow up to know that color makes no difference as to the rights of a man, that both the black man and the white man are at home; that the country is as much the country of one as of the other, and that both together must make it a valuable country. Now in the South the poor white man is taught that he is better than the black man, and not as good as the 250,000 slaveholders of former days; the result is that the slaveholders command the poor white man to murder the black man, to burn down his schoolhouses and to, in every conceivable manner maltreat him, and the command is obeyed. . . . We want mixed schools not because our colored schools are inferior to white schools —not because colored instructors are inferior to white instructors, but because we want to do away with a system that exalts one class and debases another. . . .

The New National Era, Washington, D.C., May 2, 1872

Mary Shadd Cary, the author of the following, was the daughter of Abraham Shadd and sister of J. D. Shadd, the Speaker of the Mississippi House of Representatives at the time. She was a lawyer and lecturer on temperance and other reforms.

. . . The condition of colored youth in this city and District is true of them throughout the country. But the opposition by Americans is not the only cause of this sorry state of things, though mainly so; indifference on the part of leading colored men and the deathlike silence of colored women contribute to it. A people whose leaders seek to learn the torturous ways of speculation and whose women are awed into silence, vital questions must for the time take back seats among the people. The white men of this and other countries deal vigorously now with every issue for the good of their youth, and white men are to the front with them in the work as having a common mission. . . . Our women must speak out. The boys must have trades. . . . White women are getting to be a power in the land, and colored cannot any longer afford to be neutrals. Never fear the ward meetings; get the boys started properly in life and the ward meetings will come right. . . .

The New National Era, Washington, D.C., March 21, 1872

. . . How does it happen that the movements of the Moral Education Society of Washington, radical and comprehensive as they are, have not elicited one word of comment, not to say commendation from your able paper? The ladies, members of that society, propose to make sure work by enlisting the youth of the nation in the cause of temperance and pledging against profanity and the use of tobacco. . . .

The New National Era, Washington, D.C., February 27, 1873

. . . our friends (?) . . . do not regard the colored people of Maryland as they do others. There exists within them, the same old feeling that [they] have had heretofore. They try to hide it under the guise of apparent friendship. But at intervals despite their precaution it breaks forth. In fact, they are the best friends of the colored race—as long as he is content to be seen and not heard. But as soon as he, by the least act, shows his manhood, by asking for rights which every creature God intended to enjoy, that moment they call this action impudence and audacity. There are hundreds of white men in the South today, who have not the intelligence that the colored people of Maryland have, and who are accorded all rights, without a murmur of dissent. But to the question. That our race are excluded from teaching in the public schools of Baltimore City, has been proven to us, beyond a doubt. There have been numerous applications made to school commissioners by individuals, both ladies and gentlemen among us, but they have been ignored. . . . And as far as securing the most competent instruction is concerned, we do not want ignorant colored men when we have intelligent ones who can (when opportunity is afforded) teach as well as those now teaching . . .

The American Citizen, Baltimore, April 19, 1879

Community control of education has been a persistent demand of lower-income groups, who have been prevented from exercising their right to determine their own destiny.

COLORED TEACHERS FOR COLORED SCHOOLS

We see from the different papers that we get as exchanges that in almost every state where separate schools are maintained, the colored people are insisting upon colored teachers being employed to teach them, and we have no hesitation in saying they are right, and we hope they will never cease demanding until they have put colored teachers in every colored school in the land. While we believe it is an outrage upon the civilization of the age to carry on the caste schools, yet if they must be forced upon us and if our children are always to be reminded by them that they are not entitled to the privilege of going to the same school that every other class of Americans are permitted to attend, then we shall insist upon it, that our educated sons and daughters are placed in them as teachers and not always content with sending them to some poor white man or woman who would not be permitted to teach in the white schools, but are put off on the colored people. Here in Topeka, the capital of the great free State of Kansas, a negro-hating Board of Education insists upon maintaining against both law and common sense, four or five of these caste schools and in the principle one they flatly refuse to put a colored teacher and we are told that the main reason that they employ one of the white teachers is because the said teacher is buying a farm and the Board desires to help pay for it and hence all colored applicants are refused, and payments on the farm are made regularly. When another election for school officers takes place in this city, we give notice now that we shall be found opposing every candidate who favors caste schools. The time for such relics of the dark ages is past in Kansas. We have been much surprised to see that some of our papers are willing that such schools be kept provided they were supplied with colored teachers; for our part, we should be against a race school, if we knew by their abolition every colored school teacher in America would be compelled to dig in the earth for a living for all time to come. We cannot afford to help keep up race prejudice for the sake of giving employment to any class of people whatever. Race difficulties will always exist in this country while race barriers are allowed to exist. We say down with every race institution in the land and the sooner we learn that we are all Americans the better for all concerned.

The Colored Citizen, Fort Scott, Kansas, December 14, 1878

Education in the new black communities of Kansas became especially crucial, and segregation was vigorously fought.

. . . Contrary to all exceptions the school board has again opened and set in operation two or three little colored schools in different parts of the city and thus again offers insult to every colored resident of the city. We hear of no Irish schools, no German schools, no Swedish schools. No, not one. All the children in the city are at liberty to attend the school nearest them, except the poor child that God for some reason chose to create with a black face instead of a white one. Our board of education, contrary to the law of the State, the law of God, and the laws of humanity persist in keeping up race distinction. . . . We say to every colored man and woman in the city to come together and resolve that you will no longer submit to unjust discrimination on account of your color. This thing has gone on long enough and now if it can be stopped, let's stop it. . . .

The Colored Citizen, Fort Scott, Kansas, September 20, 1878

The following editorial by P. B. S. Pinchback is characteristic of the attempt to thwart the increasing repression of Southern white society.

. . . It is not necessary that we should suffer in order that the nation may live. If its life or existence were threatened we would gladly lay down our lives in its defense. No such question presents itself now. We are at peace abroad. Domestic peace is disturbed at home. One class of citizens are at the mercy of another class, who deny or abridge their rights by intimidation or actual violence.

We have been honestly striving for peace and harmony between the races and classes in the South. We have borne the taunts of former political associates, and have had our integrity questioned because of this desire. Candor and justice compels us to say that the condition of our people is more pitiable now than ever. Under Republican rule the excuse given by our Democratic friends for their violence was bad government. Now no such cause exists. The sum total of the whole matter can be easily seen and understood. No community, where life, liberty and property are insecure, can prosper. Men will shun it. Capital will not seek to aid it; and plenty cannot abound in it, because its labor is not protected. The landowners here must understand that all our troubles grow out of politics, and the sooner they relegate to private life the men who encourage, defend or wink at these outrages, the sooner will our property and credit enhance in value and the sooner will domestic tranquility wane in our borders.

The Weekly Louisianian, New Orleans, January 11, 1879

The necessity and advisability of pooling resources had long been promoted by black editors, as many of the black papers were founded on that principle.

How we can help ourselves . . . if you guarantee . . . the bulk of the colored trade *on condition that they employ a fair proportion of colored salesmen,* the thing will be promptly done; but if this is met with point blank refusals, or evasions, the only course open is in organizing establishments on the joint capital of the colored people themselves. . . .

The People's Advocate, Washington, D.C., February 28, 1880

The black press constantly emphasized the need for racial unity and racial pride as the basis for a cohesive and strong black community.

The colored people will never amount to anything so long as they refuse to combine. All civilized races have arisen by means of combination and co-operation. . . . We believe that the average colored man will go a mile out of his way and pass a first class store of one of his own race in order to give his money to some white man who hates him. This is the result of jealousy and envy. It is the misfortune of our race that the impression prevails, "one nigger is as good as another." Now, this is a great error. There are colored men in this country as far ahead of others of their own race as Webster and Sumner were superior to the average white man.

Then again we have no confidence in each other. We consider goods from the store of a white man necessarily better than can be purchased from a colored man. We ignore colored doctors and lawyers and patronize men whose only recommendation is the color of their skin.

We speak disparagingly of our colored educational institutions, of our colored churches, of our colored newspapers, though all may be officered and managed by as able men as can be found in the same position among the other race. Our people will never be a power in this or any other country until they cease to worship the Caucasian and underrate their own capabilities. No man ever succeeded who lacked confidence in himself. No race did, or ever will prosper, or make a respectable history which had no confidence in his own nationality.

The Kansas Herald, Topeka, February 20, 1880

The black colonization of the Sea Islands proved to be the first and most successful experiments in agricultural co-ops. The following article originally appeared in the Southern Workman, edited by General Samuel Armstrong, president of Hampton Normal and Agricultural Institute, Hampton, Virginia.

The relations between the races, and the condition of the colored people on the Island is reported as the most gratifying and progressive. Day labor is becoming scarce, owing to the improvement in the condition of the laborers. Colored men who ten years ago worked as field hands for 50¢ a day now own their own lands and earn a comfortable support from them. Every inducement is offered by the planters to the colored laborers to settle on their places. On some of the Islands laborers work two days a week for the planter who gives them a house and 7 or 8 acres for himself; on other he works one and a half acres of the planter's land for the use of five acres for himself. On John's Island, the colored people own 4,300 acres; on James Island 1,600 acres; on Wadmala, 500 acres; and on Edisto, 4000 acres and make two-thirds of the entire crop of the Island. In 1872 a co-operative association of 35 colored men purchased a tract of 750 acres on Edisto Island, for $6000. Their agent, Mr. John Thorne, is now one of the most prominent colored planters on the Island. . . .

The People's Advocate, Washington, D.C., August 21, 1880

Perhaps the most crucial aspect of the quest for national identity was the emphasis on racial pride. In the 1880's, black journalists, in the midst of brutal repression, gave voice to their silenced people and strength to their resistance.

. . . The history of the world records no more gratifying evidence of advancement under the most disadvantageous circumstances than is shown by the Negro in America during the past 15 years. Starting from a depth of ignorance and poverty, smarting under centuries of oppression and injustice and harassed and hampered by a cruel and bitter prejudice such as no people ever suffered, every respectable avocation barred, every avenue for advancement closed to him, the progress which the Negro has made in spite of these almost insurmountable obstacles is something wonderful. . . . No black man can look upon it without pride and confidence in the ultimate future of his race. The Negro is advancing. Although not yet up to the world's standard of civilization and enlightenment, he is advancing toward it with giant strides. And as a quickened sense of justice and a proper enforcement of the law break down the barriers which are now imposed and open the opportunities which are now closed to him, his advancement will be rapid and irresistible. . . .

The Sentinel, Trenton, New Jersey, June 26, 1880

It has become the fashion of late to sneer at the progress of the Negro in America; to argue that he has halted in the march of improvement which prevents his emancipation from slavery; to speak of the present generation as being little better in morality and the mental power than the last; to consider his competency to make an even headway with other races in the struggle for life, all things being equal, as yet in doubt and to look with apprehensions towards his future. Even the Negro himself has to a great extent fallen into these errors and begun to think the equality of his race impossible to successfully demonstrate.

. . . men whose hands even now are heartened by ill paid drudgery, whose heads are already silvered and hearts scarred and wounded by ceaseless buffetings with a hydra-headed proscription may yet live to see the time in America when the lie with which the Republican lived more than a century past shall be made enduring truth for all time to come; when indeed, all men shall be free and equal—equal under the law, equal in every condition, equal in every avenue and walk.

The Colored Patriot, Topeka, Kansas, April 20, 1882

C. L. de Randamie, the author of this letter, was an agent for the Freedman's Bureau, following the Civil War. He later moved to Kansas, where he was assistant auditor under E. P. McCabe. In 1892 he was appointed chargé d'affaires by the president of Liberia. In 1898 he practiced law in Topeka.

Native Americans though we be, we are nevertheless looked upon as constituting an alien and heterogenous class in society and in the same light as though we emerged from slavery 20 years ago, no allowances are made for the improvements we have made in all the various avenues of life. We are promiscuously lumped together and labelled "nigger." We are herded together as much as possible in separate colonies as if we were lepers. It is only when compelled by necessity that our mechanics are permitted to work at their trades among the whites. Our educated young men unable to enter counting houses, or acquire trades or handicrafts through the rulings of the trade unions, or find any other profitable and honorable openings anywhere, are only crowding the liberal professions or becoming barbers, pullman car porters, or laborers or something without a future to it.

Our women have no careers before them other than washerwomen or domestics with families, exposed to all the evil influences and temptations these dependent positions expose them to. They are not allowed to work in factories, or in stores no matter how well qualified they may be. Besides being generally poor, we are haunted every step by disparaging comparisons and disheartening predictions. Willfully ignoring the causes of our general condition, the degradation of centuries of slavery, with the whole civilized world against us we are told that we have done nothing for the advancement of mankind—that we have produced no great men in the arts, science, literature, government, or religion, as if slavery in the South and social ostracism and proscription in the North and an unreasoning prejudice everywhere could found a college of philosophers and train men to deep thought and profound research in the higher activities of life. In the face of existing facts, it becomes manifest that if we are to grow in wisdom, power, and distinction we must depend entirely upon ourselves. The civilization of the world loves hardihood, strength and mightiness. . . . The world has no time to waste on ragged imbecile beggarism. Hence, we just trust in ourselves and co-operate with each other as much as possible; our exceptional condition must necessarily make its own laws.

We must secure for ourselves a position in this great and growing commonwealth. We must cultivate, foster, and increase the fairly favorable general sentiment of the people of this state toward us for our improvement and well-being.

With a homogeneous population pouring into the country from Europe, we must secure an equal chance in the race of life now. If this opportunity be lost, all is lost. We must learn to conform to the conditions that surround us. We must learn many new things and forget many old ones. If we are to have so much religion, let its manifestation be more rational. We must fret and chafe and never be satisfied. We are generally too frivolous, light-hearted and light-headed. Nothing serious or earnest about us. Our boys and girls must be trained to be more ambitious and aspiring and self-dependent. We must be menials and pariahs no longer. We must get education. . . .

The Colored Patriot, Topeka, Kansas, April 27, 1882

The necessity of integrated schools in breaking down racial prejudice was emphasized in the black press, which fought against the "separate but . . ." doctrine.

Compulsory separate schools, based on color cannot be defended on legal grounds; for they are in violation of the spirit of the amendments to the Constitution and the Civil Rights Bill which prohibit any discrimination based on "color or previous condition of servitude." . . . There is another argument against proscriptive schools in the sections in which they have been abolished, and this argument exerted a powerful influence towards their abolition. The colored population is so sparse, compared with that of the whites, that the expense of separate schools is relatively greater than that of the white schools, and successful grading is rendered out of the question. In all such places separate schools was another name for inferior schools and a reproach to our much boasted public school system, besides doing more to perpetuate discriminations based on color than all other causes combined.

Indefensible as compulsory separate schools are, their establishment and continuance as a matter of public policy in such a place as Washington, for instance, where the colored population is sufficiently numerous and compact for properly classified schools for efficient teachers, giving substantially the same benefits in both white and colored schools is quite another and different question from that presented for consideration in the North and West. It needs separate treatment.

Let it be distinctly understood that any law which compels a parent or guardian because of color to send his children to a designated school is unjust and humiliating, because proscriptive, and it is the first duty of Congress to have the law properly amended. But such a law need not close a single colored school now in existence. All that is necessary is to permit any parent who chooses to do so to send his child to the school most convenient of access. . . .

Only a few avocations are open to the Negro. His voice is constantly raised against the discrimination manifested against him in business houses, in trades and the civil service. All his conventions are directed to the foundation of plans and organizations by which his proportionate representation can be obtained; therefore, to advise a policy which would at once close many a now open door would be suicidal. . . .

The People's Advocate, Washington, D.C., September 24, 1881

The controversy between supporters of academic or industrial education
was a topic of concern during the 1880's and laid the ground for Booker
T. Washington's views to find ready acceptance.

. . . While the whites may be in a condition to foster academical
training and to require those mental luxuries it will not be doubted
that the colored people as a class are not quite ready for it. . . . We
feel that the colored people of the country can expect to rise to permanent equality mainly by industrial education—intelligent labor in
every department of industry—and that the public mind should be directed to that end is only too patent. When the masses become intelligent through the medium of Normal and Industrial Schools there will
be a sufficient number, whose natural bent will incline them to the
higher grades of intellectual culture to fill all the colleges of the South,
white or black or both. . . .

The People's Advocate, Washington, D.C., February 18, 1882

Where black children were prohibited from attending high schools or
trade schools, black journalists demanded separate schools.

Most of the education journals of the country are arguing the
proper management, and the best instruction for properly fitting the
different Normal schools, for active life. The STAR and all the better
thinking people of our race in the city and state, are asking for a Normal school *proper*. One, where boys and girls can be instructed by
teachers of their own race, who would be able to fit them in every particular to fill their part in the great drama of life. Give us a High and
Normal School where our young people may be instructed by those
who have their interests at heart. We are tired of having the treadles of
all the machines run by the whites. Noble descendants of Ham, stand
up for pride of race. Faint not by the way. Do your whole duty, and
teach your sons and daughters to do the same.

The Virginia Star, Richmond, November 18, 1882

One of the major concerns of blacks during the 1880's and 1890's was
the establishment of a strong commercial base on which to develop the
black community.

INDUSTRIAL ENTERPRISES AMONG US

No people will attain that standard of personal importance which will command respect if they disregard the claims of industrial enterprises. Education, Religion, good morals, refinement, all go to make a people; but these alone cannot do so. Money or that which will command it is as indispensable to the make up of a people as good manners are to the make up of the gentleman or lady. And no people who will not foster industrial enterprises will ever be wealthy. We desire to enjoy the respect and good opinion of our fellow men. We would be less than men if we did not. But it is foolishness to desire that to which we are not entitled, because it will not be granted us except as a charity. Seeing that wealth is indispensable to the end we seek, let us examine as to whether or not we are on the road to that much desired means. Are we really on the road to wealth? Let us ask a few questions, and the answers to them will determine the complexion of the one that should be given to the first. Is there a corn or flouring mill in all this great State owned and controlled by colored men? Is there a saw mill? a cotton mill? a tobacco factory, worth the name? a manufactory of any kind employing from fifty to a hundred hands and paying these hands promptly? Is there a ship or vessel of any kind, steam or sail whose master and owners are colored and who claim Virginia as their home? Are there any colored Virginians who own enough shares in any of our railroads to entitle them to sit in the meetings of the shareholders of such railroads? Have we any banking institutions? And lastly but not least, have we any newspaper or periodical that receives one-tenth the support and patronage from us as a people that it should?

. . . There will be those who will say that there are white Virginians who own all of these things; that we are part and parcel of the population of Virginia and the American nation, and all that sort of thing. Which, we confess, sounds very pretty to listen to, but will never make us wealthy nor respected. Because we would become possessors of the means of obtaining wealth and of wealth itself, does not hinder us from being part and parcel of the population of Virginia nor of the American nation. Nor does it compromise our professions of friendship for our white brethren. We want living wages for our labor. Our white brethren who own and control all such industrial enterprises as we described above will not give them to us. What then are we to do? Sit and supinely bewail our condition and quarrel and find fault with them? Must we sit and pray and hope for better times when the white man will see our need and give us better wages? Certainly not. Let us put our shoulders to the wheel; imitate our white brother instead of abjectly depending upon him; establish and carry on every species of industrial enterprise for ourselves, employing and paying fair wages to our people. And when the white people see this spirit in us, they too will be willing to give and will give us fair wages. Let us do something for ourselves, and do it quickly. We cannot do it, some say; we are too poor. But we can combine and unite our means. "United we stand; divided we fall." In this State we are half a million strong. How many white people are there in the city of Richmond? Less than fifty thousand! And yet this less than fifty thousand white people have all these things of which we write above while over five hundred thousand colored people in the whole State have none of them. Shame on us. Let us be up and doing. There is no time to lose. The sooner we begin, the sooner we will reach the end.

The Virginia Star, Richmond, November 18, 1882

Many black politicians were rewarded by their party with patronage positions. This practice was criticized by C. H. Brown, editor of the Defiance.

. . . Manhood says I have rights as a citizen of these United States and those rights must come. I am a part and a parcel of this nation, and I intend to trouble it until every right comes. We want no petty office. That is only a bone of contention. We want our rights, and nothing less, and nothing more. We want our rights as citizens and as officers and the same recognition as other citizens in every department of life. Until this manhood is manifested in the colored people, and respected by everyone in authority there can be no sentiment of the question of what and how we are to get this race, where it will not be the only question in politics. We have only this to say, in our conclusion, that until we are recognized as men we will never cease to agitate this question. The Negro is in fault in many instances for in most cases, only those of the race that can be used as employed, and allowed to rest upon the bed of ease, while many hold positions who will speak out, yet they are only given positions to shut them off. But there is no manhood in holding on to a petty office, and seeing your race outraged, and not say stop, you oppressor.

The Weekly Defiance, Atlanta, February 24, 1883

Agreeing with the efforts of Booker T. Washington, Fortune and others insisted on the need for training in basic skills and a useful trade.

INDUSTRIAL EDUCATION NEEDED

. . . There was never a time when educational effort was more needed in the south than at the present—education that will prepare the boy and girl for the serious duties of manhood and womanhood. The flowery education, the education which develops the mental but neglects the physical man, is not what we need most at this time. Colleges for higher education are good things and necessary, but they presuppose by their existence conditions auxiliary and consonant, conditions of the highest civilization which give encouragement and support to the polished man. College preparation presupposes conditions such as do not obtain among us; hence the large number of educated failures among us. . . .

The Globe, New York, December 15, 1883

Various forms of cooperation were tried (based on the principle of the joint stock company), and one of the most important was in the area of housing. This was of particular interest to T. T. Fortune, who clearly saw the dynamics of ghetto building and urged his readers to resist exploitation.

The Annex Improvement Company in this city is an enterprise which deserves to succeed and every colored man in this city who has to rent a house, or apartments, is not only interested in its success, but should aid it by absorbing all its stock. The company has done well up to this time. The object is to control decent houses to let to colored people, who are cruelly discriminated against not only in locality but in prices by white landlords and real estate agents, who class all colored people alike—one as dirty and dishonest as the other. It is a real agony for a decent colored man to start out to get a house. The locality offered him is always the meanest in the city and the rental demanded is not only exaggerated but really usurious. . . . The only relief from the proscriptive tyranny of others is to strike out for yourself, and that we do not strike out more is to be attributed to a great many hardships which avarice and meanness heap upon us.

The Globe, New York, January 20, 1883

. . . The colored people of New York City suffer more injustice in the matter of rental than any other class of citizens. They are not only forced to colonize in the worst sections of the city, and into the very worst tenements, but they are charged fabulous prices for the luxury of having a place to sleep and eat. . . . Several Building Associations have been started of late years by colored men to own and control property to be rented to the people at living rates, but they have not amounted to anything. Why? Because the race is wanting, in a most marked degree, in the qualities of co-operation; it has no confidence in itself; it prefers to be fleeced year in and year out, instead of combining and co-operating for mutual protection. . . .

The Freeman, New York, March 7, 1885

Though industrial training was recognized as essential, H. C. Smith, editor of the Gazette, *suggested that it was not enough.*

Much is being said at present in favor of industrial training, but it is to be hoped that a more intelligent person thinks that we have a sufficient number of skilled and professional laborers. There is not any danger of the colored race having too many skilled and professional men for *many* years to come, such is the demand for them, and so inadequate are the facilities for the education of colored youth generally.

The skilled laborer should have the best common school education, if not a collegiate education, that is possible.

To make a professional man, it is absolutely necessary that the person have the best collegiate education possible. This is apparent to all intelligent persons, and it behooves parents to use every effort in giving their children a collegiate education, which does not mean simply finishing the High School.

The Gazette, Cleveland, September 1, 1883

. . . We need to marshal our forces into one solid phalanx. Without union, we cannot hope to compete even with those who are constantly putting forth organized efforts to win, although by far much in advance of us. Again, we lack race pride, the necessary sympathy that is possessed by all other nationalities and is ever being exhibited among them. The consequence of this is that we are deprived of the enjoyment of rights, in many instances, justly ours. . . . Education we want, and education we must have! It is the lever that is to elevate us from the unenviable position which is now ours. We cannot expend too much effort in this regard; no sacrifice is too great for its attainment; no legacy so important: Let the cry be educate! educate! educate! Wipe out the hindrances that have been so tenacious and so detrimental to our welfare. . . .

The State Journal, Harrisburg, Pennsylvania, February 2, 1884

Mob violence ruled the south in the 1880's and 90's as the federal government ignored the oppression of its black citizens.

. . . The colored people of this country are not to be blamed for the universal poverty, ignorance and immorality which obtain among them. The Government owes them for 200 years of labor; the States not only debased the man to a brute, crushed out, as far as they could, the divine spark of reason, by laws which would make an Ashantee chieftain blush, but the white men of the South set such an example of immorality and unbridled license that a saint would have been corrupted by contamination. . . . Let the government of the United States establish a Bureau of Education. Let it place within the reach of every child in the South the means of liberal industrial education. It is necessary to train the head and the hand. It is useless to talk about leaving the matter to the States. *The South will not educate the black child; it does not educate the white child. The two grow up in ignorance and vice and stupidity. And so the whites grow up to lawlessness and the blacks to crime.* Anarchy is the natural result. The South is today a sleeping volcano. The fires of revolution and death are slowly but surely germinating. . . .

The Globe, New York, March 1, 1884

References to Africa were not unique in the black press, and from the very beginning, narratives, travelogues, stories, etc. occur to bind the black American to the rich heritage of his past. The following article is also important in its emphasis on the future of Africa.

Africa is coming rapidly to the front. . . . Trade is bringing the African face to face with civilized methods and customs, and he is daily Africanizing the spirit of modern progress. Mohammedanism is spreading rapidly, marching down from the north with wonderful ease. It is abolishing the fetish of the gree-gree and it is suppressing cannibalism and human sacrifice. It undoubtedly exercises a powerful influence upon the moral, political, and social condition of the Ethiopian tribes. It introduces the Arabic language, it establishes schools for instruction, it thus spreads among the tribes a common language, and it is thus unifying them.

Civilizing influences are going into the Soudan and Central Tropical Africa from the West Coast. In time, the people will be united by one common language and by the same tastes and desires. Tribal wars will cease. Tribal intercourse will become absolutely friendly. Intermarriages will take place. As the tribes of Great Britain gradually united their destinies until they became a great Empire, so it will be in Africa. Great Britain in the beginning of the Christian era, was as Africa is. Her growth was slow. It was not a leap from Druidism to Christianity, nor from feudalism to imperialism. Napoleon I was the product of centuries of civilization. Now that the inhuman slave trade has been suppressed, an incubus that hung like a mill-stone around the neck of Tropical Africa has been removed. The work of civilization and unification will go forward.

Tropical Africa contains what the world wants. It is a country of exhaustless resources. This will lead to human intercourse with foreign lands. . . . Growth and development will come from within, not from without. The spirit of modern progress will be Africanized. People of the same blood, dwelling together on the same soil, having the same aims, aspirations, and interests will unite, and move on in the same lines. A great mind will be a product of the changes in growth that are even now taking place in Tropical Africa. Influences will go out of Liberia and Sierre Leone that will give shape to such a political possibility as an African Empire. Perhaps the great African general and statesman will come out of one or the other of these two countries. . . .

The Globe, New York, April 5, 1884

We are not dying out as predicted. The Negro is the junior race of the world with the possible exception of the Australians; we have a great and grand future. Our race will be waxing for centuries after the white race will have commenced to wane. The Negro is a boy; the white, a man. When the man shall reach old age and the same kind of dotage that characterizes the American Indian, the Negro will be in his prime and glory and ruling the world. I think in a few years the better class of colored men in this country will go to Africa and build up a mighty nation while the riff raffs of our race will remain here. The advantages of migrating to Africa are many. Recently vast discoveries of untold wealth have been made in nearly every part of that continent. God has his hand upon our race and will give us means and marvellous agencies. It may be that the Supreme Court's decision was designed by Providence to arouse the Negro to his sense of responsibility. . . . In America black is supposed to symbolize the devil and white to represent God. But this is partially wrong, for the devil is white and never was black. There are as many blacks as whites in the universe. There are black worlds and I believe millions of black angels in heaven. In fact there are angels of all colors there. I know I do not represent my race in taking the position I do as the great mass of them are anti-Africans in the emigrational sense. But it is only a matter of time before they will awake from their slumber and see things in a different light.

The North Carolina Republican and Civil Rights Advocate,
Weldon, May 22, 1884

✸

Black editors constantly sought to examine the roots of caste prejudice and its effects.

There is no sentiment more ennobling to individual and natural character than the love and respect felt for one's race. Evidence of this is seen in the manifest interests taken in the welfare and advancement of the people. The effect of such interests has led to mutual sympathy and concert of action in carrying for whatever concerns the happiness and dignity of that race. . . . The cause of the deficiency of race pride in this country has its origin in the abominable crime of the old slave system. It was conceived in the misplaced views of a morbid sensibility, growing out of the idea that the white race, the dominant class, rules and whatever approximates to that in complexion has a right for priority. The evil as it now exists has been felt for many decades in every shade of American society. It grew and became more arrogant with the increasing wealth of those who inherited means and received aid from their former owners. For years there has been a tendency on the part of a certain class to ignore their own race and to be known as a distinct people and not able to be white, yet would not be identified with the long suffering and oppressed kindred. The result has been mischievous. It is a fact, too, that the feeling of American caste has become so strong that even among the intelligent whites a most depressing tendency to despise and reject the blacks permeates and contaminates the entire circumference of modern life, all arising from the blighting evil of slavery. It is the most glowing evil of our times—is seen at once in the different phases of its existence. The effect of that evil has its influence in the working human nature and vitiating the moral instincts, contracting the intellectual powers and disqualifying man to discharge his duties as a citizen and neighbor.

The Gazette, Cleveland, September 26, 1885

The Freeman *was one of the few papers with a woman's department, edited by Mrs. Nellie F. Mossell, and T. T. Fortune supported her aims "to promote true womanhood, especially that of the African race."*

. . . We regard the work which women have to do in the world as of equal if not greater importance than that which falls to the lot of man; and we contend, therefore, that the rudiments and the finish of

her education should be as carefully and conscientiously superin-
tended. It is the woman who brings the man into the world; it is she
who prenatally and subsequently molds his mind and character up to
the stage of manhood; in short, it is the woman who prepares the man
for success or failure in the fierce battle of life. . . .

The women of our race have a vast work to do. Upon them more
than upon any other influence depends the development of a race of
men in every respect different from those of us now upon the stage of
activity. We must develop a manhood wherein shrewdness, courage,
fidelity to race, commercial enterprise, and high moral and religious
convictions are prevailing and predominant elements. If we are to
have such men our women are to give them to us. . . .

The Freeman, New York, April 10, 1886

*The following observation gives us a clue to the means by which Ameri-
can racism was transmitted to Europeans and how it was used effectively
to divide the working class.*

The late scene of battle at East St. Louis, Chicago, and Milwaukee
is not surprising to me. Just as soon as the white foreigners arrive at
Castle Garden they are taught and disciplined by the white Americans
to hate the native born colored man and to oppose him in everything
he attempts. They also read and see that shooting, torturing, burning
and mobbing colored men and women is a common thing and an
every day occurrence, without the interference of the law. . . . Can
anyone expect anything more from these foreigners when they see that
law and order do not exist in this country?

The Freeman, New York, May 15, 1886

*With educational opportunities restricted for black people in the South,
the black press turned to the federal government for assistance.*

The question of Federal Aid to public education is one of the first
and most important questions that should occupy the attention of
Congress. . . . As a matter of principle no money from the National
Government should be used to perpetuate directly, or indirectly, race,

class, or caste distinction; and it seems to us that if the white people of the South who clamor so much for aid to education, desire to receive this boon from the National Government, they should be willing to receive it on the only equitable basis on which the National Government can grant it, on the basis of perfect equality before the law for all men. . . .

The Weekly Pelican, New Orleans, December 4, 1886

The experience of German unification had special meaning for Fortune, who saw similar possibilities in Africa.

It is written on the wall that there will one day be an African Empire whose extent and power will be inferior to that of no government now denominated as a first class power. . . . In the course of time, the people will become educated, not only in the grasping and cruel nature of the white man, but in the knowledge of their power, their priority of ownership in the soil, and in the desperation which tyranny and greed never fail to breed for their own destruction. Out of the convulsions, which are sure to come, an African Confederation, not unlike that of Germany, will certainly be evolved. It can hardly be prevented, save by Omnipotent interposition. So out of toil and privation and long agony, good will eventually come to the swarthy millions of our Fatherland.

The Freeman, New York, January 15, 1887

Minstrels here, there, or anywhere, in as much as they engage in the business of caricaturing the Negro race, tend to belittle and degrade them rather than elevate and dignify them. They never were intended to benefit the people whom they deride. They excite only a feeling of ridicule and contempt. . . . The minstrels, like the low comedy, seems to be gathering a secret influence which if not brought into disfavor will demoralize the whole social system. The practice is maintained at fearful odds against the Negro and it is time that every good citizen and every colored man commence an uncompromising system of warfare against this villainy perpetuated upon the colored people throughout the world.

The Gazette, Cleveland, February 19, 1887

The necessity for some form of protective agency for black people be-came imperative. With its roots in the early vigilance committees, and convention, Fortune's proposal for such unified action was widely ac-cepted.

A PROPOSED AFRO-AMERICAN LEAGUE

There should be some way to suppress mob law in the South. Not a day passes that the papers do not record some hideous outrage of this kind by "our best people," and the victim is invariably some one or more colored men who are suspected of some sort of crime, but who are entitled to a fair and impartial trial by a jury of their peers and who are in the sight of the law presumed to be innocent until proven guilty.

There can be no possible excuse for this constant murder of colored men by irresponsible citizens. If the sources of injustice were in such a shape that fair trial of the persons charged with crime could not be had, there might seem to be some excuse for overriding the law and meting out punishment in the absence and defiance of judge and jury. But in the South, the whites have absolute control of the entire ma-chinery of justice. There is never in any Southern state the remotest possibility that any colored man charged with a crime will not have that crime hitched upon him, and receive more than necessary punish-ment by the courts.

. . . We think it has been thoroughly demonstrated that the white people of this country have determined to leave the colored man alone to fight his battles; especially is this true of the treacherous, self-seek-ing politicians. There is no dodging the issue; we have got to take hold of this problem ourselves, and make so much noise that all the world shall know the wrongs we suffer and our determination to right those wrongs.

It can be done. We can make such a noise that the whole world will be compelled to listen. There are some eight millions of us in the United States alone. . . . Let the entire race in this country organize into a protective league; let it be organized on the same plan that the Irish National League is. What shall we call it? Call it the Afro-Ameri-can National League if you will. There are thousands of colored or-ganizations in this country which could be immediately resolved into this grand organization. . . .

The Freeman, New York, May 28, 1887

✿

The league was an important predecessor of the Niagara movement,
which became the foundation for the NAACP. The first meeting of the
league was held in 1890, in Chicago. It was, in a sense, the high point of
Fortune's decade-long resistance to tyranny and oppression.

THE AFRO-AMERICAN LEAGUE

There come periods in the history of every people when the necessity of their affairs makes it imperative that they take such steps as
shall show to the world that they are worthy to be free, and therefore
entitled to the sympathy of all mankind and to the co-operation of all
lovers of justice and fair play. To do this, they must unequivocally
show that while they may solicit the sympathy and co-operation of
mankind, they have the intelligence and the courage to know what are
their rights and to manfully contend for them. In the last issue of *The
Freeman* I took occasion to propose a vast organization of the colored
people of the United States for the purpose of creating a just public
opinion in the special matter of lynch and mob law. I now feel that the
reasons then given for so vast an organization, while in every respect
ample, might seem to some insufficient; therefore I have proposed to
myself the task of stating more in detail the reasons, as I understand
them, why we should take this important step.

I am in no sense unmindful of the vastness of the undertaking, but
this instead of being a drawback is rather an incentive to prosecute
the matter with more earnestness and persistence. There are thousands of what are termed "societies" among us, whose object in the
main is beneficiary. Whether any considerable number of these can be
used directly for the purpose of the League or not, they certainly have
served as a preparatory school for a central National organization
such as I have suggested, and such as we need. Therefore, if it shall be
found impossible to divert these organizations from their present local
nature and circumscribed purposes, they will still serve as feeders for
the National League, as they have already served, in ignorance of
such a purpose, as educators for it. The work of preparation which
they have accomplished seems almost as a special providence, and if
the great central organization shall ever become a fact, it will certainly
appear to have been such.

REASONS WHY THERE SHOULD BE SUCH A LEAGUE

I shall here state the reasons why I think such a League should be
formed. (1) The almost universal suppression of our ballot in the

South, and consequent "taxation without representation," since in cities, counties and States where we have undisputed preponderating majorities of the voting population we have in the main no representation and therefore no voice in the making and construing the laws under which we live. (2) The universal and lamentable reign of lynch and mob law, of which we are made the victims in the South, all the more aggravating because all the machinery of the law making and enforcing authority is in the hands of those who resort to such outrageous, heinous and murderous violations of the law. (3) The unequal distribution of school funds collected from all tax-payers, and to the equal and undivided benefits of which all are alike entitled. (4) The odious and demoralizing penitentiary system of the South, with its chain-gangs, convict leases, and indiscriminate mixing of males and females. (5) The almost universal tyranny of common carrier corporations in the South,—railroad, steamboat, and other,—in which the common rights of colored men and women are outraged and denied by the minions of these corporations, acting under implicit orders in most cases, as well as by common passengers who take the matter in their own hands as often as they please, and are in no instance pursued and punished by the lawful authorities, who in every instance sympathize with them. (6) The general, policy of those who conduct places of public accommodation, and are granted a license for this purpose, such as keepers of inns, hotels and conductors of theatres and kindred places of amusement, where one man's money, all things being equal, should usually be as good as another's. These matters reach down in the very life of a people; they are fundamentally the things which in all times have moved men to associate themselves together in civil society for mutual benefit and protection, to restrain the rapacious and unscrupulous and to protect the weak, the timid and the virtuous; and whenever and wherever a condition of affairs obtains where these principles are disregarded and outraged, it becomes the imperative duty of the aggrieved to take such steps for their preservation as the condition of affairs seems to warrant.

SCOPE OF THE ORGANIZATION

I think this League should have its stronghold in the Southern States. It is in those States that the grievances we complain of have most glaring and oppressive existence; it is in those States that the bulk of our people reside. The League in the North and West will serve to create public opinion in those sections and to coerce politicians into taking a broader view of our grievances and to compel them to pay more respect to our representations and requests than they have ever done before. This will follow fast upon organization and capable management; because we have learned by experience that intelligent sympathy can only be created by intelligent agitation, and that the respect of politicians can only be secured by compulsion, such alone as thorough organization can bring to bear. In the North and West we are not restrained in the free exercise of the ballot, but aside from this what benefit accrues to us? Elections come and pass, parties are successful or defeated, but the influence of the race remains simply worthless, the victor and the vanquished alike treating us with indifference or contempt after the election. And if we continue in the future as in the past a disorganized and leaderless mass there will be no change for the better, rather for the worse. Every year the indifference and contempt are shown in more pronounced and different ways. It is only by proper organization and discipline that anything to our advantage can be accomplished. In the South like results will follow, save in larger measure, and perhaps at greater cost to individual members of the League, since free speech and action are things that must be fought for there. For it cannot be denied that in the South free speech and free action are not tolerated. The white men of that section, in defiance of all constitution and law have taken affairs in their own hands, and crush out, or attempt to do it, all opinions not in accord with those of the dominant class. And this is not only true in matters of political nature but in such as are economical as well. Within the past six months two men have been killed outright, one in Mississippi and one in Georgia, and many others have been "warned" and browbeaten, for attempting to explain to colored laborers the injustice practiced on them by employers; so that the colored laboring masses of that section are fast falling into a condition not unlike in its terrible features the chattel slavery abolished by constitutional enactment.

We have it in the newspapers and we have it from the lips of our own men fresh from all sections of the South that the condition of the colored laborers of their section is simply atrocious and appalling, that the employers of such labor, backed up by ample legislation and by all the machinery of the law, are simply tyrannous in the conduct of their affairs, in so far that colored laborers have no "appeal from Caesar drunk to Caesar sober."

ATTITUDE OF THE PRESS AND THE POLITICIANS

It is a remarkable state of the case that the entire press of the North has ceased to dwell upon the state of affairs in the South in other than a wishy-washy way, chronicling such outrages as cannot well be passed over in silence as news matter, but putting such matters in such shape as invariably to make the colored person guilty of all that is charged upon him and excusing those who constitute themselves judge and jury in the execution of the mob's decree; while it is in exceedingly rare instances that the misdeeds of individual offenders ever find a voice in the press. The people suffer in silence. This should not be. They should have a voice. The grievances they are forced to suffer should be known of all the world and they must be. An organization national in its ramifications, such as we propose, would be such a voice, and so loud that it would compel men to hear it; for if it were silenced in the South, it would be all the louder in the North and the West. Indeed, the first work of the League, it seems to me must be that of thorough organization, and then of agitation. When once the organization is effected the work of agitation will, in some sense, be easy.

THE COLOR LINE BUGBEAR

Whenever colored men talk of forming anything in which they are to be the prime movers and their grievances are to be the subject to be agitated, a vast array of men, mostly politicians, and newspapers, more or less partisan, and therefore interested in keeping colored voters in a helpless state as far as disorganization and absence of responsible leadership can effect this, cry aloud that "colored men should be the last persons to draw the color line!" So they should be; so they have been; and they would never have drawn any such line, or proposed that any such should be drawn, if white men had not first drawn it, and continue to draw it now in religion, in politics, in educational matters, in all moral movements, like that of temperance for instance. We have not drawn the line. The A.M.E. Church, probably the strongest and most influential colored organization in the United States—did its founders establish it because they did not care to worship with their white co-religionists? Not a bit of it. They established that magnificent religious organization as a rebuke and a protest to

the peanut gallery accommodations offered by white Christians, so-
called, to colored Christians. The same spirit actuated the founders of
the Zion A.M.E. Church, another grand and enduring monument of
Negro manhood and Christian fortitude, and the colored M.E.
Church, and colored Baptist churches were outgrowths of the same
spirit.

It was not the colored Christians, but the white Christians who, to
their eternal shame and damnation, drew the line, and continue to
draw it even unto this hour. Turn to the Masonic, the Odd Fellow and
the Knights of Pythias orders—did colored men draw the line in
these? Did they set up colored lodges all over the country because
they did not care to fraternize with the white orders? The answer can
be inferred when it is stated that white Masons, white Odd Fellows
and white Knights of Pythias even at this hour refuse to fraternize
with or to recognize the legality or regularity of the orders their actions caused colored men to establish. Do colored people desire separate Grand Lodges in the Temperance Order? Did they ask for such?
No! But the British and American Good Templars reunited last week
at a conference at Saratoga, N.Y. and the only condition on which the
American order would consent to reunion was that the British order
would acknowledge that its action of eleven years ago in seceding
from the order on the color question was odious and unsound in principle. So that the second section of the articles of agreement provides
that in any jurisdiction of white and colored Templars there must be
separate Grand Lodges, provided either side insists upon it; and we
know the whites, especially those of the South, will insist on it every
time, the same as they do now in church conferences, in all charitable
and philanthropical works, educational and other. We do not object;
we simply seek to make it plain that we have not been the ones heretofore to draw the color line. But we have this to say: We advise all colored Templars to draw out of this reunited order. If they must be separated because they are colored, let them stand up like men in their
own order, where color will not be a brand of odium; let them form
an order of their own, the same as they have churches of their own.
The eternal compromises of our manhood and self-respect true of the
past, must cease. Right is right, and we should at no time or under any
circumstances compromise upon anything but absolute right. If the
white man cannot rescue our drunkards and evangelize our sinners
except by insulting us, let him keep away from us. His contamination

under such conditions does us more harm than good. It is not we who have drawn the color line. That is pure nonsense.

TAKE OUR PUBLIC SCHOOLS;

take the schools and colleges throughout the land—who drew the color line in these? Is there a colored school of any sort in the South where a white applicant would be refused admission on account of his color? Not one! Is there a white school in the South where a colored applicant would not be refused admission on account of his color? Not one! The thing is plain. The white man draws the color line in everything he has everything to do with. He is saturated with the black mud of prejudice and intolerance. What political party has ever treated colored voters as other than voting dummies and colored leaders as other than convenient tools? We have controlled a million votes annually for twenty years and what have we to show for them? Where are the colored men who have been honored above their fellows by the men we have placed in high places? One or two diplomatic places of the third class and a few minor places now mostly covered by Civil Service rules fill up the list. The elective officers do not count here. They were the result of our own votes. Where are the laws anywhere outside the three constitutional amendments enacted to insure us in our rights? Where are they? We protest that we have squandered our voting strength and our brain power long enough! We protest that we owe it to ourselves and our children to take another and more intelligent and manly stand in all matters where our rights and feelings are concerned, and I submit this can be effected in no way better and with more facility than through a National organization and the proper leadership, and we have an abundance of this latter material in every State in the Union. It only requires to be brought into fair play to demonstrate its fitness, and it will never be brought into play as long as the masses remain a disorganized mass. Leadership must have a following, otherwise it will run to seed and wither up, be of no benefit to the race or to the persons possessing the superior capacity. An army without a general is a mob, at the mercy of any disciplined force that is hurled against it; and a disorganized, leaderless race is nothing more than a helpless, restless mob; and, on the whole, the colored people of the United States are substantially that sort of thing, and have been since the close of the war, at the mercy of schemers and unscrupulous self-seekers. This should not be allowed to continue.

SOME DIFFICULTIES AND DANGERS

Already have persons, personally and through correspondence, assured me that such an organization as I have proposed will meet with strenuous opposition and that bloodshed may follow in some instances in the wake of the work. I have no doubt that this will be the case. All those men who have profited by our disorganization and fattened on our labor by class and corporate legislation will oppose the movement, and in the intensity of their opposition may resort to the coward argument of violence; but are we to remain forever inactive, the victims of extortion and duplicity on this account? Not a bit of it. We propose to accomplish our purposes by the peaceful methods of agitation, through the ballot and the courts, but if others use the weapons of violence to combat our peaceful arguments it is not for us to run away from violence. A man's a man, and what is worth having is worth fighting for. It is proudly claimed that "the blood of the martyrs is the seed of the church." Certainly the blood of anti-slavery champions was the seed of Garrison's doctrine of "the genius of universal emancipation!" Certainly the blood of Irish patriots has been the seed of Irish persistence and success; certainly the blood of Negro patriots was the seed of the independence of Hayti and San Domingo; and in the Great Revolution of our own country the cornerstones of American freedom were cemented with the blood of patriots who were not afraid to die; and the refrain will reverberate down the ages—

> Long as in freedom's cause the wise contend,
> Dear to your country shall your fame extend;
> While to the world the lettered stone shall tell
> Where Caldwell, Attucks, Gray and Maverick fell,

Attucks, the black patriot—he was no coward! Toussaint L'Ouverture—he was no coward! Nat Turner—he was no coward! And the two hundred thousand black soldiers of the last war—they were no cowards! If we have a work to do, let us do it. And if there come violence let those who oppose our just cause "throw the first stone!" We have wealth, we have intelligence, we have courage; and we have a great work to do. We should therefore take hold of it like men, not counting our time and means and lives as of any consequence further than they contribute to the grand purposes which call us to the work. Wherever there are gathered together ten colored men anywhere in this country let them resolve themselves into a branch of the Afro-American League, and elect a set of the best men in it as officers, the same as is done in any other social or church society. Let the work begin at once. Let us prepare for the National meeting of the League within as short time in the future as will be consistent with a decent representation to draft laws for the management of the League and its branches. Let every man of us feel that it is his peculiar business to take hold of this work of preliminary organization and to impress the importance of it upon his friends and neighbors. Let each man and woman take hold and do his duty and the results will speak for themselves. Yours for absolute right,

T. THOMAS FORTUNE (June 2, 1887)

Black settlers in Kansas, many of whom had come from the South, vigorously resisted attempts to deny them educational facilities.

We have been watching the progress of the school question at Fort Scott [Kansas] with much interest. It is a case where the colored people of Fort Scott brought against the school board for refusing to admit their children on account of color. The trial was tried in the District Courts of Fort Scott, and the school board gained the cause. An appeal was taken to the Supreme Court where it came up on March 5th. The Court held that the school board erred in not admitting the colored children at the time they applied. For Fort Scott was then a city of the second class. Separate schools for the education of black and white children can be maintained only in cities of the first class. Since the suit was brought, Fort Scott has been made a city of the first class, and thus practically will continue to discriminate on account of color. . . . The Negroes of this country are free men, or slaves. If they are citizens, they are justly entitled to all the privileges of citizens. If they are still half-slaves, they want to know it. This discrimination in our public schools is right, or it is wrong. Which is it? If it is wrong in theory, it is wrong in practice, and should be stopped.

The American Citizen, Topeka, Kansas, March 15, 1889

The Freeman, Indianapolis, December 21, 1889

Index